T0152995

DONALD CULROSS PEATTIE LIBRARY

Published by Trinity University Press

≈

An Almanac for Moderns

A Book of Hours

Cargoes and Harvests

Diversions of the Field

Flowering Earth

A Gathering of Birds: An Anthology of the Best Ornithological Prose

Green Laurels: The Lives and Achievements of the Great Naturalists

A Natural History of North American Trees

The Road of a Naturalist

A NATURAL HISTORY OF NORTH AMERICAN TREES

Donald Culross Peattie

Illustrated by
Paul Landacre

TRINITY UNIVERSITY PRESS

SAN ANTONIO, TEXAS

PUBLISHED BY TRINITY UNIVERSITY PRESS

San Antonio, Texas 78212

ISBN 978-1-59534-166-2 (paper)

ISBN 978-1-59534-167-9 (ebook)

Cover design by Chris Hall

Cover illustration: Kazuhiko Yoshino/iStockphoto.com

Book design by Robert Overholtzer

Trinity University Press strives to produce its books using methods and materials in an environmentally sensitive manner. We favor working with manufacturers that practice sustainable management of all natural resources, produce paper using recycled stock, and manage forests with the best possible practices for people, biodiversity, and sustainability. The press is a member of the Green Press Initiative, a nonprofit program dedicated to supporting publishers in their efforts to reduce their impacts on endangered forests, climate change, and forest-dependent communities.

CIP data on file at the Library of Congress.

23   22   21 | 5   4   3

CONTENTS

FOREWORD

See him now, walking along some western trail. It can be anywhere — in the lonely canyons of the San Jacinto Range, in the foothill chaparral behind his beloved Santa Barbara, or sauntering along the San Simeon Highway where the Santa Lucia Mountains, mantled in lupine and vermilion paintbrush, plunge precipitously into the Pacific. Or perhaps he strides along a path deep in the great redwoods, or pauses at the foot of the snow-covered Olympic Range in Washington to pick a flower among a small patch of moss laid bare by the midautumn sun.

But chances are that, whether he is wandering among the fan palms of the Mojave Desert or standing in the shade of a live oak in the Lompoc Hills, he will present a singular figure: a dark green Stetson on his head, a coat and tie — he never went anywhere outside without them — binoculars around his neck, and slung over his shoulder his dark green vasculum, that sturdy oval cylinder of metal in which he collects plant specimens. When he is not gazing at the far horizon, his eyes sweep the ground for California poppies and bluebells, or creosote bush and sage if his walks are in the desert.

If he is near home, he will bring back his floral treasure and will take out each captive and lay it between large, thick gray sheets of blotting paper to be placed with others in a stack pressed between two plates of slatted wood, the whole then stood on either by me or one of my brothers, while he buckles it tightly together. Days later, the blotters will be opened, releasing fragrances throughout the house, and the specimens labeled and carefully taped into a series of huge albums, which would come to constitute a veritable encyclopedia of western plants. (In the years to come the Peattie collection of western flowers and plants will become known throughout the botanical world, but their ultimate destiny will be a mystery.)

So, his sons came to know that kindly, searching figure as we grew up in various rambling homes in Santa Barbara, California. We learned to respect his hours in his study, the smoke curling up from his pipe as he sat in front of his typewriter producing the pages that so deservedly won him fame as one of America's most cherished nature writers. He was ever the courteous, beloved, but slightly distant figure, even to his sons, and if he held to the habit of wearing a coat and tie, whether at dinner at home or on a picnic near a waterfall, it was only the physical manifestation of his courtly demeanor. As a neighbor once remarked to me, "Your father has the manners of a Spanish ambassador."

His love of plants came early, and he sensed it first in the Appalachian Mountains where, as a frail young lad, he spent the winters to avoid the endless coughing fits brought on by the cold of Chicago. His fascination soon fixed on all that grew in those lush mountains. Family legend has it that, walking along a dusty road in the Blue Ridge of North Carolina, he met another boy carrying a gorgeous flowering dogwood branch with which the boy kept hitting his shoes to keep the dust off. Young Donald was so struck by the floral glory so callously treated, that on the spot he exchanged a brand new pen-knife with inlaid mother-of-pearl for the dogwood branch.

He tried his hand at other things, including two years studying French poetry at the University of Chicago, but his keen interest in living things always brought him back to the green world. So it was that he transferred to Harvard to study with Merritt Fernald, one of the greatest of America's botanists. After some years working a desk in the Bureau of Plant Introduction in the Department of Agriculture, now equipped with both scientific training and the eye of poet, he turned himself and his talents loose upon the printed page. All aspects of plant life became matters of intense interest, study, and constant writing. He collected specimens in the Indiana dunes along the windy shores of Lake Michigan and turned out a small classic from his findings. He found wonder in pondering the algae of Archaeozoic times, in reflecting on the place of the lowly billions of tiny diatoms that form the bottom of the marine food chain, and gloried in the story of the great ferns of geologic times that laid down the coal seams that were to fuel a nation. More than occasionally he wrote of the romance of plant life. He wove his magic in his account of the mystery of that delicate and long-lost flower, *Shortia*, found only in the inner recesses of the Appalachian mountains. His fascination with plant life extended to the kelp leviathans that form great marine forests off the California coast, an interest that, for a short time, was to drive his family to distraction since he filled every bathtub in our house with the seaweed he was studying.

And always, his scientific rigor was matched with a voice that was golden in the illumination of his subjects, a combination which lit the pages of a score of works that earned him honors and respect among his professional colleagues, as well as the public. A very few of the former, in crabbed jealousy, could not bear this combination of style and substance. One curmudgeonly specialist, whom he asked to fact-check his work on wheat, returned the paper, which he pronounced as factually flawless, adding sourly, "I see you could not resist the temptation to be interesting."

But it was this continent's sylva that fixed his purpose and filled the pages of his last and master work that you now hold in your hands. He confirms to us that he became a "plantsman" at age twenty, appropriately beginning in the Appalachian mountains where he had come to wander alone among the hemlocks, the balsams, and black spruces, with the sound of waterfalls in the distance. Along the way to literary renown he covered a myriad of botanical subjects: protoplasm, photosynthesis, the fertilization of flowers by insect life, tree rings, the use of timber for naval construction in the Great Age of Sail, medicinal herbs, and all the miraculous qualities of plant life upon which we and all living things on this earth depend. But always he thought of compiling a great sylva of north America. "The American sylva," he tells us in *American Heartwood* (1949) "has lain upon the rim of my mind like a blue landfall, raised twenty years ago, when I first schemed how I might come up to it."

And what a landfall he made at last. For there was and is, to my knowledge, no work quite like it, and it follows my father's own dictum to all aspiring writers: write the book that you're longing to read, but can't find anywhere. The two large volumes it comprised, one on the trees of eastern north America and one on the western trees (north of Mexico), were published at midcentury. In them, each tree was not only identified with its proper Latin designation and its common American name or names, but the reader was also provided with its geographic range and with an exacting botanical description. The jewels on each page were the woodcuts of the leaf or needles of the tree drawn by the great illustrator Paul Landacre as precisely as the textual description, as well as my father's illuminating discussion of the tree — its particular qualities, its uses by man if there were any, and its place in American life and history.

There was to have been a third volume on the sylvan exotics — apple and peach, eucalyptus, and weeping willow — and all the rest brought into this country from abroad. But it was not to be; like a great trunk invaded by borers, he was weakened by long illness and borne down at last to the forest floor. At all events, his passing has made the publisher's task easier in bringing out this one-volume edition of my father's sylva, for three volumes could hardly have been compressed into one.

Before I leave you to stroll among these leafy pages I should make some last observations about my father, Donald Culross Peattie, renowned naturalist and acclaimed writer. He worked as hard as any man I know; he was a devoted husband to his life's soul mate, and a caring and thoughtful parent to all his children. But the quality that stands out above all others was his serenity in the face of trouble and the chaos of an unruly planet. The trivia, the selfishness, and the vulgar noise that fills much of our world never shook him, fixed as he was on listening to "the roar of a mountain river, and a higher, frailer sound above the churning water, the singing of a forest in the night wind."

Mark R. Peattie
Redwood City, California
August 15, 2006

INTRODUCTION

Whenever I open Donald Culross Peattie's *A Natural History of North American Trees,* I find myself wondering, Who would write such a book these days? I don't pretend the question is fair. It's like asking who would write *Moby Dick* or *The Lives of the Poets* in the twenty-first century. But I'm always astonished by what Peattie accomplished, by the scale of the work — its geographic and botanical and historical range. These days, a natural history of American trees would have a general editor, a managing editor, and perhaps a dozen contributors. Above all, it would have photographs and maps and — for the oaks at least — a series of line drawings to help readers distinguish one species from another. Peattie had something more important: a faith in the power of words. He believed that language alone could make trees come alive in his readers' imaginations. And he was right.

That is partly because Peattie has done such a good job imagining his readers. They are surprisingly like us. We look out at Texas and marvel at the peach trees, little knowing that they are actually mesquites. We are utterly perplexed by all the alpine species of conifers. We know the aspen not only by its white bark and quaking leaves but because "it grows in the very spots most sought out by the vacationing camper." In other words, Peattie's readers are not botanists, nor are they driven by a mania for identification. And that, as I know from my own experience, is a good thing.

When my wife and I first moved to our small farm in upstate New York, I spent several seasons — guidebook in hand — trying to identify all the trees that grew around us. It was a kind of homage, I think, and also a way of taking possession. I examined the bark, the leaves, and in some cases the flowers or the buds. I compared them to photographs in the tree guides or worked through part of a botanical key until I was sure I knew what I was looking at. I watched spring overtake the woods and winter denude it. But identifying a tree is not the same as knowing it. When I was done I had a list of names, and what mattered most about any one species on the list were merely the attributes that distinguished it from all the other species on it. Something was missing.

That something is exactly what Peattie offers us, a feeling for the character — the nature — of every tree he writes about. He can be very good on the subtle points of discrimination, but he is best at something much harder: describing what it's like to stand, say, on the California plains in the presence of a Valley Oak, whose shade "is not dim and stuffy like that in a dense growth of young Redwood, Douglastree and Laurel, but luminous and breezy." In these essays Peattie reminds us again and again that perhaps the most important thing to know about the trees we live among is the effect they have upon us. And that can only be captured in words, by a writer whose greatest work is an arboretum of the mind.

This book is also a national history told in board-feet. Peattie is as moved, in his own way, by the economic chronicle of American wood as he is by the beauty of the American woods. He tries to resist — he is a conservationist at heart—but even he gives in at times to the Bunyanesque heroism of logging, especially the work of donkey engines and the high lead, a cable slung across the great stands of Douglas fir carrying giant logs on their "giddy course" through the sky. Wherever the opponents are nearly equal in strength he cannot help cheering, even as he worries about the inevitable outcome. Species by species, he shows us the American course westward. It is, of course, a tale of raw opportunism and almost feverish inventiveness, a constant failure to appreciate what we have, while knowing — to the nearest dime — what it is worth.

And so *The Natural History of North American Trees* is also a moral tale defined by the mute stoicism of the trees themselves. Here, for instance, is a scene from Peattie's essay on the Chinquapin Oak. It could be set to music.

> But the generations pass, farms are abandoned, and fences left to fall. And when, in the great days of Ohio river boating, steamships were first sent down from Pittsburgh to New Orleans, it was

discovered that these old rails of Chinquapin Oak (along with many other Oak and Hickory fences, of course) made the best obtainable fuel for the devouring engines of the steamboats. So farmers came to heap them in great piles on the shore for sale to the engineers, and stops to take on these rails of seasoned, completely combustible timber were as frequent and important as ever the stops at scheduled landings where goods and passengers waited.

You get a very good feel for Peattie's imagination here and, just as important, for the cast of his language. He may list the names the Spaniards left behind in California and call them "resounding monickers," but Peattie is never as blunt and demotic as the Kansas State Board of Agriculture, which said on the subject of the Box Elder, "There is no excuse for planting this tree." There is always a quality in Peattie's prose that it might be tempting to call formality. Really, it is a kind of honorific poetry, a sense of rising to his subject. Here is a particularly good example, a single sentence from his entry on the Alpine Fir: "Many kinds of trees that love the mountain heights must for long seasons bear great weights of snow." Yes, this is anthropomorphic, but what is more important is Peattie's unusual placement of the phrase, "for long seasons." It insists on the dignity of the occasion. It bows to the Alpine Fir and the reader.

We do not write like this any longer. That has changed. So have most of the economic facts that Peattie gathered in these pages, which were current circa 1953. Yet that archaism is valuable in itself. Peattie captured a seam in American history — after World War II but before plastic and other synthetic materials became ubiquitous and changed the way we use many trees. He belonged himself to an earlier world, where the old elms had a million leaves apiece and it was believed that sassafras drove away bedbugs and food tasted better cooked in "appetite-sauce." We would tell his economic story differently now, with a sharper moral driven by the battles over logging and preservation, by the effect that manmade climate change is having upon the distribution and survival of some species.

What has not changed is the trees themselves or the consequences of getting to know them in the presence of an observer as keen as Peattie. I find myself wondering at some outdated statistic in *The Natural History of North American Trees* or pausing to think about the sometimes venerable lilt in Peattie's prose, and I worry that his work is caught in his own time. I worry, that is, until I'm outside again, looking at the sugar maples that border our pasture, at the stand of beeches, at the hickories that are just now going yellow, at the dark hemlock edge of the woods around us. I see them differently now that I have read Peattie. It is as though he has somehow walked them onto the historical stage, where they enter fully into their own characters. What I also see, of course, is that they have taken possession of me and not the other way around.

Verlyn Klinkenborg
October 2006

EDITOR'S NOTE

For more than sixty years, the Houghton Mifflin backlist has included a pair of volumes aptly described on their back covers as "the most eloquent, informative, and entertaining books ever written about the trees of North America": *A Natural History of Trees of Eastern and Central North America*, published in 1950, and its western counterpart, *A Natural History of Western Trees*, published in 1953. These volumes, both written by Donald Culross Peattie, are "genuine classics of natural history."

In his time, according to Joseph Wood Krutch, Peattie was "perhaps the most widely read of all contemporary American nature writers." Sadly, although both books have remained in print, fewer readers discover them every year. And so to introduce a modern audience to the lyrical prose of this unique writer, I am thrilled to present a combination of the two volumes. Some of the more unwieldy descriptions and minor trees have been trimmed, leaving only the gems of Peattie's best observations in what I hope will be "a volume for a lifetime" (*The New Yorker*, 1950). Peattie's writing remains largely untouched; the original language has not been corrected or updated. The result is a book that tells as much about early America as it does about the trees described within.

We have also retained from the original books the stunning illustrations by Paul Landacre. These fine etchings were made using a technique known as scratchboard, one of the more rarely used media for creating fine art. Scratchboard consists of a rigid base, coated with white clay and topped by a layer of black ink. The artist etches the drawing into the board by making thousands of tiny cuts with a sharp tool. The result —

as you can best see in the pictures of the pines and other coniferous trees — is more dramatic than a pen and ink drawing would be.

I am excited that a new generation of readers will be able to enjoy the text and illustrations in *A Natural History of North American Trees*, and I sincerely hope that it will be in print for another sixty years.

Frances Tenenbaum
October 2006

SEQUOIAS

Giant Sequoia

Sequoiadendron giganteum (Lindley) Buchholz*

OTHER NAMES: California Bigtree Sierra Redwood. Mammoth-tree.

RANGE: Western slopes of the Sierra Nevada in California, between 4500 and 8000 feet altitude, Placer County south to Tulare County, chiefly in some twenty-six isolated groves.

THE KINGDOM OF THE PLANTS has a king, the Giant Sequoia or California Bigtree. It is, as a race, the oldest and mightiest of living things. Not even in past geologic times, apparently, were there greater trees than *Sequoiadendron giganteum*. Only the Bigtree's closest of kin, the Redwood of the California coast, approaches it in longevity and girth. In grace and height, indeed, the Coast Redwood, *Sequoia sempervirens,* is a queen among trees, a fit mate for the craggier grandeur of the Bigtree of the Sierra Nevada.

Constituting all that is left of the once widespread genus *Sequoia,* these two species have found asylum in California, but they salute each other from widely separated mountain systems. The Redwoods inhabit the north Coast Ranges where they are maintained in a coolhouse atmosphere by long baths in sea fogs, unviolated by storms. In contrast, the

---

*Editor's note: Formerly *Sequoia gigantea* (Lindley) Decaisne.

home of the Giant Sequoia, lying between 6000 and 8000 feet altitude on the western slopes of the Sierra, is Olympian, as befits this Jovian tree. There the winters have an annual snowfall of 10 to 12 feet, but drifts may pile up among the titans almost 30 feet deep — a mere white anklet to such trees. The summers are exceedingly dry; if rain does fall it is apt to come with violent thunderstorms and lightning bolts that have been seen to rive a gigantic Sequoia from the crown to the roots. Those who know the species best maintain that it never dies of disease or senility. If it survives the predators of its infancy and the hazard of fire in youth, then only a bolt from heaven can end its centuries of life. Perhaps, if this majestic tree had a will, it would prefer to go this way, by an act of God.

The province of the Giant Sequoias is measured out on the planetary surface between the 36th and the 39th degrees north latitude, a distance of 250 miles. But you will not happen upon any single Bigtree in this range, for it grows only in groves, to be sought out by pilgrimage. Each Sequoia grove has its associations and history, and thus they have all received names — the Giant Forest, the Mariposa, Calaveras, and General Grant groves, to mention only the most famous and accessible. Others bear such suggestive titles as Lost Grove, Dead Grove, Surprise Grove, and Big Stump Grove. Some are so remote from roads and sightseers that they are seldom visited save by forest rangers on their rounds. In all, there are, by the most particularized classification, some seventy-one of them, or there were until several of the finest were ruthlessly destroyed with dynamite, ax, saw, and fire. It is certain that all have been discovered, and all too likely that Nature will never spontaneously create any more.

Stranger still, there seem to have been no more even long before the coming of the white man. At least, so thought John Muir who for years combed the mountains looking for traces of extinct groves and a more continuous distribution. Logs of Giant Sequoia, which are now straddled by other living Bigtrees of great age, show no signs of decay in the heartwood after perhaps ten thousand years since they began to grow. So it should have been possible, surely, to find traces of Sequoia growth outside the present groves had there been any. But Muir's fruitless search drove him to conclude that in postglacial times, at least, the Bigtrees had already found all the places where they could flourish.

Thus, to see the Bigtrees you must travel far and climb high. It is the better part of a day's run to them by car from San Francisco or Los Angeles, with an inescapable crossing of the flat San Joaquin Valley — in summer a furnace for heat. Then you wind for a long way through the foothills, among shadeless Gray Pines and Interior Live Oaks whose glittering foliage hurts the eyes. There it was that the forty-niners toiled, in their lust tearing up the beds of rivers and sluicing down the very hills. But, serene above such ant-work of a day, stood the Giant Sequoias, undreamed of by the fevered Argonauts, holding themselves aloof with the confidence of a thousand years.

Up through groves of Black Oak and Blue, of grand Western Yellow Pines and Incense Cedars, you mount, up and up into the realm of White Firs, symmetrical with tier on tier of whorled boughs, the trunks as satiny as flesh. Somber Douglas Firs darken the late afternoon as with oncoming night. At last the Sugar Pines with rugged purple trunks, the mightiest Pines in all the world, close ranks about you.

It will be dusky, no doubt, when you reach the giant groves. And the forest will be still, yet watchfully alive. A deer may come to your outheld hand and put an inquisitive black muzzle in it. It will be a long moment before you realize that the vasty shadow behind the little doe is not shade but a tree trunk so gigantic that you cannot comprehend at first that this is a living thing. Were that great bole put down in a city street, it would block it from curb to curb. That mighty bough, the lowest one, is still so high above the ground that it would stretch out over the top of a twelve-story office building. If it were cut off and stood in the ground, it would in itself appear as a tree perhaps 70 feet high, and 7 feet in diameter at the base. As for the crown, it is as lost to accurate measurement and comprehension as your head would be, seen by a beetle at your shoe.

Yet the trees conceal their true immensity by the very perfection of proportion. For each part — breadth at base, spread of boughs, thickness of trunk, shape of crown — is in calm Doric harmony with the rest. There is no obvious exaggeration of any part, no law-defying attenuation. Even the enormously distended bases by which the giants grip the mountainside and brace the gigantic superstructure have a look of functional tightness, so that we hardly realize that they may be 100 feet in circumference.

On second view, by morning light, the impression of the Giant Sequoias is still not so much of outsize as of color and candor. The ruddy trunks, especially in the more southern groves, are richly bright. The metallic green of the foliage is the gayest of all Sierra conifers'. In winter a Sequoia grove has the simple colors of a flag — a forest-soft red, white, and green. In summer the white ground is changed for the faultless blue of Sierran skies. The bright world is never shut away, as in the misty dimness of the Coast Redwood groves with their overarching canopy. The sunlight here reaches right to the floor. The bracing air, a shining but invisible god, moves proud and life-giving in its temple. Instead of the hush of the Redwoods, you hear among the Bigtrees the lordly racket of the pileated woodpeckers at irreverent carpentry on Sequoia wood. The Douglas squirrels frisk up the monstrous boles as familiarly as children on their fathers. Running out on the boughs, they cut the cones and then scamper 200 feet to earth, to despoil them of their seeds.

Sooner or later everyone asks which is the largest of all the Bigtrees. Yet no pat answer should be given. For the tallest are not the greatest in girth, the thickest are not the highest. Further, trees that were felled long ago give indications that they were larger and loftier than any now standing. The General Grant tree is 271 feet high. The Boole tree, at 16 feet above the ground, is 25 feet in diameter — the record among standing trees — while the Hart tree is the tallest of all, at 281 feet 6 inches. These measurements were made in 1928–29 by a trained engineer with the best of instruments, but time does not call them final.

In the Calaveras North Grove lies prone the tree called Father of the Forest, inside whose hollow trunk a man rode horseback without having to bend his head. In the Big Stump Basin are two truncated witnesses of boles that were once 30 feet in diameter when their bark was still on them. Of the same diameter was a colossus of the Calaveras North Grove, traditionally believed the first Bigtree ever seen by a white man. In accordance with the ebullience of our pioneering spirit, it was speedily cut down and made into a dance floor where thirty couples could waltz.

The discovery of this tree was made one spring day in 1852 when a miner from Murphy's Camp pursued a grizzly bear far up into tall timber. When Mr. A. T. Dowd (for history has preserved the name of this Nimrod) encountered the Bigtrees, his astonishment was so great that he allowed the bear to get away. True, the Bigtrees seem to have been sighted several times before by exploring parties, but as the journals and diaries that mention them were not published till long afterward, hunter Dowd's discovery stands, like Columbus's of America, as the first effective one. At any rate, his fellow miners came, incredulous, and beheld 50 acres of what we now call the Calaveras North Grove, covered with trees, some of them 325 feet high and 19 feet in diameter. The men departed, to spread the fame of the "Mammoth-trees" as they were at first called. And within a month or so of their discovery by Dowd, somebody now forgotten gathered specimens of branches, leaves, and cones which somebody else passed on, in June of 1852, to the excellent Dr. Albert Kellogg, pioneer botanist of California. But Dr. Kellogg was a man of leisurely habits and did not hasten to publish in a botanical way on the great discovery. In fact it does not appear that he had roused himself to visit the Mammoth-trees when, two years later, he showed his specimens to William Lobb who had recently arrived to collect plants for a British nursery establishment. With swift initiative Lobb set out for the Calaveras Grove, hastily gathered herbarium specimens, hurried back to San Francisco, and, without saying a word to any American scientists, took the first boat to England.

There he turned his specimens over to John Lindley, an English botanist who rushed a formal botanical publication into print by December of 1853, naming the mighty conifer *Wellingtonia gigantea*, in honor of Arthur Wellesley, Duke of Wellington and victor of Waterloo, who was then still alive to be flattered by having the mightiest production of Nature named in his honor.

Loud was the patriotic anguish of the American botanists. But fortunately the generic name of *Sequoia* for the Coast Redwoods had been published in Germany six years before *Wellingtonia*, giving it priority, and when it was realized that the Bigtrees too are Sequoias, Americans were satisfied. For the name was bestowed in honor of Chief Sequoyah, the great Cherokee who devoted his life to inventing an Indian alphabet and teaching others to read it.

It was a disappointed gold seeker, G. H. Woodruff of New York State, who climbed up into the Bigtree groves in the early fifties and threw himself down, homesick, upon his back. As he lay gazing into the green crowns, the cones snipped off by the chickadees came plumping down all about him. He began to examine them and shake out their seeds. Soon he had a great many and put them for transport in an empty snuff box. Back at camp he wrapped up the little box and prepaid a charge of $25 to send it east by Pony Express. So the first seeds reached the nursery firm of Ellwanger and Barry in Rochester, New York, and from them sprang up in 1855 four thousand tiny trees. They did not sell very fast in the eastern states, but in England where they were retailed, as Wellingtonias of course, they sold so rapidly that orders could not be filled. Botanical gardens in England, France, and Germany wanted specimens. Cities planted avenues of Sequoias. Soon every man of wealth or title must have a specimen for his grounds. "The great event of the year 1864," wrote Tennyson's son in a memoir of his poet father, "was the visit of Garibaldi to the Tennysons, an incident of which was the planting of a Wellingtonia by the great Italian and ceremonies connected with it." Eventually Ellwanger and Barry paid over to the fortune hunter Woodruff the sum of $1036.60 as his share in the profits — on a snuffboxful of seeds!

Californians were even then unabashed in the claims they made for their state, including the age of Bigtrees. They asserted that these trees were old when the Pyramids were abuilding. Even so eminent an authority (on fishes!) as Dr. David Starr Jordan assured the press they had endured ten thousand years. John Muir counted the annual rings on the biggest stump he ever saw and found over 4000, but not more. Even that can no longer be verified and is suspect of error. Accurate ring counts in recent times have never put the age of any logged tree at more than 3200 years.

Yet surely thirty centuries of life are awe-inspiring. There is something comforting about handling a section of Sequoia wood that seems scarcely less living now than when it grew before the time of Christ. For the proof of its age is there under your naked eyes, the annual rings which you can tick off like dates on a calendar — the years and the decades, the centuries and the tens of centuries. Somewhere about 2 inches inside the bark of a tree recently cut will be the rings laid down in 1849, year of the gold fever, and of the still more feverish 1850. Yet nothing of moment is graven for that time on the wooden tablets of Sequoia history. And it is humbling to notice that those particular rings may be 15 feet from the center of the tree, the starting point of its growth. The calm deposition of the rings (rosy pink spring wood ending in the sudden dark band of summer wood) has gone on millimeter by millimeter for millennium after millennium — advancing ripples in the tide of time.

Why, out of a world of trees, do these live longest? Why is a Cottonwood decrepit at seventy-five years of age, why does the Oak live three hundred summers? And since it can do so, why does it not endure a thousand? How does the Giant Sequoia go on growing, without signs of senility, until literally blasted from the earth by a bolt from heaven, a consuming fire, a seismic landslide, or a charge of dynamite?

One answer may lie in the very sap, for that of the Bigtrees contains tannic acid, a chemical used in many fire extinguishers. Though fire will destroy the thin-barked young Sequoias, when bark has formed on the old specimens it may be a foot and more thick and practically like asbestos. The only way that fire can penetrate it is when inflammable material becomes piled against the base and, fanned to a blowtorch by the mountain wind, sears its way through to the wood. Even then fire seems never to consume a great old specimen, no matter how it devours its heart. And the high tannin content of the sap has the same healing action that tannic acid has on our flesh when we apply it to a burn. The repair of fire damage by a Bigtree is almost miraculous. It begins at once, and even if the wound is so wide that it would take a thousand years to cover it, the courageous vegetable goes about the business as if time were nothing to it.

So we might say that Bigtree lives long because fire and parasites seldom succeed in storming its well-defended citadel. We might say all this and more, yet there remains some quantum of the inexplicable, and in the end we are forced to admit that Sequoias come of a long-lived race — whatever that means — and so outlast the very races of man.

All this semieternal life, all these tons and tons of vegetation, come from a flaky seed so small that it takes three thousand of them to make up 1 ounce. The kernel is but 14 inches long, and inside it lies curled the embryonic monarch. There are commonly from 96 to 304 seeds to a cone, and the cones themselves are almost ridiculously small for so mammoth a tree. They do not mature till the end of the second season, and not until the end of the third, at the earliest, do they open their scales in dry weather and loose the seeds, which drift but a little way from the parent tree. Their method of transport is not only weak, but their viability is low; perhaps only half of the seeds have the vitality to sprout. And long before they do so, they are attacked, in the cone and out of it, by untold multitudes of squirrels and jays. Many do not fall upon suitable ground — mineral soil laid bare — but are lost in the duff of the forest floor. Of a million seeds on a tree in autumn, perhaps only one is destined to sprout when the snow-water and the sun of the late mountain spring touch it with quickening fingers.

First the sprouting seed sends down a slim spear of a root. Swiftly this makes its way down about 2 inches and puts out its suckling root hairs. Only then does the first shoot appear, bearing four or five baby leaves still wearing the jaunty cap of the seed hull. Within a week or ten days the blades burst apart and the infant bonnet is flung away. Only now the tiny seedlings face further perils. They are attacked from below by cutworms, above by armies of black wood ants. Ground squirrels and chipmunks, finches and sparrows cock a bright eye at them and pull them up for a toothsome salad. Deer browse them by the thousands. If a seedling survives its first year, it may face the centuries with some confidence.

Underground, the taproot is descending faster than the shoot goes up, but at six to eight years it stops, and thereafter only lateral growth takes place. Eventually the side roots will become gigantic and spread out in all their ramifications over two or three acres. A tree 300 feet high has roots whose circle has a radius of 200 feet, and occasionally the roots are longer than the height of the tree.

Up into the light and air grows the princeling. The youthful leaves are soft, glaucous blue green; the bark is still smooth and gray with no hint of red about it. The stocky shape of childhood gives way to a conical outline, and the young tree stands clothed to the base in boughs that droop gracefully at the tip, of wood strong yet supple. These lower boughs help to brace the trees against the weight of the great snows of the Sierran winter, which will drift higher than young trees and bury and bend them. When the snows melt, the striplings shake off the last loads from lithe arms and lift shining heads, and they are "gey bonny," as Muir might have said in his Scots idiom, as they stand ranked close about some dewy, iris-spangled, deer-browsed meadow formed where one of their ancestors has fallen and blocked a stream to make a sedgy bog.

In the second century of life, the trees begin to assume a "pole form" — that is, with strong central trunk clear of branches for a long way, and a high peaked crown. Gone now are the drooping limber boughs of youth. In their place great arms begin to appear, leaving the trunk at right angles and then, bending up as if at elbows, lift leafy hands in a gesture of hosanna. The soft blue green foliage is replaced by metallic green. The smooth gray cortex gives way to the richly red bark of maturity. At last it is furrowed thicker than the brow of Zeus, and in the gales its voice begins, these years (and hundreds of years), to take on the deepest tone in the world's sylva.

When the Giant Sequoias flower, the trees are loaded with millions of male and female conelets from as early as November to late in February. The greeny gold pollen showers all over the giant's body and drifts in swirls upon the pure sheet of snows. A single tree will bear hundreds of thousands of cones when in the full vigor of its life.

Great age brings to the trees a diminished fertility — fewer cones, that is, but not less viability of seed. It sees the heroic self-pruning of the older boughs, which at last break off of their own weight. Electric bolts may repeatedly strike the monstrous lightning rod, topping it unmercifully. The once broad and symmetrical crown becomes broken and craggy. The tremendous strains of the superstructure have resulted in gigantic buttressing at the base. The whole tree is now as far past the manly beauty of its prime as that is past the pretty charm of its childhood. It is, after thirty centuries, practically a geological phenomenon.

In the wood, corresponding changes take place with the slow passage of time. The fibers of young trees are supple, and all the wood, for the first hundred years, is light yellow sapwood with dark orange bands of summer wood to mark the years. Only in the second century does the dark rose heartwood, deeply impregnated with tannin, begin to form, first a slim pencil that increases, in a thousand years or so, till it becomes most of the vast cylinder of the trunk. The wood at the base of an ancient tree is all contorted and tough with the compressions and strains of carrying some 600 tons of body above it. That at middle heights is straight grained, rose red, and, when fresh, so wet that it sinks in water. At the top of the tree the wood is pink and lightly buoyant.

All the properties of Sequoia wood save one are inferior to those of nearly every other timber tree in our sylva. Its chief virtue is that it lasts perdurably. In consequence, it was early sought out by lumbermen for shingles, shakes, flumes, fence stakes, and poles. The giant groves promised ready fortunes, by the look of them. Stumpage that scaled at from 20,000 to 120,000 board feet per tree promised fair!

So logging railroads were hurried up the mountains, mills were set up, and the Lilliputian lumberjacks fell to work among these woody Gullivers. First a 6-foot platform was erected to clear the flaring buttresses, and on it stood two men to chop a cut; chips 18 inches long flew out, till a gigantic notch was cut. When this was 10 feet deep, the fallers took a 20-foot saw around to the other side of the tree, and for several days they dragged it back and forth, all the while greasing it to make it slip, and stopping to drive great wedges behind it lest the tons of wood above begin to settle and vengefully trap the saw. At the last a few heavy gluts were sledged home, and the vast structure leaned, toppled, kicked back with a terrible lunge, then struck the earth with a cracking of limbs and a seismic shock that could be felt and heard a mile away.

In this wise was accomplished the destruction of the Converse Basin grove, probably finer than any now standing. Today in the Converse Basin there are few seedling Sequoias to give hope that this species will grow there abundantly again. Instead there are thousands of logs that were never utilized because they proved too big or costly to handle, millions of board feet gone to waste because the wood smashed to bits in its fall. The whole ghastly enterprise ended in financial failure, but not a failure of destruction. That was complete.

To the ruin of lumbering there was soon added a worse one, the fires deliberately set by sheepherders to improve the annual browse; these consumed thousands of young trees, Sequoias of the future. And this havoc was wreaked not upon private lands but upon the public domain. The long battle to save the Bigtrees was begun, so far as the Giant Forest is concerned, by Colonel George W. Stewart, a newspaper editor of Visalia, California, who roused public sentiment where there had been apathy. He was joined by one public-spirited citizen after another, by newspapers and magazines in California and finally in the eastern states. When fraudulent surveys and applications for possession of the Sequoia groves were made under the old timber and stone law, Colonel Stewart detected them and brought about suspensions of the applications. When a secretary of the interior lifted the suspensions, forty men of Visalia marched into the nearby groves to file private claims and so save the trees for the nation. Victory came in 1890 when Sequoia and General Grant National Parks were created. Even then, without a national park service to patrol these reserves, stockmen and timber thieves continued to violate the public domain, until John Muir's demand for a troop of cavalry to patrol the parks was finally acted upon by President Theodore Roosevelt. Today General Grant Park has been merged with the much larger Kings Canyon Park (the dream of Muir's life), and thus, with the inclusion of other fine Sequoia groves in Yosemite Park, the future of the king of trees seems assured. It seems so, but the forces that wish to unlock the national parks for private exploitation never sleep, and the vigilance of the forces of conservation must not do so either.

Coast Redwood

Sequoia sempervirens (Lambert ex D. Don) Endlicher*

OTHER NAMES: California Redwood. Coastal Sequoia. Sempervirens. Palo Colorado.

RANGE: In the fog belt of the California coast, though usually, at present, not at the shore but 1 to 30 miles east of it, in the lower Coast Ranges and intermountain valleys, from the Oregon boundary (and 8 miles north of it) south to Marin County, north of San Francisco Bay. Reappearing in the Santa Cruz and Santa Lucia mountains and down to sea level at Big Sur.

T HE COAST REDWOOD, the ever-living Sequoia, sempervirens, is the tallest tree in the world. Not just occasionally taller, in individual specimens growing under unprecedentedly favorable conditions, but taller as a whole, as a race, a titan race. Also it produces logs with the greatest diameter among all timber trees. Only the Redwood's big brother, the Giant Sequoia, *Sequoiadendron giganteum* of the Sierra Nevada, is ever greater in girth, but the Sequoia is not today in the class of prime timber tree.

True, too, that the Giant Sequoia lives longer, but Redwoods live long enough to awe the mind. A Redwood has a normal life expectancy of 1000 to 1500 years. The oldest specimen whose rings have been counted is estimated to be 2200 years old; a section of this log is preserved, for the doubting, in the Richardson Grove, part of California's state park system. So that tree began to grow when Hannibal was taking his elephants over the Alps; it was more than 200 years old at the birth of Jesus.

In all the world there is no other forest growth like that of the Redwood. It is at once the tallest and the densest of stands — not dense like the jungle's tangled quantities of trees, lianas, and undergrowth, for the Redwood groves are spaciously open to your footsteps — but dense in sheer volume of standing timber. Instances are on record of a growth of 2.5 million board feet to the acre, and from a single tree have been sawed out 490,000 board feet of lumber. Up in the Redwood country they show you churches and banks and mansions, each built out of one tree.

The Redwood forest stretches all the way from extreme southwestern

*Editor's note: Formerly Sequoia sempervirens (Lambert) Endlicher.

Oregon south for 450 miles. It is, however, a narrow belt, averaging only about 20 miles in width and lying sometimes close to the Pacific, again 30 or 40 miles inland from it, as it follows the wandering crest of the Coast Ranges from Oregon to the Golden Gate. A detached province of it lies south of San Francisco in the Santa Cruz Mountains, and another in the Santa Lucia Mountains south of Carmel. But it is in northwesternmost California that these trees grow tallest and most densely; there the growth is most ancient and the quality of timber best, where the annual precipitation runs as high as 100 inches. Such a drenching would do credit to a tropical rain forest, the more as it falls all in the winter and spring months. The summers are rainless, but even then the Redwood belt is almost nightly blanketed in heavy sea fogs, and though these burn off in the morning, they frequently roll back during the day to saturate the atmosphere in which grows so deep the vegetation carpet of the Redwood forest floor — all the evergreen mosses, and the ferns of a Carboniferous luxuriance. Nowhere is the Redwood separated from these summer fogs.

To see the heart of the greatest Redwoods of all, take U.S. Highway 101 north from San Francisco. For nearly 200 miles you travel through the brilliant sunlight of the dusty interior California summer. Fields are open, or, if there are woods of Oak and Pine, the light fills all their glades; wild flowers are gaudy, jays are clamorous, the swift-running stream of cars a loud, metallic current. The eyes are tired of color, the ears of sound. Then suddenly you are enfolded in the first of the centenarian groves, and for the next 40 miles, to and through the Avenue of the Giants, you are seldom out of their ancient shade. The transition is like stepping into a cloister, one infinitely more spacious and lofty than any ever raised by man, and closing the door behind you upon the bright secular world.

Your footfalls make no sound on the needles and moss that have lain there for centuries. Your body casts no shadow in that green, lakelike diffused light. The goose honking of a car, the calling of a child, fade into the immensity of silence. Time, the common tick-tock of it, ceases here, and you become aware of time in another measure — out of an awesome past. For this forest has stood here since the Ice Age, and here, together with this transfixed past, is the future too, for these immense lives will outlast yours by a thousand years or so.

But this solemnity is not like that of church or tomb; it is enlivened by the soft dispute of a stream with its bed, or the swirling, blurred whistle of the black-throated gray warbler so high in the clerestory of the woods that he cannot be seen. And now and then the treetops utter a slow, distant sea-hush, a sigh that passes, and then comes again, as if it were the breathing of a life beside which our lives are as a single day. At any time in the day the mist may roll silently through the forest aisles. It may rest on the forest floor, drenching the beds of oxalis and moss; it may wander, like the incense smoke in a temple, among the trees; it may move through their crowns, leaving the forest floor quite dry. But always the strong sun comes piercing through the fogs in beams of smoky light, slant shafts that fall with unerring drama upon some high altar log swathed in the emerald cloth of *Hypnum* moss or bearing aloft the great tuft of a translucent fern or a spray of the phantom orchis. Many of the wild flowers of the Red-woods — the oceanspray, the sugarscoop, the deerfoot, and the inside-out-flower — are pale and delicate and small of corolla, as if the great trees had used up all the bigness at the time of creation.

And they are mighty past telling. Their enormously swelled bases are buttressed with great lynxlike claws, as if the trees gripped the earth to keep their balance. The ruddy shafts rise up, unlike almost all other trees, with scarcely any discernible taper, the sides parallel as those of columns for a hundred feet or two hundred, till they disappear in the high canopy of branches. The effect of gigantism is increased by the burls often seen on the trunks. Many other kinds of trees also produce those lumpy swellings, but the Redwood's burls are in proportion to the rest of the tree — as much as 6 and 8 feet thick. The cause of these burls is not understood, but the result is the production of a heavy, hard, dark wood figured with fantastic grain. Like a potato with its "eye," a burl contains buds, and the small burls sold by the roadside will, if you put them in a dish of water, send out a ferny sprout.

When a Redwood is cut down, the high stump often sprouts from the base, giving rise to a lovely circle of sister trees. Yet they are not truly daughters of the old tree but a continuation of the same life. Again, a fallen log may send up shoots resulting in a straight row of close-ranked trees which put down roots straddling the log. This too is a continuation of the same tree life, not a new generation from seed. So that it is nearly impossible to say where a Redwood life ends; rather it changes direction and grows on — as nearly immortal as anything under the sun.

From the beginning, a Redwood is beautiful. In its seedling stage, its childhood, it is straight, graceful, covered with a lovely foliage of needles rather like a Hemlock's, dark green and glittering above, delicately silvered with lines of stomata below. Unlike the Pines, the Redwoods do not go through an awkward age, but in young and middle life they retain all their grace, all their military straightness, as they crowd down to the curving banks of the rivers, climb the slopes of the Coast Ranges, fill the flats and benches of the terrain. At this stage a Redwood forest is dusky as you walk under it, owing in part to the crowding of the trees before competition has weeded them out, but still more to the dense shade cast by the accompanying California Laurel and the Douglas Fir. But time is all on the side of the Redwoods. In the fullness of it, the fast-growing young trees will crowd out competitors, by root and by crown, till they reach the stage that ecologists call a climax forest — one which cannot be displaced by another sort unless ax or fire violently intervene.

In the climax forest there are or were specimens that pile climax upon climax! The "Captain Elam Tree," that stood on the holdings of the Little River Redwood Company, was found by log sealers to have a diameter of 20 feet and a height of 208 feet, containing enough lumber to build twenty-two average-sized houses. It was cut down a few years ago. A giant in the Mill Creek woods is known to be 340 feet tall and 16 feet 6 inches through. The tallest of them all, the highest tree in the world, is the Founders' Tree, in the woods at the North Dyerville Flat. It is 364 feet high, yet so lofty are its neighbors that without the figures to prove it, you would not guess this chieftain to be greater than its brothers. The age of the Founders' Tree is not known, but it is probably less than that of a tree felled in 1943 by the Union Lumber Company on Big Flat, Mendocino County. The count of its rings tallied 1728 years. Its height was 334 feet, with a stump diameter of 21 feet 6 inches. With a power-driven 22-foot saw, this ancient was laid low.

The mind pauses over the fact of such a magnificent tree, felled and sawed up into lumber. The fact brings us sharply to the realization that behind, and not far behind, the Redwood Highway and its slim ribbon of parks preserved for the public, there lies by far the greatest part of the Redwood stand, which is in the hands of lumber companies or private owners who will presumably sell if the stumpage price is attractive enough. The Redwood lumber industry is one of the most active in the country, but the public sees far less of its activity than that of most industries; public roads do not wind through most of these holdings, and visitors in the region where giants are crashing to earth are in too much danger to be welcome. The truth is that this industry, according to its own statistics, is cutting into the Redwoods at a rate that is seldom less, in recent years, than 300 million board feet a year, and sometimes rises to 600 million.

Backed by all the inventive genius of our people, this industry has overcome, with power-driven saws and modern tractors, the obstacles to lumbering among giants which looked almost insuperable to the pioneering fathers and grandfathers of the present owners of what are among the greatest sawmills in the world. There are now about four hundred sawmills, large and small, in the Redwood country, as well as some forty shingle mills, and in the period 1899 to 1948 the industry cut about 22 billion board feet — at least a third, perhaps more, of the amount now standing. Salesmanship which can be admired for its resourcefulness is taking orders right now for Redwood in Australia, New Zealand, Central America, and the eastern states, as well as in the fast-growing timber-consuming state of California itself. Trees being felled as you read this will soon be railroad ties in Peru, or banana boxes of the United Fruit Company's subsidiaries.

Must we be proud of this, or indignant? It is easy to give a quick, emotional answer, depending on our economic persuasions or our esthetic faith. But if one were appointed an arbiter with sole responsibility to do perfect justice to every conflicting interest, one would have to walk all around the question, viewing every aspect. To do that is impossible in these pages. The best that can be accomplished is to sketch very briefly the story of the white man's discovery of this tree, his great need of it, and his finally awakening consciousness that this heritage of the ages calls for some responsibility in him.

On October 10, 1769, Fray Juan Crespí, chronicler of the Portolá expedition (the first exploration that the Spanish made by land of the California coast), recorded that on the Pajaro River (near present Watsonville) the party traveled "over plains and low hills, well forested with very high trees of a red color, not known to us. They have a very different leaf from cedars, and although the wood resembles cedar somewhat in color, it is very different and has not the same odor; moreover the wood of the trees that we have found is very brittle. In this region there is great abundance of these trees and because none of the expedition recognizes them they are named redwood from their color." Then, in 1776, Fray Pedro Font, chronicler of d'Anza's expedition to San Francisco Bay, recorded that on March 26, they saw "a few spruce trees which they call redwood, a tree that is certainly beautiful; and I believe that it is very useful for its timber, for it is very straight and tall." On March 29, on the return journey, the party descried in the distance "a very high redwood . . . rising like a great tower." Next day they came up with it; Font measured it and recorded: "I found it to be . . . some fifty *varas* high, a little more or less. [Fifty *varas* is 137 feet 6 inches.] The trunk at the foot was five and a half varas [about 14 feet 9 inches] in circumference and the soldiers said they had seen even larger ones in the mountains."*

So the Redwood enters into recorded history, named on sight though never seen before, and, it is significant to notice, immediately appraised for its value as lumber. Time swiftly brought increasing appreciation. When saintly old Padre Junípero Serra, founder of California's chain of missions, knew that his end was near, he ordered the mission carpenter to build a coffin out of Redwood, and in this he was buried in 1784 at Mission San Carlos Borromeo at Carmel. When the roof of this abandoned mission fell in 1852, the burial place of the good Father could not be found in the ruins, but in 1882, or ninety-eight years after the burial, it was rediscovered, the Redwood coffin in perfectly sound condition.

The Spanish settlers used a little Redwood for beams in their churches; the Russian colonists used rather more, to judge from the numerous saw-

---

*Font's *palo alto*, his "tall tree," is still standing; from it the town of Palo Alto takes its name. As it was once a council tree of the Indians, so it is sacred in the traditions of Stanford University students, who used to guard it, the night before the football game with the University of California, from being cut down (they said) by their rivals. It is figured on the seal of the university.

pits and stumps around Fort Ross and Bodega Bay. The Muscovite church at Fort Ross, built in 1812 of local Redwood, stands to this day. But the first real assault upon Redwood came with the Gold Rush. As early as 1850 sawmills appeared on the hills south of San Francisco, and soon Redwood was cut for houses, barns, fences; it was carried to the mining country for sluice boxes, rockers, sheds. In 1855 the first shipment by sea went from Humboldt County to San Francisco, and that mushrooming settlement soon became a city of Redwood houses. Wharf piles, piers, bridge supports, and even curbs were soon built of Redwood. Redwood gutters and eave troughs for houses became common. Aqueducts and flumes for irrigation canals were early built from it, and for outfall sewers and wooden water pipes and conduits it was found to be peerless, for not only does it not decay, but the longer water runs through it the smoother become the inside walls, while iron grows rougher with grit and accretions. Every part of the United States has at some time used Redwood pipes and flumes as parts of municipal water plants or in mines. Railroad water tanks of Redwood have been built all over the country. Because Redwood splits so evenly and lasts so long, shingles were early made of it. The pioneer children of California were rocked in Redwood cradles and, in school, learned from Redwood "blackboards" made from a single plank 4 or 5 feet wide and as long, of course, as necessary. And soon the Milwaukee brewers were using Redwood vats. Presently Redwood reached the South Seas, and pearl divers in the Society Islands were making boats, with outriggers, of three Redwood planks. A more versatile wood never invaded the lumber markets of the world.

This versatility rests upon the inherent properties of the wood. For Redwood is so durable in contact with the soil and freshwater, though not saltwater, that it is matched by few American woods. It has slight tendency to shrink or swell and holds paint well, making it ideal for drawers, sills, sashes, and doors. Because it is so nearly immune to the attacks of termites, it is exported to tropical lands extensively, and in California a law requires that wooden uprights under buildings be made of Redwood sunk in concrete. Owing to its lack of resin it is highly absorbent of water; when the hoses are turned on a burning Redwood house, it soaks up the water promptly. Redwood imparts no flavor of its own to liquids stored in it; in consequence the wine industry in California early began to make casks of Redwood and continues to do so to this day. Though it is not a very strong wood, absolutely speaking, it is strong in comparison to its weight. So, for light trestles and bridge supports, it early came into use, and in World War II immense quantities of it were rushed to the Pacific.

Redwood is a joy to carpenters, so knot free, straight grained, and smooth as cake under the plane. So it goes into balusters, newels, porch rails, posts, columns, moldings, flooring, and siding as well as uprights, beams, doors, and shingles. As a wood for fine paneling it is a beauty. The heartwood needs no coloring but its own natural soft rich hue. More, it has an inexplicable golden gloss of its own, a halation as delicate as the shimmer on a tress of blond hair. White Redwood is produced by some of the trees near Crescent City, marvelously clear of blemishes and knots. The rare black Redwood comes from trees with extremely dark heartwood and on account of its lasting qualities is sought for tanning vats, which are set below the surface of the ground. Curly Redwood comes from stumps and is highly valued for flamboyant cabinet work. But the finest grade of regular commercial timber is cut in the forests of Humboldt County. It is very soft, with a satiny surface, whitish sapwood, and a terra-cotta-colored heartwood, has a straight grain, seasons well, and commands the highest price.

Although Redwood accounts for only 2 percent of the timber cut in the country today, it is plainly high on the list when it comes to quality. In multiple use it is all anyone could ask of any one species, though it is spared the ignominy of being reduced to pulp, for in that direction it is of almost no promise. In sum, this is a tree around which a great lumber industry was predestined to arise; this country and many others would be poorer far without it and will not be denied the use of it while there is Redwood to cut and the price remains within bounds. The bark, once considered a dead loss, is now sold for insulating electric water heaters, cold-storage warehouses, fur vaults, butcher shops, and dairies; it is used for sound deadening and mattress filling, for fishing floats and cork jackets, soil mulch, and even cloth and felt hats.

The first to lumber the Redwoods, back in the 1830s and 1840s, merely nibbled at the woods, dropping trees small enough to be handled with poleaxes and whipsaws. By 1850 a side-wheel steamer, its paddlewheels turned into pulleys, powered a steam mill of sorts on the Mendocino coast. It is said that the Chinese of Mendocino utilized the incoming and outgoing tides to drive a water mill rigged up with a Muley perpendicular saw. Later, double-bitted axes came into favor. "Fallers, or choppers, as they are known locally, work in pairs," so the veteran logger H. I. Bower recalled before the Pacific Logging Congress in 1936. "An outsider is impressed by the number of tools a set of choppers carry around with them in a Redwood operation — two axes, two eight-foot saws, one twelve-foot saw, two dozen plates, one dozen shims, ten wedges, two sledges, one pair of gun stocks, one plumb bob, twelve springboards, six pieces of staging.

"Areas are felled as units. The chopping boss — bull buck — plans the strips. A set of choppers may work anywhere from a month to three months on a strip. The timber as far as possible is felled uphill, heavy leaners being an exception. The choppers' primary concern is to fall the tree with the least amount of damage.

"After determining the direction of the fall, smaller trees, called 'bedding,' are felled into the layout to build up the low spots. The undercut is now put in. The back cut is the next step."

If the tree is out of plumb — and it easily may be as much as 4 feet, at the top of its 300-foot length, though appearing straight enough to the unaided eye — the bottom of the cut may have to be raised 1 inch to "take out the lean," and then raised another to make it fall in the right direction. The slightest miscalculation may send hundreds of tons of wood crashing on the loggers.

For a Redwood in death, Walt Whitman himself has spoken:

Farewell my brethren,
Farewell O earth and sky — farewell, ye neighboring waters;
My time has ended, my term has come.

Along the northern coast,
Just back from the rock-bound shore, and the caves,
In the saline air from the sea in the Mendocino country,
With the surge for bass and accompaniment low and hoarse,
With crackling blows of axes sounding musically driven by strong arms,
Riven deep by the sharp tongues of the axes, there in the Redwood forest
*   dense,*
I heard the mighty tree its death-chant chanting . . .

Nor yield we mournfully, majestic brothers,
We who have grandly filled our time . . .

Thus on the northern coast
In the echo of teamsters' calls and the clinking chains, and the music of
*   choppers' axes,*

The falling trunk and limbs, the crash, the muffled shriek, the groan,
Such words combined from the redwood-tree, as of voices ecstatic, ancient
  and rustling
The century-lasting, unseen dryads, singing, withdrawing . . .

The chorus and indications, the vistas of coming humanity — the settle-
  ments, features all,
In the Mendocino woods I caught . . .

Whitman saw Redwood lumbering still in its heroic age of falling by hand, when teams of twenty yoked oxen dragged the giants down the skid road to the splash dams or the harborless coast where the great logs traveled by cable from shore to schooner, or put to sea as gigantic rafts of logs towed by small steamers. But in 1881 John Dolbeer, a pioneer operator among the Eureka Redwoods, brought out of his blacksmith shop an invention that made the bullwhackers guffaw. It was a sort of donkey engine with a vertical boiler, a horizontal one-cylinder engine, and a big drum on which to wind up the tentacles of steel cable. He made these fast to a gigantic log, then opened up his engine wide. The log came thrashing down the skid road faster than the bullwhackers could cuss an ox, and the smirks died from their faces, for their jobs were gone. Today, super-tractors take the place of the donkey engine, and powered saws cut short thousand-year-old lives like guillotines. The tempo of felling has risen to a *presto furioso*, with larger mills cutting up to 600,000 board feet a day. Their storage sheds may roof over 10 and 12 acres each.

This is not to say that all the logging practice in the Redwood region is bad practice. On the contrary, many, though still not all, of the operators are carrying on selective logging, with the minimum of destruction to young trees. Mature and overmature trees are logged, leaving the "young" (under four hundred years of age!) the light and space and soil water which they were denied by their tyrannous elders. Waste has now been cut to a low minimum, a saving at the mills that means a saving of standing trees. Fire is fought like a demon. Diesel tractors have largely replaced the donkey engines and cable systems of the past, with a great saving in damage to young trees.

The Redwood industry, with a view to reforestation, has set up about 100,000 acres, to date, in tree farms. More important, the current practice of logging with diesel engines makes it possible to leave scattered "seed trees" for natural reforestation. Selective logging instead of clear-cutting is now the practice on the best-regulated private holdings. Immature trees 24 to 48 inches thick on the stump are left, with the result that by the time the operator has cut the last acre of his ownership, the immature trees will have become prime for cutting, and in the meantime, they will have reseeded the land with another crop. Thus, says Professor Emanuel Fritz of the Department of Forestry of the University of California, the timber is cut on a maturity basis, and the land is kept in continuous production. Speaking of the outlook, he says: "At the expected rate of logging, 500 million board feet per year, it would appear that we are overcutting the growth by just that amount during the first year, because the virgin timber itself is believed to make no accretion in volume. In the second year we will appear to have overcut by one million board feet, less the growth on the area cut the previous year. But if logging and growth on new cutover lands are projected forward 50 years it becomes less and less apparent that the forest area is being overcut. The cut in the fiftieth year will still be, for the purpose of this exposition, 500 million board feet, but there would be accumulated [by that time] . . . 500,000 acres of cutover land. . . . The annual growth on such an area of selectively logged cutover land should produce 500 million board feet per year. This is equal to the annual cut."

Like a good scientist, Professor Fritz honestly acknowledges that this is the picture of what should be, and only in part the picture of what is. He points out that his "present rate of cut" is merely assumed for purposes of argument; no one can know that it will not increase as the population of the country increases. And the whole industry, not merely the best of it, must practice selective logging. To bring about sustained yield in the Redwood Empire, all operators, not just some of them, must leave the lands in such a condition that the Redwood's marvelous regenerative powers can assert themselves, instead of being left in such a state of ruin that no Redwood can grow there again in centuries, if ever.

It is true that virgin forest is not necessarily the best forest, from the point of view of lumbering; a fine, healthy, even-aged, second-growth stand is in many ways more satisfactory to log. But from the point of view of preserving forest grandeur that it has taken a thousand years to produce, virgin Redwood groves have values that belong to the world, and the future. How much of this old-growth Redwood is there left? The estimates vary. The Forest Service thinks there are only 31 billion board feet of it uncut, but the lumbermen believe it amounts to 50 billion. Taking their more optimistic view, virgin Redwood would last just one hundred years more at the present rate of consumption if only virgin timber were cut. But selective logging is our hope. New growth on lands selectively logged is expected to produce 1000 to 3000 feet per acre per year.

Unfortunately the progressive elements in the Redwood industry have no coercive power over their brethren still operating on the cut-out-and-get-out philosophy, while singing the old canticle of "inexhaustible abundance." Nor can the federal government take a hand. It has no authority to prevent owners of forest land anywhere from recklessly destroying their own capital. It possesses very little Redwood land of its own today, though once, in the Redwood Empire, it was monarch of all it had never surveyed. For soon after California joined the Union, Uncle Sam began giving away this empire under the then popular persuasion that the main thing was to get the country "settled up." Trees everywhere were regarded as usurpers of land that should be raising corn and hogs; they were ambush hiding murderous redskins. So for the pittance price of homestead claims, we gave away the finest timber in the world, on the same terms as saw-grass swamps and alkaline deserts!

Worse still, too many of the homesteaders in the Redwoods made fraudulent entries. Russian sailors just off the ships, for instance, were brought by interested persons to the Land Office, their claims were written out for them, a dummy cabin (transportable from place to place) was stood up briefly on the claim, to comply with the law, and the "homestead" then changed hands, for a few dollars. At least one clerk in the Land Office confessed later to connivance in the theft, in this way, of millions of dollars' worth of Redwood timber, and many others must have known what was going on and cynically closed their eyes. From one speculator to another these originally stolen claims then passed. The ultimate operator often had to pay a fair price for the trees he cut, but the profit had been taken by profiteers, to the great loss of the government, the consumer, and all the American people.

When the Forest Service and the national parks were formed at last, they were given lands out of the public domain then remaining. By that time the Redwoods no longer formed a part of it. Thus, the preservation of the Redwoods has been the work of private individuals and the state of California through its park system. It all began with a trip through the Redwoods taken in 1917 by Dr. Henry Fairfield Osborn and Dr. John C. Merriam, the naturalists, and Madison Grant, an amateur scientist. The devastation they beheld caused them to found the Save-the-Redwoods

League. Today, with headquarters in San Francisco, it has over 15,000 members, has collected the funds — $5 million to match state money — to buy some 60,000 acres of the noblest Redwoods, and with a master plan of what it hopes ultimately to accomplish, it is constantly working to secure other tracts of matchless beauty.* For instance, World War II was not yet over when the League went to work to set aside, by purchase, the National Tribute Grove, to express the eternal gratitude of the nation to the men and women in the armed services. Today this magnificent virgin wilderness has been secured to that high purpose by contributions from all over the country. And there is the Children's Forest — one of the League's most moving projects. Anyone can add to its existing acreage by a contribution; most gifts to it are made in memory of beloved children who have died. With meadows and streams, paths and bridges to enchant a child, the grove is a serene and smiling monument in which to enshrine such lost little lives. Other groves have been purchased, with funds given the Save-the-Redwoods League by such organizations as the Garden Clubs of America, and by individuals, to be preserved from the ax forever.

And it is moving, as one travels slowly through the nickering light and shade of the Redwood Highway, to realize that many of these groves were given, in part at least, by people who have never seen the Redwoods and perhaps do not expect ever to see them. For the members of some of the sponsoring organizations live in Iowa or Vermont, in Georgia or New York. The great majority of them are probably not persons of wealth at all. They gave anonymously, they gave purely, they gave to the future, to people yet unborn; they gave not only to the country but to the world. And they gave out of a deep religious feeling that the beauty and age and greatness that here have risen from the earth to tower above us are holy and shall not be profaned.

Editor's note: As of 2006, the Save-the-Redwoods League has purchased and protected more than 165,000 acres. More information is available at www.savetheredwoods.org.

PINES

Eastern White Pine

Pinus strobus Linnæus

OTHER NAMES: Soft, Sapling, Pumpkin, or Weymouth Pine.

RANGE: From Newfoundland to Manitoba and south to Iowa, northern Illinois, central Indiana, eastern Ohio, and Pennsylvania, thence south on the Appalachians to Georgia.

FOR THREE HUNDRED YEARS, till well after the turn of the last century, Eastern White Pine was unrivaled as a timber-producing tree. Perhaps no other tree in the world has had so momentous a career. Certainly no other has played so great a role in the life and history of the American people. Fleets were built to its great stands, and railroads bent to them. It created mushroom fortunes, mushroom cities. Earlier it was a torch in the hands of American liberty. Though now it has fallen dramatically from its high estate to a modest place among the other conifers, its saga is a tale worth recalling.

The hero of this saga may be distinguished at a glance, almost as far as it can be seen, by its pagodalike outline and habit of growth. The whorled branches grow in well-separated tiers, as if they formed successive platforms of a tower. This structure is as clearly marked (where the trees have room to attain natural development) in very young specimens as in the oldest, though this characteristic outline is less obvious in dense groves

26

where the older, lower branches have died and the congested crowns are deprived of full development.

The White Pine is a northern tree; in the aboriginal American forest it was perhaps the most abundant species almost throughout its range. Over vast areas it formed pure or nearly pure stands, or with only Red Pine for an intimate associate, according to the testimony of early "land lookers" (timber cruisers, as we would say now). The fact that today in those same localities it is intermixed with Spruce, Balsam, Aspen, Hemlock, Canoe Birch, Jack Pine, and many other North Woods species, only means that the kingdom which White Pine once held as its own has been invaded, since the days of the sawmills, by an influx of trees that once were its humble subjects. Much of Pennsylvania and almost all of New York outside the Adirondacks — so it has been asserted — was one vast White Pine forest. Pioneers used to say that a squirrel could travel a squirrel's lifetime without ever coming down out of the White Pines, and save for the intersection of rivers this may have been but slight hyperbole. When the male flowers bloomed in these illimitable pineries, thousands of miles of forest aisle were swept with the golden smoke of this reckless fertility, and great storms of pollen were swept from the primeval shores far out to sea and to the superstitious sailor seemed to be "raining brimstone" on the deck.

Nor can one easily conceive, from the second growth that is almost all that is left to us, of the toppling height of the virgin White Pines. Trees 150 feet tall astounded the first settlers and explorers; 80 feet or more of the trunk of such a specimen might be free of branches, marvelously straight and thick. On the present site of Dartmouth College, a specimen 240 feet in height was measured. This would surpass anything in the eastern United States and would do credit to the Douglas Fir of the West, and even the Redwood. Similar heights were recorded from Maine, Quebec, and both eastern and western New York, in pioneering times. How many others were felled unmeasured or unrecorded, we cannot know. It was possible for the old "land lookers" or "timber hunters" or "spotters," as they were variously called, to climb some lofty Spruce and from its top sight these mighty groves miles away on the horizon — "clumps," they called them, or "veins of Pine" running like sighing rivers through the primeval forest. A branch was thrown down on the ground, to point the direction of the groves, and the way was then found through the trackless wilderness by compass.

The first account of this tree in English appeared in John Josselyn's *Ac-*

count of Two Voyages to New England (1674): "The Pine-tree is a very large Tree, very tall and sometimes two or three fadom about; of the body the English make large Canows of 20 foot long, and two and a half foot over, hollowing them with an Adds and shaping of the outside like a boat." But Eastern White Pine had undoubtedly been carried to Europe by the earliest navigators in Canadian waters. Before the middle of the sixteenth century it was growing at Fontainebleau and was mentioned then by the French naturalist Belon.

In 1605, Captain George Weymouth of the British Royal Navy sailed his vessels up one of the Maine rivers, and, first of Englishmen perhaps, he got more than a coasting sailor's look at the White Pine. Away with him he took specimen logs of mastwood, and seeds of young trees. These were planted at Longleat, estate of Thomas, Viscount Weymouth, second Marquis of Bath, since when the English have called our tree the Weymouth Pine. But it has never proved adaptable to the English climate. Only in its own country was White Pine destined to a great role.

Certainly it was the first gold that the New England settlers struck. The exploitation began immediately and was so intensive that it was soon necessary to pass our first forest conservation laws. Not that anyone then could have envisaged the day when the virgin stands would all be gone, so vast and dense was White Pine's empire, but the wastefulness in the mills began with the first one, built about 1623, at York, Maine, and was never to cease while the virgin timber lasted.

It was not the wood needs of the puny colonies which threatened this great resource, but the fact that, aside from fish and fur, timber was the only great export of early New England. Within thirty years she was selling her White Pine not only to England but to Portugal, Spain, Africa, the West Indies, and ultimately even densely forested Madagascar.

How one could sell trees to jungle countries can only be explained by recalling that most tropical timbers are heavy and hard; they lack the very qualities of lightness and softness in which the White Pine excels. It is the softest of all the Pines of eastern America, yet in proportion to its weight it is strong. In proportion to its strength, it could be had in solid "sticks" of prodigious lengths for masts, such as no other known part of the world was then producing.

Certainly no wood light enough and strong enough for masting was grown in Europe in such lengths. And England, mistress of the seas and forever at war with the other navies of the world, had no mastwood at all. She pieced together her proudest masts out of Riga Fir (Scots Pine —

Pinus sylvestris) but Prussia, Russia, and Sweden held monopolies in it on which England was dependent, to her own great discomfort. The Danes had only to close the Sound to cut off her supply entirely. So that the arrival of the first White Pine masts created a sensation in the Navy Board. Contracts were let at once to American agents like the Wentworth family of New Hampshire, and, with great mast sticks selling at £100 apiece, it is no wonder that the Wentworths grew rich and occupied a position of political power commensurate with their wealth.

In the meantime other colonists were growing rich. A great three-cornered trade was set up when, in all-Oak ships of their own building, the New England merchants exported White Pine to the Guinea coast of Africa, shipped on a load of human ebony, sold it into bondage in the West Indies, loaded up with sugar and rum, and raised sail for Portsmouth, Boston, Newburyport, or Salem. Of White Pine boards, and of the wealth that came from this trade, were built the quiet mansions of the seaport cities, the dignified doors, the exquisite fanlights. As tastes grew more sumptuous, an exchange might be made direct with the West Indies — light, utilitarian Pine for heavy Santo Domingo Mahogany to be made into the most elegant of early American furniture.

More and more the New England sailing ships came to be decorated by the famous American wood carvers with figureheads of a very special sort of White Pine, so smooth and soft of grain that it could be cut with almost equal ease in any direction. The woodsmen called it Pumpkin Pine, and they contrasted it with the coarser-grained Sapling Pine. To the lumberman, as to the wood carver, the distinction was profound. They asserted that Sapling Pine had more sapwood and that its trunk tapered more from base to crown, while the Pumpkin grew on uplands, and "held its contour better." Botanists and foresters today believe that the difference was a matter of age; they point out that in our day of second-growth Pine, Pumpkin is almost unobtainable; it was a product of centuries of undisturbed virgin timber growth.

Few historians mention it now, but Eastern White Pine was one of the chief economic and psychological factors in the gathering storm of the American Revolution, at least in New Hampshire and Maine. The trouble began in the reign of William and Mary, when by decree those monarchs began to reserve the grandest specimens for the use of the Royal Navy. In her desperate timber shortage, and her endless wars to keep the seas, the mother country naturally looked on aghast when pioneers, advancing far beyond the land grants, into the "Crown Lands" or royal domain, chopped down, or even burned down the finest trees along with the least, simply to farm the land. It seemed to the British that they were fighting the empire's battles for the colonists as well as the home country; they could not understand what looked to them like the greed and short-sightedness and refractory spirit of the American pioneers.

To the colonists the same facts looked entirely otherwise. What the Crown called Crown Lands, reserved to His Britannic Majesty for sale, perhaps, to London land speculators, appeared to the Americans then (as the wilderness was to do for centuries) as Indian country, theirs for the taking. Unexploited, it was at once an impregnable fortress for cruel savages, and wealth, vast wealth, desperately needed by a struggling people. The man who could find his way 50 miles beyond the nearest settlement, into the primeval forest, cut down gigantic Pines, work them with boom and tackle to the river, ride and pole them down the whirlpools, rocks, and falls, to a secret market, perhaps in another colony, was (whatever else you called him) a man indeed. And as for masts for the wars of the English, the colonists had their own wars — with the Indians — and felt capable of winning them, if not called on to help fight Spain and Holland and France.

So one law, proclamation, or royal instruction after another was passed to restrain the colonists from what was called timber stealing on one side of the Atlantic, and on the other was practically considered the Lord's work. John Wentworth, baron of the New Hampshire pineries, later to become the last royal governor of that colony, was made Surveyor General of His Majesty's Woods in America, with authority to mark for the Navy Board every great Pine with a resented blaze known as the King's Broad Arrow. Tactful, cultivated, genial, he was a conscientious servant of his king. But well though he was personally liked by his fellow Americans, the King's Broad Arrow infuriated the pioneer, as the Stamp and Townshend acts infuriated the merchants, as the tax on tea the city dwellers. Not for this did the woodsman fight his way into the wilderness to make himself a home — only to find that his trees, as he thought of them, were branded with that hateful symbol of royal privilege. No wonder that he chopped them down, obliterated the blaze, sawed the giants into smaller lengths, and floated them down the Connecticut River to New London or some other Sound port for sale and export, perhaps, to England's enemies.

The Crown retaliated. In 1761 it instructed the royal governor that in all future land grants a clause was "to be inserted to reserve all white or other Sort of Pine Trees fit for Masts, of the growth of 24 Inches Diameter and upwards at 12 inches from the Earth, to Us our Heirs & Successors, for the Masting our Royal Navy, and that no such Trees shall be cut — without our Licence — on Penalty of the Forfeiture of such Grant, & of the Land so granted reverting to the Crown; & all other Pains and Penalties as are or shall be enjoined or inflicted by any Act or Acts of Parliament passed in the Kingdom of Great Britain."

More, a spy system was set up against those who cut trees in violation of these instructions, the spy to receive the land grant of the lawbreaker. In retaliation, the pioneers disguised themselves as Indians and did their cutting at night. A law decreeing that all who cut trees in disguise should be flogged had no known deterrent effects. American officers would not arrest other Americans for breaking British forest laws made in Britain for the sake of Britons, nor would juries convict them, or judges impose sentences. British agents drove the loggers from their homes and burned their sawmills, but the loggers had their own law — "swamp law" they called it, and it was not healthy for agents unaccompanied by troops.

When the storm of the Revolution broke, the Americans foresaw that their own White Pines might come back to them as the masts of armed ships bringing armed men. In 1774 Congress stopped the export of every-thing, mastwood included, to Britain. In April 1775, after Lexington had been fought, the lumbermen were patriots, to a man. A British agent and his mastwrights were captured on the Kennebec, with several masts. When the armed ship *Canceau* sailed into Falmouth to protect a Tory rig-ging and fitting the mast ship *Minerva*, Maine men drove her off. Putting to sea, the men of Machias overtook the armed ship *Margaretta*, boarded and captured her, and fitted her out as a privateer. In revenge, the British flattened Falmouth to earth with shot. Down at Portsmouth, the patriots seized the great masting pools on Strawberry Bank. The last cargo of American White Pine reached England shortly after Bunker Hill. From then on, the British fought on sea with heavy, jointed masts of Riga Fir, while coasting within sight of Pines that would have enabled them to meet the French on equal terms.

The first flag of our Revolutionary forces bore for its emblem a White Pine tree. But out of Portsmouth, November 1, 1777, sailed the *Ranger*, Captain John Paul Jones, fitted with three of the tallest White Pine masts that ever went to sea, and from the mainmast fluttered a new flag, the Stars and Stripes, to carry the war to Britain's shores.

Independence won, the New Englanders turned to their pineries as the richest natural resource they had. This is not the place to tell the story of

White Pine lumbering, the greatest chapter in the history of any nation's forests. There is a wide literature of the American lumberjack, the old-style lumber baron, the whirlwind exploitation, romanticized in such classics as John S. Springer's *Forest Life and Forest Trees* (1851), bemoaned by Thoreau in our most beautiful forest idyll, *The Maine Woods*, detailed in some twelve hundred pages in Deffebaugh's unfinished monument, *The History of the Lumber Industry in America*, recounted with gusto for the Rabelaisian details in Stewart Holbrook's *Holy Old Mackinaw*, keened as a wake in his *Burning an Empire*, and exposed in all its grime of ruthless waste, greedy exploitation, bribery, corruption, labor wars, and timber thefts in *The Great Forest* by Richard G. Lillard. To sum up a mighty epic in a few poor lines — it was under the boughs of the Eastern White Pine that there evolved the greatest woodsman the world has ever seen, the American lumberjack (though much of the time he was a Finn, Dane, Swede, Norwegian, or Russian by birth), an embodiment in himself of the Paul Bunyan legend, a hero of courage and skill amidst toppling giants and river jams, a demon of accelerating destruction. The industry built fortune after fortune acquired by ruthless exploitation, spent, in many a case, with the highest benevolence, evolving ever new methods, ever higher efficiency, including efficiency at lobbying and holding the forces of conservation at bay until the end of the northern pineries was reached.

In the days of its greatest utility and exploitation, White Pine gained its importance from factors partly environmental, partly inherent in the special properties of the wood. Most of the White Pine grew in a region of heavy snowfall, so that the logs could be, at low cost, sledded with oxen power to the river. The abundance of rivers made transportation to the mill inexpensive. Add to this that the extreme lightness of White Pine greatly aids it in flotation; heavy logs like White Oak or Black Locust would be floated with much less success. The great abundance of the forest, the continuity of its stands, made it possible to develop a concentrated industry, with mass production and mass marketing, and correspondingly cheap rates to the consumer. Then, too, the old-time lumberman was able to operate, in successive localities, on virgin timber. This yielded a much finer grade of wood — longer, smoother, free of defect and knot, and more easily worked than second growth can easily boast.

In the three hundred years of its exploitation, Eastern White Pine, more than any other tree in the country, built this nation, literally and figuratively. It would be impossible, in the scope of these pages, even to list all the uses of White Pine, the most generally useful wood our country has ever possessed. They range from the paneling of fine old colonial interiors to the famed bobsleds of New England, from hobby horses to the 72 million board feet of this now precious wood which was still being split into matches in the year 1912. (Western White Pine has now taken over the burden of matchwood.) Of White Pine were built, according to François Michaux, speaking of the period around 1805, half a million American homes, those frame houses that are the most typical form of dwelling, save in great cities, from Maine to Florida, and west as far as White Pine was ever shipped on the treeless plains — houses viewed with amazement by foreigners, accepted complacently by natives. No other wood served so well for window-sash material, for it could be moved at a touch of the hand, yet did not warp. No other furnished such great clear boards for doors and interior finish. In every sort of millwork White Pine reigned supreme while it lasted. It was the favorite material for heddles of looms, since the weaver must lift or lower the heddle for every thread that goes into the woof. Because it is so light, smooth, easily planed and polished, untold amounts of cheap furniture have been made of it. It takes paint and gilt better than almost any rival.

The amount of shingles made of this Pine for the roofs of American homes is beyond calculation. In twenty-four years Michigan, Wisconsin, and Minnesota produced 85 billion of them. For two centuries they were hand rived with a froe. An expert (and he was indeed an artist at his profession) could rive five hundred a day and earn a dollar doing it. He professed to know when a given specimen in the forest would rive well, but if he had any doubt he whacked out a big block from the standing tree to test its splitting qualities. If they were unsatisfactory, he simply left the tree to bleed its resin from the cut, providing thereby a wick that would ignite the tree to its crown in the next woods fire. "The pioneer custom in Kentucky of killing buffaloes for their tongues was little more wasteful than the primitive white pine shingle maker's procedure. He used only the choicest parts of pine trees. The sapwood, the knots, much of the heart, and practically the whole trunk above the first 20 feet were left in the woods to rot. It was not unusual to sacrifice a 3000-foot tree to get 1000 shingles — throwing away about fourteen-fifteenths and using one-fifteenth. The introduction of shingle-making machinery put a stop to that enormous waste, for the saws could make shingles of knots, slabs, tops, cross grains, and all else, from stump to crown. The old-style method of shingle-making died hard, for the shavers opposed the introduction of machines, and declared the ruination of the country would follow so radical a revolution in a widespread industry."*

The famed covered bridges of America were built of White Pine in preference to almost any other wood, because of its long-lasting qualities and its lightness in proportion to its strength. Of this wood was built the bridge over the Charles, connecting Boston and Cambridge, the same on which Roger Taney passed his momentous decision in the Charles River Bridge case, dealing a blow at monopoly. The Delaware River Bridge at Trenton (where Washington had crossed through ice floes) and the aqueduct for the State Canal over the Allegheny River at Pittsburgh were White Pine structures. This aqueduct, considered a miracle of its day, was 16 feet wide, 1020 feet long; with seven spans, it carried one watercourse, and the commerce borne upon it, over another.

"Many of the bridges in the interior of Pennsylvania and West Virginia, by which the old pikes crossed the numerous streams, were built of white pine," say Hall and Maxwell, "and it is said of some of them that no man had lived long enough to witness their building and their failure through decay. Some of these structures were marvels of efficiency. Extra-large timbers were unnecessary, and though slight in appearance, they carried every load that came during periods often exceeding half a century. They were roofed — usually with white pine shingles — and were weatherboarded with white pine or yellow poplar, and though painted only once or twice in a generation, they stood almost immune from decay."

In each state the White Pine brought sudden wealth; all the great rivers of northeastern America, except the Hudson with its alternating tides, were choked at one time or another with tremendous rafts of logs, each bearing its owner's mark or brand, like cattle going to market. The longest haul was from the pineries of Pennsylvania, 200 miles above Pittsburgh, to New Orleans, 2000 distant by the windings of the streams. One raft that passed Cincinnati covered 3 acres and contained 1.5 million board feet of Pine, valued at $5 a thousand in Pittsburgh, at $40 a thousand in the Creole capital. When the timber was gone, the farmer followed, at a temporal distance of about twenty-five years.

Or he did so in the most rosy pictures of exploitation. Actually much of the land could never be profitably farmed. Between the millions of stumps it was acid or rocky; in place of the forest giants of yesterday spring up the Aspen and Spruce, the brambles and the fireweed. Too often the end came

*William Hall and Hu Maxwell, "Uses of Commercial Woods of the United States. II. Pines," *Forest Service Bulletin* 99, 1911.

in fire and smoke. Forest fires in northern Michigan in the 1890s sent palls of smoke 200 miles up Lake Michigan to Chicago. The Peshtigo fire in Wisconsin killed more people than the Great Fire of Chicago that began on the same day. The story of what happened to Hinckley, Minnesota, is an almost unreadable record of human agony. The end was miles of ashes, like a landscape of hell, or ghost towns, or sawdust piles.

By 1900 there was nowhere to turn for virgin White Pine except the southern Appalachians. And certainly there were some dense stands of White Pine in the high coves. Trees 150 feet tall were then known there. At Shady Valley, Virginia, the yield reached an all-time record, for the South, of 100,000 board feet of White Pine to the acre. So here the industry turned for a last skid to the mills. Not that many of the old-time lumberjacks of Bangor or Alpena came this way — they followed the lumber barons and the saws to the "big sticks" of Oregon. In the Appalachians, the industry developed with local resident labor; no great lumber camps ever evolved. Everything that had given the North Woods lumbering its characteristics was lacking in North Carolina; there was no snow, there were no rivers capable of carrying big logs, no great central mills. Instead steep inclines, narrow-gauge railroads, migratory mills, and stationary labor created a pattern far less picturesque, though not lacking in effectiveness.

The wood, too, was different. Appalachian Eastern White Pine is heavier and coarser than the northern grades, with a somewhat reddish color. In consequence it has never commanded the high price of the best northern Pine. The southern boom in White Pines lasted from 1900 to 1915. Today the stand of White Pine is in the neighborhood of 14 billion board feet in the United States and 8.7 billion in Canada. Maine, which was one of the first states to lose its paramount position in White Pine production, is once again the leading region in the United States. This is because the second growth has, after nearly a century, reached maturity.

The glory and tragedy of the White Pine epic had its lessons, and its lasting results. The boom was, in the nature of historical factors and economic and social pressures, inevitable. The "bust," by dramatizing the situation as in the case of no other American tree, roused public opinion to the support of the conservationists who had fought for twenty years without allies. Though public opinion came too late to save the virgin White Pine, it made itself felt just in time to save the great forests of the western states, to back Theodore Roosevelt and the Forest Service and the national parks in their battle for timber conservation.

Western White Pine

Pinus monticola Douglas ex D. Don*

OTHER NAMES: Silver, Soft, Fingercone, Mountain, Idaho, or Little Sugar Pine.

RANGE: Southern British Columbia and Vancouver Island, below 2500 feet, south to the mountains of northern Idaho and northwestern Montana, and through western Washington (sea level in the Olympic Mountains to 6000 feet in the Cascade Range), the Cascades of Oregon (2500 to 7500 feet), the northern Coast Ranges of California (4500 to 8500 feet), the Sierra Nevada (7000 to 11,500 feet) and in southern California on the San Gabriel, San Bernardino, and San Jacinto mountains above 8600 feet. Also in the Blue and Warner mountains of eastern Oregon above 7500 feet, and in the Reno and Lake Tahoe region of Nevada.

F AR REMOVED FROM THE EXPERIENCE and rounds of most of us, the queenly Western White Pine reigns over the "Inland Empire," as its inhabitants like to call it — the central parts of the northern Rockies, in the "pipestem" or "panhandle" and other northerly sections of Idaho, and adjacent parts of Montana, Oregon, and Washington. Even when you visit this region, on your trip from Glacier National Park, let us say, through the beautiful lake country of the Northwest, you

*Editor's note: Formerly *Pinus monticola* Douglas.

may fail to distinguish this tree, splendid though it is, from its fellow conifers the Hemlock, Spruce, Larch, and Fir that make up the dense, the somber forest of the empire, almost as lofty and as lush as that of the Olympic peninsula. For one thing, mature Idaho Pine (the lumberman's preferred name for it) has such a long stem clear of branches, carrying its crown to 100 feet overhead, locked in a dark arch with the crowns of the other trees, that from the ground you do not easily distinguish the bundles of five slender blue green needles, nor the long, finger-slim, drooping cones which proclaim this tree a Pine, and one of the aristocratic White Pine group, at that. It is easiest, perhaps, to recognize this species by its bark, which is not furrowed even in age but is broken into many rather small and irregular but smooth blocks by narrow, shallow lines and crosschecks. The bark when fresh is purplish but is soon weathered to a silvery color. If scoured by constant mountain winds, it may show cinnamon on the exposed side.

Yet though the living tree is known to so few of us, it plays such a large role in our daily lives that every American handles its wood on an average of 2300 times a year! We are familiar with its weight (or rather its extreme lightness), with its color — or lack of it (for its sapwood is very pale) — and even with its faint, sweet smell. For this tree, almost exclusively now, yields us our wooden matches. Formerly they were made from the Eastern White Pine, but as the first growth of that species approached exhaustion, the western species, its closest relative and similar to it in the physical and chemical properties of its wood, began (from about 1914 on) to bear the whole burden of matchwood production. This may not seem a great drain — a match is so slight a thing — but remember that twelve thousand wooden matches are struck, by the American people, every second. That makes more than 103 million in twenty-four hours. To produce a year's supply of matches, three hundred thousand mature pines must yield up their lives. If grown to a pure stand, they would cover an area 2 miles wide and 10 miles long.

Not all of any White Pine tree will do for the making of matchwood. A match plank, to be marketable, must yield 60 percent or more of high-grade wood — that is, wood which has no diagonal, twisted, coarse, or hard grain, no knots, pith, compression wood, weak wood, or discoloration. Good match plank is sawed out into 2-inch thicknesses and cross-sawed into blocks exactly equal in length to that of a match stick. These are fed into machines where a row of some forty circular knives, flashing up and down at the rate of five strokes a second, slice off individual sticks on the down stroke, and on the up stroke they punch them into perforations in a steel plate. If you have noticed that one side of a match stick is usually rounded, you will understand that it is the squeezing of the stick into the perforation which gives it that shape. An endless belt then conveys the sticks through a paraffin bath to increase their inflammability; they pass next through a chemical bath which shortens the afterglow, so that, once blown out, the ember will die quickly, not linger as a coal.

In almost all respects, the Western White Pine carries on the great tradition of the Eastern White Pine as nearly peerless in its class as a softwood. Its best grades of wood are even grained, light yet comparatively strong, remarkably free from warping and shrinkage. As a result, it is used in great quantities for window sashes, which must not warp with changes in the weather and should be so light that they can be moved at a touch, and for doors, panels, finish, columns, siding, shelving, sheathing, flooring, ceiling, and lattice and pantry work. Because of its lightness and freedom from resin and decay, it goes into window blinds and shutters. Because it takes paint and gilt so well and is light and smooth grained, it is a favorite for picture frames, cabinet work, and veneer backing.

Much of the "knotty Pine" so popular now with interior decorators, especially if it is of a pale tone and with dark reddish knots, is Idaho White Pine. "Clear" — that is, not knotty — paneling of this species is also increasingly popular; it is almost without visible grain, that is, the summer wood is scarcely darker than the spring wood and so presents a beautiful, light, satiny surface. The wood, moreover, is a joy to the carpenter, under his plane, so soft and smooth it is. For patternmaking it is ideal, since it can be cut across the grain with almost as much ease as with it. It seems a wood made by Nature for man's hand to fashion at his will. Straight and true, tractable, fine — these are words one may apply to it both by analogy and quite literally. Only the virgin White Pine of the East, in its day, ever produced a softwood lumber of such refinement and versatility. But the eastern species was, half a century ago and more, ravaged and wasted. The western species has taken its place before the saw.

Wherever Western White Pine occurs on a commercial scale it is almost certain to be the most valuable timber tree in its region, no matter what its competitors. It fetches a higher price than Western Red Cedar or even Douglas Fir when growing side by side with them. The annual cut at the present time is running around 261.5 million board feet a year, most of it in the Inland Empire, but this rises at times to twice that amount. In

British Columbia it would be probably the most valuable timber resource in that greatly forested province, if only it did not form so slight a percentage of the stand, and the same is true in California.

Yet Western White Pine lumber has but a small market in the very regions where it grows. Its great reputation with buyers is in the eastern states, where the tradition of the Eastern White Pine's marvelous wood still lingers. Eastern customers accept the western species as a satisfactory replacement for their native soft Pine in all the millwork enumerated above and are willing to pay the high price of hauling the lumber across the continent. To reduce the cost of the rail haul, Western White Pine is usually kiln-dried near the sawmills. It is then shipped east, manufactured into all sorts of millwork and stock sizes of doors, frames, panels, and the like, including "mail order" window sashes with their glass already set in them, and is then frequently shipped back to the West and sold to the house builder right in the Inland Empire.

David Douglas, the great Scottish explorer-botanist who first discovered so many western trees, made this species known to science after he found it in 1825 growing on the slopes of Mount St. Helens, in what is now the state of Washington but was then unexplored "Oregon," a vast area neither clearly British nor clearly American. But the true home of this tree — where, at least, it occurs in its greatest abundance and finest dimensions — is deep in the interior of the northern Rocky Mountain system. And here it was that lumbering of this valuable timber began at a remarkably early date. For the year 1840 found Idaho still a howling wilderness, when that intrepid Presbyterian missionary, the Reverend Henry H. Spalding, employed his Nez Percé converts to dig a millrace from the Clearwater River and erect a sawmill, at his pioneering mission school of Lapwai, Idaho. The waterwheel for this mill was constructed of Western Red Cedar and Idaho White Pine, and the saw was obtained from the celebrated Dr. McLoughlin of the Hudson's Bay Company post at Fort Vancouver. It was brought all the way from the fort to Lapwai, on horseback and in canoe, by Dr. Marcus Whitman, the medical missionary who was so soon to lay down his life as a martyr to the treachery of the Cayuse Indians. Spalding, who had with Whitman brought out the first wagons, the first printing press, and the first white women, over the Oregon Trail, was so horrified by the Whitman massacre that he became obsessed with a conviction that the Cayuse had been stirred to the act by the Catholic missionaries, and finally he left his sawmill, his school and mission altogether to stump the country with lectures on the subject. There is no evidence that the Catholic missionaries instigated, even indirectly, any such deed as resulted in the deaths of the saintly Dr. and Mrs. Whitman, and several others.

After Spalding's pioneering venture in White Pine lumbering, the business moved but slowly. The great bulk of the stand was almost wholly inaccessible for a long time, and the market was flooded with fine coniferous woods. But the approaching end of the supply of Eastern White Pine almost coincided with the building of the first railroads across northern Montana and Idaho — the Northern Pacific in 1881, the Great Northern in 1890, the Chicago, Milwaukee, and St. Paul in 1908. These railways, at the start, offered special rates to homesteaders, and many special inducements to settlement in the last great forest frontier of this country. Some of the railroads themselves were owners of vast timber holdings, acquired from the government, in alternate sections of land on each side of their rights of way (as inducement for the great initial cost of laying the tracks), and these were disposed of to lumber companies and speculators. As the eighteenth century drew to a close, then, all the forces of exploitation were drawn up before the virgin stands. These forces included an approaching dearth of softwood lumber in the East, a "high" market, railway systems to take the wood to that market, a highly advanced technology of rapid lumbering and milling and seasoning, an influx of settlers and investors on cheap land, an open-handed policy on the part of the government, and the old frontier psychology of "getting rid of the woods and settling up the country."

Certainly the aboriginal growth of White Pine was temptation enough to set the saws to whining. There were areas in which sound trees, 150 years old or thereabout, cut out at 51,000 board feet to the acre. On the White Pine's preferred site of deep porous soils on gentle north slopes and flats, individual trees towered up 100 and 175 feet high and produced boles as much as 8 feet in diameter at breast height. How beautiful such growth appeared before the destruction began is recalled in the memoirs of an Idaho settler who was about eleven years old, in 1901, when she first raised the curtain of the tourist train that was bringing her to her new home: "Trees surrounded us; tall, graceful trees; great trunks waving like timothy and exuding the exhilarating odor of pine. There were still mountains, but draped mountains, fold on fold of silvery green, a little darker than the breast of a teal, but with the same billowy sheen. As we wound around the shores of Lake Pend Oreille, the men gathered in an exclaiming group about my father, listening to his explanations of this splendor with avid interest. . . . Bay after bay swept by, green and blue and blue and green, drenched in the golden sunlight of a spring morning; and then, as we neared Hope, a startling sight met our eyes. Great trees lying prone, crisscross and tossed about, as if a tremendous tornado had swooped and slapped and slain. I heard the word 'slashings' for the first time and never can I forget its appropriateness. . . .

"Everyone was soon homesteading in the splendid Marble and Mica Creek district. . . . Logging was the only industry and at that time competition was brisk and haste the watchword. . . .

"Time passed. I married a homesteader who had just proved up. Homesteading was not farming in those days, but just a subterfuge to gain possession of timber. . . . The money from the sale of this . . . went into more timber and the financing of other homesteaders — a grubstake was tripled when the homesteader sold — and we used our stone and timber rights beside. Quick turnovers and more investments, and our stake was made. We were ready for a clean-up, all titles clear and the patents ready to turn over. The timber companies were planning a monstrous cut in the spring. Cruisers were making their final estimates, and thousands lay in the banks awaiting the word. We were jubilant. A new house and new clothes, a trip to the city, and a solid investment were the promises of the morrow."*

To understand what happened next, in that breathless, expectant August of 1910, we must leave the homesteader's young wife, Nancy Warren, and study the meteorological and political conditions prevailing over Idaho for many weeks previous, for the murk about to envelop her was of vast extent, affecting hundreds of thousands of lives, and great fortunes. Back in Washington, Congress in its wisdom had just voted to deny the newly organized Forest Service any fire-fighting funds. The winter over the northern Rockies had been normal enough, but drought started in spring. The hills that year scarcely grew green with grass before it was withered. Crops were seared, and the forests became dry as tinder. All during June, July, and August, dry electrical storms started small fires, while careless railroad crews and wandering prospectors, loggers, and homesteaders were responsible for others. The force of the Forest Rangers was thinly scattered in the Lolo, Coeur d'Alene, and Pend Oreille forests; there were no lookout stations, then, few telephone lines, no firebreaks, few trails.

*Nancy Rovena Warren, "White Pine — My Lady of the North," *American Forests*, September 1928.

As the small fires increased to some three thousand, a curtain of resinous smoke spread over the whole region. Lights burned by day in people's houses. Train conductors had to read the passengers' tickets by the light of their lanterns. The oppressive air was strangely quiet — sounds seemed to be swallowed up; birds staggered in their flight, and horses rolled their eyes, straining at their halters. Then on the night of August 20, the superheated atmosphere over the whole area, rising, sucked in winds of hurricane force. Forest rangers were almost blown out of their saddles; acres of timber went down like kindling. And the small fires were whipped, in a matter of moments, into great ones.

Young Mrs. Warren stepped outdoors to get some fuel for the evening meal, when she says, "a smoking twig fell at my feet. . . . I sniffed, but the air was usually laden with smoke. I looked at the horizon and saw nothing. A blast of hot air swept my face — just that and the smoking twig, but a sudden fear gripped my heart."

"On the Lost Horse Trail, deep in the Bitteroot Range, a forest guard stirred uneasily in his sougans (a thin, generally shoddy, quilt). Something pattered on the tent roof. . . . Wind was moaning through the trees, dropping needles and refuse on the tent. . . .

"A few minutes later one of his crew . . . called him out. . . . A star, he said, had fallen on the hillside across from the camp, setting a small fire. The forest guard swung around into the wind. There on the western horizon, a fiery glow lit the sky for mile after mile. He knew then what the 'star' was and what it meant."*

Mrs. Warren had also, about the same time, and a hundred miles away, seen a "star" fall. The church bell began to ring. Women gathered in groups. Children were awakened. The fire rolled down the hills like a gigantic curtain, while the able-bodied men hurriedly plowed and shoveled a fire line on the forest side of the town. Water pipes were hastily laid and all the available fire-fighting apparatus was called in.

The "stars" that these two had seen, the blast of hot air that hit Mrs. Warren's face, were but the perimeter phenomena of as frightful a calamity as ever befell a forest. For as the thousands of small fires were lashed by the winds into seething holocausts, an area hundreds of square miles in extent became so superheated that the resins in the virgin and mighty coniferous stands began to volatilize until great clouds of inflammable hydrocarbon gases were formed. And these, catching fire all at once,

*Stanley Koch, "Remember 1910!" *American Forests*, July 1942.

simply exploded in one screeching detonation after another. Tongues of flames shot into the sky for thousands of feet. Whole burning trees were uprooted and sent hurtling far ahead as gigantic brands. Flames tore through the crowns of the forest at 70 miles an hour. Settlers' cabins, railway trains, towns, were suddenly engulfed in seas of flame.

At Wallace, Idaho, the telegrapher for the Northern Pacific Railroad tapped out, "Every hill around town mass of flames Whole place looks like death trap Men women children hysterical in streets leaving by every possible conveyance."

The telephone girl at Avery, Idaho, where the St. Paul tracks cross the Continental Divide, was broadcasting her warnings up to the moment when the line went dead — the poles leading to the telephone office were down in flames. One refugee train with a thousand souls aboard hid from the flames in Tunnel Thirty-two, while, outside, the ties were burning and the steel rails buckling.

About ten miles from the burning town of Wallace, Ranger Edward C. Pulaski, grandson of the Polish Count, Casimir Pulaski, who gave his life for American Independence at Savannah, was in charge of a crew of forty-three men, most of them volunteers. As the flames closed in around this band from every side, Pulaski led his men into an abandoned mine shaft. Two or three blankets had been salvaged in the flight, and wetting these in an underground trickle, Pulaski made a fire curtain of them over the door of the shaft. As the heat and smoke grew too intense for endurance, and the mine timbers began to burn, men became insane and tried to dash outside. Pulaski held them back with his revolver until he dropped, suffocated. But at the words, "Come on outside, boys, the boss is dead," he revived to say, "Like hell he is," and scramble to his feet. Five men died in the tunnel before the flames passed. The survivors were led to safety by Pulaski through a landscape charred beyond recognition.

All through the national forests similar scenes of heroism and tragedy were being enacted. Not till the twenty-third of August did a general rain, with snow on the high peaks, descend in torrents and quench the holocaust that no power of man could have stopped. An area the size of Connecticut, in the aggregate, had been destroyed, eighty fire fighters had been burned to death, hundreds of homes destroyed, millions wiped out in fortunes large and small.

Supervisor Koch of the Lolo Forest set out to tramp the embers' wrath: "The still warm ashes were knee deep where once I had walked in cool forest aisles. For mile after mile, as far as the eye could reach, lay a smoldering, desolate waste. Stunned and heartsick, I never wanted to see the country again."

Mrs. Warren and her husband, their lives saved by the rains which came too late to save their little fortune, walked over the scene of their green hopes, that was now a blackened ruin. Then, as their eyes slowly swept the scene, they saw a fluttering tuft of pine, a single tree on a hilltop that by some miracle had, though scorched, not been killed.

It was from such as these that the burned-over area began its natural restocking. Today, nearly fifty years later, an even-aged stand of second growth has, in some places, entirely healed the dreadful scars of 1910, but in too many other spots, Aspen and Fir and other inferior trees are still in the slow process of making the ruined land habitable again.

There were many lessons taught by this, the worst forest fire in history. The most obvious and painful was that the lessons of Alpena, Peshtigo, Hinckley, and the other disasters in the Eastern White Pine had not taught the succeeding generations a thing. Haste, recklessness, waste, greediness for quick profits, all played their part in the starting of the innumerable fires that went out of control when the high winds arose. And this responsibility, as usual, must be scattered over a wide field; it applied to great railway systems and to small landholders alike. The only force for conservation on the scene was the Forest Service, which before the fire was widely unpopular with lumbermen, stockmen, and prospectors but emerged from the flames with enhanced reputation.

Lumbering on private holdings in Idaho White Pine today is carried on along the scientific lines advocated years ago by Forest Service. At least this is true in the best-conducted operations. Slashings and other wood waste are reduced to a minimum and carefully disposed of before they become a fire menace. The lower limit of diameters of trees suitable for logging has been raised. Adequate numbers of seed trees are left to restock the cutovers. Thus an area logged in, say, 1926, will be available for a second cut in 1961 and, seed trees again being left, a sustained yield of this high-grade lumber should continue into perpetuity, if fire and the insidious blister rust can be kept out.

To the lover of wilderness scenery, of course, these second growths, cut just when they are beginning to attain their full beauty, can never mean what the virgin White Pine means. For that we must look in the future to our national parks, and even there, even in the sanctuary of Glacier, we see the ravages of fire. In this semiarid climate, with such highly inflammable and resinous trees, it will remain a danger always.

Sugar Pine

Pinus lambertiana Douglas

OTHER NAMES: Big or Great Sugar Pine.

RANGE: From the central Cascade Range of Oregon (2000 to 3000 feet, or on the east side to 5000 feet) to southern Oregon (down to 1000 feet in the inner Coast Ranges and Siskiyous); at 4500 to 6500 feet in the desert ranges of southeastern Oregon; in California in the Siskiyous, Trinity Alps (1800 to 6000 feet), south on the northern Coast Ranges (but not in the coastal fog belt), especially in the Bully Choop and Yollo Bolly mountains (2300 to 6000 feet) to northeast slopes of Mount St. Helena but not around San Francisco Bay; reappears (2000 to 7000 feet) in the Santa Lucia Mountains of Monterey and San Luis Obispo counties. Found around Mount Shasta and Mount Lassen (3000 to 7500 feet) and south in the Sierra Nevada (west slopes, 3000 to 9000 feet), in the high mountains of the Santa Barbara region, and from 4000 to 10,500 feet in the San Gabriel, San Bernardino, and San Jacinto mountains of southern California. Also in the Lake Tahoe region of Nevada and from 8000 to 10,000 feet on the Sierra San Pedro Mártir of Baja California.

THE GREAT GENUS OF THE PINES stretches around the north temperate zone and on mountains far into the tropics and numbers some eighty species. Many of them are of the highest use or the greatest beauty, and many of them attain splendid proportions. But there is one species, the Sugar Pine, that towers above them all. It is the king of Pines, undisputed in its monarchy over all others.

In magnificent dimensions the Sugar Pine ranks after the two Sequoias and the Douglas Fir; it is, therefore, the fourth greatest of all American trees in size. A specimen standing today in the Stanislaus National Forest, California, is 200 feet high and has a trunk circumference, at breast height, of 31 feet and 8 inches. Some of its neighbors in the mountains of California are almost as tall and mighty of bole, and it is quite possible that before the lumber mills began, over a century ago, the whirlwind destruction of the finest of accessible stands of Sugar Pine, there were other specimens larger still.

A grand old Sugar Pine two or three hundred years old can stretch out its lower limbs high above the heads of many other species — the Incense Cedars, Yellow Pine, and the Firs. Even in the company of the Giant Se-

47

quoia, the Sugar Pines are not dwarfed but stand as worthy associates of the largest and oldest living things upon earth.

As you mount up the western slopes of the Sierra Nevada, you first meet the Sugar Pine at altitudes as low as 2000 feet in the north, but in the southern Sierra it scarcely occurs below 6000 feet, and on the high mountains of southern California it is first met with at 8000 feet and ranges up to 10,000 feet altitude. It thus occurs in what are the most grandly forested portions of this great mountain range, where the rainfall is in the neighborhood of 40 inches and the snow at times may lie 12 feet deep. But in summer, which is the dry season, this is the most enjoyable part of the Sierra Nevada — a region of open groves with very little underbrush but a wealth of wild flowers and small flowering shrubs. Here mule deer step proudly and unafraid, through the groves of the Sugar Pine; a lumbering bear goes by intent on his business and not in the least hostile to man; the Douglas squirrel dances and chitters on the boughs perhaps a hundred feet overhead, the needles are deep underfoot, and views of snowy peaks, canyons, and waterfalls, open at every vista of the groves.

In this magnificent setting the Sugar Pine is at home. Its mighty boles rise straight as the shafts of columns, but colored a rich purplish brown and livened with tufts of the yellow green staghorn lichen. The incense of its needles and resinous exudations fills the aisles of this forest temple. Overhead the majestic crowns of the Sugar Pines just touch each other, making a vaulted roof that is airy and full of light. Everywhere is a sense of light and space, of hope and time — time enough to grow a kingly tree, a long time that has gone before you, to clothe a mountain range thus nobly.

Young Sugar Pines are all alike in their slender, close-grown, conical form. In winter their youthful limbs easily shed the snow, never breaking under it. Before the season is done the drifts may have sifted so high that the little trees are buried many feet under it, and many tons of weight may lie upon them. Yet the snow is the friend of these trees, for, softly but firmly encasing them, it keeps them for months of the year in a rigidly upright position, so that a crooked stem is almost never seen in a Sugar Pine. Once started straight, the tree, as it grows older, is able to keep the martial tenue it gained in youth. The lower branches are self-pruned as the young groves grow older, with the result that few Pines have so little limbage, or a larger bole so clean of branches. At the top of the long stem an old Sugar Pine bears a palmlike crown, though grander than any true palm's, for the lowest limbs may be 40 feet in length — very fair trees in themselves were they cut off and set upright. As it enters old age, the Sugar Pine allows it-

self endless eccentricities. No two old trees look alike; each is an individualist of the most rugged sort, grandly asymmetrical, disdaining the pretti-
ness, the uniformity of Fir tops, or the winsome nodding of the tips of
Hemlock. Instead, an old Sugar Pine's crown looks storm racked but indomitable, sometimes almost absurdly sprawling or overreaching.

Yet this tree has its grace; for from the underside of the foliage hang the
swaying, slender cones, 15 to 26 inches long, green shaded with dark purple on the sunward side. After they ripen in September and October, their
scales open and the winged seeds slip forth upon their errands through
the forest. Now the color of the scales alters to a warm yellowish brown,
and thus the cones remain swinging on the wind all winter and through
the following summer. Fallen at last on the forest floor, they are still so big
and beautiful that he who wanders a Sugar Pine grove for the first time is
almost certain to pick up the first few cones he sees, convinced that he has
come upon specimens of an unusual size. But he soon discovers that the
woods are full of them and he drops his armful back to earth, conscious
that he is in the presence of treasure so bounteous that he need not carry
away any; that all he has to do, to be rich in the best things of earth, is to
stay where he is, breathe this air, hear the sound of the wind in those great
singing crowns, and rest his hand upon the serene boles.

It was the enormous cones of this tree which led to its first discovery
by science. For David Douglas, pioneer botanist of the Northwest, was
shown a single cone of this tree when he was in the valley of the Columbia
River in 1825, and the sweet seeds, too, which the Indians carried in their
pouches for food. So great a cone could only come from a great tree, he
reasoned, and with this single cone for clue, he set off from Fort Vancouver on September 20, 1826, when the present states of Oregon and Washington were under the British flag, holding few white settlers outside the
forts, and hostile Indians and grizzlies roamed a land unknown, un-
mapped, unspoiled. Now let him tell his own story, which he wrote by the
flickering light of a Pine torch, on what is now Sugar Pine Mountain, just
west of Roseburg, Oregon:

"Thursday, 26th. I left my camp this morning at daylight. . . . About an
hour's walk from my camp I was met by an Indian, who on discovering me
strung his bow and placed on his left arm a sleeve of racoon-skin and
stood ready on the defence. As I was well convinced this was prompted
through fear, he never before having seen such a being, I laid my gun at
my feet on the ground and waved my hand for him to come to me, which
he did with great caution. I made him place his bow and quiver beside my

gun, and then struck a light and gave him to smoke and a few beads. With a pencil I made a rough sketch of the cone and Pine I wanted and showed him it, when he instantly pointed to the hills about 15 or 20 miles to the south. As I wanted to go in that direction, he seemingly with much good-will went with me. At midday I reached my long-wished *Pinus* (called by the Umpqua tribe *Natele*), and lost no time in examining and endeavouring to collect specimens and seeds. New or strange things seldom fail to make great impressions, and often at first we are liable to over-rate them; and lest I should never see my friends to tell them verbally of this most beautiful and immensely large tree, I now state the dimensions of the largest one I could find that was blown down by the wind: Three feet from the ground, 57 feet 9 inches in circumference; 134 feet from the ground, 17 feet 5 inches; extreme length 215 feet. The trees are remarkably straight; bark uncommonly smooth for such large timber, of a whitish or light brown colour, and yields a great quantity of gum of a bright amber colour. The large trees are destitute of branches, generally two-thirds the length of the tree; branches pendulous, and the cones hanging from their points like small sugar-loaves in a grocer's shop. . . . Being unable to climb or hew down any, I took my gun and was busy clipping them from the branches with ball when eight Indians came at the report of my gun. They were all painted with red earth, armed with bows, arrows, spears of bone, and flint knives, and seemed to be anything but friendly. I endeavored to explain to them what I wanted and they seemed satisfied and sat down to smoke, but had no sooner done so than I perceived one string his bow and another sharpen his flint knife with a pair of wooden pincers and hang it on the wrist of the right hand, which gave me ample testimony of their inclination. To save myself I could not do by flight, and without any hesitation I went backwards six paces and cocked my gun, and then pulled from my belt one of my pistols, which I held in my left hand. I was determined to fight for life. As I as much as possible endeavoured to preserve my coolness and perhaps did so, I stood eight or ten minutes looking at them and they at me without a word passing, till one at last, who seemed to be the leader, made a sign for tobacco, which I said they should get on condition of going and fetching me some cones. They went, and as soon as out of sight I picked up my three cones and a few twigs, and made a quick retreat to my camp, which I gained at dusk. . . . The position I am now in is lying on the grass with my gun beside me, writing by the light of my Columbian candle — namely a piece of wood containing rosin."

The Sugar Pine takes its name from its sweet, gummy exudations. "The sugar," John Muir explains, "is to my taste the best of sweets — better than maple-sugar. It exudes . . . in the shape of irregular, crisp, candy-like kernels, which are crowded together in masses of considerable size, like clusters of resin-beads. When fresh, it is perfectly white and delicious, but, because most of the wounds on which it is found have been made by fire, the exuding sap is stained on the charred surface, and the hardened sugar becomes brown.

"Indians are fond of it, but on account of its laxative properties, only small quantities may be eaten. Bears, so fond of sweet things in general, seem never to taste it; at least I have failed to find any trace of their teeth in this connection." The sugar in this resin is said to be as sweet as cane sugar, but belongs to an entirely different class of the sugars known as pinitol. If you are a chemist it may mean something to you to learn that pinitol is a monomethyl ester of dextroinositol.

No other Pine in the world has such length of trunks clear of limbs and with very little taper. Taken all in all, the delightfully fragrant wood with its lightness, satin texture, close grain, ease of working, and ability to take a fine polish makes it an outstanding lumber Pine. And no other produces so much to the acre. Small areas are known which will yield 100,000 to 200,000 board feet to the acre. So it is not surprising that from the earliest days of settlement in the Sierra foothills, the Sugar Pine was cut in preference to any other. Indeed, it was to cut Sugar Pine that John Sutler set up his famous mill at Coloma, where gold was discovered on a momentous day in 1848. And when the sudden influx of settlers brought a great demand for house timbers and shingles, the Sugar Pine answered best of all. Sugar Pine roofed the shacks of the forty-niners and their followers and descendants.

The first shingles were, more exactly, shakes; that is, split, unshaved pieces of wood usually 30 inches long and from 4 to 6 inches wide, and often only one-fourth inch thick, rived out by hand. Those early shake makers were experts with the froe, but wastrels in the way they used this precious wood. Trees that would have sawed out at 10,000 or 20,000 feet of lumber were cut down by the shake makers and oftentimes left to rot in the woods if it was found that their splitting properties were less than excellent. And even when they were outstandingly good, usually more than one-half of the tree was wasted. The shake makers would go up in parties of two to four and make a camp in the pineries to spend the summer and, without stirring more than 300 yards, they could provide themselves with a season's work, for four or five giant Sugar Pines sufficed. Needless to say these were all stolen trees. Any sort of tree on government land was then considered to be the property of him who could get to it first and cut it down.

But though shakes might roof the early houses of California and provide siding too, large buildings and barns demanded structural timber, and so the sawmill early made its appearance. Sugar Pine was sawed, in the days of the forty-niners, for flumes, sluice boxes, bridges, houses, barns, fences, and mine props. Like the shake makers, the pioneer mill men simply stole the government's trees, and soon more Sugar Pine was being cut in the Sierra than all other woods combined, for it was lighter and softer than the Yellow Pine, its nearest rival. Before railroads brought in lumber from other regions, ox teams were toiling up steep grades to altitudes of 4000 to 6000 feet and hauling off Sugar Pine for building and fencing material from the mountain mills to treeless valleys below, for a distance of as much as 100 miles. At the same time, the old shake makers were giving way to shingle mills, only a little less wasteful than the crew they had displaced. Then, as the fruit industry developed in the Sacramento valley, Sugar Pine was cut for orange and raisin boxes. Sugar Pine wood, because it imparts no flavor to what it touches and is so light and handsome, has remained the ideal packing box for fruits.

As the White Pine of the East began to give out, toward the end of the eighteenth century, Sugar Pine came to replace it. For it has about the same weight per cubic foot and is sometimes considered preferable to Eastern White Pine for doors and sliding sashes since it shrinks and swells even less and holds its shape better. White Pine was long considered the one ideal wood for patternmaking, but Sugar Pine matches it today. Planing mills utilize it for molding and panels, railing and stair work, doors, sash, blinds, and the decking of boats. Because of its freedom from odor, it is used for the compartments in which to store coffee, tea, rice, and spice, and for druggists' drawers. Its straight grain qualifies it for service as the pipes in church organs, a role in which comparatively few woods are at all satisfactory.

When, roused to its duty by the stinging words of John Muir the government at last began to take charge of its own forests in the Sierra Nevada, the first thing it did was turn out the wandering bands of shake makers. Its struggle with the sheepherders was longer. It had been their wont to build corrals on the edges of the meadows by felling Sugar Pines in such a way that, stretched at length on the ground, they made a huge triangular or circular enclosure — all this, of course, as a trespass upon government land. Longest of all was the battle with the cattle ranchers, who had for years been dropping Sugar Pine logs end to end to make fences to turn cattle. Regarding themselves as lords of the land, as pioneers who had won their way, as tenders of a vested interest with precedence over any other interests, they went armed and took orders from government foresters only a little more respectfully than they would have taken them from sheepherders. Decades of tact, education, patience, and firmness were required to bring about the present and still precarious balance among the interests of the sheepherders, the ranchers, and the foresters, on the Forest Service's own lands.

And, even now, by far the largest part of the stand of Sugar Pine in California and Oregon is out of the government's hands and in those of lumber companies or private individuals who might sell whenever the stumpage price goes high enough. The national parks and the national forests protect the magnificent groves of Sugar Pine when these fall within their boundaries. But the countless visitors who each year motor or climb through the Sierra Nevada seldom realize that some of the Sugar Pines which they most admire are not within the jurisdiction of the government, and that their destiny is the sawmill — if not next year, then ultimately.

Knowledge of this fact rouses the emotions of us all, and it is meet and right that groves of great antiquity and beauty should be included in the bounds of national parks and national forests whenever possible. It is also right and necessary that there should be a lumber industry, and that a tree of such high utility as this one should be cropped in a scientific way which will permit a sustained yield from one generation to the next. Unfortunately that goal has not been reached yet by most lumber companies in the Sugar Pine region, and with some it is not even an ideal. At the present time the cut is still well in excess of the natural replacement, and until the two come into balance we can expect only increasing destruction of this superb tree and a corresponding rise in the price of its fine lumber.

Western Yellow Pine

Pinus ponderosa P. Lawson & C. Lawson*

OTHER NAMES: Bull, Black Jack, Western Red, Western Pitch, Big, Heavy, Sierra Brownbark, Western Longleaf, Ponderosa White, or Ponderosa Pine.

RANGE: Almost throughout the mountains of the western states at low altitudes in the north and increasingly higher in the south, from southernmost British Columbia, western Texas, and the high mountains of southern California, occurring sporadically on the high plains of Montana and Nebraska, and high mesas of Arizona and Oregon, rare in southwestern North Dakota, absent from the desert ranges of California and Nevada, from the Coast Ranges of British Columbia and Vancouver Island, and the Olympic peninsula. Varieties are found on the mountains of Mexico.

I F YOU KNOW YOUR WEST AT ALL, you know its Western Yellow Pine. It is found in every western state and parts of Canada and Mexico, from near to sea level in Washington to 10,000 feet in Arizona. In general, it chooses the life zone that ecologists call the Arid Transition — the very range of conditions that man himself finds most agreeable and the eastern tourist most exhilarating. So the Yellow Pine grows most abundantly in the West's prime "vacation land" as the travel posters call it. Its dry and spacious groves invite you to camp among them. Its shade is never too thin and never too dense. Its great boles and boughs frame many of the grandest views, of snow-capped cones, Indian-faced cliffs, nostalgic mesas, and all that brings the world to the West's wide door. Untold millions, for example, have taken that ride by train or car from Williams, Arizona, to the south rim of the Grand Canyon, through the flickering light and shade of the Western Yellow Pines. Wide spaced as if planted in a park, stately of trunk, with colorful orange or cinnamon or buff yellow bark, the Pines of that fine plateau are all of this one species. And they look unlike any other western tree.

If you get out of your car, you discover that no conifers are finer than these for a walk beneath their boughs — so ample and open their groves, so clean the forest floor of all save needles and grass and pungent sagebrush, with here and there a fleck of wildflower red or blue — some bugler

*Editor's note: Formerly *Pinus ponderosa* Lawson.

penstemon or lupine with its pouting lip. And the voice of these Pines is a grand native chanty. "Of all Pines," thought John Muir, "this one gives forth the finest music to the winds." If you have been long away from the sound of the Western Yellow Pine, you may, when at last you hear it again, close your eyes and simply listen, with what deep satisfaction you cannot explain, to the whispered plainsong of this elemental congregation.

And you will breathe again, with a long, glad inhalation, the cleanly incense of these groves, which is nothing so cloying or seductive as a perfume. It is an aroma, rosinous and timbern, that pervades much of the life of all the West, and many towns, like Bend, Oregon, and Flagstaff, Arizona, are perpetually steeped in its wholesome, zestful odor. Indeed, the town of Flagstaff takes its name from the incident, on the Fourth of July, 1876, when a group of scouts stripped a lofty pine of its branches and "with suitable ceremony" raised the American flag upon it, with rawhide strings. With time the gigantic flagpole became a landmark of the trail, known from Santa Fe to San Francisco. "'Travel straight West, stranger, till you come to that flagstaff,'" immigrants used to be told. "'There's a good spring there, and it's warm alongside that mountain, and a good place to camp.'"*

Of all western Pines this one seems to the beholder most full of light. Its needles, of a rich yellow green, are burnished like metal. When the shadowless summer winds come plowing through the groves, waving the supple arms and twigs, the long slender needles stream all one way in the current, and the sunlight — astronomically clear and constant — streaks up and down the foliage as from the edge of a flashing sword. Then, when the wind is still and the trees stand motionless in the dry heat, a star of sunlight blazes fixedly in the heart of each strong terminal tuft of needles. Each tree bears a hundred such stars, each clump of Yellow Pines a thousand, and the whole grove blazes like a temple with lighted sconces for some sacred day. The Western Yellow Pine covers an area of 1 million square miles on this planet's surface! And no tree that grows, and few works of man, one feels, could satisfactorily replace an acre of this, the foremost lumber Pine of all the West. Deep-rooted, aromatic, and sparkling, the forest stands exultant, with the mule deer bounding through its aisles and overhead the ravens, jet and stertorous, cruising the timber.

The Western Yellow Pine is a tree gregarious in high degree. It will associate with other species on occasion — Pinyon in the south, Lodgepole

*Arizona, A State Guide, Hastings House, 1940.

57

in the north, and Douglas Fir in California. It tolerates the red-trunked Incense Cedar in the Sierra Nevada, and the White Fir, many-tiered and fragrant, in the Rockies. But best it likes to grow alone, to see nothing but its kindred to the horizon. It is not fastidious as to geology and soil, will thrive upon limestone or basalt, gravel or sandy clay loam, or endure with little soil at all on cliffs and rocks. It mounts the cinder cones of the West's not long-dead volcanoes and gives shade even on the pitiless malpais, the pumic rock of old lava flows. It springs up freely on burned-over lands but is seldom or never a true alpine tree. The high altitudes to which it goes in the southern Rockies are still squarely in the temperate zone.

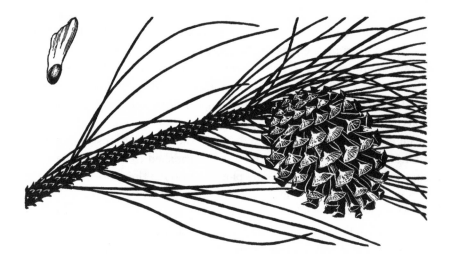

The preferred habitat of this great tree is on level or rolling land. Even in the Sierra Nevada, it elects the floors of the U-shaped valleys carved out by glaciers, and, in the Rockies, silted-up beaver ponds. Over a great part of its range it is found on the high plains of the interior, or on those lofty plateaus that the westerner prefers to call mesas — taking from the Spanish pioneers the word for table. Most of this area is located deep in the interior of the country, where the summers are very dry. Indeed, as you travel through a vast forest of Yellow Pine in midsummer, when the air is like a furnace breath and the bunch grass is withered to straw, you marvel that trees of such size can grow under such desertic conditions. Yet remember that the winters have a heavy snowfall, and the melt in spring does not run readily off these level lands; most of it sinks to the subsoil and is captured by the extensive root systems of this tree. No Pine has a more efficient equipment of roots, for it is deep and in its branchings almost as extensive as the limbage of the crown. So, searching for water, the roots and rootlets expand in an inverted hemisphere until they meet the subterranean competition of another Yellow Pine. Thus the mighty trees hold each other at a distance in those parklike groves that characterize it.

And mighty this tree certainly is. In the more arid Rocky Mountain states it does not grow so high as on the Pacific coast. Sixty to 125 feet is usual for mature specimens in the Rockies, with a diameter, at breast height, of 20 to 30 inches. On the coast, where the growth is much denser, owing to the greater precipitation brought from the Pacific by the prevailing westerlies, it is still greater in all its dimensions. Near Lapine, Oregon, one specimen was found to be 162 feet high and 27 feet in circumference around the trunk. In Washington State, on the south slopes of that perfect, snow-capped cone, Mount Adams, stands a Yellow Pine 175 feet high and 84 inches in diameter. But John Muir measured one tree 220 feet high, in the Sierra Nevada, with a diameter of 8 feet. With such a magnificent physique, its great plates of bark 4 and 5 feet long, its boles soaring, almost without taper till the lowest branches are reached, for 60 feet and more, its short heavy crowns of foliage, and the prodigious spread of its middle branches, well does this species merit the name of *ponderosa* suggested by David Douglas when that famous Scottish explorer of the Northwest wilderness first made it known to science.

But even before his day, it had been distinguished and admired by Lewis and Clark in their immortal journey from the mouth of the Missouri to the mouth of the Columbia and back. It first came to their attention when they noted "pine burrs," borne on the swift current of the White River where it reaches the Missouri in what we now call South Dakota. Lewis, if not a trained botanist, was a keen observer, and he seems to have recognized that these were not such cones as he knew in his native Virginia; they promised great forests, somewhere far in the mysterious interior, and indeed we know now that they came from some of those outlying stands of Western Yellow Pine found on the high plains of westernmost Nebraska, or else from the Black Hills. The explorers, as they toiled up the Missouri into western Montana, undoubtedly collected specimens of the new Pine, which they speak of in their journal as the "longleaf pine," but unfortunately those specimens were damaged beyond salvation when they were buried at the foot of the Lemhi pass, and only those collected on the return journey were ever brought back to civilization. One of these was a specimen of *Pinus ponderosa* taken in 1800 near present-day Orofino, Idaho, where the canoes were abandoned and horses mounted for the crossing of the continental divide. It was Meriwether Lewis's intention to publish his extensive notes on natural history, and had he done so he might have named this great Pine, but violent death cut short one of the most promising careers in American history. His natural history notes were completely passed over when the expedition journals were first published; his specimens were shuffled through by Frederick Pursh the botanist, in search of novelties, but so superficially that this Pine was not even recognized as distinct, and so, just as Lewis's friend Thomas Jefferson feared, it fell to foreigners to rediscover and name far too many of his pioneering "finds."

But the discovery and naming of a tree are small matters compared with the impressive story of the living tree itself, a monarch that expects to reign (man and fire and beetle permitting) for 250 to 500 years. A seedling just starting life has come even so far by a series of lucky accidents, for the seeds are a favorite with numberless animals like quails, squirrels, chipmunks, grouse, and those gray crows known as camp-robbers or nutcrackers. Even so, provident chipmunks are sometimes the friends of Yellow Pine reproduction. On the dry pumice soils of the upper Deschutes basin in Oregon, for instance, as much as 85 percent of the seedlings come up in chipmunk caches that have either been forgotten by these little scatterbrains or have been left as a legacy by the demise of one of these misers. Foresters found one such hoarding in which twenty-nine seedlings had sprung up, and similar clumps dotted the volcanic barrens. For some reason chipmunk-sown clumps are far more likely to survive drought in their early years than wind-sown seeds falling singly on the bitter waste. Where an old tree has fallen and then been burned in a ground fire, perfect hedgerows, 25 to 75 feet long, of Yellow Pine seedling will spring up, fertilized by the minerals in the ash.

The seedling is cruelly subject to heaving of the soil by frosts, to nipping by late spring frosts, to the long summer drought characteristic of most of the West, to browsing by mule deer, which, in season, make it their favorite food. Bushes afford the youngster much protection from sun and wind so that sagebrush, bitterbrush, and squaw-carpet are its nurses in youth. Later, Lodgepole Pines afford it protection without seeming to compete seriously with it as parent Yellow Pines would do.

The first effort of the little tree is to put down a taproot. This will be 7 to 12 inches long, while above ground only 2 or 3 inches of growth will be made by the shoot in the first year. But the second year more of a top is formed, and by the time it is eight years old the young tree will be about 1 foot 4 inches high — a slow growth. Indeed, few first-class lumber Pines grow so slowly as this one unless it finds unusually favorable conditions such as prevail in the Sierra Nevada and the west slopes of the Cascades. Broadly speaking, Yellow Pine grows very slowly for the first ten or fifteen years; but for the next seventy-five or one hundred years the growth is fairly rapid; exceptional trees will increase 2 feet in height a year and 1½ inches in diameter. At the age of 150 years the increment has fallen off almost completely; the tree is now mature and prime for lumbering, for from this point on only breakage and decay can be expected, in progressive amounts.

In its fiftieth year or so a Yellow Pine begins to bear cones in abundance. But time brings many changes in appearance. The bark of young boles is often furrowed, with slender blackish ridges, the inner bark in the crevices showing somewhat orange or yellowish. Lumbermen call this "blackjack," as though it were a different kind of tree. But "blackjack" bark gradually changes until it assumes those great smooth plates, sometimes 4 or 5 feet long by 18 inches wide, that give the old trees such a noble look. No other western Pine approaches this one in the thickness, the smoothness, the bright color of its bark. Only in the Pines of the Gulf states does one see the same sort of plated bark, on the Longleaf, Loblolly, and Shortleaf Pines. And this is for the very good reason that our Western Yellow Pine belongs to the same subsection "southern pines" (*Australes*) of the genus *Pinus* as do those southern trees, while no other western Pines do so, except the Jeffrey and Apache Pines. The long needles, too, remind one of the Longleaf Pine, and there is some similarity in the wood, so that the western and southern Yellow Pines compete fiercely in the eastern lumber markets.

That wood, which lumbermen prefer to call Ponderosa or even Ponderosa "White" Pine, makes a very high grade lumber at its best — fine grained and so light and soft textured that it sometimes passes for true White Pine and is often so marketed. It is turned to almost every purpose to which Pine lumber anywhere can be put. In the Northwest many houses are built entirely of Yellow Pine — even the shingles, floors, trim, paneling, doors, and sashes and frames for windows. It is exported, even by the high expense of rail haul, all the way to the eastern states as a general all-purpose factory material in the production of stock sizes of doors, sash, finish, shelving, bevel and drop siding, pattern material, and rustic ceiling and flooring. Much of the "knotty Pine" so much in favor at present is Yellow Pine; it is known from Western White Pine paneling by its brownish, not dark reddish, knots.

In the early days of western settlement this wood was extensively employed for mine props and stulls, and in some localities it met the whole demand. Quartz mills for crushing the ore from the mines utilized Yellow Pine for fuel, and a single mine would strip hundreds of acres of forest in a few years, to feed its uproarious stamp mills. Early railroads like the Denver and Rio Grande laid the rails of their heroic engineering through the Rockies on ties of Yellow Pine, and others set them in the sod of the high plains, in the days when buffalo were stopping the first trains and toppling the telegraph posts of Yellow Pine as they scratched their hides against them. Time has shown that Ponderosa is not durable in contact with the soil unless treated with preservatives, and in case of a fire in a mine, its resins, when superheated, gave off gases that exploded. Its future is all above ground.

The outlook for Ponderosa Pine as a timber tree is good for a long time to come; that is to say, we are far from the end of it. But we are also far from bringing the rate of cut and of losses by fire, insects, and overgrazing into balance with the rate of reproduction. To be sure, the stand of merchantable timber is great, with 185.441 billion board feet. It thus ranks third in the country, exceeded only by Douglas Fir and the southern Yellow Pines. In cut, it ranks fourth — 3.65 billion board feet a year.* But the annual gross growth or replacement is only half as much as the yearly cut. One reason for this is the serious toll taken by insect damage. The pine butterfly and the Pandora moth in their caterpillar stages defoliate the trees. The pine-engraver beetles destroy young growth, and the western pine beetle and other coleoptera attack the bark. Laws and chemicals are arrayed against these insects, but their depredations are best halted by cutting timber before it becomes overly mature.

Ground fire is calamitous to young trees and regarded with too much indifference by the population because the flames never break into terrifying crown fires endangering lives and homes. Worse still is overgrazing. Cattle and sheep raisers were well established in the West before lumber-

*The statistics include the Jeffrey Pine, which is not distinguished by lumbermen, but neither does it account for a large share of the total.

ing or forestry became common; they think of their rights as an eminent domain, something wrested by their own efforts from the Indians and practically assured by the Constitution. And the open, usually flat groves of the Western Yellow Pine, with their grass cover but little shrubby undergrowth, seem to the stockman as if made for grazing by a God who loves the cowboy. Scientific studies show, however, that heavy browsing of seedlings by stock is one of the worst, perhaps the most objectionable, of deterrents to satisfactory reproduction by this valuable and noble tree. Reduction in the number of cattle per acre, especially on lands stocked with seedling Yellow Pines, is the answer. It will not only aid greatly in the perpetuation of the forest but will bring about improvement in the stock.

Naturally, a tree with such an immense range of climates, altitudes, and soils (perhaps the greatest among all the Pines of North America) exhibits marked variations. Among them are the following:

Variety *scopulorum* Engelmann, the ambiguously called Rock Pine, Rocky Mountain Yellow Pine, or Rocky Mountain Ponderosa Pine, characteristic of the east slopes of the Rockies and sometimes found to the east of the mountains, on the Great Plains in Montana, Nebraska, and so forth. It is a smaller tree, both in stature (75 feet is about the average maximum), and in its organs. The leaves are only 5 to 7 inches long and sometimes only two to a bundle; they are somewhat curved and definitely more rigid and blue gray than the Pacific coast form. The cones tend to be smaller (2 to 4 inches long) than those of the typical species.

Variety *arizonica* (Engelmann) Shaw, the Arizona Pine, has usually five needles in a bundle (but the same tree may also bear bundles with two and three needles); the twigs are rather glaucous, and the brownish, stalked, nonprickly cones are, on the whole, shorter than those of the true species, and the needles slenderer, but only by one twenty-fourth of an inch.

Pitch Pine

Pinus rigida P. Miller

OTHER NAMES: Black, Torch, or Sap Pine.

RANGE: Rare in western New Brunswick; southern Maine, across New Hampshire, Vermont, and at low altitudes in New York to the Thousand Islands in Ontario, west to southeastern Ohio and western Kentucky, south at low altitudes to New Jersey and Delaware, and in the mountains to Georgia.

ALMOST BLACK AGAINST THE SKY, the tufts of the Pitch Pine's dark green and shining foliage stand out upon the twigs nearly at right angles. Usually the tree has a short thick trunk, more so than any of our other pines, with whorled, contorted, and often pendulous branches that form a thick, round-topped crown. Where sea winds or mountain winds torture the tree, the crown may be flat topped or lopsided or picturesquely broken and irregular. The cones tend to persist on the tree, not as living unopened cones, as in the Jack and Pocosin Pines, but dead and black, as if hundreds of black birds were clustered on the boughs. Or, after long weathering, they turn gray like the color of an unpainted, abandoned house down in the Jersey Pine barrens, while at a distance the trunk seems to be black.

The Pitch Pine is *the* Pine of Cape Cod and of storm-swept Montauk Point on extreme eastern Long Island. It is the most important Pine of rocky ledges in the Pennsylvania mountains. Above all, it predominates in the famous Pine barrens of New Jersey. This is a lozenge-shaped area, lying west of the great coastal marshes, on the average 80 miles long and 30 miles broad, corresponding almost exactly with what the geologists call the Beacon Hill formation, a nearly flat, shield-shaped area composed of alluvial deposits when this region was under the sea in Miocene times, nineteen million years ago. Since then other parts of New Jersey have been under the sea, leaving the Beacon Hill formation as an island; it has never been submerged again, nor glaciated. When the white man first entered this region, he found it one vast forest of Pitch Pine and Southern White Cedar, with more or less Shortleaf and Virginia Scrub Pine on its perimeter.

It was a region of sterile sands and bogs, and in the bogs was found abundant bog iron ore — some of the first iron available to the early colonists. In the era before the use of coal, iron was smelted by charcoal, and the Pitch Pine, right at hand, was an ideal wood for the purpose. Tar, pitch, and turpentine were extracted by crude distillation from the intensely resinous knots.

Down at Cape May a large boat-building industry grew up, and the Pitch Pine, though not a durable naval construction material, was heavily cut for it. Pitch Pine went also into barn floors, bridges, inexpensive houses. So began the intensive exploitation of the great Pine barren resources. During the Revolutionary War, and the War of 1812, the Pitch Pine charcoal and the bog iron ore at Batsto forged weapons for our armies, and there was made the steam cylinder for John Fitch's *Perseverance.* Today the hundreds of small forest forges of the Pine barrens are but picturesque ruins, if they survive at all; the weed-grown circular hearths of the charcoal burners are still discernible, to those who penetrate the sandy wood roads.

But a century of exploitation and of terrific, unchecked forest fires among these pitchy trees which become living torches have destroyed all the virgin timber. The Pine barrens are now invaded by the worthless scrub Oaks, and the Pines themselves are stunted, never growing 50 and 60 feet tall as once they did, and sometimes, when repeatedly fire swept, ceasing growth altogether at knee height. Agriculture, however, has not been able to replace the vanished forest on such sterile soils, and today the Pine barrens remain a wilderness some 2400 square miles in extent yet only one hour by motor from Philadelphia, two from New York.

Dwelling in these Pine barrens is an isolated people known to the outside world as the "Pineys." Some, at least, of their ancestors were deserting Redcoats, others were hunted Tories, others still escapists from religious intolerance in the days of stocks and pillories and whipping posts. To these were added the "Pine Robbers" whose "cruelty and lust" were dreaded by every man and woman within their reach. The first sociological report on these people, cut off by the Pitch Pine wilderness from law, medicine, education, and commerce, was made by Elizabeth S. Kite of the Vineland Training School, who shocked the country with her article in *The Survey* for April 1913.

Conditions have probably changed much since the black picture she drew of the Pineys' lives. Today they cut lumber, gather sphagnum moss for the florist trade, and raise cranberries in their bogs. Those who have known them best have not found them violent. A tale is related by a detective who came among them to discover the body of a murdered man. He enlisted the aid of the men who knew their wilderness best. As he tracked the woods with them he was amazed to find that they watched the tops of the Pitch Pines instead of the ground. At a certain point they stopped and exhumed the body. The reason, they said, was that where the roots have been disturbed, the needles turn yellow.

The Pitch Pine's wood today enjoys no better reputation than the Piney's worst fame. It is full of knots, coarse grained, hard to work. It holds nails and bolts so poorly that ships built of it have been known to pull apart at sea. Yet its resistance to water decay made it invaluable for ships' pumps and the old water wheels of primitive American mills. A barn floor laid in this wood in Pike County, Pennsylvania, was found so good, after 160 years of use, that it was taken up and relaid in a new house.

Pitch Pine knots, which weaken and disfigure the wood for carpenters' use, are yet so filled with resin that they resist decay long after the stump has rotted away, and in regions where the tree was abundant, they used to cover the forest floor. Pioneer children were kept at work, stooping and gathering these, day after day. The knots were then tied to a Hickory withe. Burning for hours, such torches lighted the pioneer for miles through the forest at night. These flambeaux made ideal lights, too, for "shining" deer — their eyes fascinated and illumined by the flame while the hunter drew his bead upon them.

The tar obtained from Pitch Pine was considered the best axle grease for wagons, and no wagon in the old days but had its tar bucket and paddle swung from the rear axle. Though today it is still employed for wharf piles, mine timbers, and above all for cheap crate material, the great days of Pitch Pine in the domestic economy of Americans are over. But as long as our forests stand, as long as trees march down to the sea or climb the wind-swept ridges of the Alleghenies, its dark plumy crown, its grand, rugged trunks, the strong, sweet, pitchy odor of its groves, and the heavy chant of the wind in them will stand for something that is wild and untamable and disdains even to be useful to man.

Lodgepole Pine

Pinus contorta var. *latifolia* Engelmann ex Watson*

OTHER NAMES: Black, Spruce, Prickly, Jack, or Tamrac Pine. Tamarack.

RANGE: From the Nutzotin Mountains of eastern Alaska south through the Rockies of British Columbia and Alberta to Colorado and northern Utah, and on the east side of the Cascades in Washington and Oregon, south, at increasingly high altitudes (6000 to 10,000 feet), in the mountains of California: in the north, in the Trinity Mountains, Siskiyous, and Mount Shasta; abundant south through the Sierra Nevada; on very limited areas high on the mountains of southern California: the San Bernardinos, San Gabriels, and rare at 10,000 feet on the San Jacintos. Also on the Sierra San Pedro Mártir of Baja California.

A S YOU CROSS THE GREAT PLAINS of Montana or Alberta and reach at last the foot of the Rockies, you see that the slopes are swathed almost to their bases in a great zone of even-aged Pines. When living, the foliage of these Lodgepole Pines is yellow green and thus paler than that of most conifers, though darker than the leaves of their twinkling companions, the Aspens. Frequently, though, hundreds of acres will be crowded with dead yet still standing Lodgepoles, killed by fire or the far more insidious beetle. But even these "ghost forests," as westerners sometimes call them, are arresting and by moonlight cast an eerie spell, and they but serve, these tree cemeteries, to accentuate by contrast how much of wiry vitality there is in the surviving stands. Often these look as if they had been sown from seed all at the same time — so uniform are they in height and dimensions, and this (for reasons to appear) is probably just

Editor's note: Formerly *Pinus contorta* var. *latifolia* Engelmann.

what happened. Martially straight — straight and slim as poles — these Pines, if not individually noble, yet make, when densely grown over a vast tract of mountain slope or valley, an impression of forest grandeur, as great today as when Lewis and Clark in their toilsome journey by canoe up the Missouri first beheld their multiple dark lances.

But very different will be your impression if you have come from the magnificently forested Pacific coast — through the western gate of Glacier National Park, for instance — where gracious Hemlocks, giant Cedars, and Douglas Firs grow lushly. For there, when you emerge on the eastern slopes of the Rockies, the Lodgepole forests seem arid, monotonous, spindling, and thin of shade. Campers and trampers who have tried to make their way through a dense Lodgepole stand, fighting against the dead branches to which it perversely clings instead of neatly self-pruning them like other trees, will find little good to say of the Lodgepole. For when one of these Pines dies it finds no room to fall decently down, but, caught in the dead branches of its neighbors, it slants halfway to the ground. So an old Lodgepole grove is a perfect jackstraw pile, exasperating and exhausting to the explorer. Yet this is one of the most curious and significant of all western trees; it has played a great role in the lives of red men and white; its vast domain and numbers would be impressive even were it not rich in human associations. It is at the same time a forest weed and a commercial timber crop, a tinder box in case of fire and a phoenix after it. And, finally, it is not one sort of tree but two, utterly unlike in every trait except botanical.

At different altitudes and under different conditions of crowding or freedom of growth, Lodgepole takes on these two distinctive forms. They do not differ in flower, cones, or leaves, but in the outline of the tree and the shape of the trunk they are strikingly unlike. Timberline trees, and those with ample room to develop, have nothing polelike about them. Much nobler in aspect, they have no value as timber. So (and because it is much more abundant), consider first the typical form of the Lodgepole Pine, which is that of a spindling tree growing in a close grove; it may be 50 feet high yet possess a trunk only 5 or 6 inches thick — a true pole.

This form is due to the intensive crowding of the trees where they grow together and form a pure stand of this species alone. And that very crowding is due, in turn, to the behavior of the seedlings, and of the seeds which gave rise to those seedlings, and of the cones in which the seeds were borne. For the cones are often retained, unopened, on the trees for years, but sooner or later fire is almost predestined to sweep through a Lodgepole forest. This was true even before the coming of the white man, for the Indians probably started many fires, and certainly lightning, from the Rockies' abundant and savage summer storms, must for ages have started fires among these trees. The tinder-dry deadwood of the lower branches, the dead trees carried in the arms of the living, the thin bark of the living trees, and the resinous crops of successive seasons' cones feed a holocaust sometimes unappeased till every Lodgepole within reach of its wind-whipped breath is consumed to the roots.

Yet the seed life, sealed between the scales by a heavy coat of stiff resin, is not killed by the fire. Indeed, the resin is melted, the cones are roasted till their scales pop open, and out leaps the seed crop that has been dormant for years. Thus as many as a hundred thousand seedling trees will spring up on a single acre of burn. Most of them are destined to be crowded to death, but even so, a great number will survive to maturity and produce a dense stand. So, where the excessive light, heat, cold, drought, and lack of humus of a burned-over area would be fatal to many more aristocratic trees, the indomitable Lodgepole surmounts, indeed it thrives upon, these harsh conditions. If the Lodgepole is gravely subject to fire, it is incomparably adapted to survive and triumph over it. Further, since all the seedlings after a given burn will be of the same age, the stand will be remarkably uniform — which is ideal for the lumber industry, making cutting and milling easy. Many North American Pines are similarly adapted to natural reforestation after fire, and even in similar measure dependent on fire for release of the seed crop. But Lodgepole is the archetype of the fire forest, which is as distinctive a formation as the coniferous rain forest of the Olympic peninsula.

Few Pines grow more slowly than this one. It takes about a hundred years to produce a saw log of the smallest size — quite a while to wait for a pole to grow! A trunk 3 feet in diameter is probably the outside limit. And though such poles eventually grow to 50 or even 60 feet tall, that is nothing much in the great coniferous forests in the West. In compensation, there is the fact that Lodgepole may come of cone-bearing age at six years and seldom later than fourteen — a precocity that, linked with its fertility, is almost unparalleled.

Slow as is the growth of Lodgepole, this species has probably greatly increased its acreage in modern times. For with the increased incidence of fires and the heavy cutting of more valuable trees in so many parts of the West, the Lodgepoles have sprung up over vast areas once occupied by other trees. Moreover, the Lodgepole is a pioneer tree in the invasion of small, flat, springy meadows in the Rockies and the Sierra Nevada, such as grow when old beaver ponds fill up with silt, sedge, brush, and grass. Slowly but steadily the Lodgepole, encircling such meadows, will creep out upon them and on the flood plains of mountain rivers, such as the Merced in Yosemite Valley. Within the memory of persons still living, spots in the Yosemite which now support a close stand of Lodgepole were once open meadows bright with wild iris and browsed by deer. The cottages of Yosemite Lodge are set in just such a Lodgepole grove.

Both on a small and a large scale, then, the Lodgepole is an aggressive pioneer of a tree, much like its associate the Aspen. In the ecological succession of trees, Lodgepole should be ousted at length by such shade-tolerant trees as Western Hemlock, but sometimes one fire succeeds another so soon (as time is reckoned in the life of a tree) that Lodgepole, which is shade intolerant and sun loving in the seedling stage, tends to succeed itself decade after decade. Today, Lodgepole covers something like a million square miles, from Alaska to New Mexico and the Sierra Nevada, and much of this is burned-over land that would not be ready for over a hundred years to support finer but less vigorous forest types. No one knows from year to year, in so vast an area, how many billion board feet of timber are standing in the form of this species, but there is little doubt that in sheer abundance the Lodgepole is the seventh most common tree in North America.

Lodgepole takes its name from the custom, among the Rocky Mountain Indians, of cutting the trunks into lengths 10 to 15 feet long, in the spring, and peeling off the bark. Then they would set out on their summer hunts, leaving the poles to season until fall. By that time these would have become light and easily dragged or carried by the women into winter camp. Owing to the growth habits of the tree, these poles were nearly of the same thickness (or thinness) for their whole length. Such a pole 15 feet long may be only 2 inches in diameter and, when seasoned, would weigh only 7 or 8 pounds. Furthermore, it is extremely strong, stiff, and nearly impossible to split. When the red men wished to set up a wigwam these poles were arranged in a circle inclined inward to the top and there lashed together. On these poles were then stretched the buffalo hide which made the walls of the tepee.

Lodgepole sticks were also the favorite for the making of the travois, the litter or drag sled which, in default of any wheels in the life of the Indians, were dragged by dogs or women. With a piece of hide stretched from the two poles, the travois became a platform to which bundles could be tied when the tribe was on the move. So great was the demand for poles of this particular tree that the Indians of the Great Plains, who had no trees or only the unsuitable Cottonwood or Willow, went all the way to the Rockies to cut Lodgepole Pines or bought them by barter.

When the first white settlers began to move into Lodgepole country, this tree, more than any other, was a boon to their immediate wants. Its polelike trunks made it ideal for fencing corrals, and of it the pioneer built his sheds, stables, and sometimes even his cabin. Later, when orchards began to produce fruit in the northwestern states, Lodgepole furnished a cheap and excellent material for fruit boxes. Then came a need for the first telegraph poles, and later for telephone poles, and again this species, when properly treated with preservative, proved ideal — straight growing yet of twisted sinew within.

From the earliest days of ranching in the West, Lodgepole served, too, for poles and rails in fences and for corrals, small bridges, cattle pens, sheds, and barns. For mine props it is a cheap and substantial timber; even wood that has been standing dead from fire for many years can be treated with creosote and thoroughly seasoned and, very light as it is, proves valuable in mines. When creosoted, Lodgepole crossties will serve a railroad bed without decay for many years; the very first railroads to enter the Rockies utilized Lodgepole ties. At Horse Creek, in the Wyoming Range, the forests are still levied upon for railway ties. "Lumberjacks fell the lodgepole pines for this purpose in winter, saw them to six-foot lengths, trim them with razor-sharp broad-axes, and then stack them near frozen streams. Pole ties, the most durable, are made from small trees and the tips of larger trees, with only two sides surfaced; slab ties are made of larger poles, split once, with three sides surfaced; quarter ties are made of poles, split into four segments, with four surfaces finished. An experienced trimmer can leave the surfaces of a tie almost as smooth as if planed. In early summer, the timbers are floated 15 or 20 miles to the Green River, where they are boomed (held back by cables stretched across the creek mouths), until the waters are at the best height for the drive to the city of Green River. The boomed timbers extend upstream for miles. If they jam when the booms are removed, men with spiked boots and long pikes walk out to the middle of the stream, upon the treacherous floor of sticks, and work them loose."*

In complete contrast to the Lodgepole that the lumberman knows — that is, the pole-shaped specimen of the dense, even-aged stand in the fire forest — is the high-altitude and timberline growth of what is, botanically, identically the same tree. These high-mountain specimens grow not in pure stands, but scattered amidst Alpine Larch, Mountain Hemlock, Red Fir, and others. They wear a completely different expression from that of the close-packed typical Lodgepole, as different as is the behavior of a sheep in a flock kept in line by dog and herder, from a lone sheep brought up with children and dogs for playmates. For every close-grown Lodgepole is perforce like the others; every open-grown specimen is an extreme individualist. Shaped by the torque of gales, crouching from the lash of snows, or bent to its knees by mountain slides, its stems often look as if they had writhed as they grew. Comparatively small trees may be — and look — already old, their crowns preternaturally broad in proportion to the foreshortened stem, or lopsided or one-sided. The trunk may become so thickened and shortened as to have a bottlelike swelling at base — this in a Lodgepole! But if conditions are not too harshly arrayed against one of these trees it may attain, as in the high hanging valleys and "flats" of upper Yosemite, a rude nobility. One specimen measured there is 106 feet tall, with a bole 19 feet around.

These high-mountain trees, like the grove trees, often retain their lower branches obstinately, but as living, not dead, wood; this gives such specimens a look of indomitable vitality. The bark of polelike trees is a thin skin of a hue varying from the gray of ashes to the black of cinders,

*Wyoming, American Guide Series, Oxford University Press.

but in all cases without luster. The bark of the high-mountain specimens is thicker, softer, with a warm, living, yellow brown to ruddy hue, or even a charming pink tint, as if it kept some of the afterglow of alpine sunsets.

Fire probably plays but an infrequent part in determining the life span, the opening of cones, the occurrence or nonoccurrence of seeding, in these open-growth mountain trees, and thus neighboring specimens are not even-aged but may be long tree-generations apart. Possibly the mountain trees are longer lived, too, since less threatened with fiery death. The thick and crooked-boled individuals could never have been used for the poles of lodges or of travois, and no more would most of them be worth logging today, even if they grew in accessible spots.

Truly these trees have life stories quite as different from those of the pole-stemmed specimens as they are unlike them in appearance, and they deserve a distinctive English name even if they cannot logically be granted a separate botanical one. But there seems to be none as yet, and, when it is given, let us hope it is not made known by revealed authority of some deus ex machina nomenclature but is born out of the imagination and experience of the western people, just as was the name Lodgepole itself.

Jack Pine

Pinus banksiana Lambert

OTHER NAMES: Gray, Black, Black Jack, Scrub, Princess, or Banksian Pine.

RANGE: Local in Nova Scotia and New Brunswick, north in Ungava almost to James Bay, and northwest to the Yukon, south to northern and eastern Minnesota, locally on sterile soils to south-central Wisconsin, northeastern Illinois, and northwestern Indiana, southern peninsula of Michigan, southern Ontario, and southeastern Quebec; rare in northern Vermont and northern New Hampshire, and locally plentiful in Maine.

THE GREAT NORTH WOODS OF CANADA and the northern United States boast three Pines, the stately White, once the most valuable of all their timber trees, the Red, hard and strong and noble of aspect, and the present species, the Jack Pine, a mere runt as to

height and grace, a weed in the opinion of the lumberman, fit for nothing but pulpwood.

The French Canadian woodsman has — or used to have — his own opinion of Jack Pine. He believed that a woman who passed within 10 feet of its boughs would become sterile, her womb closed — an analogy suggested perhaps by the way the cones remain on the tree for years, obstinately unopened, never seeming to shed their seeds. Jack Pine was supposed to poison the very soil where it grew, a superstition easy to understand since this tree is driven by its tall competitors to seek the most sandy or sterile soils, granitic rocks of the glaciated regions, and acid bogs. Cattle browsing near it might droop and die, it was thought. Almost any misfortune that befell a man's ox or his ass or his wife could be blamed on the nearest Jack Pine, and the only thing to do was to get rid of it. Yet so powerful are the spirits of perversity supposed to inhabit this ill-omened tree that no one who valued his life would cut it down. So wood was heaped around it, and the owner then set fire to the kindling. If in its turn it set the tree ablaze, the powers of evil could not blame the man!

Jack Pine constitutes the Pine barrens of central Michigan, famous for their infertility. In Minnesota it covers a wilderness 20,000 miles in extent, or about the combined areas of Massachusetts, New Hampshire, and Connecticut with, however, some large enclaves of Spruce forest in the boggiest parts. This area is, of course, not bounded by the International line but extends over a glacier-scoured, granitic, and lacustrine area, north of Lakes Superior and Huron, and west to the Lake-of-the-Woods.

Fossil cones of Jack Pine from the glacial period have been found as far south as Spartanburg County, South Carolina, washed out, no doubt, from the Blue Ridge Mountains, where this Pine must have grown in a cold epoch that brought a Canadian flora far down into Dixie. If in historic times the Jack Pine has not changed its boundaries, it has not suffered such loss of territory as have some of its betters. For the old-time lumberman left the knotty, stunted Jack Pine contemptuously alone. As for the forest fires, the strange cones that remain closed for so many years upon the tree will sometimes open only if fire has forced them! In consequence, Jack Pine does better in burned-over land than its aristocratic kin.

If it is a low tree, sometimes only 25 feet tall, never over 70, its twisted stocky form is not uprooted by great winds, as are taller and more slender trees. If its wood is weak, soft, and light, its lack of worth has had a negative survival value. Complain as one may of its misshapen form, Jack Pine covers thousands of square miles of cold, sterile, wind-swept ground which might otherwise be bleak as the tundras that lie beyond the northern limit of its distribution.

Reckoned as a nurse tree, too, as foresters say, Jack Pine takes possession of lumbered or burned ground, able as it is to endure wind and heat and light and drought, growing rapidly at first, and thus it forms a shelter for the tenderer Red Pine seedlings. But the Red Pine is even faster growing. After fifteen or twenty years it outstrips its nurse and can live without its protection.

When growing well in the open, Jack Pine is likely to have a crooked trunk; only under conditions of forest competition does it grow straight enough, in its search for light, to produce saw logs. The cones have a humpbacked look in maturity. They may cling on the tree almost indefinitely before they drop their seeds with pale lustrous wings that bear them, insectlike, upon the northland's winds. Of all the features of the tree that enable one to identify it, these crops of curved-back, stubbornly unopening cones are the most visible at a distance.

Now that he has cut the great virgin stands of White and Red Pine to ribbons, the lumberman has come to have a belated respect for Jack Pine. It is cut for bed slats, staves for nail kegs, plasterer's lath, keg headings for slack cooperage, posts, fences, and boxes. Out of the largest and straightest trees a certain number of dimension timbers can be sawed. It was valued once as frames for the Canadian Indians' canoes; it is useful today for railway ties. Above all it is an inexpensive firewood, and with its resinous content it burns readily. Today pulp mills are chewing up Jack Pine where sawmills whined once for the flesh of Eastern White Pine. Thus Jack Pine carries the burden of many plebeian uses for which, otherwise, finer woods would be taxed.

A Jack Pine which is sixty years old is fast approaching its last days. At an age when the Eastern White Pine is in all the charm of youth, the plebeian Jack Pine is already an old crone of a tree which has not, in all likelihood, grown an inch for twenty or thirty years but has merely hung on to life in the hard-bitten environment where it is forced to live. After its death the winter winds soon whip away its branches; then the bark falls off, leaving a naked stick of a tree to stand a few more desolate years.

Monterey Pine

Pinus radiata D. Don

RANGE: Along the California shore from Pescadero, San Mateo County, intermittently to Cambria, San Luis Obispo County, and on Guadalupe Island, Mexico.

P ROBABLY NO OTHER AMERICAN TREE, certainly no western conifer, has been so abundantly planted all over the world as the Monterey Pine. Sometimes under that name and sometimes called Insignis Pine, it has been grown as an ornamental for well over a hundred years in England, especially the western and southern parts, and in Mediterranean Europe and in North Africa, while in South Africa and Australia it is planted as a valuable timber tree. In many of the cities, towns, and gardens of California, Monterey Pine is considered the best of possible Pines for shade and beauty, attaining in thirty or forty years a height of 60 to 80 feet, with fine, sturdy boles, a magnificent sweep of boughs that is neither too symmetrical nor too eccentric, rich but cheerful green foliage, and scarcely any special demands in the way of watering or protection from pests. Moreover, the Monterey Pine, unlike most trees, produces a far more luxuriant growth away from its native setting.

And that setting is confined to three small localities, all within the fog belt of the central California coast. The first (that is, the largest and most famous of these) is the Monterey peninsula. Here, between the town of Monterey itself and over the interior hills of the peninsula, to Carmel, it forms its densest growth. It extends also inland some 6 or 7 miles on the ridges above the Carmel valley, and again, south of the Carmel River, it is found at Point Lobos State Park and on a narrow strip of the ocean bluffs as far south as Malpaso Creek. Some sixty miles down the coast, there is a picturesque small stand of Monterey Pine on the Cambria hills. This is the southernmost outpost of the Monterey Pine today, and the northernmost is a grove just south of Point Año Nuevo, close to the shore and just south of Pescadero. But in interglacial times the Monterey Pine was more widespread up and down the coast; its fossil cones have been found, along with the sabertooth tiger's fierce tusks, in the La Brea tar pits of Los Angeles, while up in northern Marin County other cone fossils were suddenly revealed by the San Francisco earthquake of 1906. But in the past, as now, Monterey Pine was strictly a maritime tree.

Yet though so closely tied to the coast, the Monterey Pine does not so often grow, as do the Monterey Cypresses, on rocks directly overhanging the salt spray of high-tide mark. In such localities the Cypress seems better able to endure the harsh conditions. Or perhaps when the Cypresses attempt to spread inland, they meet opposition from the Monterey Pine. These are faster growing and perhaps in other ways more aggressive; so, by root below and shade above, they carry on a subtle warfare with their gnarled fellow conifers and keep them pushed to the very shore.

Like these Cypresses, the Monterey Pines, especially those within a mile of the sea, where the air is most often saturated with the thickest fog, drip with the misnamed Spanish Moss — in reality the lichen *Ramalina reticulata,* which gives the woods a gray and sorrowful look. Though it is not a true parasite (like the dwarf mistletoe that often attacks conifers), but merely a perching plant, the lichen harms the Pines mechanically by shutting out the light and blanketing the leaves, so that boughs are smothered and starved to death, and sometimes whole trees may die from the high cost of playing host to this dependant. But these wavering shrouds of lichen are an inseparable part of the solemnity of the groves and belong there, for weal or woe, as naturally as the pouring fog, and the pervasive and ineluctable reek of some soil- or log-inhabiting mold that, especially at night and in the mist, exhales, as Robert Louis Stevenson called it, "a graveyard odor."

Sometimes when these Pines grow on dunes, their struggles with the shifting sand may result in half-buried trees with sprawling prostrate limbs. Again, their form, when they grow densely in groves, is apt to be spindling — the boles and crowns both unimpressive. It is only farther back from the sea, away from the fogs, the shifting sands, the shrouds of lichen, where these Pines begin to feel the unrelenting cheer of California sunlight and to associate with wide-spreading, normal Live Oaks instead of the tortured Cypresses, that the Monterey Pines begin to stand out as individual trees and take on their inherently ample and even lusty forms. Here the sun runs a glistering finger along the polished surface of the foliage tufts; here the bark grows thick, showing between the corky ridges a ruddy glow, and the air smells sweetly of this Pine's natural rosin. When given such improved conditions — plenty of sunlight, depth of soil, and space — an individual Monterey Pine will shoot up 80 and 100 feet high, cast what is for a Pine a wide pool of shade, and begin to branch its trunk with some ease. Yet just where this tree seems to reach its finest proportions, it stops abruptly short, apparently unable to live far, except in cultivation, from the enslaving fogs.

Naturally so fine a tree in so striking a position came to the notice of the very first explorers of the California coast. Only fifty years after Columbus discovered America, Juan Rodríguez Cabrillo, in his battered little galleon, sailed past here and named the peninsula the Cabo de Pinos, while Monterey Bay itself he called the Bahía de Pinos. But a savage sea was running, the fogs were treacherous, and Cabrillo kept his little bark well out to sea without landing. Not until Vizcaíno in the year 1602 anchored in the bay did any other European see our Pines. Vizcaíno surmised that they might furnish masts of any size, and perhaps he had visions of launching a fleet here. At any rate, he changed the name of the bay to do honor to the Mexican Viceroy, the Conde de Monterey, and he named the peninsula the Punta de Los Pinos. Then, having clapped these resounding monickers on the landscape, he too sailed away.

At last arrived the first overland expedition under Portolá, bringing with it Padre Junípero Serra himself to found San Carlos Mission, today popularly known as the Carmel Mission, amid the Pines. After the sword and the cross came the Spanish settlers. And now the sound of the ax was heard, the woods were set alight in order to provide better browse for the white man's cattle, a great space was cleared in the Pine groves for the Presidio, and from every direction the stately Pine forest began to shrink. By the time Robert Louis Stevenson reached Monterey, in the year 1879, the destruction had advanced far, though not nearly so far as in our times.

Fires deliberately set for the purpose of burning off the woods, or allowed to rage unchecked, are a thing of the past. And so, one would have thought, would be the whine of the sawmills which for many decades in the early period of American settlement laid waste these unique and noble groves. But for a short time, beginning in 1946, tractors and bulldozers went roaring and bucking through these lovely groves. In one year 3 million board feet of timber were felled on the Monterey peninsula, according to an author* who seems to have thought it a grand accomplishment. An electrically driven mill with a 25,000-board-foot daily capacity showed how swiftly these groves can still be exploited. Except for the small stand in Point Lobos State Park, all the Monterey Pines are still in private hands, to be managed as private owners see fit.

As a timber tree, the Monterey Pine is indeed tempting, and if we ever come to a day when we start planting commercial forest instead of living on our forest capital, this species should have a great future. The wood is hard, strong, tough, and durable away from soil. In the days of the Spanish Californians, selected trees were used in boat building. The cutting of the early American period was for flooring, for the planking of wharves, and in bridge construction. Its value as fuel is great, and formerly the Montereyans exported as much as 25,000 cords of fuel wood a year. Today it is used mostly locally, for building the bungalows among the Pines of the pretty seaside town of Carmel.

The reproduction of the Monterey Pine is, fortunately, abundant. The cones may remain upon the tree for many years, maturing their seeds, and sometimes only a forest fire will force the scales to open. Yet if fire is kept away, there will come a year when conditions seem just right, and then on some warm day in the fall when there is no wind to tear them off, the cones begin to drop off of their own accord. On the twig that is left there is

*Charles H. Stoddard, "Forestry in the Monterey Pines," *American Forests*, June 1947.

a little pitch-lined pocket, and the stem of the cone will show the heavy drip of golden brown pitch. But often the cones open while still on the tree. This usually happens in the hottest weather, which in Monterey is autumn. One walking in the woods then may hear a great crackling and snapping like the first licking of fire through brush. But this is the sound of the cones bursting open, and it may continue all through the night that follows the warm day. Once opened, the thick elastic scales look, when fresh, like so many (a hundred or more) flower petals. For they show under their tan tip a wine red color with lacquerlike finish. Meantime, thousands of little black seeds have escaped. Each fluttering on its single wing, they glide or gyrate as far as the wind will take them into the forest. They are wonderfully viable, and a seedling only four or five years old may be a tree 10 or 15 feet high. Fertility and hardihood have so far saved the Monterey Pine from all the assaults that have been made upon it.

One cannot leave this lovable tree without brief mention of the affinity which is shown for it by butterflies. Especially in the spring, thousands of the common but handsome monarch butterfly will settle on some favored specimen, and next year the same tree is likely to play host again to these fluttering guests. In the sunlight, giddy swarms of them drift around and over the tree. But if the chill fog comes rolling in, they hang from every bough and twig like bunches of brown oak leaves. It is not known why certain individual trees are so beloved by the butterflies that they are sought out by succeeding generations of these frail ephemeral creatures.

Literary historians have pointed out that the Monterey peninsula and its pines furnished the setting created by Robert Louis Stevenson for the immortal *Treasure Island*. The author, in 1879, was at Monterey and writing of it both in his letters and his essay "The Old Pacific Capital," and two years later published *Treasure Island* under its original title of *The Sea Cook*. Again and again are Pines mentioned in *Treasure Island*, as well as Live Oaks, and such Montereyan sights, odors, and sounds as the bellowing of sea lions, the strange, fungoid odor of the woods, the gray and sorrowful appearance of the island groves, which is identified in his Monterey descriptions as given by the beards of Spanish moss. In fact, almost every plant and animal alluded to in *Treasure Island* is definitely identified with the fauna and flora of Monterey, and conversely almost every organism, even every natural sound and smell which Stevenson mentions from his sojourn on the peninsula is carefully inserted on his imaginary island.

Knobcone Pine

Pinus attenuata Lemmon

OTHER NAME: Narrowcone Pine.

RANGE: In the Coast Range mountains of southern Oregon and northern California (on the Siskiyou Mountains, Trinity Alps, Mount St. Helena summit, etc.), on the Santa Cruz Mountains, on Point Pinos, near Carmel, Monterey County, and the eastern slopes of the Santa Lucia Mountains, Monterey County; on Mount Shasta (4000 to 5600 feet); on the west slopes of the northern Sierra Nevada, at 1500 to 4500 feet, south to the south side of the San Bernardinos at 2500 to 4000 feet. Lacking otherwise in the southern Sierra Nevada and southern Coast Ranges.

T HERE CAN NEVER BE ANY DIFFICULTY in identifying the Knobcone Pine at a glance, because its cones occupy so unusual and conspicuous a position on the tree. Instead of being borne at the end of the branches and far out on twigs, like those of most Pines, they are pegged by a short stalk to the wood of the main trunk and branches. Rigidly attached and bent downward, they encircle the stems in whorls or clusters of three to five at a node, or abnormally seventeen! While unopened, they are remarkably long and narrow, very lopsided at base, and show a most curious development of the scales facing away from the branch and an odd warping or foreshortening of those on the side next to the branch. They may remain upon the tree until the second or third or fourth year, when they expand, losing their narrowly conical form, and fall off after releasing their seeds. But more commonly this is not the case. The tree, on the contrary, tends to hoard its cones, sometimes until they are twenty-five years old, and the growth of the wood may actually engulf the base of the fruit, so that this has been called "the tree that swallows its cones." So they cling there as weathered knobs, awaiting the breath of fire — the destroyer of the parent tree and liberator of the next generation locked away in the prison of the unopening cones.

The seed will germinate in the most barren soils, and from the start the seedlings are hardy. So that the Knobcone Pine, like the Lodgepole, is distinctly a fire forest type — gravely subject to fire and yet marvelously adapted to reforestation after its ravages. About 85 to 160 seeds are formed in a cone. When a young field is springing up with Knobcones after a fire they stand, as Jepson says, "as thickly as stalks in a cornfield." Like the Lodgepole, the Knobcone begins to be fertile at a very early age, and trees only five or six years old will soon be covered with cones. Unlike the Lodgepole, this tree does not produce wood of any value commercially except as firewood. However, it has even more constitutional vigor, will grow in even more desolate situations, and is not nearly so subject to the attacks of beetles and fungi as the Lodgepole. In reforestation it may yet have a great role to play.

Twenty to 30 feet high, with trunks only 6 to 12 inches in diameter, the average Knobcone is an unimpressive tree among the great conifers of the West, but specimens in favorable situations may grow to be 60 or 70 feet high, with a trunk 30 inches in diameter. When given room to expand, the tree is generally forked and subdivided into a wide irregular crown, with a short trunk and slender branches coming well down to the ground. The thin foliage is usually rather faded in appearance, no matter what the age of the tree, and in general nothing much can be said for this species on the esthetic side. But if man does not admire it, Nature evidently does, for within the spotty range of this species it often grows abundantly. It thrives where better trees would die, so that at least it may be called the best of possible trees where one finds it.

SPRUCES

Sitka Spruce

Picea sitchensis (Bongard) Carrière

OTHER NAMES: Tideland or Menzies Spruce.

RANGE: Islands and sea slopes of the Alaskan Coast Ranges from sea level to timber line (up to 3000 feet), from Kodiak Island and the length of the Alaskan peninsula, all around the Kenai peninsula and south through the Panhandle (maritime southern Alaska) to the islands and Coast Range of British Columbia, from sea level to 4000 or rarely 5000 feet; in Washington mainly at the mouths and bottomlands of rivers and extending up valleys to the foothills of the Cascades, 50 miles from the sea; in Mount Snoqualmie National Forest at 1800 feet in the valley of the Nisqually; in the Olympic National Forest only up to 1000 feet; confined to the coast in Oregon except in the Columbia valley reaching the Cascade Range foothills, south to the Mendocino County coast in northern California.

T HE GREATEST TRACT OF UNBROKEN FOREST in the United States is that on the Olympic peninsula where the temperate rain forest (12 feet of rain a year) clothes an area the size of Connecticut. There has been heavy lumbering on the south and east sides of the peninsula, but from timber line on the Olympics down the north slope to the Straits of Juan de Fuca and the west slope to the Pacific Ocean, hundreds of thousands of acres are virgin wilderness. A single auto highway traverses it, and so vast is the forest that even traveling at 50 and 60 miles

per hour, hour after hour, you seldom see a house or slightest clearing in the woods. Only trees — towering, majestic, dark coniferous forest — their crowns interlocking till they shut out the sky. And the farther you go on, the more the trees become an element like the sea without shores, like the rocks when you go down in a cave, or like space, when you think too long about the distance of the stars. If you have companions, they and you have long since ceased to speak; you only look in each other's faces and see there a reflection of your own awe, as Western Hemlocks, Cedars, titanic Douglas Firs, and great Lowland Firs come rushing toward you, are passed, fall behind, and then seem to spring reborn out of the horizon ahead.

But there is one tree here that seems grander than all the rest, for it is on the Olympic peninsula that the Sitka Spruce attains its greatest stature. Trees 200 feet high, with a diameter of 10 feet above the much greater, swollen and buttressed bases, are sighted towering above the rest of the forest, and some have been scaled by foresters at 280 feet. Such a tree has probably lived eight hundred years or more, but so fast-growing is this species, especially for a Spruce, that trees 200 feet high have been shown by their annual rings to have shot up to such heights in a single century.

Yet the majesty of the Sitkas is not all in their size, but rather in the noble bearing of the crowns, the monumental cleanly straightness of their boles. The branches of this king of Spruces have an upward sweep suggestive of strength and rejoicing; from these the branchlets hang down in a beautiful weeping habit, and the twigs too, ending in the pendant cones. The young tree, and the trees by the side of the highway with room to expand, are clothed to the base in thick-set numberless boughs. The ancients of the deep woods, on the contrary, have tall bare trunks — and what trunks! The strains and stresses above, perhaps, and the boggy nature of the ground beneath, have resulted in greatly swollen and buttressed bases, whence the roots start, clawlike, from the stem and grip the earth as if to balance the immense superstructure. Above, the trunks soar, columnar and incredible, to disappear in the canopies of crowding, lesser trees; their own crowns may be quite shut away from you, far overhead. But the voice of the varied thrush may drift down to you, where the bird in the Sitka's topmost branches faces the sunlight that never penetrates below.

Some women's beauty (say those who know about such matters) imperils them, but their virtues never do. Just the opposite, Sitka Spruce, one of the most imperiled trees in all the American sylva, is in danger not because of its surpassing beauty but for its high qualities. For man has so many uses for this tree that the competition between its suitors is fierce. But whatever the outcome among them, it is the tree that suffers.

First, the general lumber industry has the highest regard for the properties and qualities of Sitka Spruce. Though soft it is strong, and it has a uniform texture and a high affinity for glue and paint. This makes it ideal material for doors, especially overhead garage doors, which must be so light as to move at a touch. The wood has little tendency to bleed through the finish, so it is excellent for interior trim and paneling, bungalow siding, and furniture. It does not split, warp, or crack, in the position of hatch covers for vessels, and being both light and strong is unexcelled for workmen's scaffolding.

One of the most select of all this great tree's uses is in the soundboards of pianos and violins and for the pipes of organs. A satisfactory soundboard must have qualities not found in every wood; indeed, resonance, in a high degree, and with fidelity to pitch, is found in few woods. Such a wood must be uniform in texture and without irregularities in the grain, so that all parts of the wood, when vibrating, will respond equally. The annual growth rings should be narrow as well as uniform, to produce the greatest elasticity. The instrument builders of Europe long ago settled on the Norway Spruce for sounding boards. In this country, Sitka Spruce is found to yield most frequently the close-ringed, defect-free, straight and true boards.

Of all the woods in the world, Sitka Spruce has the highest strength-to-weight ratio. Many a wood is strong, but usually strength implies corresponding weight, and weight, in the last analysis, is a form of weakness. Many a wood is admirably light, and consequently cheap to ship and easy to handle, but usually it is weakish to very weak. Sitka Spruce of the best grades combines remarkable strength and toughness with lightness and freedom from cupping and warping under severe strains.

The simplest example of the need of lightness and strength combined is in a ladder; it must be light enough, even if exceptionally long, to be handled readily, but human life depends upon its strength. So the best ladders are Spruce ladders. Similarly, but with more lives depending on it, is the lightness of Spruce combined with strength in portable bleachers for sports events. But these must have an added quality — they must not splinter with use. To all these needs Sitka Spruce answers admirably. College racing shells, too, must be made of the lightest of possible woods having also strength. The seat of such a shell of Sitka Spruce, for instance, will carry a 200-pound man, yet it weighs only 1¼ pounds. As constructed by the famous builder George Pocock, of Seattle, the racing shells are built of Oregon-grown Spruce for its toughness and strength; pound for pound it is stronger than steel.

But airplane construction tests a wood to the last degree, and in two world wars, Sitka Spruce met the demands of heavier-than-air craft. Experience in combat has taught that wood has greater ability to absorb shock than has metal. When a metal propeller is dented it may develop an unseen fatigue crack that will explode later; not so with Spruce props. A bullet hole in wooden wing or wooden fuselage is repaired by plastic wood in a jiffy; repairs of holes in metal is a major operation involving time and resulting in additional weight. Gunfire through wooden planes results in no extensive tearing.

Going back to the field of plane production, manufacturers find the construction of a metal plane requires hundreds of hours of work by skilled riveters, welders, and metal workers. But wooden planes can be produced with a minimum of manpower in a minimum of time. Kiln drying of Spruce cuts the time required for curing the wood from two years to twenty-one days and yields a better product.

The arguments for Spruce in wing beams, wing ribs, and as plywood are conclusive enough, but the amount of Sitka Spruce actually suitable to aircraft construction does not present so bright a picture. Strength, of course, is the first factor, and a strong wood is a straight-grained wood with a divergence of no more than 1 inch for every 15 inches; it must also be free of knots and blemishes. Such trees are not common at any time, and only about 12 percent of logs are judged, after cutting, to be suitable. Of this lumber only 10 percent is likely to prove acceptable when sawed out in boards. At best, 1 board foot in every 50 is of plane quality. So the search for airworthy Spruce has been called the jewel trade of the lumber business.

The needs of planes for defense cannot be denied, and under the stress of national survival, the cut of Spruce has gone on, in the past, without thought to the wasteful methods involved. More, the drain of three fighting nations in the last wars has been leveled almost entirely upon Oregon and Washington Spruce, for wood grown in those states was considered superior. So intense was the demand, however, that Alaska sent her Sitka Spruce in rafts of a million board feet at a time, towed 900 miles along the coast to Puget Sound. But large though Alaska's Spruce resources, much of her stand is quite inaccessible and so is British Columbia's. Only in Washington and Oregon is this species growing where it is easy to cut and move, and even here the merchantable stand is but a fraction of the total growth that includes both immature and superannuated trees.

And still the list of uses of this versatile tree is not complete. For Sitka Spruce is today one of the continent's great raw materials for paper pulp. Indeed, you could not ask for a better conjunction of favorable conditions for industry in the Northwest, where the forests, the water power, the transportation, and the climate are all conjoined for a tremendous output. At Ocean Falls, British Columbia, for instance, oceangoing steamers dock just below the pulping mills which utilize the water power from a big dam holding back a long lake which, further, furnishes the immense quantities of pure water required for washing the pulp. On this lake are rafted the Spruce logs, which have been cut in the heavily timbered mountains. And so dense is the growth of Spruce, so much does the mild rainy climate favor rapid replacement after logging, that it is hoped that the supply of pulpwood will be a self-renewing resource that will never give out, and the pulp plant and the town that depends on it will be permanent.

Here, as elsewhere in all modern pulping plants, the processes of converting Spruce logs into paper have been worked out to near perfection in mechanical efficiency. The logs are taken from the lake or river by conveyors and sawn into proper length and piled. When needed, the raw log material is mechanically conveyed to the mill where big steel revolving drums wear off the bark. The enormous machines hold the peeled "stick" against a grindstone turned by water power and kept cool by further large volumes of water.

The ground-up mass that results is a dirty slush which is then run through screens of successively finer caliber to strain out all coarse material. Now the water pulp must go to a Hollander or beating vat where it is whirled and further macerated with blades against an adjustable anvil. Then are added the fillers — clays and other substances to give polish and body to coated papers, and rosin, alum, and gelatin for sizing so that the paper will take ink without blotting. And, last, the dyes are added to tint the pulp the desired color.

But now the mass, with all its chemical elements added, must be dried by a machine that may measure 30 feet wide, 300 feet long, and 30 feet high and weigh 2000 tons. Into it flows, day and night, every day in the year, a continuous stream of slush which is 199 parts water to 1 part solid pulp, and the problem is to expel the water and dry the pulp. First the mass is shaken on a screen so that the fibers will lie in every direction and not arrange themselves in the direction of flow — lest the ultimate paper product tear too readily in that direction. Then the screen and its watery sheet are run across suction boxes and through suction cylinders. Much drier now, the papery sheet is put through felt-lined wringers and mangles and then pressed between a series of some fifty enormous steam-heated rollers. Now the half-formed paper is sent between steel rolls that polish it and finally it is rolled up on a mandrel or core, like towel paper on a kitchen roll.

So effective are all the inventions that have been brought together at the pulping mill that the pulp travels sometimes at the rate of 1200 feet a minute, and a sheet of paper is unrolled which never stops, year in, year out, unless the sheet breaks.

The question arises, in view of all these demands, whether Sitka Spruce can stand the drains upon it. If it served any one of its masters exclusively — the pulp industry, the general lumber industry, or plane production — the answer might be a clear yes. But when for all uses the cut runs to 240 million board feet a year in Oregon and Washington alone, while annual growth in that region amounts to but 21 million board feet, it is plain that we are cutting Sitka Spruce more than ten times as fast as it is replacing itself. Of all the great industrial trees on this continent, Sitka Spruce stands in the most deadly peril, and under the stress of war or even preparation for war, the peril may be nearly doubled. The tree, as a species, is not in danger of extinction as a very rare and local species might be. But when the great stands of it are gone, no other tree will do its many jobs so well, since no other has quite the same strength-weight ratio or the high quality of fibers for pulp. We shall then have to wait for second growth, and it will be cut under pressing demand as fast as it matures.

There is one bright side to the picture, and that is the large amount of Sitka Spruce held in national forests and national parks. That in the parks can never be cut, under the present laws; Spruce in the national forests can be logged at the discretion of Forest Service whose regulations permit it to mark mature trees for falling; private companies then bid for the timber and are allowed to take it out under government supervision. Thus the Spruce in the national forests constitutes a national reserve which could meet a national emergency. But it should not, in the judgment of the conservative, be called on to help out private industry just because the lumber and pulping companies are running short. They will have to solve their own problems and bring into line the rate of cut with the rate of natural reproduction.

Red Spruce

Picea rubens Sargent

OTHER NAMES: Yellow Spruce. He-Balsam.

RANGE: Nova Scotia to southern Quebec, and south throughout Maine, New Hampshire, and Vermont to Cape Ann, Massachusetts, and the Berkshires, Catskills, Adirondacks, and Hudson valley, south on the higher mountains of New Jersey, the high ridges of the Alleghenies in Pennsylvania, above 3500 feet in the Virginias, and above 4500 in the Tennessee and North Carolina mountains.

SELDOM IS THE RED SPRUCE seen save in the company of its constant companion the Fir tree, or Balsam. The southern mountaineers, indeed, call both Spruce and Fir "Balsam"; they speak of a certain type of mountain as a balsam — meaning one conspicuously crowned with these two trees, for their evergreen, very dark and pointed tops contrast in the sharpest way with the paler green and broad crowns of the de-

ciduous forest zones beneath them. The southern Appalachians have no true timber line and no snowcaps; usually trees march to the very summits of the highest peaks. All the highest, save some of the grass or heath "balds," are crowned with these black caps of Spruce and Fir, and from them the Black Mountains, culminating in Mount Mitchell itself, take their name.

The mountain people recognize the intimate association of the Spruce and Fir by calling them respectively the He-Balsam and the She-Balsam. Observing that the Fir has swollen blisters of resin under the bark, they fancifully compared them to breasts filled with milk, hence the She-Balsam. And supposing perhaps that a mate must be found for the She-Balsam and noting that its companion tree had no resin blisters, they named it the He-Balsam.

To tell the "He" from the "She," when you find yourself among these two companion trees, crush the needles in your fingers and discover the two distinct odors — the orange-rind aroma of the Spruce, and the balsam-pillow smell of the Fir. Yet in these high groves there is only a delicious commingled fragrance, reminding you of Christmas morning even though it may be a day in July when, panting in the thinner air after a 6000-foot climb, you rest beneath the intense shade of these trees, on the deep bed of mosses.

The Red Spruce is much the commonest Spruce of the White Mountains of New Hampshire, and as one climbs Mount Washington it is soon met with, amidst the Birch, Beech, and Maple of the lower forests. But, companioned by the Balsam Fir, it leaves the other trees behind, and for a while we climb easily in fine groves of these two trees; though their canopy is close, and the shade is perpetual — cool and damp — the forest room in which we seem to be walking has a high ceiling, and there is a striking lack of understory trees and shrubs.

But at about 5000 feet above sea level, we find ourselves looking out over the tops of the Spruce and Fir, for they have shrunk to breast height, and, intricately branched, the branches thick and tough with years, they make a thicket through which it would be impossible to force one's way. Only the trail, hacked out by ax, makes any going easy here, though one may try walking on top of the dwarf trees. When the Spruce is down to ankle height, no taller than the Labrador-tea bushes, you are at timber line.

As a saw-log tree, Red Spruce is all that the softwood lumberman could ask, with fine straight stems, the knots sound, the wood strong in proportion to its weight, and elastic. So heavy cutting and fires have, in the short time between the end of the age of the Eastern White Pine, when lumber companies first deigned to look at Spruce, and the present, done execution on this valuable timber resource. On the high southern Appalachians the virgin Spruce-Fir forests do not, when removed, replace themselves. A hardwood forest, when cut over, sprouts from the stumps, but the Redwood is the only conifer that shows any regular ability to reproduce by sprouting. A cutover Spruce growth must reproduce from seed, and if lumbering is followed by slash fires, the deep bed of humus, the kindly protection of mosses are destroyed. Or the Spruce seedlings die soon after germination in the sun-bitten, wind-scorched desert left after fire. Instead, the brambles move in, then Fire Cherry and Trembling Aspen.

To the pulpmill goes Red Spruce whenever the paper manufacturer catches a stand of it not included in a national park or forest. The wood has a long list of other uses; to enumerate them would be almost a repetition of White Pine's versatility, and indeed if ever eastern forests are managed by the government, as Swedish forests are, with controlled cutting and a long-term policy of planting for sustained yield, Red Spruce will be a great natural resource.

Red Spruce has one precious quality for which it is cut in small but choice amounts, and this is its resonance. Musical resonance in any wood is superior to that of the resonance of metal because it enriches and softens the tone and also damps it off quickly; metals make it hard and prolong it, and heighten the pitch. The wood selected for musical instruments is chosen with exquisite care. It must have an absolutely uniform texture and be free from all defects and irregularities of grain. Spruce measures up to these qualifications in the highest degree — at least the best quality does so — being a wood with fairly narrow growth rings of uniform width. So it is preferred for guitars, mandolins, organ pipes, piano soundboards, and violin bellies. For the latter Spruce is considered by the best makers to have no substitutes. It is often asserted that the old violin makers had secrets, in the selection of wood, in design, in the nature of the varnish or the way it was dried, that made their instruments better. But the serious historians of the violin all doubt this; modern techniques and materials are certainly the equals of the old ones. There is, however, an undeniable difference between a violin that has been used for many years, and a "green" one that is not "broken in." Here the wood technologists step in, to tell us that the wood cells become more and more elastic with constant vibration; old violins are, as it were, aged in music. But the finest of instruments, if neglected, stiffen up again. The fiddle of Paganini, after lying in the museum of his native Genoa, was found in fifty years to be a ruin, so far as tone was concerned. At the Library of Congress in Washington the historic instruments are, on the contrary, taken out and played regularly to keep them in condition.

White Spruce

Picea glauca (Moench) Voss

OTHER NAMES: Skunk, Cat, or Single Spruce.

RANGE: Newfoundland and Labrador to Alaska, south on the Alberta Rockies to Montana, Minnesota, Wisconsin, northern Michigan, northern New York, Vermont, New Hampshire, and Maine. Also on the Black Hills of South Dakota.

T HE MOST BEAUTIFUL APPROACH to the North American continent from Europe is up the St. Lawrence to Quebec. The grandeur of this estuary, the greatest, save the Amazon's, in all the world, the storm of gannets from the bird rocks, the white cliffs of the Gaspé peninsula, would be enough to make it incomparable. But most impressive of all is the vast coniferous forest, so dark a green that it looks almost black, stretching from the north shore away and away to the horizon and beyond, for hundreds of impenetrable miles, to the arctic limit of

trees. In this forest are set the little villages of French Canada, the inevitable white steeple and gold cross gleaming bright against the evergreens and the raw, elemental blue of the sky. Each of these villages seems, from the deck of the ship, a collection of toy houses and churches pressed closely by Christmas trees. And of all the conifers there, the fairest is the White Spruce, the beauty of its family.

It was in the basin of the St. Lawrence, indeed, that the White Spruce was first seen by Jacques Cartier when in the autumn of 1535 he sailed up the Saguenay River. "From the day of the 18th to the 28th of this month we have sailed up this river without losing an hour nor a day, during which time we have seen and found as beautiful a country and lands and views as one could wish for, level as aforementioned, and the finest trees in the world, to wit oaks, elms, walnuts, cedars, spruces, ash trees, willows and wild vines."

In youth the White Spruce forms a fine spirelike top, with a central stem straight as a mast, ending at the acute symmetrical tip; the lowest arms sweep benignantly down almost to earth, then turn up at the twig, like fingers lifted, in a gesture of easy grace. The foliage tends to curl, no matter from what side of the branch it may spring, toward the top of the twig, and so appears combed up and out. When crushed, it gives out a pungent, almost skunky odor.

Banks of streams and lakes, and borders of swamps, are the habitat of this fine tree; it seeks out ocean cliffs along the coast of Maine, where the salt spray of the Atlantic burns the needles on the windward side, and the sea winds sculpture it into fantastic forms. On the eastern slopes of the

Canadian Rockies it attains its greatest height — sometimes 150 feet, with a trunk 3 or 4 feet thick. It reaches almost to the Arctic sea in scattered groves, and every one of the rivers of the Mackenzie and Yukon provinces is choked with the naturally fallen logs of White Spruce, while its driftwood is piled, whitening, on their banks and shoals.

In Canada, especially the western provinces, White Spruce is often a fine lumber tree, used for interior finish. Its greatest use, though, is in the making of paper pulp; the least hymned of all forest industries, pulping is, since the disappearance of the great stands of virgin White and Red Pines, the most important forest industry of eastern Canada. For pulp manufacture is requisite a very abundant tree with very soft fibers. White Spruce answers exactly to this description, and so tremendous has become the drain on our pulp woods that many great newspapers in the United States own their own Spruce forests in Canada, and by operating on successive tracts over a sufficiently great area they hope that this fast-growing Spruce will furnish them a self-renewing crop to perpetuity. In vain have American pulp manufacturers sought to raise a tariff wall against Canadian Spruce; for once, the pulp interests have met their equals in the press, and Canadian pulp still comes in duty-free as a needed raw material just like rubber, silk, and coffee.

In the making of pulp, the fiber is torn apart by great grindstones kept cool by water, till the once proud log is reduced to a dirty slush, or else the pure cellulose is freed by dissolving out the gummy lignins with sulfite or soda. To this sludge are added all the fillers, such as rosin, alum, and gelatin for sizing, and clays to give body and polish to coated papers, and dyes for colored papers. Then the pulp is drained and mechanically dried, in principle as one dries clothes with wringer or mangle, but by a series of machines that are a marvel of inventive skill. There emerges at last a continuous flowing sheet of paper which in the great mills never stops, year in year out, unless the paper breaks. To produce a ton of newsprint requires one cord of wood, 2800 tons of water, nearly 2000 kilowatt hours of electrical energy or 100 horsepower for twenty-four hours, and a capital up to $50,000 per ton of daily output. And thus it is we get, each morning, our bad news and our comics.

Colorado Blue Spruce

Picea pungens Engelmann

OTHER NAMES: Blue, White, Silver, or Parry Spruce.

RANGE: From the mountains of western Montana and central Idaho (at 6000 to 9000 feet), south in Yellowstone and Grand Teton National Parks through the mountains of Colorado to New Mexico (Sangre de Cristo, Mogollon, and Sacramento mountains, at 8000 to 11,000 feet), and from the Uinta and Wasatch Mountains of Utah to Arizona (Kaibab Plateau and White Mountains, 7000 to 11,000 feet altitude).

E WHO HAS SEEN THIS TREE only in formal cultivation in well-tended grounds has little notion of its wild beauty in the grandeur to which it is native. It is a popular tree indeed in the eastern states, where it is the most planted of western conifers, under the name of Blue Spruce or sometimes Silver Spruce, for it is no end admired by the suburbanite as a lawn tree, and the newly wealthy man likes to order it in quantity as a windbreak, or to line the curving approaches to his summer place. As a hedge, it is so close-growing and cruelly prickly as to be boy-proof and is indeed impenetrable to still smaller animals.

If you don't yet know it in cultivation, the nurseryman's catalogue is sure to carry a color picture of young specimens of this insistently pretty tree, displaying its charms of tier on tier of branches graduated in perfect symmetry from the longest boughs that sweep the ground to the slender but strong tip. Above all, the feature that brings the customers in off the street is the cast or bloom, like blue moonlight, upon the foliage of young trees and the tips of the new or summer growth of older trees. All specimens exhibit more or less of this glaucous beauty, for a time, but some more than others, and these are carefully selected in seedling stage for they are in most demand and fetch the highest price. A very showy form called Silver Spruce has foliage tips of an argent frostiness, and these are propagated by grafting them on stock of less silvery individuals.

But when the easterner comes west, he does not find the middle slopes of the Rockies covered with neat, blue, symmetrical little trees like those on the lawn at home. Instead, dark cohorts, proud as lances, march up the noble slopes with a look unconquered, unrestrained. These trees are not consistently powdered with that look of stage moonlight; they are predominantly dark green, even somber, like most Spruces, with little blue about them except, for a brief season, the tips of the new growth or, here and there, a young specimen that is fairly azure or glaucous all over. And as the summer wanes the blueness on older trees tends to weather away, since it is nothing, after all, but a superficial waxiness or powder, and not at all the underlying color of the needles.

But let the Aspens turn from green to glowing gold, let them spend all that gold and shiver nakedly in the swift-driving snow, let the snow pile deep, and still proudly above it, though heavy laden with it, march these Spruces upon their sky-piercing conquest of the Rocky Mountain scene. In this wild state they are in beauty far above the mere symmetry of the lawn-grown specimens; here they have the proud look of fighters. For forest competition soon kills off the younger boughs, and the trunks become polelike, the crowns carried high and irregularly sculptured by the elements. Forgotten is the connotation with the lawn mower and the upholstered hammock. Instead, after a vacation in the West, you will have stored, beneath the flickering shade and in hearing of the seething murmur of the Colorado Spruce, some of your most treasured memories — of the flash and thunder of whitewater, of a line tautened by the rainbow trout, of a family of dippers teetering on the edge of the fall or plunging right under the flood. And when you go back east you will look on the cultivated specimens of the Blue Spruce with changed eyes. How all too blue the fancy-dress little things appear, how juvenile in their self-conscious symmetry, how stingy of shade, and voiceless in the wind!

Engelmann Spruce

Picea engelmannii Parry ex Engelmann*

OTHER NAMES: White or Mountain Spruce.

RANGE: At 1500 to 5000 feet in the Canadian Rockies (central British Columbia southward) through the southern Rockies (10,000 to 12,000 feet) to southern parts of New Mexico and Arizona; frequent in the Cascades and rare in Shasta County, California.

THE MOST DRAMATIC TREE of your first trip in the Rockies will almost certainly be the Engelmann Spruce. Your memories of it will be linked with the towering Grand Tetons, the long, forested valleys of the Yellowstone, the breathtaking beauty of Lake Louise, the parklike spaciousness, the exciting dry air, of Rocky Mountain National Park. And the meeting with a bear, glimpses of bounding deer, the insolence of crested jays, the racket of nutcrackers, the chill of high mountain lakes, the plop of a diving beaver, the delicious taste of camp food cooked in appetite-sauce, and mountain meadows glorious with larkspur, columbine, and lupine — all these are part of your composite recollections of the realms where this fine Spruce grows. But you would not recall it as distinct from other trees had it not an inherent personality of its own. Fifty and 100 feet and more tall, it is, in dense forests, slender as a church spire, and its numbers are legion. So it comes crowding down to the edge of the meadow where your tent is pitched, to the rocks surrounding the little lake that mirrors its lancelike forms upside down. And when the late mountain light begins to leave the summer sky, there is something spirit-like about the enveloping hosts of the Engelmanns. Always a dark tree, this Spruce's outlines are now inky, and its night silence makes the sounds of an owl, or of an old moose plashing somewhere across the lake, mysterious and magnified in portent.

When daylight comes again the friendliness returns to the Engelmanns, and they are seen in the light of reality to be trees that are merely dramatic by their very nature, with those short, dense, downsweeping boughs. But there is nothing impenetrable about their groves and little that is ever dangerous. Fragrant and glittering, the hosts of this Spruce

Editor's note: Formerly *Picea engelmannii* Parry.

clothe vast areas in the Rockies with a beauty equaled by only some of the conifers on the Pacific coast.

At high altitudes the Engelmann behaves like most other timberline trees and is dwarfed, straggling, naked on the windward side, and even sprawling. It is not truly an alpine tree, however, since its real home is lower down. When growing in the open, of course, it retains its lower boughs more completely and takes on more ample outlines.

The commercial stand of Engelmann Spruce is reckoned at some 29 billion board feet. The wood is relatively strong and yet lighter in weight than White Pine. Mill work and interior trim are sometimes worked up from Engelmann, but it is the very straight stems that recommend it to its most common use — for telephone and telegraph poles.

Fire in this pitchy, close-growing tree may soon become a demon out of all control, but Engelmann Spruce is a tree endowed with great vitality and the necessary tolerance for recapturing what it has lost. For its seedlings are able to endure deep shade. So they come up under any and all other growth. Thus a forest may become so umbrageous that other tree seedlings do not thrive beneath their parents, but this Spruce's children continue to seed and come up year after year. They grow very slowly under such conditions, but they do not give up, and they can afford to wait, for some day old age, decay, windfall, or lumbering operations will remove their superannuated rivals. Then, when the sunlight reaches the young Engelmanns, and the roots of their tyrants wither away, these Spruces will put on a spurt of amazing growth, and eventually Engelmann Spruce may take over entirely. But no other tree is so well fitted to succeed them as it is to succeed itself, year after year, so that the triumph of the Engelmanns is likely to be final till flames or axes or avalanches intervene.

WILLOWS

Black Willow

Salix nigra Marshall

OTHER NAME: Swamp Willow.

RANGE: New Brunswick to the region north of Lake Superior, and to southern North Dakota, southeastern South Dakota, Nebraska, Kansas, and Oklahoma; south to Georgia and eastern and central Alabama and into the south-central states — Arkansas, Louisiana, and eastern Texas.

O
UR GREAT BLACK WILLOW, perhaps the largest Willow in the world, occupies many habitats over its vast range and takes on many forms. On the dunes of Cape Hatteras it is but a shrub; beside the brooks, streams, and smaller rivers of the eastern seaboard it is a moderately tall tree 40 to 50 feet high; in the deep muck of the bottomlands of the middle South it may be a forest tree with a single straight bole fairly thick and very tall and clean of limbs a long way up. But beside the Father of Waters and its mighty tributaries, the Willow is a sprawling giant of a tree. In such sites Black Willow has usually several forks, beginning low down, each fork leaning somewhat outward; or trunks arising from the same root system seem to separate at the base. These leaning riverbank trees, when grown to large estate, have a sort of slouching picturesqueness, not unlike the lazy brown streams themselves.

Water-loving at all times, the Black Willow is especially fitted for its life

102

as a riparian tree of the great slow rivers, for its twigs snap off easily at the base, as every American with a country childhood knows, and are capable of rooting if thrust in the ground. Most of us have known a native Willow, in some familiar dooryard, that was planted by this very means, and doubtless untold numbers of giant riverbank Willows were once floating twigs.

The bark of the root is intensely bitter and used to be an ingredient of spring tonics to "purge the blood." In Revolutionary and pioneer times Willow was much employed in the making of a fine charcoal for the black gunpowder of those days. As a wood compared with others, Willow would seem at first to have few good points. One of the lightest and probably the softest of all our eastern hardwoods, it is extremely weak in a structural sense; at least no one would think of building a bridge of Willow beams! Yet it has a strength of its own. When nails are driven into it, Black Willow does not readily split; on the contrary, its springy fibers hold a nail far better than most woods. Flexible, it serves for wickerwork furniture and baskets.

And though it has the worthless lazy look of some old riverbank loiterer, it plays, too, a heroic role. For where engineers have to face the problem of reinforcing levees, the Willow is unsurpassed for revetments. No other wood is so pliant yet tough, no other is so cheap, nor so ready at hand. Right on the banks of the Mississippi, the Ohio, and the Missouri, thrives the tree that can hold in check the fury of their powers in flood. Probably no other American tree is worth so much in property that, thanks to it, has not been destroyed; none, it may be, has saved so many human lives.

Pussy Willow

Salix discolor Muhlenberg

OTHER NAME: Glaucous Willow.

RANGE: Nova Scotia to Manitoba, and south to Delaware, southern parts of Indiana and Illinois, southwestern Iowa, and northeastern Minnesota. Also in the Black Hills.

OF ALL THE NATIVE WILLOWS of the eastern United States, the Pussy Willow is the favorite. In earliest spring, or even in the last weeks of winter, the flower buds begin to burst their scales, and the male catkins, still much shortened, peep out on the naked wood of the twigs, clothed in their silky soft hair. This constitutes the "pussy fur" known to everyone from childhood on. Even in florists' windows, in the city streets, pussy willows are displayed for sale and find purchasers who must, surely, be people with old memories of a country or a village past.

But you will enjoy them best if you go out in the country and cut your own Pussy Willow twigs. Take your galoshes, or whatever you choose for dry footing, for the Pussy Willow delights to grow around sloughs and swamps and riverbanks, and even when it takes up a position that in summer is comparatively dry, at this season the melting snows and high brimming of the streams will make your way an amphibious one. As you go sloshing into the mucky ground, you will hear the sweet piping of the first spring peepers and the swamp tree frogs, and perhaps the old fence post you observed will suddenly pluck itself out of the marsh and go flapping away — for it was a bittern — with a raucous cry of *faugh!* It is a poor Pussy Willow that does not have a song sparrow perched on it at this season, his throat vibrating with the tumbled, jingling notes of his early love song.

If you will keep the pussies in water after they have begun to turn into flowers, and wait a week for them to pass through an awkward age in which they have lost the charm of babyhood and not gained the splendor of maturity, you will be rewarded at last by the appearance of the beautiful golden stamens. Out in the woods these are sought by swarms of bees gathering pollen to make pollen-cakes for their young. It is doubtful, though, that they effect pollination, since there is little about the modest female catkins to attract them. Wind is the true pollinator. The Pussy Willow has therefore to produce enough pollen to satisfy the needs of the bees and to waste in unthinkable quantities upon the chill winds, for only a minute part will actually alight upon the female flowers. That is why the male flowers are so intensely laden with this golden dust that it drifts sometimes in swirls upon the cold waters of the woodland pool.

Leafing comes after the flowers, but in full leaf the Pussy Willow is in no way disappointing. The contrast of the dark green upper surface of the foliage with the bluish silvery undersides is lovely all season, and when fall comes the leaves turn a buttery yellow before dropping.

The leaves and twigs of Pussy Willow frequently become involved in a gall (*Rhabdophaga strobiloides*), which takes on the appearance of a pine cone or strobile and is sometimes mistaken for a fruit. It is so curious and handsome that it manages somehow not to be disfiguring like most of the galls.

FIRS

Douglas Fir

Pseudotsuga menziesii (Mirbel) Franco*

OTHER NAMES: Douglastree. Douglas, Yellow, or Red Spruce. Oregon Pine.

RANGE: The true species found from the head of the Skeena River in British Columbia south through Washington and Oregon (Coast Ranges and Cascades, from sea level to 7200 feet) and in the mountains of California, south on the Sierra Nevada to the headwaters of the San Joaquin, and in the Coast Ranges south to the Santa Lucia Mountains of Monterey County. The variety *glauca* (Beissner) Franco, the Rocky Mountain Douglas Fir, found from Tacla Lake, British Columbia (latitude 55° north), south for 2200 miles through the Rockies at 4000 to 11,000 feet altitude, in Alberta, Montana, Wyoming, Idaho, Utah, Colorado, Arizona, and New Mexico to western Texas and the highlands of Mexico; also in the Black Hills of South Dakota, the Big Horns of Wyoming, and, *somewhat* rarely, on the mountains of eastern Nevada.

WHEN THE IMMORTAL FRIGATE *Constitution* first put to sea in 1798, she carried as masts three lofty Eastern White Pines felled in the state of Maine. But when in 1925 these had to be removed, there was left no White Pine in all the eastern states tall enough to replace those glorious sticks. From the Northwest came, instead, three

Editor's note: Formerly *Pseudotsuga taxifolia* (Poiret) Britton.

towering shafts of Douglas Fir, and these "Old Ironsides" bears in her decks today where she rides in honor at the dock of Boston Navy Yard.

Thus has Eastern White Pine fallen from first place among the timber trees of the continent; thus has Douglas Fir (which no American had ever seen or heard of when the keel of the *Constitution* was being laid) risen to the position of premier industrial tree of the world. For it was to this great western conifer that the lumber industry turned when, at the close of the nineteenth century, the end of virgin Eastern White Pine was in sight. Luckily for them and us the noble species which took its fallen sister's place is quite as versatile in fulfilling a hundred vital uses and manyfold as abundant.

And it is mightier in stature. Towering up to heights as great as 220 feet, with sometimes 100 feet of trunk clean of branches, arrow straight, and with almost no taper below the crown discernible to the naked eye, an ancient Douglastree may be 17 feet in diameter. This tree is thus the tallest and most ponderous in North America, save only the two Sequoias. And except in their presence it is almost everywhere in its immense range the most majestic species, as it is the most commercially important.

One-fourth of all the standing saw timber in the United States is Douglas Fir. In volume cut it surpasses any other one species. It occurs in every western state and in parts of Canada and Mexico. Its somber shape, its serrated crowns and sharp lance-point tips and long swaying boughs become printed like a lasting eidolon on all our memories of the Pacific Northwest. And even deep in the desert states of the Southwest we meet it again, on high peaks, with gratitude for its dim, cool groves, after the glare and heat of the rocky wastes below.

Yet this important and abundant and beautiful tree has never had a universally accepted common name. Formerly in this country it was known as Oregon Pine and is still so called abroad. In Canada, and commonly in the lumber trade in this country, it is simply called Fir — *the* Fir, since no other can approach it in economic importance. In the literature of forestry it has wavered between Douglas Fir and Douglas Spruce, though it is no Spruce and no true Fir, as botanists see matters. Some years ago the Forest Service officially settled on "Douglas Fir" and if this impaction seems to you to clear up matters, you may use it with the blessings of the Government Printing Office. The least misleading of proposed names is Douglastree, since it leans on no analogies and still does honor to that noble pioneer among explorer-botanists of the Northwest, David Douglas. In the pages that follow, this name will be used for the living forest tree, but for its logs, lumber, and wood products, the lumberman's name of Douglas Fir (or Fir for short) seems best.

The veriest beginner will have no difficulty in distinguishing a Douglastree in the field by its cones, for between their soft, broad scales are thrust out ribbon-shaped bracts that look like three-forked tongues. Many species of *Abies,* the true Firs, also have extruded bracts, but they are never tridentlike. With experience one comes to recognize Douglastree in the field from almost as far as it can be seen, by subtle points and traits. The dense, compact crowns, the lusterless, dark blue green of the foliage (relieved only for a few weeks by bright new growth), the darkly, deeply furrowed old boles, the mastlike stems, and the grand downsweeping of the boughs, all go to make up the character of this species.

But one feature there is which is peculiarly distinctive, and that is the way that numberless long slender twigs, clothed in a spiral of needles, hang vertically from the branches. Though the general habit of the tree is not what gardeners call weeping, these long pendants have a sort of sorrowful grace. When the summer winds blow lightly through the forest they stir this shawl-like fringe in an idle, ferny way; when winter rains come driving through the forest, level and endless from the storm-bound Pacific, then these long pennants lie out waving upon the gale in a way that gives the whole tree a wild and streaming look.

To see a growth of virgin Douglastree in all its venerable grandeur — for these trees may live five hundred to a thousand years — perhaps the most impressive of easily accessible spots is on Grouse Mountain which rises behind the fine seaport city of Vancouver in British Columbia. A highway takes you up in hawklike, soaring swoops, and from the excellent hostel at the road's end a footpath leads you directly up into the undisturbed and solemn stand where Douglastrees of towering height mingle with Hemlocks and Cedars only a little less tall. It is very dim and cool under the close canopy; seldom does a sunbeam reach to the forest floor where the mosses seem not to have been trodden since the Ice Age. And everywhere you look the great shafts of the Fir close up the aisles with their dark, deeply furrowed bark. From time to time the mountain wind goes seething through the high canopy above you, as if the whole forest were breathing as one ancient organism. And, if you are still, you will hear a spirit voice. It seems to begin far away at the auditory horizon and to bound toward you — a "bump . . . bump . . . bumpadump" — as if some creature were knocking on the great Fir trunks as it approaches. This is the call of the blue grouse for which the mountain is named, and as each bird utters it the next one takes up the proclamation. So the sound approaches, passes right by you — for the nearest bird is probably right over your head in some grand Fir, close to the trunk — and goes bounding into the distance. Somehow the stentorian bird seems the very voice of this profound and aboriginal wilderness and its cry, once heard, will be linked forever with your memory of Douglastrees.

Once, presumably, the entire Northwest was more or less covered with wilderness like this. It marched right down to the shores in the days of 1792 when Archibald Menzies, a naturalist of the famous Vancouver expedition that explored the Puget Sound region, saw, first of European scientists, the "impenetrable stretches of Pinery," among them the Douglastree that then bore no name. Menzies, who was also the first to collect specimens of the Coast Redwood and so many other great western trees, brought back herbarium specimens of the Douglastree and on their basis Lambert, the leading English authority on conifers, published the new species — as a sort of Pine! Then, when David Douglas reached the mouth of the Columbia in 1825, he saw from the deck of the ship "a species which may prove to be *P. taxifolia*" — the tree that was to be named for him and carry that name, in a hundred useful products, to the ends of the earth. Proceeding inland, Douglas began to measure some of the gigantic logs of the tree he knew as *Pinus taxifolia*. The largest specimen he could find was 227 feet long and 48 feet in circumference. He wished to collect seeds, but found trouble in procuring them from such lofty trees; his buckshot would not reach the cones so high overhead and his hatchet could not cut down such lusty giants. When he finally procured seeds, he set out on a race for the coast, knowing that the ship *Dryad* was soon to sail. Only a day was left him to pack his collections of a year, which included 125 pounds of seeds, but he got his cargo aboard in time, and from those seeds grew the first European trees of this forest monarch. Soon Douglas's life would be cut short by a cruel death on the Hawaiian islands where he fell into a trap pit set for wild animals, and was trampled to death by a bullock.

Douglas's host, Dr. John McLoughlin, the celebrated Hudson's Bay Company agent, in 1828 erected the first sawmill on our Northwest coast and began the cutting of Fir. But it was not until the lumbering of Eastern White Pine had laid waste the virgin growth of that species that the great days of Northwest logging really began, toward the close of the nineteenth century. Some firms came as a unit, bringing their lumberjacks with them; one old Maine firm transported its mills in sections around the Horn. Many bought up great blocks of forest from the railroads, which had received them from the government as grants to compensate them for building transcontinental lines into country almost uninhabited. Other companies bought up large tracts from homesteaders, and in Oregon there was even a thriving business done by one government clerk in making false homestead entries which then went to lumber companies for a song; eventually he and some much bigger fish went to prison.

Indeed, lumbering in the Northwest in the early days was often a "two-fisted" business, in which one would say that neither the lumber barons (who came to be known as "tyees") nor the lumberjacks, had learned a thing from the wastage, the fires, the boom-and-bust days, and stump counties of eastern history. Nothing, that is, except greatly increased efficiency at whirlwind exploitation. But that was in a cruder age, in the days when labor troubles went to the shooting stage, when pirates on Puget Sound stole whole rafts of timber and secretly sawed up the logs after obliterating the brands (each legitimate company had its own, like cattle ranchers), when fires burned over forests the size of many a European principality, when the Forest Service was jeered at and obstructed, when saloon bars in the coast towns were a mile long and brothels were big as hotels. Those days are gone. Progressive companies now hire their own trained foresters and follow practical conservation. Well-located lumber towns have become permanent cities, with fine schools, churches, hospitals, parks. Employees are usually married, own their homes, eat the best of food, sleep in clean beds. Fire is fought like the Devil. Those who wish to read more of the sociology and business history of this raucous saga with the prosperous and respectable ending should turn to *Holy Old Mackinaw* and *Green Commonwealth* by Stuart Holbrook, *The Great Forest* by Richard G. Lillard, and *Time, Tide, and Timber* by Edwin Truman Coman.

The geographical setting of the Douglas Fir industry shows why the Northwest was destined to become the lumber capital of the world. For that region is the tidewater country around Puget Sound, Georgia and Juan de Fuca straits, and the lower Columbia River and its big tributary the Willamette, occupying an extensive area in British Columbia, Vancouver Island, Washington State, and Oregon. True that this region was, for a century and more after its discovery by mariners, trappers and explorers, remote from the lumber markets of the world. But the coming of transcontinental railroads, and still more the Panama Canal, changed all that, and made it possible to sell Fir to the eastern United States and even Europe.

More important still has been the lay of the land, much of it being level or nearly so, and thus making transport from timber to mill inexpensive. The intricacies of Puget Sound, and the waters between Vancouver Island and mainland British Columbia, have made possible the movement of great log rafts, some of which have gone to sea as far as San Diego. The great harbors permit oceangoing vessels to dock right at the mill yards. The small harbors have proved ideal for the location of a host of small mills (and at one time for sheltering the log pirates).

But most important of all has been the climate, with rainfall up to 100 inches a year and over, and a mild winter, permitting a long growing season. In very wet mild climates all trees grow swiftly and very densely, grow tall and mighty in bole, and tend to live long. But the inherent greatness of Douglastree made it king in the Northwest tidewater. Add to this one lucky fact: this king in size is also, by the physical properties of its wood, a timber tree of the very highest grade, with potentialities for multiple use in our complex civilization undreamed of by the first tyees who saw in it only its dimension timbers in abundance.

From the beginning, the task of getting those giants out of the big woods has called upon all the skills, courage, and inventive genius gained by the fallers and buckers in a hundred years of experience with eastern Pine. Undercut notches as much as 5 feet deep are first chopped by these living Paul Bunyans. Then on the opposite side of the tree the long falling saws are started on Herculean work, with steel wedges driven in to keep the tons and tons of living wood from settling on the saws, until at last only a thin pivot between the undercut and the saw supports the fatally swaying monarch.

"'Timber! Timber!' the fallers loudly warn everyone of danger," writes a veteran of Northwest logging, "and with a few final blows on wedges they withdraw their tools and place themselves on each side of the severed stump. With increasing velocity the top describes an arc, the trunk hinging on the uncut wood of the undercut and saw cut. Faster and faster, with mounting crescendo of sound through nearly 500 feet of an arc, the top sweeps to the ground, shattering the smaller trees in its way and finding its resting place with a thud, roar and rush of wind that shakes the earth for hundreds of feet and sets all the other trees to swaying as though an earthquake had shaken the forest."*

The next task is to get the big sticks out of the woods and here ingenuity and invention have made their greatest progress. First came the old skid roads, with logs laid on the ground to act as rollers stretching from deep timber to the nearest splash dam or logging railhead, or even to the mill, with long strings of oxen dragging the giant sticks till the rollers smoked with the heat of friction and the air was blue with the oaths of the bullwhackers. But the arrival of the donkey engine to drag the logs by a steel cable wound on a great drum so speeded up the delivery of timber that it came too fast for the mills. Then the mills grew so vast that a speed-up (workmen call it highballing) in log delivery was called for. This was met by the "high-lead," where logs shot along on cables slung high over the tops of the forest. This operation demanded a great spar on which to rig the pulleys and cables, and this in turn brought into existence the high-rigger, the most spectacular kind of logger ever known, a steeplejack of the big sticks who at some point 100 to 200 feet up the trunk saws off the top of a giant tree that is to act as a spar. Then a block weighing up to 1½ tons is fixed at the top of the spar; through this will pass the cable. Rigging slingers then hook the steel chokers to the logs to be dragged to the foot of the spar tree. Chasers hook them to the main line; the flagman

*Frank F. Lamb, *Sagas of the Evergreens*, W. W. Norton Company.

waves to the whistle punk who blows signals for starting, stopping, and backing up by the donkey punchers at the engine's levers.

Today the donkey engine has grown into something as great as Babe, the Big Blue Ox, for it is a giant powered by diesel, steam, or electricity. In its grip logs weighing 50 tons are moved like jackstraws; ropes of braided steel fly at a thousand feet a minute through the forest; in eight hours a single crew has been known to handle 10 million pounds of Fir.

The need of cutting areas where the merchantable timber is scattered has summoned from the farm and battlefield the track-laying tractor, which tows the great logs from stump to dam or truck. Yet this 150-horsepower slave is under the control of one man, the cat-skinner, who can take his monster up steep grades, through deep mud and among big rocks, pushing down trees 6 to 8 inches thick which obstruct his path, till he finds his way to the spot where the fallers are bringing down the giants. Arrived at the mill, the logs are dumped by crane into a storage pond, then pulled by an endless chain to the head saw, a band of thin steel running over two large pulleys at the rate of 25 miles per hour. The approaching log is handled by a "nigger"* which flips it over from one face to another to receive the shearing cut of the saw. Then the big cuts or cants of lumber have next to be cut into the desired finer and precise dimensions. So they are raced over rollers and run onto a platform where they are slid sideways past a battery of circular saws. These can be raised or lowered by a man in a cage who plays upon a bank of keys like a skilled pianist. Finally the lumber, cut and dressed to order, green or seasoned, marked for grades by experts, is lifted by an automotive spider that runs out over the wood, straddles the piles with its wheeled legs, raises the lumber under its throbbing body and bears it off like a predatory creature, to drop it right into waiting railroad car, or storage pile, or in the hold of a ship.

Out of this complex called a modern sawmill still come Fir timbers measuring up to 24 by 24 inches wide and thick and 100 feet long. And dimension timbers remain today of outsize importance in the Fir business, just as they were back in the days when the Mormons cut trunks of huge Fir, in the mountains, and brought them down to Salt Lake City to arch over the roof of their great fane, the Tabernacle. Enormous Fir timbers and masses of solid wood are more than ever called for in structural beams and trusses for big buildings, docks, trestles, bridges and spans and

*Editor's note: A long-toothed lever arm used to position logs.

for planks in the floors and ceilings of factories. Also, in the construction of reinforced concrete buildings there is a demand for wooden forms into which to pour the concrete, which shall be both long and strong and able to hold rigidly in place the heavy masses of restless, wet concrete. For this purpose Douglas Fir's superiority is recognized at home and in distant lands.

Taking the place of Eastern White Pine, Douglas Fir is now a favorite with carpenters and architects, since the wood does not warp or pull its nails, for sills and posts, beams, floor and ceiling joists, roof rafters, floor boards, and studding. Kiln-dried Fir makes a beautifully figured, easily finished interior woodwork, both in vertical and flat grain.

Thousands and thousands of miles of railroad track in the West are laid on Douglas Fir ties, which can be cut from second-growth trees, since large dimensions are not needed. Beside the tracks march telegraph and telephone poles of whole Douglas Firs. Fir makes, too, a hot firewood, inflammable even when green; the mills commonly sell off their slabs and waste for this purpose in the Northwest. The bark, once considered a total loss, is now ground up and then variously treated to serve as a soil conditioner, as absorbent filler in plaster acoustical products, as a substitute for the expensive and sometimes unobtainable natural cork, as soles for shoes, in radio recording for electrical transcriptions, and patented inventions which have already passed five hundred in number.

In World War II Douglas Fir, more than any other tree, played a vital role. Every man in the service knew it well, for his foot locker was generally made of it. He crossed rivers on pontoon bridges of Douglas Fir, and if he was wounded he was carried from the field on stretchers whose rails were, very likely, of this strong yet light wood. Fir went into the tanks for gasoline storage, at advanced bases. It was a favorite wood for the Pacific huts that housed our soldiers all the way to Japan. Every few minutes, 24 hours a day, factories completed another Pacific hut; it was then shipped in knock-down form to the remotest atoll or Aleutian isle.

Both in war and peace, the most revolutionary thing that has happened in the field of structural wood is the rise of the plywood industry. Though many trees may be made into plywood, Douglas Fir has taken, and will probably always hold, the lead. Plywood is not exactly new, since its basic principle was known to the Egyptians. Nor is it a complex process involving a reconstruction of the very fibers of cellulose into something unrecognizable as wood, as in the case of plastics. Plywood is simply a glue-up of thin sheets of wood, usually kiln-dried. The extremely thin wood is cut from the log by a rotary veneer knife, which unrolls from the log a continuous sheet of wood, as one unrolls paper toweling. This is the veneer, which is then sliced by guillotine knives into the sizes desired. When the veneer is to be used structurally, as in the case of Douglas Fir, it is built up in layers (commonly three-ply), each layer or ply lying with its grain at right angles to the pieces above and below. This gives a resistance to splitting that makes plywood stronger than steel of the same weight. Any householder who ever thought to make kindling wood out of pieces of plywood left by carpenters by swinging an ax on them has found that he and his ax are worsted. Nails and screws can be put in the very edge of plywood without any possibility that they can tear loose under strain, or that the wood will split.

Of course a bonding agent is required to unite the plies, and this is one of the marvelous modern glues, united under heat and pressure with the plies. These glues are even stronger than the wood, and new glues with special properties are appearing on the market. Glue and ply together form a structural system that can be extended to any length, bent into any shape. As a result, synthetic structural timbers are now made of ply, which even so titanic a tree as Douglas Fir could never produce in the forest. Great hangars, and arches for enormous warehouses and halls are made of glue and wood almost as thin as paper, which yet surpass steel in strength, lightness, and cheapness. Plywood has proved ideal, too, for the Navy's lifeboats, saving a ton of steel on each boat, and floating 7 inches higher out of water than its steel counterpart. Plywood also goes into coastal patrol and torpedo boats, into PT and assault and landing boats. In the field of prefabricated housing, which has revolutionized the building business, plywood is the magic name, and Douglas Fir is in the lead for a dozen reasons. One of the least important of them economically, but esthetically pleasing, is the beauty of the grain; this is not destroyed by the veneer knives or lost in the bonding, but stands out, as vivid and handsome as that of Yellow Pine, in plywood paneling in your room.

Can even the great stands of a Douglas Fir withstand the demands presently made by the greatest of all lumber industries? It is said that in some thirty years one-half of all the virgin Fir in Washington and Oregon has been lumbered, and in the neighborhood of railroads and highways it is all gone. Lands cut over by wasteful methods in early days have too often reverted for delinquent taxes to the counties — but as desolate stump lands from which even the hardiest lumberjack or tyee averts his eyes. True that plywood may eventually take away some of the drain upon virgin timber, since trees of great dimensions are not needed for it, but that will happen when the profitable virgin growth is still scarcer, and will merely mean that second growth will be cut as fast as, or even before, it wholly matures.

On the bright side — and it is brighter than for almost any other important tree now being cut — there is the tremendous regenerative power of Douglastrees. They are fertile; they are vigorous; they are very fast growing. These inherent qualities are favored by the reliable and abundant rainfall and the mild climate. True, under virgin conditions a forest tract dominantly Douglas Fir in one tree-generation is likely to be supplanted in the next by the far less valuable Western Hemlock. The reason for this is that a heavy stand of old Fir is too shady for its own seedlings, which are light demanding, while the seeds of Hemlock will sprout in the dimmest woodland light, and their saplings shoot up and eventually take over. But when a tract in the Northwest is thinned by selective cutting or clean-cut (completely razed of all trees), then Fir seedlings rejoice, but Hemlock's are sun smitten. So Douglas Fir will succeed itself over and over if repeatedly cut — providing, always, that the cleared areas are small enough to allow for natural reseeding from neighboring strips of woodland, and that fire is kept out of young growth.

Young Firs under favorable conditions come on lustily. We can count even now upon 4.7 billion board feet a year of renewed growth on cutovers in this country, if they are well managed. The lumbermen promise themselves an eventual increment of 7.4 billion feet annually. That will still be short of the present cut and loss, however, and there is no reason to think the present cut will not increase as our population and industrial civilization increase. But the losses to fire could be cut, and the most progressive lumber companies are now carefully managing their cutover lands and planting where planting is needed. They believe that they are already started on a cycle of balanced cut and regrowth which will keep them in business on their own present acreage forever.

Alpine Fir

Abies lasiocarpa (Hooker) Nuttall

OTHER NAMES: Balsam or White Fir. White or Mountain Balsam Fir.

RANGE: Coast Ranges of southeastern Alaska from sea level to timber line (3000 feet), and southern Yukon Territory, in the Rockies and east slopes (not west) of the Coast Range of British Columbia and Alberta, south through the Rockies of Idaho, Montana, Wyoming, Colorado, Utah, and Nevada, to southern Arizona and New Mexico (Tunitchta Mountains, Pecos Baldy), at or near timber line (10,500 feet in the southern Rockies); also in the Olympics of Washington, the Cascades of Washington and Oregon, the Wallowa Mountains of eastern Oregon, and the Trinity Mountains of California.

THE OUTLINE OF THE ALPINE FIR, so outstandingly slender and martially erect and rigid, is the most dramatic statement made by any native tree. The Engelmann and Black Spruces, when crowded for space, may take on such a cathedral-spire form, but given room they will expand; under all circumstances the Alpine Fir, at least in all but the lower third of the tree, keeps this pencil-slim form. Not the Lombardy Poplar or the Italian Cypress is more ejaculatory in the landscape. And they are but horticultural sports of trees which normally have wide-spreading boughs. The Alpine Fir comes by its outline naturally, through the extreme shortness of all but the lower branches. Its statement in the subalpine and subarctic scenes is that of an exclamation point!

And the scenery where, in the United States, the Alpine Fir grows most triumphantly is something to exclaim over. For though it grows so widely, from Alaska to the Colorado Rockies, this tree displays its beauty to the most striking advantage where at high altitudes it rings round those snow-capped and extinct volcanic cones — eleven of them, and each more than a mountain, each a majestic spirit — that soar above the Cascade Range of Washington and Oregon. Greatest is Mount Rainier, a peak that rises up from almost sea level to 14,409 feet, which, in relative height of peak above base, makes this the highest, as it is the most beautiful, peak in the United States. Indeed, it is more than any ordinary peak; in its vastnesses it is the equal of a great range. Scores of waterfalls leap from its sides; twenty-six great glaciers glitter on its flanks, and trees beyond all estimating swathe it round.

120

Among these the most striking and yet fitting is the Alpine Fir, which frames all those views so beloved of the photographer, of long, flower-spangled meadows leading toward the great cone that seems, in its clearness and abruptness, about to break as a white wave. Indeed, it would require a tree of the most dramatic shape, of almost incredible symmetry, to draw attention to itself in all this splendor. Yet so eye-taking is the Alpine Fir that even in photographs of Mount Rainier and Mount Hood, Mount Olympus, Mount Baker, and the rest, it wrests attention away from the sensational peaks, so that people who have never seen the West inquire its name. They do not say, "That is a mountain I would like to climb," but rather, "That's a place I would like to camp" — in just such a meadow, with just such a view, amid such trees.

Many kinds of trees that love the mountain heights must for long seasons bear great weights of snow. Some, like the graceful but weak-tipped Douglas Firs and the Hemlocks, bend under it, especially while young, till they look like sheeted ghosts all doubled up, or crouching, as if convulsed either with mirth or with pain, but scarcely recognizable as trees. Not so the Alpine Fir. No matter how immature it is, it is already rigid as a mast, with tier on tier of whorled, perfectly horizontal branches that are too short and stiff to bend. Many other conifers have flexible needles, but those of this Fir are at once stiff and all, as it were, brushed upward to the top of the twig. So the foliage instead of being a flat spray, as in the Eastern Balsam Fir, is a spiky bed on which the snowfall is speared and held in cottony tufts. If it is to escape these leafy fingers it will have to melt; the sturdy needles refuse to yield to it and spill it.

Around the mountain meadows in the United States the Alpine Fir will grow to some 50 or 75 feet in height, at the most. At timber line it may be only 3 or 4 feet high, yet it is still erect — a miniature of its greater self — and never prostrate like so many alpine trees. But it is in north-central British Columbia that Alpine Fir attains its greatest stature, up to 175 feet. Here, where it is the only true Fir, it grows so closely, so loftily, and casts such a somber shade that Theodora Stanwell-Fletcher, who has probably written more of it than any other author, speaks repeatedly of it, in her book, *Driftwood Valley,* as forming a "jungle." No Indian camps, she says, seem ever to be pitched in the shadowy depths of its groves — so dank and deeply drifted in winter, so windless and mosquito haunted in summer.

The late northern or mountain spring brings to the Alpine Fir many touches of subtle color to lighten its coniferous solemnity. The tips of new foliage are gleaming silver. The male flowers are a dark blue, turning violet, the female violet purple. With the coming of the brief summer, the deep purple cones mature; as the hot weather beats upon them, silvery blobs of resin drip from the scales. When the cones open in the fall, they loose ivory gray seeds that twirl away upon large, lustrous purple or violet-tinged wings. Usually gray, the bark of the trunk is sometimes chalky white. In its youth, big resin blisters are found upon the stem, but these disappear in age and the bark becomes quite flinty.

The lumberman has little use for the soft, weak, coarse, nondurable wood. According to Mrs. Stanwell-Fletcher, even the Northwest Indians find trouble in making a fire with Alpine Fir. But mountain sheep, Richardson's grouse, and Cascade pine squirrels devour the seeds.

Variety *arizonica* (Merriam) Lemmon, the Corkbark Fir, differs from the typical Alpine Fir in having soft, corky, thick bark made up of large, overlapping yellowish white scales; the cones are longer and narrower than those of the Alpine Fir, the scales at base halberd shaped. This variety, which is found at 8000 to 10,000 feet altitude in the mountains of southern Colorado, northern and southwestern New Mexico, and central and southeastern Arizona, grows 50 to 75 feet tall, with a trunk up to 1½ feet thick. Within its range and on the thin gravelly or rocky soils where it grows, it may accompany or replace Alpine Fir.

Northern Balsam

Abies balsamea (Linnæus) P. Miller

OTHER NAMES : Balsam or Balm-of-Gilead Fir. Blister, Fir, or Silver Pine.

RANGE : Newfoundland to the Yukon Territory and northeastern British Columbia, south to northern and eastern parts of Minnesota and Wisconsin, northern Michigan, throughout northern New England, the Berkshires, eastern New York, and south on the mountains to southwestern Virginia.

E XCEPT WITH THE OLD-TIME LOGGER, who had no use for Balsam save to make himself a natural sweet-smelling mattress laid on a springy frame of Spruce boughs, this is the most generally popular of all the trees of the great North Woods. To anyone whose childhood summers were luckily spent there, the delicious spicy fragrance of Balsam needles is the dearest odor in all of Nature. Merely to remember it is to raise before the eyes lake waters, or the soft high swell of the northern Appalachians, or the grandeur of the St. Lawrence gulf. It brings back the smell of wild raspberries in the sunlit clearing, the piercing sweetness of the white-throated sparrow's song, the birdlike flight of the canoe from the gurgling paddle stroke. For Balsam loves the rocky soil close to water, where its familiar is often the Paper Birch. At the edge of any sparkling lake in the great glaciated province of eastern Canada and the northern United States, these two grow in the happiest of contrasts, the Balsam with its darkly gleaming but motionless evergreen foliage and its militarily straight stem and precise whorls of branches, and the white-barked, leaning, and gracile Birch, with its showers of pale green, restless, and talkative foliage.

For success in the eternal forest battle for survival, Balsam depends upon its adaptability, the speed of its growth, its fertility. The seeds, which fly through the woods on trim bright wings, are many and highly viable, but the grouse and the red squirrels and the pine mice eat them, just as moose and deer browse on the foliage. Balsam is, too, a danger to itself because of the resin blisters under the bark, which, in case of forest fire, ignite so that the whole tree is soon a blazing torch.

These resin blisters yield what is called Canada balsam, a sort of turpentine employed in the manufacture of varnish. It is familiar to all advanced students in the biological sciences as a transparent fixative for mounting and preserving specimens for the microscope. It not only seals the cover glass to the glass slide, but as a matrix for the specimen holds and preserves it from drying and decay. More, balsam has the fortunate property of refracting light to exactly the same extent that glass does so that the balsam matrix, the cover glass, and the microscope lenses become one optical system with the same refractive index.

One of the odd things about the lovely aroma of Balsam branches is that many of those who live with it constantly can no longer smell it. The city child has the sharpest pleasure in it. If he collects the needles to make a balsam pillow to sleep on, he dreams of the North Woods for the time that he can smell the pillow. But presently he may fail to do so, though the smell is there for others, and may not do so again until the fresh Christmas tree is brought into his house. Balsams are the ideal Christmas trees — fragrant beyond all others, with long lower branches and thick, spire-like tops. The needles do not drop like those of the Spruce, even after a month without water, nor do they stab the hand when one is decorating the tree, since they are not tipped with prickles.

The Christmas tree industry is now a big, though a seasonal, business. On forest land the proper selection of little trees will merely result in betterment of the stand. On farms and estates the raising of trees, from seedlings supplied free or at cost by state forestry nurseries, offers, on land not otherwise profitable, possibilities that were dramatized by the highly successful plantations at Hyde Park by President Roosevelt. Yet from time to time some overzealous moralist decides that we are depleting our forests by cutting millions of young Christmas trees every year for a momentary pleasure, thus robbing ourselves of tens of million of feet of lumber. But out of every ten young trees in the forest nine are destined to lose out and die. No harm, but only good, can follow from the proper cutting of young Christmas trees. And the destiny of Balsam, loveliest of them all, would otherwise too often be excelsior, or boards for packing cases, or newsprint bringing horror on its face into your home. Far better that the little tree should arrive, like a shining child at your door, breathing of all out of doors and cupping healthy North Woods cold between its boughs, to bring delight to human children.

Southern Balsam

Abies fraseri (Pursh) Poiret

OTHER NAMES: She-Balsam. Fraser Fir.

RANGE: High mountains of North Carolina, Tennessee, and the Virginias.

L IKE MANY ANOTHER SCOT, JOHN FRASER, for whom this tree was named, came to London, in 1750, to get rich. In Paradise Row he set up a linen draper's establishment; but a visit to Chelsea Botanical Garden gave him a taste for botany. Forsaking calicoes and dimities, he sailed in 1784 for the then young United States, landing at Charleston, and set off for the southern Appalachians. He was indeed the first plantsman who ever explored their highest peaks, in the days when they were still wild and largely trackless country.

On his wanderings he fell in with a rival — the celebrated André Michaux, and for a while they traveled together. But in spite of the identity of their interests, or perhaps because of them, they did not get on well. Michaux believed Fraser was dogging his footsteps perhaps to be sure to discover for the British any new flower or tree that Michaux sent back to Louis XVI. So, offering as an excuse that his horses had strayed and he must catch them, Michaux let Fraser go on ahead. And that is how it happens that John Fraser was the first — by his nose perhaps — to discover this deliciously aromatic tree, which grows right to the top of Mount Mitchell, Clingman's Dome, and all the most famous peaks of North Carolina and Tennessee.

After four visits to America, Fraser entered into the service of Catherine the Great, and subsequently of Czar Paul. So he revisited the New World as a Russian official, but after expending large sums in collecting our finest conifers, azaleas, rhododendrons, and Magnolias, he was not reimbursed by the new Czar, Alexander, and his previous appointment was not recognized. However, he had a little nursery business of his own in Chelsea, and, returning once more to America, he brought back from the sweet-smelling high groves of our southern mountains the first living specimens of the Southern Balsam that England had seen.

But this tree has never done well in cultivation, and to see it in its perfection you too must take the climb up from the blazing heat of the Carolina piedmont, under Tuliptree and Magnolia, up through Maple, Beech, and Oak, through the thickets of purple rhododendron, to the groves of Red Spruce and Southern Balsam. True that you can motor close to some of the summits in half an hour, but if you do you will never know the sense of contrast, or of conquest, as you find yourself at last in the damp and fragrant climax forest.

The depth of the perpetual shade in these woods is due in part to the darkness of the foliage itself, to its density upon the boughs, and to the interlocking of the crowns above your head. And a large part of the year these groves are swept by mists and clouds; in winter they are deep in snow. As a result, the ground is covered with a carpet of lichens and mosses, hepatics and ferns. Especially on the trunks and logs of the Balsam do the lichens delight to grow, and usnea moss drips from the dead lower boughs like waving beards upon old prophets. So everything conspires to give these trees, which are really not long-lived, a look of hoary age. A child would call the Balsam groves a fairy-tale wood, and it is doubtful if the ecologists, with all their synthetic terminology, could more aptly characterize this woodland type.

Lowland Fir

Abies grandis (Douglas ex D. Don) Lindley*

OTHER NAMES: Grand, White, Silver, Yellow, or Stinking Fir.

RANGE: Vancouver Island and the adjacent mainland of British Columbia, west to the Rockies of Montana and Idaho, and south in the Cascades to Oregon and in the Coast Ranges to Sonoma County, California; also on the mountains of the eastern parts of Oregon and Washington.

A LL THE WESTERN FIRS are beautiful trees, and many are grand. But the Lowland Fir is grandest of all, fulfilling honestly the boastful Latin of its name of *Abies grandis*. In the great coniferous rain forest that covers the lowlands of the Olympic peninsula, the Puget Sound region, the tidewater country around the mouth of the Columbia, the Lowland Fir rises like a tower for 150 to 200 feet, and exceptional trees have been measured which were 250 to 300 feet high, with trunks up to 6 feet in diameter. Such individuals rank with Douglas Firs, Sitka Spruces, and Redwoods in their majesty, and even lesser specimens stand out handsomely in the rain forest. In the "Inland Empire," or forested area of northern parts of Idaho and Montana, the Lowland Firs are not great in dimensions, but at all times they are beautiful. The foliage, on

*Editor's note: Formerly *Abies grandis* (Douglas) Lindley.

the upper surface, is a dark but glossy green; on the under surface it is almost silvery white. The cones, looking rough-hewn but handsome, are so big that though they are borne chiefly near the top of the tree, they show conspicuously and still further carry the honor of this Fir's specific name.

Like so many Firs, this species has big resin blisters under the bark of the young growth, and when you cut down a little Lowland Fir for a Christmas tree you may get a shot of balsamic gum right in the face. The needles when crushed have a sweet, balsamy aroma that steals forth into the room when the tree is being decorated. The wood is too soft, yet too heavy in proportion to its little strength, to make first-class lumber. Pulpwood offers its only commercial future, and there are so many finer pulping species in the woods that Lowland Fir is little felled for any purpose and is usually left in the forest to make music and distill incense.

White Fir

Abies concolor (Gordon & Glendenning) Lindley ex Hildebrand*

OTHER NAMES: Balsam or Silver Fir. White Balsam. Fir.

RANGE: Cascades and Siskiyou Mountains of Oregon, south in the high Coast Ranges of northern California, and throughout the Sierra Nevada (4000 to 8000 feet) and in the high mountains of southern California from the San Rafael Mountains of Santa Barbara County south through the San Bernardinos (up to 10,000 feet altitude) and the San Jacintos to Baja California; and in the Rockies from the Wallowa, Blue, and Warner mountains of eastern Oregon, and in Idaho west and south, through the mountain systems of Utah and Colorado, Arizona, and New Mexico to the highlands of Sonora and Chihuahua; on some of the desert ranges of Nevada; rare in Wyoming and Montana.

O F ALL THE WESTERN FIRS, the White Fir is the most widespread. You see it abundantly on the mountain slopes just above the floor of Yosemite Valley, its beautiful, light gray and smooth bark shining between its tier on tier of regularly whorled branches, its deep green or almost silvery gray needles cheerfully matching the clear

*Editor's note: Formerly *Abies concolor* (Gordon & Glendenning) Hoopes.

mountain sunlight. In Colorado it lines the exciting mountain drives and crowds into the canyons where the streams come seething down. A particularly noble grove of it is seen in North Cheyenne Canyon, one of the favorite tourist sights in the neighborhood of Colorado Springs. Always the springing boughs, the symmetrical broad cone of the outline, have a look of strength and health and the ability to grow almost anywhere in the drier mountains of the West and endure all that the Rockies and Sierra Nevada can bring of snow and storm and long dry summers. Balsamic fragrance breathes from them, squirrels bound in their branches, grouse devour their seeds, porcupines commit lamentable depredations on their bark; the black-tailed and mule deers are highly dependent on them for food, and you may practically count on seeing some of these beautiful creatures, sooner or later, in any good growth of White Fir.

There are no complete statistics on the amount of logging of this tree, for it is cut along with all the Firs without botanical distinction. It would make a good pulp wood but is not needed now in that well-supplied market. Its lumber "compares favorably" with Eastern Hemlock, which is faint praise, and holds paint and nails well when used for boxes or construction lumber in small houses.

Rather does the future of this tree lie in its value as an ornamental. It takes with the most accommodating good nature to cultivation, developing pretty charms not nearly so visible in the wild. It will even survive and make growth in the dense shade of older, higher trees and of city buildings. So, long life to it — and may it attain wherever it grows its full fine stature of 100 and even 200 feet.

JUNIPERS

Eastern Red Cedar

Juniperus virginiana Linnæus

OTHER NAMES: Pencil Cedar. Virginia Juniper.

RANGE: Southern Maine, across north-central New Hampshire and Vermont to southern Ontario and Hull, Quebec, west through the southern half of the lower peninsula of Michigan, southern Wisconsin, and Minnesota to the Badlands of South Dakota, and south to eastern Texas and the Gulf states, but absent from the Gulf coast itself and from the high Appalachians.

N O STONE-WALLED HILLTOP TOO BLEAK, no abandoned field too thin of soil but that the dark and resolute figure of the Eastern Red Cedar may take its stand there, enduring, with luck, perhaps three centuries. In aboriginal America the Cedar probably formed extensive groves, sometimes excluding almost all other trees, and remnants of such are still to be seen occasionally on the limestones of eastern Tennessee and Kentucky, where the tree reaches a height of 100 feet. As the country has been cleared of trees for farms and pastures, the Cedar has come out of the forest and invaded abandoned fields. It troops along the fence rows, where it is common with poison ivy, and along roadsides where its seeds have been dropped by birds sitting on telegraph wires. For the berries are eagerly devoured by a long list of birds, headed

by the handsome cedar waxwing, who takes his very name from his fondness for the fruit of this tree.

Our Eastern Red Cedar takes two very different shapes. Most familiar to millions living on the eastern seaboard is the form with a narrowly conical, spirelike outline, much like that of the Italian Cypress, with its branches ascending at a very sharp angle and hugging the trunk to make a compact mass. Indeed it may be called the farmer's Cypress, for he is fond of lining the road to his house with it, or setting it as a windbreak along one side of the farmyard. It is a favorite in old country graveyards, where, to the imagination of our forebears, perhaps, its finger seemed to point to heaven; its evergreen boughs spoke symbolically of life eternal. This has been called, by botanists, variety *virginiana* Linnæus. It is common from southeastern Maine to Pennsylvania and in southernmost Michigan, northern and western Indiana, northeastern Illinois and southeastern Wisconsin, and, occasionally, in eastern Missouri, southern Illinois, northwestern Tennessee, and the foothills of the southern Appalachians.

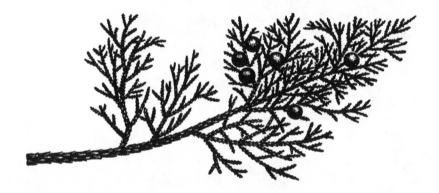

The other form of the tree is not at all spirelike; it takes on a broadly conical form, with the branches widely spreading. The range of this form, which is considered to be the true species (or at least the first form to be discovered and described to science), is, on the whole, more southerly and westerly. It is the typical form of the Red Cedar from the piedmont of Maryland southward and from the western slopes of the Alleghenies westward (except in a wide zone around the southern end of Lake Michigan). There is considerable intermingling of the two forms, however, and there are many trees intermediate in form.

The earliest explorers of the Atlantic seaboard did not fail to mention so handsome, so fragrant a tree as this one — "the tallest and reddest Cedars in the world," wrote Arthur Barlowe and Philip Amadas in their opening sentences of description of the New World, which they touched for the first time at Roanoke Island in 1564. The early colonists recognized the value of the Virginia Juniper from the start — for fences and shingles, benches and tables, coffins and the superstructures of boats. So easy was it to split with the froe and to smooth with the plane that it could be worked even by people as woefully ill prepared for wilderness life as the theologian-tradesmen and overdressed gold hunters who first sought our shores. When the log cabin and the snake-rail fence appeared on the American scene, Red Cedar was a favorite because of its endurance when exposed to rain and soil.

The better craftsmen of colonial Virginia were soon producing in Cedar such complex types of furniture as bedsteads, secretaries, and virginals. The fragrance of the wood and the showy contrast in color between the red heartwood and the creamy sapwood compensated, to the tastes of those days, for the fragility of the material. In our times Red Cedar finds employment chiefly in the linings for mothproof chests and closets. How repellant the odor may be to moths is less certain than the psychological attraction it has for the careful housewife.

For over a century Red Cedar bore the brunt of the attack of pencil makers. It was a perfect wood for this purpose on account of its lightness and the ease with which it can be sharpened. However, only the very clearest knot-free heartwood was employed, and pencil making wasted 70 percent of the bulk and 90 percent of the weight of every log cut for that purpose. As pencil manufacturers could afford to pay higher prices than anyone else, they consequently got all the best wood. For nearly a century our Cedars supplied the world with pencil wood. The famous Faber Company used them exclusively. Tennessee, in 1900, sent 3 million feet of fine quality Cedar down the Cumberland River in great timber rafts. But only ten years later Cedar "cruisers" had searched out the last virgin stands, lumbermen were working over the stumps of their previous destruction, and buyers were snapping up log cabins, barn floors, and even rail fences that had stood exposed to the weather for fifty years.

Fortunately it does not pay the lumberman to cut down roadside, dooryard, and cemetery trees, or he would do to the friendly fence row and old-field Virginia Juniper what he does to the Black Walnut. The easterner is spared his Cedars only because the pencil industry has transferred its affections to the Incense Cedar of the West. So once more we have escaped the consequences of our economic sins — our wastefulness and lack of planning — by cheerily moving out West and finding a gold mine.

Cedars are often disfigured by the galls of a fungus disease (*Gymnosporangium juniperi-virginianæ*), the cedar-apple rust. In dry weather these galls are small, hard, and relatively inconspicuous, but in wet weather in spring, long, yellow, gelatinous processes are extruded and render the disease obvious. Spores from these extrusions next infect the leaves of Apple trees, producing damaging yellow blotches. From these, again, spores may reinfect the Cedars. Different as the infections on Apple and Cedar may appear, they are the same disease, and the Red Cedar, which carries the rust as a chronic but not a fatal malady, thus becomes a reservoir of infection, in woods near orchards, for a harmful disease of Apples.

Pathologists pointed out that the easiest control of the disease was the destruction of all Cedar trees within a mile radius of the orchard. "Cedar eradication is the cheapest form of orchard insurance that you can buy. The cost on the average is less than the cost of a single spray application." So declared the *Annual Report* of the Virginia State Horticultural Society for the year 1918. Acting on this, the apple growers of Virginia, particularly in the famed orchards of the Shenandoah Valley, went to the legislature and got Cedar-eradication laws enacted. West Virginia did the same. These laws permitted the destruction of all Cedars in a large area, upon the certification of "ten freeholders," without any recompense to the owners of Cedars. In 1929 there was a short, sharp clash between them and the Apple orchardists, in which one Cedar owner at Shepherdstown, after exhausting every legal resource, attempted to prevent the destruction of her trees by clasping them, one after the other, as axmen sought to cut them, and only when she dropped with exhaustion could the trees be felled. Where they stood, their embattled owner planted forty-eight American flags, for the states.

That the legislation eradicating the Juniper is high-handed and one-sided seems obvious. If the slogan of the orchardists, "Cedar or cider," were changed to "cider or pencils," the relative merits would be more truly set forth. And the statement that "Cedar eradication is the cheapest form of orchard insurance" might not certainly be true if the orchardists had to pay for the value of the destroyed Cedars. One wonders, too, what would happen if the orchardists of Tennessee should demand the felling of the sacrosanct Cedars set out at The Hermitage by the hand of General Andrew Jackson. Plainly there are cases in which it would be as reasonable to pass a law that all Apple trees must be cut down for a mile in the vicinity of valuable Cedars, as that any and all Cedars must fall for the sake of any and all orchards!

Common Juniper

Juniperus communis Linnæus

OTHER NAMES: Dwarf or Ground Juniper. Horse Savin. Hackmatack. Gorst. Fairy-circle.

RANGE: Greenland and Newfoundland and across Canada to Alaska, south to Pennsylvania, thence south on the Appalachians to South Carolina, and to the shores of the Great Lakes (as in northwestern Indiana) and in southern Illinois, and west to Nebraska; south on the Rockies to western Texas, the high peaks of Arizona, and in the Sierra Nevada to central California. In Asia, across Siberia and south to the Caucasus and Himalayas; in Europe throughout the northern countries south to the Maritime Alps, the Riviera, and Portugal and the high mountains of southern Spain, and on the Italian peninsula (but not Sicily), and Greece.

T HE COMMON JUNIPER has what is perhaps the widest natural range among all trees; certainly it is the only tree native both in North America and Europe. On the other side of the ocean it is commonly of tree size in the Mediterranean basin; in this country, as in northern Europe, it is usually only a shrub, sometimes with creeping stems, forming circular clumps which, as they expand, may die at the center — hence the old English name of Fairy-circle. Yet in the mountains of New England, in eastern Pennsylvania, and, reportedly, sometimes on the high mountains of North Carolina, it grows up to 24 feet high. The trunk may be as much as a foot in diameter but is always short and eccentric and irregularly lobed or fluted. The erect branches form an open, irregular, or broken crown. The spinelike tips of the bristling leaves make this a fiercely hostile thing; to thrust one's hand in among the branches and gather the handsome berries from the female tree is an act of courage!

The leaves have an agreeable fragrance when crushed; though technically evergreen, persisting about three years, they change in winter to a deep bronze color, which again freshens in spring to the beautiful whiteness of the upper surface, the shiny green of the lower.

When the ovules are ripe for fecundation, they secrete a drop of clear stigmatic liquid at their enlarged and open apex. The fruit at first looks like a flower bud and does not enlarge much during its initial year, but when the flowers again bloom in early spring, the upper scales become consolidated around the ovules, and by the commencement of the second winter the berry is about three-fourths grown and is then a light green, hard and globe shaped, the seeds still soft and milky. In the following autumn (the third season since fertilization), the berries are mature and covered with a glaucous bloom over the dark blue skin. The flesh is fragrant, sweet, and resinous tasting and much devoured by birds. If not eaten, the berries may remain a year or two on the tree after ripening.

It is the flavor of the berries which imparts to gin its characteristic aroma and tang, for they are used in the preparation of this alcoholic drink which would otherwise be a nearly tasteless *eau de vie*. Indeed our word "gin" comes from the French *genièvre*, as gin is still called in Flanders and Belgium. And that, in turn, derives, of course, from the name of the tree in French, *genévrier*. Formerly the berries were in high repute medicinally, and the oil is still sometimes used therapeutically in India and Europe.

Juniper wood is used in Europe for vine stakes because it is so durable in contact with the soil, and in India is burned as incense.

Back into ancient times stretches the cultivation of this tree for hedges. For topiary it is probably the favorite — if one likes to see trees trimmed to look like lions and pyramids balancing balls, and such. Forms with weeping branches or with golden foliage, and dozens of other horticultural sports, are known in gardens but not in the wild.

Utah Juniper

Juniperus osteosperma (Torrey) Little

OTHER NAME: Desert Cedar.

RANGE: Mountains of southeastern Idaho and southwestern Wyoming throughout Nevada and Utah at elevations of 5000 to 8000 feet, to the desert (eastern) slopes of the Sierra Nevada and northern slopes of the San Bernardinos and on the Panamint Mountains above Death Valley; on mountains, mesas, and high plains of northern and north-central Arizona.

O N THE VERY EDGE OF THE OPENED BOOK of the Grand Canyon — page upon page of red stone tablets receding away into the purple shadows of a billion years of time gone by — perches the Utah Juniper. Now erect of stem, with crown symmetrically intact, now aslant over the awesome chasm, with storm-torn, broken head, and stem contorted as by the whirl of the winds themselves or lightning-riven and stripped to the white bones of half its bark — this indomitable tree dares the south rim of the canyon for miles. And when you step gingerly to the edge and look down into the vast emptiness, you see this Juniper far below you, dotting the bridle trail, clinging to perilous ledges, springing out of crevices in the rocks, sprinkling the giddy slopes of talus, a symbol of undefeated life in an abyss of death. From this only silence wells up to you, a silence as of outer and infinite space, where interplanetary gales could blow and make no sound. But when you stand by a rim Juniper you hear the whistling of the wind in its sharp-angled foliage, a high thin vibration of an elemental harp, and it is a comforting sound; it is a sort of message from green life, in all this dead geology. Yet in its way the living tree, the older and craggier it grows, seems the most consonant of possible trees with this, the most stupendous site in all the world.

South of the Grand Canyon, from Ashfork, Arizona, for mile upon mile, the Utah Juniper forms an open forest, below the belt of Pinyon and Yellow Pine, looking handsome and vital, with its dark green masses in contrast with the gray green of the sagebrush. And indeed everywhere in the Great Basin — between the Rockies on the east and the Sierra Nevada and Cascade Range on the west — this tree is likely to be the most abundant, as it is the most widely distributed, at least in the life zone called the Upper Sonoran. It dots the mesas, descends the canyons, climbs the

mountains. In its namesake state of Utah it is as characteristic a settler as the Mormons, and in its venerable age sometimes reminds you of an old patriarch of the sect — rugged and weathered and twisted by hardship, but hard too to discourage or kill. Utah's famed Cedar Breaks ("breaks" meaning great natural amphitheaters in mountain and mesa) take their name from this tree, and so does historic Cedar City. It is the Chief Inhabitant, among trees, of Bryce Canyon National Park, that "petrified sunset," as it has been called. No other tree, it seems, is so well fitted as this one to endure the arid, wind-blown, sand-swept land of Deseret.

Like most desert trees, the Utah Juniper is unimpressive in height, for it seldom grows more than 20 feet tall, and it is extremely slow of growth. A trunk with a diameter of no more than 6 to 10 inches may show an annual ring count of 145 to 250 years of life, and some of the ancients near the Grand Canyon with trunks 3 feet thick have been claimed as trimillennial. This may be doubted, but old they certainly are, as they are grand, with their broken, leaning crowns, their contorted stems, and heavy coats of long fibrous bark strips which are generally so weathered by sun and sand that they are whitish instead of their natural brown.

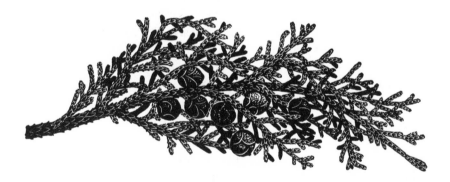

Almost every Utah Juniper is heavily infested by parasitic mistletoe, so much so that these tufts of pale yellowish green foliage — a sickly color appearing more dead than alive — are a characteristic feature of this tree. The lusterless lead-white of the mistletoe's berries mingles with the Juniper berries, red brown washed by a soft bluish gray cast, and both are highly attractive to western birds.

The short, branched, contorted stems of Utah Juniper have never allured the lumberman, though fence posts are made of the durable wood, and it makes a fine fuel that burns, however, without the fragrance of

some of the other species. But in the lives of the desert Indians, from ancient times, this tree has figured importantly. In the Gypsum Cave dwell-
ings of the prehistoric red men in Nevada, M. R. Harrington discovered
that Juniper bark had been used extensively for cordage. The vanished
race, pedantically called the Basket Maker II people, manufactured an
unfired clay pottery which was molded in baskets and given a strengthen-
ing of Juniper bark, just as we make bricks with straw. Basket Maker II
infants were carried in cradles of Juniper bark bound with yucca fibers,
and the bark went into the making of sandals and was woven into bags. In
the famed pit houses of the Southwest, Juniper bark was used as a thatch
under the earthen covering of the roof, and as a cordage to lash the
wooden uprights of the house to the stringers. On the walls of the pit
houses were hung coverings of Juniper bark matting.

In a side valley of the Grand Canyon today lives the small tribe of
Havasupai, a people of the Yuman stock. In the life of the Havasupai the
Utah Juniper figures from babyhood to the grave. When the child is born
he is covered with Juniper bark which his mother has rubbed very soft for
his tender skin, then swaddled in a blanket and placed in a Juniper cradle.
From the bark are fashioned the dolls with which he first plays, and he
sleeps on an oval mat of the bark. When he is weaned, he begins to eat the
berries of the Juniper, and in winter he is warmed at a fire which has been
made by his father's starting a spark in tinder of the dried bark. When
he reaches puberty, the Havasupai boy carries a slow-match or spill of
twisted Juniper bark, running toward the dawn as far as he can with it,
touching his ankles, knees, wrists, and elbows with the fire, to keep him,
so goes the belief, from getting rheumatism. Then he throws the slow-
match over his head so that he will be able to recall forgotten articles
when he sets out from camp. When he marries, the young Havasupai
brings his wife to a bed of Juniper bark.

The closely related Yavapai Indians give a woman a drink of tea of Juniper leaves after the birth of her child, to promote muscular relaxation
following the violent contractions she has endured, and later she will be
"fumigated" with smoke of the leaves laid on hot coals. If the Havasupai is
wounded, he uses Juniper gum as we use "New-Skin," to make a protec-
tive membrane over the sore until it can heal. When a Navaho dies, the
two men who attended him to the last back carefully away from the grave,
sweeping their tracks with Juniper boughs so that deathliness shall not
follow them from the grave.

Cherrystone Juniper

Juniperus monosperma (Engelmann) Sargent

OTHER NAMES: Oneseed Juniper. New Mexico Cedar.

RANGE: Mesas and mountains from Utah and western Colorado to eastern Nevada, Arizona, except the southwestern section, and Texas (Panhandle, Big Bend, and Edwards Plateau). In northern Sonora and Chihuahua, Mexico.

O NE EVENING IN THE AUTUMN OF 1851 a solitary horseman, followed by a pack-mule, was pushing through an arid stretch of country somewhere in central New Mexico. He . . . was trying to find his way back to the trail. . . . The difficulty was that the country in which he found himself was so featureless — or rather, that it was crowded with features, all exactly alike. As far as he could see, on every side, the landscape was heaped up into monotonous red sand-hills . . . exactly the shape of Mexican ovens, red as brick-dust, and naked of vegetation except for small juniper trees. And the junipers, too, were the shape of Mexican ovens. Every conical hill was spotted with smaller cones of juniper, a uniform yellowish green, as the hills were a uniform red."

Thus, in the opening pages of *Death Comes for the Archbishop,* does Willa Cather describe the Cherrystone Juniper's interminable monotony. It is not a dreary repetition, since this is rather a bright tree and likely to yield from its growth the flashing blue of a pinyon jay, the call of a Gambel quail, the slinking form of a coyote, a handful of mistletoe, an unexpected burro, or an even more unexpected Indian urchin. But reiterant it certainly is — in form, in color, in sun-baked fragrance.

It is hard, if possible at all, to think of another southwestern tree that, unaccompanied by another species, covers so vast an area — uncalculated thousands of acres of the old Spanish country. Again, it may have a single companion, no taller, no more varied, than itself, the Pinyon Pine. Together these two come to haunt all our memories of the red hill country of New Mexico. And they are happy memories, full of the high curved turquoise of her skies, full of sweet aromas, of the startling liquid voice of thrashers, of the spell of the pueblos, their art and their deeply religious bronze-skinned peoples. He is lost to simplicity who complains of their monotony. What is more monotonous than the streets, the buildings, the gray, damp, low-skied days to which he is apt to return from the country

141

of the Juniper? Many a time we would gladly exchange all that to see again the conical spires of this evergreen rising from the ruddy domes of the little hills down Santa Fe way.

The very air of the old town of Santa Fe entices the visitor, transporting him, from the world of speed and noise, to an older and sweeter way of life, where travel is at the burro's pace, where the commonest sounds are the tinkling of the *acequias* that slide and glitter through gardens and streets, the clangor of old bells with much silver in their copper, and the soft commingling of Spanish and Indian tongues. For in place of gasoline fumes, Santa Fe's soft dry air is pervaded by the smell of Pinyon smoke, blent with the odor of the *enebro* wood, as the Spanish-speaking people call the Juniper — a mingled perfume, sweet as the curling smoke from some church censer.

And you sniff it everywhere, upon the airs — not only in the narrow *calles* of Santa Fe and Taos, but throughout the pueblos of the southwest and in the long-settled, warm, Spanish-speaking part of Colorado. For the Indians and the Spanish Americans, even in the towns, often cook by wood fires, in those outdoor bake ovens of clay that look like old-fashioned skeps. For heating, the wood of true Pinyon Pine is preferred by many people, but Juniper is employed in cooking, because of the intensity of its heat and its glowing bed of coals. It has, however, the disadvantage, in an open hearth, of throwing sparks and is used there chiefly to clean out flues and chimneys, according to Haniel Long, the distinguished author of *Pinon Country*.

Twenty and thirty years ago if you went walking in the Pinyon- and Juniper-clad hills around Santa Fe you were almost certain to meet the head of a donkey bobbing toward you on the trail; then you saw the big faggot of *enebro* on his back, fixed there on a wooden saddle frame, and behind him paced an old man, or a small boy, carrying a stick for the better correction of the burro's innate sin of sloth. This was Santa Fe's fuel supply — perhaps four dozen crooked sticks of dead and seasoned wood at a time, advancing at the slowest rate that the burro could manage. It followed, therefore, that there had to be more than one old man and donkey, and indeed the woods were full of them, all wending their way from the surrounding hills to the little adobe city. It was the same around Taos and every other town wherever the Juniper grows and the Spanish tongue is spoken; the streets, between the adobe walls, especially toward twilight, were filled with the clatter of burdened donkeys. They delivered the wood directly to the householder's gate in the wall, without any middleman to take away the pleasures of the courteous greeting from the vendor, of the buyer's pat on the little burro's flank, a word or two in his cocked ears, and a *Vaya con Dios* as beast and man depart. Today trucks go rattling out on the roads and the wood is delivered without picturesque accompaniments.

Cherrystone Juniper grows up to 60 feet high or even more, but generally it is much shorter; often the tree is as broad as high, and usually there are several forks from near the base; in any case the trunk, however thick and old, is always short, sometimes with branches coming out close to the ground and resting their tips upon it, or, again, the trunk is bare of branches below, revealing its picturesque contortions. With age the trunk becomes fluted and buttressed, covered with twisting strands of soft fibrous bark. Some specimens are believed to be five hundred years old. A trunk only 5 to 7 inches in diameter represents, in general, a life of 175 to 195 years, while trunks 10 to 12 inches thick have yielded 315 to 375 annual growth rings.

Probably the most fantastic and ancient specimens, certainly the most exclaimed-over and photographed, are those in The Garden of the Gods, that stage set of geologic drama, that playground of centuries of erosion and droves of summer tourists, with Pikes Peak for a backdrop. Here, amid fantasies in upturned sedimentary red rocks, are ancients of this race of trees with trunks twisted and crowns lopsided as if to rival the most extravagant whimsies of this unearthly spot. The Juniper known to the Garden guides as "Methusaleh" has several enormous stems all forking from the ground and leaning out from each other, much like the trunks of a Crack Willow, each one seemingly mighty enough to be the bole of a fair-sized tree, each top with a crown of rich green foliage that, with the red of the rocks and the white of Pike's snows, paint the Garden in elemental splendor. "Methusaleh" is claimed, or rather guessed, to be nine hundred years old. There may be grave doubt of that many, but several centuries at least must have produced such a growth. Although the ground around it is littered with bark strips and dead and broken boughs, there is promise still of indefinite life in this grand old specimen.

The Navaho eats the berries of this Juniper in the winter or fall when they are ripe. In times of food shortage, these people chew the inner bark. When the snow is deep, branches are lopped off for the sheep to eat. Wool is dyed green with the bark and berries by the Navaho weavers. The Navahos say that the beautiful margins of their baskets are an imitation of the overlapping of Juniper leaves. To this day in the Navaho war dance a stick of this Juniper is carried. All the twigs except a small bunch at the tip are first pruned away and with it is bound a bunch of rabbitweed or snakeweed. Prayer sticks, war bow, and bows for the canopy of the papoose cradle are made by the Navaho of the wood of this tree, and they use it as charcoal for smelting their famous silver jewelry.

The wood is close-ringed, and in consequence hard and dense. Like that of most Junipers it is, if properly seasoned, strongly resistant to decay and is used locally for ranch fence posts, though there is never enough clear lumber to make boards of it. A pity, since it has a delicious Cedar-like fragrance and handsomely contrasting ruddy heartwood and clear pale sapwood.

The female trees are sought for their berries by the Hopi chipmunk, quail, fox, rock squirrel, and deer. Both sexes yield browse to New Mexico's omnivorous goats — but what does not?

LARCHES

Western Larch

Larix occidentalis Nuttall

OTHER NAMES: Western Tamarack. Hackmatack.

RANGE: Mountains of southeastern British Columbia south through the Cascades, Blue Mountains, and Wallowas of northern Oregon and the Bitterroots of Montana and Idaho, 2000 to 7000 feet above sea level.

THE HOME OF THE WESTERN LARCH, as one of the great lumber trees of the West, lies primarily in the region that likes to call itself the "Inland Empire" — west of the continental divide in Montana and including northern and much of central Idaho. This is, too, a re-

145

gion of fine lakes, such as Pend Oreille, Coeur d'Alene, Priest, Whitefish, McDonald, and largest of all, Flathead Lake. Around the shores of this last, and up past Kalispell and the western slopes of Glacier National Park, the Western Larch reaches its grandest size. Trees 200 feet high were known, at least formerly, before the assault in force begun by the lumber industry, half a century and more gone by, cut such wide swathes in the virgin stands of Larch, Western White Pine, and Douglas Fir. Even today one sees individuals 100 and 150 feet tall, the tapered trunk rising straight as a flagpole, and the branches astonishingly short, thus exaggerating to the eye the height of the tree. The branches are also sparse, as are the needles.

As you travel today through the Inland Empire, you may feel at times that you are gazing on an empire torn by war. Here a mountainside has been swept bare to the mineral soil by some dreadful holocaust of the past, and there lie the "slashings" of lumber operations, a jackstraw pile of logs, with the very high stumps left by the logging methods of a past generation. Second growth is coming up, though not so swiftly or densely as in regions of greater rainfall, and from it still stand forth the gaunt gray poles of trees swept by fire or decorticated by the ravages of the beetle. But high above the second growth, out of the slashings, tower scattered specimens whose bark perhaps was so thick that it resisted injury by fire, whose years were too many to make it likely that their wood was sound enough to pay for logging them. And these reminders of the Larch forest's past greatness stand like warriors who still keep their feet after a battle that has littered the ground with their dead comrades. Seen through the clouds of a gathering storm in the mountains, or through the drifting smoke-haze of some fire, each one of these becomes, as you ride or tramp, a landmark that looms up ahead, is reached, passed, and falls behind, to be followed by another sentinel ancient in years. There is an air of lofty tragedy about these grand old trees, some of which cannot have much longer to live, and we can only hope that the second growth will be saved from fire and beetle and lumbered, if at all, on a basis that the future as well as the present will call sound.

True that there are fine and almost pure stands of Larch remaining that have never been logged over — most of them now in the hands of Forest Service, which gives them a protection that they have seldom had on private holdings, where the annual cut continues at the rate of some 26 million board feet a year. But it is likely that there are no stands that have never been burned over, for "never" is a long time; and fires, in this region of violent electrical storms striking in some of the most inflammable, pitchy forests in the world, must from time to time have raged here with little to check them. Winds too, of hurricane violence, must have blown here in ages past, and have piled their own kind of slashings in their wake, so that scenes of natural devastation may well have opened to the Indians' eyes as well as ours. Yet somehow this, the king of Larches, has, like its fellow conifers, managed to reassert its reign over and over in the Inland Empire.

In youth the Western Larch is a pretty thing, far removed from the grandeur and grimness of some of the centenarian survivor specimens. The long, lithe branches of the young tree clothe it to the ground, and the rime of delicate foliage lights the twigs with a soft halo of pale green, paler than that of any other kind of western conifer, so that one can pick out Larch from as far away as colors can be distinguished. Then, when autumn comes and the sun shines through the golden foliage, the trees gleam for a while like the Aspens in an angelic light. When the needles drop, then of course the trees are left naked, a starkness the more barren and dead seeming because we are accustomed to think of the needle-leaved trees as evergreens. But the beautiful cinnamon red bark gives this species more color than the other Larches show in winter.

Few softwoods have such hard and heavy wood, yet it is easily worked with tools and takes a good polish. So it goes into interior finish and even furniture. Its great durability under conditions likely to favor decay makes it valuable for railway ties and boat construction. This durability, and the perfect straightness and scant limbage of the trunk, have caused it to be cut in great amounts for telegraph poles. Much Larch disappears underground for use in mines, and experiments indicate that the wood is suitable for pulping and would make a high-grade wrapping paper. But most of all is it used for rough lumber, that is, construction timbers where its strength and comparative cheapness recommend it. Western Larch is thus a valuable but not a precious or fine wood. It may be coarse compared with the highest grades of some woods, but it does heavy duty with an endurance that could not be expected of many another tree.

Tamarack

Larix laricina (Du Roi) K. Koch

OTHER NAMES: American, Black, or Red Larch. Hackmatack.

RANGE: Almost throughout interior Labrador, Newfoundland, Quebec, the Maritime Provinces, and Ontario, and all the way across Canada between the prairies and the tundra to the shores of the arctic in Mackenzie, and down the Yukon River to its mouth. South through Minnesota and Wisconsin to northern parts of Illinois, Indiana, and Ohio, northernmost West Virginia, Pennsylvania except the southeastern parts, extreme northwestern New Jersey, throughout New York State except Long Island and Staten Island. Absent from eastern Connecticut, Rhode Island, Cape Cod, and southeastern Massachusetts.

T HE TAMARACK GOES FURTHER NORTH than any other tree in North America, and at the farthest limits of its distribution it grows in summer by the light of the midnight sun. At that season it is one of the most tenderly beautiful of all native trees, with its pale green needles like a rime of life and light.

But in winter it is the deadest-looking vegetation on the globe. Many a tenderfoot has been horrified, coming upon a Tamarack swamp, to see miles of these trees that he concludes have been swept by fire, the bark seemingly scorched to its rusty hue, the twigs apparently seared to stumps, and the corpselike forms still standing rooted in the muck.

Then when spring comes to the North Woods, with that apologetic rush and will to please which well become the tardy, these same trees that one thought were but "crisps" begin, soon after the wild geese have gone over and the ice in the beaver ponds is melted, to put forth an unexpected, subtle bloom. The flowers are followed in a few weeks by the renewing foliage, for the Larches are the only conifers (except the Bald Cypress of the South) which drop their needles in autumn and renew them again each spring. And there is no more delicate charm in the North Woods than the moment when the soft, pale green needles first begin to clothe the military sternness of the Larch. So fine is that foliage, and so oddly clustered in sparse tufts, that Tamarack has the distinction among our trees of giving the least shade. The northern sunlight reaches right to the bottom of a Tamarack grove.

Tamarack may grow on high land and, in the far northern Rockies, even tries to climb their bases, but over most of its vast range it loves boggy land; it delights in old, silted-up beaver ponds while the soil is still quaky with water, where one can neither paddle a canoe nor walk, nor even touch solid bottom with a 10-foot pole. It is especially abundant in the interior of Labrador, where it constitutes itself the chief tree inhabitant, but reaches its finest dimensions north of Lake Winnipeg. There, and in Maine and New Brunswick, people often call it Juniper, and absurd and misleading though such a name is, the traveler must accept local names as facts, in the district where they are used.

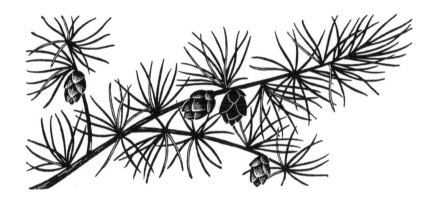

Long before the white man came, the Indians used the roots of Tamarack for sewing the strips of Birch bark in their beautiful canoes. The best roots came from trees in beaver ponds, for they were especially tough, pliant, slender, and elongated. When the white man began to build his own boats, he sought out Tamarack roots for a very different purpose. He used them for "instep crooks," or ship's knees — that is, a solid piece of durable wood with a natural angle or bend. Such bends were found in the roots of Tamaracks which grew in shallow mud underlain by a hardpan clay that deflected the growing roots at a sharp angle. However, only small knees are ever made by Tamarack; the great knees of the sailing ships were got out of Southern Live Oak and Eastern White Oak. But because it is so durable in contact with water, Tamarack is still used by builders of small boats for knees, stringers, keels, and floors.

Durable too in contact with the soil, Tamarack was ideal for railroad ties before creosoting rendered almost any hard wood suitable, and the mastlike trunks had only to be lopped of their branches to make telegraph poles. Yet it is not the ax that has decimated the great northern stands of Tamarack, but an insect pest, the sawfly, which a few years ago swept them like a plague, leaving the great trees skeleton. New growth is fortunately coming in.

It must have been the Indians who showed the first New England settlers hidden virtue in the Tamarack. Good old John Josselyn, first naturalist-historian of the Bay Colony, recorded: "The Turpentine that issueth from the Larch Tree is singularly good to heal wounds, and to draw out the malice . . . of any Ach rubbing the place therewith." As long as woodsmen know their woods, the Tamarack can prove their friend in time of need, for its curative powers are genuine.

HEMLOCKS

Eastern Hemlock

Tsuga canadensis (Linnæus) Carrière

OTHER NAMES: Canadian Hemlock. Spruce or Hemlock Pine. Hemlock Spruce. Suga.

RANGE: Nova Scotia to the north shore of Lake Huron and the south shore of Lake Superior to Minnesota (where rare) and southwestern Wisconsin; almost throughout Michigan, Pennsylvania, West Virginia, New York, and New England except the high mountains, in New Jersey away from the coastal plain, in Maryland away from tidewater, in southern and eastern Ohio, in northern and eastern Kentucky, and south on the mountains at intermediate altitudes to Georgia and Alabama. In a few scattered counties in central and southeastern Indiana.

I N THE GRAND, HIGH PLACES of the southern mountains Hemlock soars above the rest of the forest, rising like a church spire — like numberless spires as far as the eye can see — through the blue haze that is the natural atmosphere of those ranges. Sometimes even its branches reach out like arms above the crowns of other trees. But though the Hemlock's top may rejoice in the boldest sun and brave any storm, the tree unfailingly has its roots down in deep, cool, perpetually moist earth. And no more light and heat than a glancing sunbeam ever penetrates through the somber shade of its boughs to the forest floor.

The very opposite of a pioneer species, with its light-sensitive, drought-fearing seedlings, Hemlock must wait until other trees have created a forest. When the ground has become strewn with centuries of leaf mold, and the shade so dense that other trees' own seedlings cannot compete with their parents, the Hemlock moves in. Conditions on the forest floor are then more favorable for it than for any other tree. Painfully slow though the Hemlock's growth is, it will inevitably make its way above its neighbors. One by one they are eliminated, until at last only the shade-loving Beech can keep company with Hemlock. They associate together gladly, shaggy bole contrasted with paper-smooth one; somber, motionless needles with light and flickering blades; strength with grace. The hemlock has then reached what ecologists call the climax stage — that is, a vegetational group that cannot be invaded or displaced by others unless ax or fire violently intervene, or an actual change of climate in the course of geologic ages.

Besides shade, the Hemlock loves rocks; it likes to straddle them with its ruddy roots, to crack them with its growing, to rub its knees against a great boulder. The north sides of hills, the sides of mountains facing the rain-bearing winds, exactly suit it. Unlike the Tamarack, it seems never to grow on level land if it can find an incline. It loves to lave its roots in white water — rushing streams and waterfalls; it despises slow water, warm and muddy, and so avoids the Mississippi valley and all its works.

But where it grows, it has long served the mountain people. They learned from the Indians long ago that the high tannin content of the bark made it a valuable curative for burns and sores. More, the earliest settlers were quick to find that its bark could be used for tanning leather, and for two hundred years and more they stripped the trees in the most wasteful manner; only the broad, thick bark of the lower trunks was taken, the rest unutilized. The peeled logs were left in the forest to decay, though the old-time lumbermen sometimes had a use for "Hemlock peelers" in driving Pine logs down river to the mill, since the slippery naked logs helped to ease along the Pine. Still in the southern Appalachians the bark is used as a brown dye for wool, but to leather it gives a red tone and serves in immense quantities for tanning. Today, however, its chief use is for the making of pulp, especially in Michigan and Wisconsin.

But not in newsprint and cheap wrapping paper does Hemlock serve us best, but rather rooted in its tranquil, age-old stations. Approaching such a noble tree, you think it dark, almost black, because the needles on the upper side are indeed a lustrous deep blue green. Yet when you lunch on the rock that is almost sure to be found at its feet, or settle your back into the buttresses of the bole and look up under the boughs, their shade seems silvery, since the under side of each needle is whitened by two lines. Soon even talk of the tree itself is silenced by it, and you fall to listening. When the wind lifts up the Hemlock's voice, it is no roaring like the Pine's, no keening like the Spruce's. The Hemlock whistles softly to itself. It raises its long, limber boughs and lets them drop again with a sigh, not sorrowful, but letting fall tranquility upon us.

Western Hemlock

Tsuga heterophylla (Rafinesque) Sargent

OTHER NAME: Alaska Pine.

RANGE: Islands and seaward slopes of the Coast Ranges of southeastern Alaska from sea level to 2700 feet; in British Columbia, on the southwest coast of Vancouver Island and the Queen Charlotte Islands; on the Coast Range, and, inland, up to 5000 feet in the Selkirk and Gold mountains; throughout western Washington from sea level to 5000 feet on Mount Rainier; throughout western Oregon, frequent on the west side of the Cascades but rare on the east and not known from the Siskiyous; confined in California to the fog belt of the north coast (Del Norte and Mendocino Counties; reappearing in Sonoma County).

WHEREVER THE WINDS OF THE NORTH PACIFIC come bearing eight and nine months of rain (up to 100 inches a year) followed by three months of bright but deliciously cool summer, the Western Hemlock grows. It comes down almost to the beaches of Oregon and extends far up the gorge of the Columbia — the grandest river scenery on the continent. Its delicate fronds of foliage wave in the breezes set up by the numberless and enchanting waterfalls of the Cascades whose slopes it climbs for a few thousand feet, as long as the climate stays mild and rainy. It swathes the bases of the Olympics, of Mount Rainier and Mount Baker, and is perhaps the most abundant tree around the intricate fjords of southeastern Alaska. Compared with some of its constant companions — Douglas Fir, Western Red Cedar, and Sitka Spruce — Hemlock is not one of the gigantic species, though its 100 to 150 feet of height would be considered so in the sylva of the eastern states. But abundant, almost omnipresent in its range, it certainly is. For Hemlocks seem, in the Northwest, to fill all the spaces not forcibly occupied by other trees, leaving scant meadows save where the ground is actually boggy or inundated by tidal waters. True, there are many places where other trees completely dominate the scene; there are spots where the Hemlock is quite lacking, or, again, where it seems for miles around to be the only tree. But in general it is simply the commonest, most continuously distributed, of the trees of the great coniferous rain forests of the Northwest coast.

Fortunate it is, then, that it is so beautiful a tree. In its early life, when it takes the form of a broad-based cone, its branches have a deliciously youthful gesture, as of uplifted arms. In age the reverse is true; the branches, becoming old and heavily laden with branchlets, bend down at the tips, and the twigs are often pendant too, so there is something of the "weeping" habit about a specimen two or three hundred years old — or perhaps only half "weeping" — gracefully resigned, rather, to the burdens and the dignities of age.

The Western Hemlock is notable for the way that its long, lashlike leader shoot nods over at the tip, like the end of an old-fashioned buggy whip as it stood in its socket. Its needles, lying in a very flat spray, make a gracious shade. For, though small, they are closely set, and so are the spirals of boughs around the stem, of branches on the boughs, of branchlets on the branches and, in their turn, the twigs. The tiny needles by the millions thus cast some of the densest shade thrown by a conifer, and, where the Hemlock grows thickly, the forest floor may not see many sunbeams from one month to the next.

The astonishing darkness under a close canopy of Western Hemlock plays an important role in forest ecology and succession. For Hemlock seedlings are able to endure the darkness forced on their early years by their parent trees, but the young hopefuls of other species are firmly shaded out. Thus where Hemlock once gets in, even as an understory and seemingly humble and unaggressive tree, it is really preparing to inherit the earth, and, except for the intervention of fire or steel, it is likely to do so.

This was one of the reasons why the old loggers of the Northwest hated the Hemlock. It seemed to them that wherever they turned they met more of this "weed tree" than any other, and its lumber was supposed, on the analogy of Eastern Hemlock, to be well nigh worthless. True, its bark contains twice as much tannin as the eastern species, but the cost of hand labor in the Northwest is and always has been so high that there is no prospect that Western Hemlock bark will ever compete with the tannin materials coming in from Argentina and other countries. As for the logs, if one were cut by mistake, the old-time mill foreman refused to scale it; he just quietly sawed it up and sold it with Douglas Fir, with as much sense of sin as you feel in passing off a Canadian twenty-five-cent piece that has been passed off on you.

Then, toward the turn of the century it was realized that the Western Hemlock is not a bad lumber by any means, since it is strong, fine textured, straight grained, stiff, free of pitch, saws off easily without splintering, and holds nails well. So it is a good lumber for studding, drop siding, ladder stock. Flooring of Western Hemlock takes a polish almost like a hardwood; indeed, it hardens and darkens with age. Interior paneling, furniture, sash and door millwork are all served by this species, which is shipped as far as Japan and through the Panama Canal to ready markets in the eastern states.

With dramatic suddenness, in the 1930s, Western Hemlock leapt to the fore as one of the most important industrial woods in the world. Inventions that had been worked out twenty-five and fifty years before, chemical theories long known but till then little applied, caught up with this abundant and versatile tree. At the same time a lot of ill-founded assumptions fell to the ground. For, it appeared, the fast-growing Western Hemlock was just as capable of producing paper pulp as the slow-growing Spruces, which, it had always been asserted, were the only trees that yielded the right sort of cellulose. That sort is alkali resistant and is referred to in industrial chemistry as alpha cellulose, and Western Hemlock has it in abundance. The staple of its fibers is long and strong, and it can be easily separated from the other wood elements — primarily the lignin or gluey material — and economically prepared for market. This is done by "digesters" which, in the case of Hemlock, often employ the sulfite process, invented in this country by Tilghman in 1866–67. A "cooking liquor" of calcium bisulfide and sulfurous acid is ingeniously put together on the spot and heated to 250° to 300° F. Into this is fed the Hemlock; in the fierce chemical fire of the digester everything except the cellulose fibers will be eaten away. The digested wood — "the batch" — is a pulpy, dingy slush which must be screened and then washed in quantities of pure running water till every trace of acid and of noncellulose is sluiced from the precious fibers. These then go to the bleaching plant where chlorine turns the pulp to an almost snowy white. The finished pulp — now a heavily surcharged yet still partly liquid mass — travels in pipes to the paper plant, if paper it is to become. But Hemlock first and foremost supplies the alpha cellulose that goes into the making of cellophane, rayon yarns, and plastics.

Within one generation, rayon — at first called "artificial silk" — has stampeded the textile markets of the world, throwing a scare into the wool, silk, and cotton businesses by its cheapness and attractive appearance. It is true that many sources of fiber, including some that are completely inorganic, contribute to the total rayon output of the world. But

Western Hemlock is one of the great sources and yields rayon yarn by the Viscose process patented back in 1892. Essentially, the process consists of placing the pulp sheets in a box with strong caustic soda, which is later squeezed out by wringers; then the flaky "crumbs" of pulp that remain are heated with carbon bisulfide. The result is "xanthate," a viscous solution with a texture and hue something like mucilage. This is then forced through a threaded nozzle, much as the spider and the silkworm force the products of their silk glands through their spinnerets, so that the silk emerges as a strong but fine thread. Indeed, the threaded nozzle is also called a spinnerette (and thus spelled, in distinction from the insects' organs), and its holes correspond in number and size to the desired caliber of fiber. Constant improvement in rayon has resulted in a yarn that is finer and stronger than any natural silk. At the same time the price has steadily climbed down while the production has mounted. As a result, the child of the poorest parents can wear pretty, dainty rayon clothing that, a short while ago, was a murmuring Hemlock in the somber forests of the Northwest. As the child peels the cellophane wrapper from the sanitarily packaged food she eats, she is handling another product of wood cellulose, that may, in all likelihood, have come, too, from Western Hemlock.

Many are the sources of our plastics — all the handles, kitchenware, steering wheels, composition "leathers," safety films, Lucites, substitutes for tableware, lenses, buttons, and the like to which in one generation we have become so accustomed. But those made from wood cellulose are superior in toughness, strength, resilience, and brilliance, and Western Hemlock is the commonest source of much of them. The cellulose pulp is very inexpensive to cast in steel dies in any desired form, and to tint or color before the casting. Then the pulp is solidified in the die, by high pressure and heat, and the product is complete without any further finishing, coloring, or tooling — all ready to sell.

Fortunately Western Hemlock is an abundant resource. Washington, Oregon, and British Columbia possess something in the neighborhood of 161 billion board feet of this species — four times as much as the supply of that next-most-important pulp wood, the Sitka Spruce. The cones may be small, and not beautiful like the long cones of Mountain Hemlock, but their seeds fly far on those wings and are bounteously produced. They germinate well, whether they fall on the soil or in deep moss, or even on the trunks of fallen trees which they straddle with their roots. There is reason to think that the natural replacement of this species is well in excess of the present cut, which indeed is not increasing because so many other soft-wood trees are now known to be capable of producing pulp and are coming to share the burden of the cut. So often have we boasted in the past of our inexhaustible resources, only to see them sadly depleted, that it would be rash to claim that Western Hemlock, though favored by its native climate of a long growing season and tremendous rainfall, will hold out forever. But in the foreseeable future its great stands are in no danger of becoming exhausted, while the possibilities of further progress in plastics and synthetic textiles are all but limitless.

American Beech

Fagus grandifolia Ehrhart

RANGE: Throughout Nova Scotia, Prince Edward Island, and New Brunswick to the north shore of Georgian Bay, south to northern and western Florida and eastern Texas, and west to eastern Wisconsin, eastern and southern Missouri, and extreme southeastern Oklahoma.

A BEECH IS, in almost any landscape where it appears, the finest tree to be seen. There are many taller trees, and many that attain to moments of showier glory, like the Sugar Maple in autumnal coloration, or a Dogwood starred with snowy blossoms. But, taken in all seasons and judged by all that makes a tree noble — strength combined with grace, balance, longevity, hardiness, health — the Beech is all that we want a tree to be. And more besides, for it is a tree deep-rooted in the history of our people, in this new world and the old one, and figures beloved to us both in fable and fact move under its ancient boughs.

Far down the aisles of the forest the Beech is identifiable by the gleam of its wondrously smooth bark, not furrowed even by extreme old age. Here it will be free of branches for full half its height, the sturdy boughs then gracefully downsweeping. The gray bole has a further beauty in the way it flutes out at the base into strong feet, to the shallow, wide-spreading roots. And the luxuriant growth of mosses on the north side of such a

159

tree, together with the mottling of lichens, adds to the look it wears of wisdom and serenity.

The elegant clear gray of the bark extends from the trunk to the main mighty boughs, then to the hundreds of branches, and out to the thousands of branchlets. So that when the tree stands naked in winter it seems to shine through the forest, almost white in contrast with the dun colors all about it, or against the dark evergreen backgrounds of the Canadian Hemlock and Eastern White Pine with which it associates. In very early spring an unearthly pale pure green clothes the tree in a misty nimbus of light. As the foliage matures, it becomes a translucent blue green through which the light, but not the heat, of the summer day comes clearly. And in autumn these delicate leaves, borne chiefly on the ends of the branchlets and largely in one plane, in broad flat sprays, turn a soft clear yellow. Then is the Beech translated. As the sun of Indian summer bathes the great tree, it stands in a profound autumnal calm, enveloped in a golden light that hallows all about it.

As the leaves fall, late in the season, the twigs are revealed wearing a tinge of reddish brown, and the little triangular nuts can be seen, which with the first frost begin to drop. Fruit is abundant, in general, only every third year on any one tree, and commonly a heavy or a light harvest of the nuts prevails over a whole region.

In the days of America's virgin grandeur, forests of this luminous and stately tree covered a large part of Ohio, Kentucky, Indiana, and central Michigan. But they bespoke their own destruction, for the pioneers soon learned that the Beech was a sign of good soil. It loves what the farmer loves — rich limestone overlain by deep, level, dark loams. So in the Ohio valley the ax soon felled the growth of centuries, followed swiftly by the plow. Today, speeding easily through that candid country, the midwesterner may marvel at a report, written from southern Indiana in June of 1833 by that princely traveler Maximilian of Wied:

"We came to a tall, gloomy forest, consisting almost wholly of large Beech trees, which afforded a most refreshing shade. The forest continued without intermission . . . the lofty crowns of the trees shut out the sky from our view. They were the most splendid forests I had yet seen in America." He speaks of how the canals in Ohio ran through Beech forests, and even near Rochester, New York, finds them "wild and magnificent," adding with, perhaps, a homesick sigh, "The dense Beech forests constantly reminded us of the scenery of Germany."

For to the newcomer to this savage land the Beech tree had a kindly look of familiarity. Our species does not differ greatly from the Beech of Europe (*Fagus sylvatica*), which from time immemorial had already played a great role in human life. Beech nuts seem to have been a food of the New Stone Age man, just as they still are eaten by the peasants of central Europe. The most abundant tree in its wide range, Beech provided the principal fuel, both for keeping warm and for the charcoal used in the Old World's iron smelters. It supplied much dimension timber, a vast quantity of furniture wood, handles of agricultural tools, wooden shoes, and too many other uses to number. Indeed, it has long been the general utility hardwood of Europe.

And on the Beech was written, probably, the first page of European literature. For, it is said the earliest Sanskrit characters were carved on strips of Beech bark; the custom of inscribing the temptingly smooth boles of Beeches came to Europe with the Indo-European people who entered the continent from Asia. Indeed, our word "book" comes from the Anglo-Saxon *boc*, meaning a letter or character, which in turn derives from the Anglo-Saxon *beece*, for Beech. So if you find a big old Beech tree in the woods, hacked by some love-struck boy with the outline of a heart and his girl's initials in it, forgive him. He is but following a custom older than Shakespeare, who also records it:

> O Rosalind! These trees shall be my books,
>   And in their bark my thoughts I'll character;
> That every eye which in this forest looks
>   Shall see thy virtue witness'd everywhere.

And Virgil asks:

> Or shall I rather the sad verse repeat
> Which on the beech's bark I lately writ?

An epic line in pure American vein might have been read by all who passed that way, until about 1880, on a Beech tree on Carrol Creek, in Washington County, Tennessee, on the old stage road between Blountsville and Jonesboro.

> D. Boone
> Cilled A Bar
> On Tree
> In Year 1760.

This tree fell in 1916, the scars of the inscription, but not the exact wording, still visible. It was 28½ feet in girth, and 70 feet high, and its age was estimated by the Forest Service to be 365 years. So it began to grow in the year 1551, half a century before Orlando mooned about Rosalind in Arden, and was an ancient of two centuries when Daniel Boone inscribed his hunter's triumph on it.

For such glory, and for its own beauty, is the Beech tree justly famous, not for more mundane usefulness today. Though in Europe the Beech was utilized in every part, by a wood-hungry civilization, as the best of available hardwoods, in America the early settlers soon found twenty hardwood trees better than Beech. Here it has never been more than a second-rate tree for service, when compared with Walnut's beauty, Hickory's strength, White Pine's dimension timbers. Not as hard as Birch or Maple, it has the further disadvantage of being heavier than they. When green it is tough to split, yet it is all too apt to split when seasoned. It is knotty and has but half the value of White Oak in resistance to atmospheric decay. So, though it has a long list of modern uses, including furniture and flooring, they are most of them trivial, such as for boxes and crates, barrels and crossties, down to picnic plates and spoons, culminating — for humility — in the lowly clothespin.

Let other trees do the work of the world. Let the Beech stand, where still it holds its ground, a monument to past glories. Of these, none is more wholly vanished than the passenger pigeon, to which the Beech played lavish host. It was upon the mast of Beech nuts that the great flocks fed, and their seeming migration, Audubon writes, was more exactly a quest, by the million, for rich harvest of the Beech.

"As soon as the pigeons discover a sufficiency of food to entice them to alight, they fly around in circles, reviewing the country below. During their revolutions, on such occasions, the dense mass which they form exhibits a beautiful appearance, as it changes its direction, now displaying a glistening sheet of azure, when the backs of the birds come simultaneously into view, and anon, suddenly presenting a mass of rich deep purple. They then pass lower, over the woods, and for a moment are lost among the foliage, but again emerge and are seen gliding aloft. They now alight, but the next moment, as if suddenly alarmed, they take to wing, producing by the flapping of their wings a noise like the roar of distant thunder, and sweep through the forests to see if danger is near. Hunger, however, soon brings them to the ground. When alighted, they are seen industriously throwing up the withered leaves in quest of the fallen mast."

Speaking of the night roosts of the pigeons in the Beech forests of Kentucky, he goes on to write:

"It was . . . in a portion of the forest where the trees were of great magnitude, and where there was little underwood. . . . I arrived there nearly two hours before sunset. Few pigeons were then to be seen, but a great number of persons, with horses and wagons, guns and ammunition, had already established encampments on the borders.

"Two farmers . . . had driven upward of three hundred hogs to be fattened on the pigeons which were to be slaughtered. . . . Many trees two feet in diameter, I observed, were broken off at no great distance from the ground; and the branches of many of the largest and tallest had given way, as if the forest had been swept by a tornado. Everything proved to me that the number of birds resorting to this part of the forest must be immense beyond conception . . . Suddenly there burst forth a general cry of 'Here they come!' The noise which they made, though yet distant, reminded me of a hard gale at sea, passing through the rigging of a close-reefed vessel. As the birds arrived and passed over me, I felt a current of air that surprised me. . . . The fires were lighted, and a magnificent as well as wonderful and almost terrifying sight presented itself. The pigeons, arriving by thousands, alighted everywhere, one above another, until solid masses as large as hogsheads were formed on the branches all round. Here and there the perches gave way under the weight with a crash and, tailing to the ground destroyed hundreds of the birds beneath."

So together they fell, bird and tree, from their supreme place in the history of American Nature. For after the Beech forests were swept away by

the man with ax and plow, the fate of the passenger pigeon, the most marvelous bird on the North American continent, perhaps in the world, was
sealed. As much by the disappearance of Beech mast as by mass slaughter
were the shining flocks driven to extinction.

When Audubon was young, in Kentucky, in love with his young wife,
Lucy, he painted his "Passenger Pigeon" — a pair of them — and to some
of us it is his greatest picture. The curve of the soft necks, the lift of shining wings, are eloquent, unconsciously, of a tenderness and passion not all
theirs. It is on a Beech bough that he has perched his pigeon pair, and two
withered beechen leaves tell us that the season is autumn when the mast
is ripe. An autumn that will not come again but lingers, immortal, in
those leaves that cannot fall.

WALNUTS

Black Walnut

Juglans nigra Linnæus

RANGE: Western Massachusetts and Connecticut to the coast of North Carolina, west through the upper districts of the Gulf states to central Texas and Oklahoma, and from southern Ontario to southern Minnesota and central Nebraska and Kansas.

THE HOME OF THE BLACK WALNUT is the deep rich soil of bottomlands and fertile hillsides; it grew abundantly throughout the primeval hardwood forests of America. There in their days of glory it used to reach heights of 150 feet, with the first 50 feet clear of branches, making a splendid saw log sometimes 6 feet in diameter. But the Black Walnut really prefers to stand well by itself in an open field; it dearly loves a dooryard where it will be watered and pruned and protected by the hands of its human friends. Then its limbs spread widely, the head becomes a great green dome, and the whole tree seems to luxuriate in space and deep soil and abundance of sunshine and rain. At all times its appearance suggests massive strength, the trunk solid and heavily furrowed, the compound leaves like big fronds, the catkins, which appear with the leaves in midspring, heavy and vivid, and the clusters of fruits in fall hard and solid on the tree.

Of all the native nut trees of America, the Black Walnut is the most valuable save only the Pecan, and in the traditions of pioneer life and rustic childhood it is even more famous. In a more innocent age, nutting parties were the most highly prized of children's festivities in autumn throughout the eastern forest belt, and though butternut, hickorynut, hazelnut, chestnut, chinquapin, and even beechnut and kingnut were gathered, walnut was the favorite. The charm of the nutting party, of course, did not depend solely on the subsequent pleasure of cracking the rough shell and extracting the delicious, oily sweet kernel from its intricate walls. It derived much from the tingling autumn airs, the flaming forest leaves, the wild telegraphing calls of the crows, and the shouts and games of the other children. Someone still gathers the nuts, for Walnut is a valuable confection in the market, and a favorite flavoring for ice cream.

Black Walnut provides the finest cabinet wood of North America. The colonists understood its utilization from the first — indeed were exporting it to England from Virginia as early as 1610 — without, however, being able to develop its beautiful figured grains as can be done now with veneers. On the contrary, they employed solid Walnut wood and often had so little appreciation of it as a grain beautiful in its own right that they painted its surface. Walnut was used in every sort of homemade furniture of the Colonial and Federal periods, but seldom in fine styles. By the time that appreciation of rare grains was born and the rage for Walnut really began (1830 to 1860), machine-made furniture, turning out Empire, Victorian, and Revival styles, ruined many a fine piece of wood. Then, as the final irony, when styles improved, Walnut had become comparatively rare.

There is so little Black Walnut in the forest now (except in the southern Appalachians) that it is sought by lumbermen in a door-to-door hunt throughout the countryside, where owners are sometimes tempted by a small price to sacrifice a magnificent shade tree worth in some cases, if they but knew it, more than their houses.

But in pioneer times these giants were so abundant in our earth that they were used for such humble things as snake-rail fences; probably many of the rails that Lincoln split were Walnut. Millions of railroad ties have, on account of its durability in contact with soil, been made of this now valuable wood. Cradles were almost exclusively made of Walnut in our heroic era. For gunstocks it was, and is, unsurpassed, since no other wood has less jar or recoil; it never warps or shrinks; it is light in proportion to its strength, never splinters, and, no matter how long it is carried in the hand, will not irritate the palm, with its wonderful satiny surface. In every war, the United States Government has made a fresh raid upon Black Walnut for gunstocks. Unfortunately, armies are always growing larger, and Walnut grows rarer. In our day some of the old heirlooms of solid Walnut furniture are being dragged out of garrets, barns, and cellars, where they had been thrust in the first craze for Victorian elegance, and either refurbished by the cabinetmaker or sold to him to be sawed into veneer.

There is a significant difference between the solid Walnut furniture of the pioneers and the modern Walnut veneers. The old trees were mostly forest grown, hence slow growing; it took about a hundred years to produce a Walnut of timber size under those conditions, and the boards show a straight grain and very dark heartwood. Thus the old-time Walnut furniture often has a somber, heavy look, lacking refinement either in grain or design. But there is an honesty about it that links us to our past. Perhaps the best example of the middle period of American Walnut furniture is the great secretary of President Jackson, to be seen at The Hermitage near Nashville, at which he wrote his sizzling and misspelled correspondence.

The wood of the dooryard trees that are being cut now is quite other. It is lighter in color and much more varied and handsome in grain. This beauty can be brought out by skillful cutting. The first veneers were sawed out one-eighth inch thick, but it is now possible to rotate the log against a knife and unroll, as a continuous band of paper may be unrolled, a sheet of wood only one twenty-eighth inch thick. An old tree may thus yield up to 90,000 square feet of precious veneer, valued sometimes at $20,000 wholesale. This method also permits the nicest matching of mirror-image cuts of the same fancy grain, resulting in butterfly or even double-butterfly or diamond patterns that no art of man can touch for delicate intricacy and subtle shading. They simulate, too, feathers, flames, or bees' wings. In some cases the wood actually changes color, like changeable silk, when viewed and lighted first from one angle, then another, so that this once living stuff seems to keep still a secret life of its own.

Butternut

Juglans cinerea Linnæus

OTHER NAME: White Walnut.

RANGE: New Brunswick to southern Minnesota, southeastern Nebraska, eastern Kansas, and Arkansas, and northernmost Mississippi, south on the Atlantic coast to Delaware, in the piedmont and mountains of Virginia (rarely tidewater), in North Carolina chiefly in the mountains, in South Carolina, Georgia, and Alabama, wholly so.

W HEN, ALL UNWARY, you pick up a Butternut's fruit where it has fallen on the ground after a windy autumn night, you learn your first botanical lesson about this tree, for the sticky, rusty hairs of the husk leave a brown stain upon the fingers. You try to wipe it off but find that you cannot, nor can you scrub it off; only time will cleanse your hand. For this is no ordinary stain; it is a genuine dye. Even the white inner bark yields a yellow or orange dye that has been used for a century and a half by the southern mountaineers in dyeing their homespuns. During the Civil War, the backwoods Confederate troops were sometimes dressed in homespun "uniforms" of butternut-dyed cloth, and they became known as "Butternuts." So the very name of this tree has become a synonym for tattered glory.

The kernel is agreeable when fresh — oily and sweet — but soon becomes rancid. Today one seldom sees in the markets these delicious nuts; walnuts and pecans have captured the popular fancy. Yet the Indians appreciated butternuts, for Roger Williams mentions that the Indians made of them an excellent "Oyle good especially for annoynting their heads. And of the chips of the Walnut-tree, the barke taken off, some English in the country make an excellent Beere both for taste, strength, and color." Few know it now, but a good sugar is made from the sap, though the yield is but a quarter that of the Sugar Maple.

A countryman's tree is the Butternut, known to the farm boy but not his city cousin. One who takes thoughtful walks in the woods may come to know and admire it for the grand old early American it is. But the landscape architect complains that the leaves are often sparse and by summertime may be dingy looking, and that many dead branches detract from its appearance. Compared with the stately Black Walnut, the Butternut is usually a low, broad tree, seldom more than 40 feet tall, with a short thick trunk which soon branches into numerous limbs that in themselves may be very substantial stems, heavy and wide spreading. In the forest it may tower up 100 feet and develop a fine, unbranched trunk clear for half its total length.

Very light and soft and easily worked, the wood of Butternut has been largely employed as a cabinet wood and for interior finish. In the old days of carriage building, fine "shays" were often paneled in Butternut because of its beauty combined with lightness. Though soft textured, the wood of Butternut is so lustrous and satiny as to be a favorite of the architect designing rooms of dignity and luxury. The paneling of the Chicago Board of Trade grill is veneered in perfectly matched half-panels and, used in conjunction with light brown pigskin, it produces an air of sumptuousness.

Age only mellows Butternut's surface, and like Black Walnut it "stays put," never warping or cracking. It is still a favorite of the wood carver, and many fine old American altars were made of carven Butternut. Alas, the demands upon this tree have been unremitting, and today White Walnut can seldom be procured in practical lengths. This uniquely American wood is rapidly becoming a scarce and precious hardwood, nor does the future promise better things, unless that day ever comes when the American people demand that their wooden resources be restored to them by a planned forestry.

HICKORIES

Shagbark Hickory

Carya ovata (P. Miller) K. Koch

OTHER NAMES: Shellbark or Scalybark Hickory.

RANGE: Southern Maine to Delaware, thence south on the piedmont to southern Georgia, west to southeastern Texas (but not the Gulf Coast) and from Ontario through southern Michigan to central Wisconsin and southeastern Minnesota, central and southwestern Iowa and extreme southeastern Nebraska, eastern Kansas, and Oklahoma. Absent from northern New Hampshire and northern Vermont.

TO EVERYONE WITH A FEELING for things American, and for American history, the Shagbark seems like a symbol of the pioneer age, with its hard sinewy limbs and rude, shaggy coat, like the pioneer himself in fringed deerskin hunting shirt. And the roaring heat of its fires, the tang of its nuts — that wild manna that every autumn it once cast lavishly before the feet — stand for the days of forest abundance.

"The fruit," wrote William Bartram in his *Travels in North America*, "is in great estimation with the Indians. The Greeks store [Shagbark Hickory nuts] in their towns. I have seen above an hundred bushels of these nuts belonging to one family. They pound them to pieces and then cast them into boiling water, which, after passing through fine strainers, preserves

173

the most oily part of the liquid; this they call by a name which signifies hiccory milk; it is as sweet and rich as fresh cream, and is an ingredient in most of their cookery, especially homony and corn cakes."

When the Indians were gone and the white men came, "nut cracks" were a popular diversion of pioneer boys and girls. The tough hickory nuts, and black walnuts too, were cracked with hammers and flatirons and then shelled. As many were eaten at the time as young appetites could endure — which is a great deal — and the rest saved for sale and for future consumption. Quite as important as the nuts at these cracks seemed the kissing games played by the children and the courting that got done among the older boys and girls. Today it is to be feared that even on farms nut cracks are a thing of the past; the farm children get to the country store and buy packaged peanuts and pecans, like the rest of us.

A Shagbark can usually be distinguished as far as it can be seen by the smoke gray bark, which is forever warping away from the stem in great plates a foot long or more and 6 or 8 inches wide. Frequently the strip is loose and curling at both ends and is only more or less loosely attached by the middle, while its edges usually touch those of another strip of bark, so that if one tries to pull it free from the trunk, it is so engaged on both sides that one soon gives up the task. True, there are other trees with exfoliating bark, but none in our sylva with such great segments, so long or so thick. This shagginess begins to develop in comparatively young trees. Around the feet of old specimens the forest floor may be quite littered with the cast-off heavy coat of armor. But the tree is not shedding its bark preparatory to some other condition, for normally new shagginess has simply thrust the old away. Occasionally a tree has close, not shaggy, bark and is called by lumbermen "Bastard Hickory."

In rich deep soil, Shagbark attains heights of 120 feet, and under forest conditions it may form a columnar trunk, free of branches for the first 50 or 60 feet. It tends to have a narrow crown, with short branches and heavy, yet graceful, drooping branchlets. Against the winter sky the outline of form and twigs is scraggly and uncouth.

But about the first week in April the inner bud scales begin to open, arching out and twisting at the same time, but with their tips at first still adhering in a pointed arch. Shining and downy on the inner surface, and yellow green richly tinged with red, they look like petals of some great Tulip or Magnolia as finally they part and curl back. The young leaves and catkins are then seen standing up in a twist, like a skein of green wool.

The catkins now rush into growth simultaneously with but more swiftly than the delicate, pale, and lustrous young leaves.

Dark, heavy, and aromatic is the foliage all summer, but if the season is a dry one the leaves may begin to turn a dull brown even in August and drop, leaving the tree prematurely naked. Yet if they last through, they join modestly in the autumn splendor of our midwestern woods, with a soft dull gold, not without its luminous beauty when the sun of Indian summer shines through them. To all who know the Shagbark, such memories are linked with visions of the violet smoke of asters curling low through the drying grasses, with peeled October skies, with crow calls that signal your presence through the woods, and the shining of red haws, like little apples, on the thorn trees.

The fuel value of Shagbark is higher than that of any other American wood except Locust. A cord of Hickory is almost the equivalent in thermal units of a ton of anthracite and even today costs less. In our times of scarcity, it is horrifying to think that untold millions of cords of this wood were chucked into the hearths and stoves of pioneers. The log cabins, notoriously drafty if not perfectly constructed, were kept warm by a roaring fire, day and night, a large part of the year, and Shagbark was the favorite wood to feed this Moloch.

Green wood of Hickory is considered by epicures the perfect fuel for the preparation of smoked hams. The pioneers found this out, and no one has ever discovered a finer source of coals or fumes for this purpose. The aroma of burning Hickory enters into the ultimate taste of the smoke-cured ham as definitely as that of Spanish Cedar in cigar boxes blends with the taste of the finest Havanas. True that, weight for weight (not volume for volume), White Pine fuel has more thermal units, but for seasoning hams it would never have the long-lasting coals or impart the subtle flavor of Hickory.

The pioneers made boxes of the shaggy bark. They made ramrods for their guns of Hickory, and fenced in their grounds with Hickory rail fences, though it is one of the most difficult woods in the temperate zone to split and decays swiftly when exposed to the elements. The early furniture makers discovered that seasoned rounds of Hickory in posts of green "sugar wood" (Maple) made unbreakable joinery, for as the green wood shrank it clasped the iron-hard Hickory dowels forever. Green Hickory splits made perfect hinges for the pioneers' cabin doors. Yellow dye from the inner bark tinctured the homespun of the cabin housewife. Hickory hoops encircled the ubiquitous pork barrel and are not surpassed in general utility by the metal hoops of today.

That Hickory was a symbol of strength in the pioneer mind is attested by the nickname of "Old Hickory" given General Andrew Jackson. It was accorded him when, a major general of militia, he received callous orders from the Secretary of War to discharge his troops, in the War of 1812, at Natchez, when they were 500 miles from home. Flatly refusing, he marched his men back along the Natchez Trace to Tennessee in order that they might be mustered out near their homes. Sharing their poor fare with them, sleeping with them on the hard ground, he wrung from the backwoodsmen their admiration. "He's tough," admitted the tough boys from the Hickory groves, "tough as Hickory." "Old Hickory" they dubbed him, and the name chanted him to the White House. Today he sleeps beneath six towering Shagbarks, in his grave in The Hermitage garden.

Broom Hickory

Carya glabra (P. Miller) Sweet

OTHER NAMES: Brown or Black Hickory. Pignut.

RANGE: Southern and western New England to southern Michigan, Illinois, and southeastern Iowa, south from New Jersey to Georgia on the piedmont and lower mountain slopes, all of Tennessee except the Mississippi bottomlands and south to east-central Mississippi.

TO TURN FROM THE PRECEDING SPECIES, the native Walnut, prince of cabinet woods, to the incomparably tough, heavy, shock-resistant Hickory is like turning from a polished nobleman to a sinewy, hard-bitten backwoodsman. And of all Hickories the Broom is, on the whole, the most rugged of a hardy breed. Its wood is the heaviest in our range, equaled only by Shagbark Hickory (from which this species is hardly distinguished in the lumber business). Tough yet flexible, and resistant to an impact load, it is in the highest demand for ax handles and every sort of striking tool. Because of its low conductivity of heat, it is prized for wagon parts, like the hub, where the heat of friction may be great, or others, like singletrees, that may endure a sudden strain. No wonder that the covered wagons of American history rolled westward on Hickory hubs and Hickory fellies, or that Hickory sulkies have made the American trotting race famous. The terrific vibration on the big picker sticks in textile looms can be sustained only by Hickory. Skis, too, must stand violent strains, so that American Hickory is the most prized wood of skiers the world over. For Hickory is stronger than steel, weight for weight, more elastic, less brittle, less heat conductive. It is not possible to imagine another wood which could replace our Hickories if all of them were depleted — a situation now looming well above the horizon.

This species alone was cut — under the stimulus of increasing war needs — to the tune of 78 million board feet annually. This is not a high figure compared with the cuts of some of our western softwoods, but it is high when other factors are considered, such as the extreme slowness of the growth of the tree under forest conditions (sometimes twice as slow as such a notoriously slow-growing species as White Oak). Add to this the tremendous toll taken by wood-boring insects, which in inconceivable numbers attack the living trees, while other species destroy the lumber just when it has been carefully seasoned for a year. And finally there is the wasteful way in which the wood is utilized, only the pale sapwood normally being accepted by buyers, because of an unfounded prejudice that the darker heartwood is weaker, although scientific tests do not bear this out in the least.

But Hickory fights back toward survival in its own stubborn way. Like backwoods children flourishing, the seedlings can come up through dense shade. So Hickory is a "pushing" species, able to succeed other hardwoods in the ecological course of events, even to succeed itself, generation after generation, on the same land. More, it will endure poorer soils and drier situations than many of our hardwoods. And, when released from intense forest competition, it can put on comparatively fast growth where, before, it had been the slowest of all.

Spring is late in coming to most of the Hickories, and well after other trees have flowered or leafed out this one stands forth, naked and massive, on the dry ridges and hillsides where it delights to grow. Thus bare, its thin, contorted branches give it an awkward look. But the winter gales may wrench at it as they will, for its very deep taproot — remarkable even for a Hickory — makes it one of the most windfirm of trees. And if the tree be closely examined in winter, it will be seen that the outer bud scales have already fallen and the next inner pair of scales, clothed in shining golden hairs, are ready to expand till they look like petals. Finally the innermost bud scales open, and with sustained warm weather they curl back almost like Magnolia flower parts, luminous as spring sunshine and with the downy look of young life. Very different are the bold spring leaves from the weather-worn foliage of autumn, turned a dull yellow. Often the leaflets fall off separately, leaving the leafstalks clinging, bare, to the twig, like so many yellow darning needles, while the hard little fruits come rattling down in the wind. The small kernel is insipid or bitter, not in the least in the class of the nuts of Shagbark and White Hickory and Kingnut and Pecan.

The name of Broom Hickory was given it by the early settlers because narrow strips were split from the wood and made into brooms — how, is well told by Doctor Daniel Drake in his memoirs of *Pioneer Life in Kentucky:*

"Till I went to Cincinnati to study medicine, I had never seen a scrubbing brush. We always used a split broom, in the manufacture of which I have worked many a rainy day and winter night. A small hickory sapling was the raw material. The 'splits' were stripped up for eight or ten inches with a jackknife pressed by the right thumb, bent back, and held down with the left hand. When the heart was reached and the wood became too brittle to strip, it was cut or sawed off, and the splits turned forward and tied with a tow string made for the purpose on the spot. It only remained then to reduce the pole above to the size of a handle. A lighter and genteeler work was making 'scrubs' for the buckeye bowls and the good old black walnut table (bless it!) with a crack in the middle, from end to end, occasioned by the shrinking of the boards. The 'scrub' was a short hand-broom made precisely like the scrubbing broom, but out of a smaller sapling."

That Age of Wood was a stouthearted age, and the Hickories, tattered old sentinels yielding reluctantly to the screaming saw and the silent enemies boring from within, stand as its rude but noble symbols.

Pecan

Carya illinoinensis (Wangenheim) K. Koch

RANGE: Texas from the Rio Grande valley north through the central and eastern parts of the state, central and eastern Oklahoma, eastern Kansas, Missouri except the northern part, up the Mississippi River valley to southeastern Iowa, central Illinois, up the Ohio to southern Indiana and western Kentucky and east to central Tennessee and west-central Alabama.

FAR IN THE HEART OF THE NORTH AMERICAN continent, remote from any seaboard except the shores of the Gulf of Mexico, the Pecan might have stood long unknown to the white man save for its chance discovery in 1541 by the renowned Hernando DeSoto. On his wanderings, he crossed the Mississippi with his gold-seekers, who in their Castilian armor floundered through the swamps of eastern Arkansas until they emerged upon high, dry ground where the fields abounded with what DeSoto's chronicler called Walnut trees. But he describes the nut as thin shelled, and thus can have meant only the Pecan tree. So here, only fifty years after Columbus first sighted San Salvador, appears in history one of the most strictly interior trees of North America, its most famous nut tree, and the largest and kingliest of all species of *Carya*.

All the early chroniclers of French Louisiana mention the pecan, telling us that the Indians of many tribes in the lower Mississippi stored it, and that the Creoles soon came to appreciate it deeply, using it at least as early as 1762 in that heavenly confection known as the New Orleans praline.

Long before the American pioneers crossed the Alleghenies into the fertile wilderness of the Mississippi Valley, unknown traders and fur trappers brought the first pecan nuts over the mountains with their beaver skins. In consequence, pecans were first known in the east as "Mississippi nuts," or "Illinois nuts." Men curious about the wonders beyond the mountains turned them over in their palms, fingered and tasted and smelled them, and began to plant them.

So it was that Thomas Jefferson, himself a naturalist and great tree-planter and a man who always thought westward, following the explorers with his mind like an eagle who watched where they toiled, set out Pecan trees at Monticello. Presently he dispatched pecans to George Washington. Ever on the watch for new and useful crops, the master of Mount Vernon planted them eagerly, and in his journal of May, 1786, he refers to a row of "Illinois nuts" which he had just planted. Today those Pecans, gift of Thomas Jefferson, are the oldest living trees at Mount Vernon, where the visitor will find them towering above the southeast corner of the mansion.

Until almost the turn of the last century, pecans reached the market largely from wild trees. The harvesting methods in early times consisted in nothing less heroic and criminal than cutting down gigantic specimens — the bigger the better — and setting boys to gather the nuts from the branches of the fallen giants. It seemed to the pioneer then, as it did to every American, that the forests of this country were inexhaustible. Thus it came about that the wild Pecan tree had become rare before men began to realize how much was lost.

But already the farther-seeing had been at work on selection of fine varieties and their propagation. Slow growing though the tree is in its native state, under cultivation and with plenty of fertilizer and deep soil, it reaches bearing in a few years. As with most crop trees, it does best when grafted on wild stock. The earliest successful graft was made by Antoine, the black slave gardener of Governor Telephore J. Roman, at famous Oak Alley Plantation in St. James Parish, Louisiana. That was in 1846, when sixteen trees were trunk grafted and the variety known as Centennial was produced. Today perhaps a hundred named horticultural varieties of the Pecan are known, and every form of grafting has been mastered. The culture of the Pecan — the only case where a native nut tree has been extensively grown in orchards — now extends to far-off California and Oregon. Georgia is the leading pecan-producing state.

The Pecan is the state tree of Texas, for there it reaches its grandest dimensions — sometimes 120 feet high with a trunk as much as 30 feet around, and a spread of enormous limbs which gives the crown a diameter of 100 feet. It is one of the surprises of your first trip to Texas (if you are a traveler who motors deep into the country and then walks into the woods) to come upon a centenarian grove of Pecans down in the bottomlands. Even in winter, or perhaps especially then, the grandeur of the ancient trees stands forth; the trunks appear sometimes as if they had been stung by fabulously large insects, or to have grown to their elephantine shape as a result of pollarding, like the Burnham Beeches in England.

The first settlers of Texas, now well over a century ago, told of such gigantic and patriarchal trees under which they drove their wagons or pitched their camp, finding beneath the Pecans shade, fuel, lumber, and the food that fell in the wilderness like manna from heaven. If it is painful to think that it was such trees as these that the pioneers of the American bottom in Illinois destroyed for a single year's harvest of nuts upon them, it is good to think that here at least is one of America's noblest trees which is being extensively planted. True, Pecans in an orchard, planted in rows and methodically trimmed, do not have the venerable and picturesque appearance of the wild trees of the bottomlands, yet time may take care of that. In southern Europe one sees Chestnuts and Olives planted by the Romans, which are now majestic monuments to the long-dead men who set them out. So the Pecan orchards of our time may take on the same august appearance, and future generations will astonish our shades by exclaiming how wise we were and how well we builded!

HORNBEAMS

American Hornbeam

Carpinus caroliniana Walter

OTHER NAMES: Smooth-barked Ironwood. Blue or Water Beech.

RANGE: Nova Scotia to northern Florida and west to central Minnesota, eastern Iowa, eastern and southern Missouri, eastern Oklahoma, and eastern Texas. Also on the mountains of Mexico and Central America.

THE FIRST REWARD of tree study — but one that lasts you to the end of your days — is that as you walk abroad, follow a rushing stream, climb a hill, or sit on a rock to admire the view, the trees stand forth, proclaiming their names to you. Though at first you may fix their identity with more or less conscious effort, the easy-to-know species soon become like the faces of your friends, known without thought, and bringing each a host of associations.

Such is the American Hornbeam, a tree recognizable on sight by its beautiful fluted stems and branches. Each trunk and bough is spiraled with low, rounded, broad ridges that look like twisted muscles. This is a trait which begins to develop almost from the first, while the tree is still in youth; the smooth bark seems to be corrugated with some sort of swelling or twisting inside the wood itself, as if the life within showed itself proudly, as a young man will flex his arm in the joy of its strength.

The name Hornbeam has reference to the extreme hardness of the wood — "horn" for toughness, and "beam," an old word for tree, comparable with the German *Baum*. "The Home Bound tree," wrote William Wood in *New England's Prospects*, "is a tough kinde of Wood that requires much paines in riving as is almost incredible, being the best to make bolles and dishes, not subject to cracke or leake." Hornbeam has been utilized, too, for levers and handles of striking implements, but, as it cannot be obtained in large quantities from so small a tree, it is employed chiefly by local tool makers and does not figure as a wood of commerce. The hardwood lumberman thinks of this as a mere weed tree.

But the rest of us who know it deem the Hornbeam a very lovely companion of our wood walks. True, it is only an understory tree of the forest, seldom over 40 feet tall, usually only about 20 at maturity. The crooked, slender trunk is short and soon forks in a bushy way, with slightly zigzag, tough, but slender branches that toward the ends become pendulous. Late in March or early April, we see its slim catkins and dainty leaves appear together. In summer its foliage is like that of the Beech — the blades themselves thin and beautifully translucent, but the foliage in the mass dense, giving a shade cool yet not dark. In late autumn the leaves turn deep scarlet and orange.

The Hornbeam plays second fiddle to the famous taller trees of our eastern forests wherever it occurs, and sometimes an officious landscape architect or forester will urge that it be destroyed to make way for more important species. But in the judgment of more mature authorities it is seldom wise practice, in the management of the mixed deciduous woodland, to try to grow just a few species of the highest economic value. Forest trees do best in a forest and under the most natural conditions. By that standard, Hornbeam is of value as a companion tree and a contributor to the total biota. Hornbeam should be spared, if not planted, whenever a natural landscape effect is desired.

Eastern Ironwood

Ostrya virginiana (P. Miller) K. Koch

OTHER NAMES: American Hop Hornbeam. Rough-barked Ironwood.

RANGE: Cape Breton Island (Nova Scotia) through southern Quebec and southern Ontario, across the northern peninsula of Michigan to the Black Hills of South Dakota (but not north of Lake Superior), south to northern Florida (but not on the coastal plain of the south Atlantic states), thence west to eastern Texas (but not in the Delta country of Louisiana and not on the Gulf coast), and west to eastern parts of Oklahoma and Kansas.

I N OUR RICH SYLVA a little tree like the Eastern Ironwood melts into the summer greenery, or the silver intricacy of naked twigs in the winter woods, in a way that makes it difficult to pick out and identify. Not that it lacks for distinctive features; it has two — the hoplike scales around the nut that make it look as though the fruit were enclosed in little papery bags, and the bark, which somewhat resembles that of the Birches but is more scurfy than papery.

Except for the Dogwood, this is the hardest wood in our northeastern sylva, harder than Oak or Ash, Hickory or Locust or Persimmon. In proportion to its great hardness and strength, its heaviness is not disadvantageous. This should make Ironwood ideal for use wherever great toughness is required, but only occasionally does this tree grow as much as 30 feet high, or produce a trunk a foot thick, nor does it occur abundantly enough to make it commercially profitable. So Ironwood is only locally used, when someone is searching for material for the handle of a mallet or an ax, or a lever to endure great strain. Even this presupposes a man who knows of the high qualities of the wood and can recognize this rather undistinctive tree when he sees it.

For the beauty of Ironwood is subtle, with its dainty beechen leaves which turn a soft, dull gold in autumn, and in summer shut out all the heat of the sun but only a little of the light. A modest component in the mixed deciduous forest of our eastern sylva, it finds its place as a nurse tree and as a contributor to the rich and ancient mold of the forest floor. Being an understory species, it gives shade or, rather, redoubled shade, to the wild flowers and the mosses. Its tiny nuts, which no human would ever bother to dig out of their casing, feed the bobwhite and the deer, the pheasant and the rabbit. The unsensational color of the autumn foliage serves for what the gardener calls a "softener." Everything about this little tree is at once serviceable and self-effacing. Such members of any society are easily overlooked, but well worth knowing.

BIRCHES

Paper Birch

Betula papyrifera Marshall

OTHER NAMES: Canoe, White, or Silver Birch.

RANGE: Newfoundland and Labrador west to Hudson's Bay, eastern Manitoba, eastern Wyoming, and central Colorado; south to Long Island, northern New Jersey, northern Pennsylvania, around the shores of the Great Lakes, and west through northern Illinois to Iowa and Minnesota; also on Mount Mitchell, North Carolina, above 5500 feet, and in the Black Hills of South Dakota.

O F ALL THE SITES THIS FAMOUS BIRCH may choose none is more dramatic than its stand on Goat Island, at the very head of Niagara Falls. Here where great clouds of mist, rising like battle smoke from the tumult below, perpetually assault the rocks with drenching spray, the Paper Birch and the Arborvitæ flourish in abundance. They make a telling contrast, the filmy green of the Birch feminine beside the dark spires of the Arborvitæ, its slim whiteness gracile against the shaggy bark of the twisted and more ponderous tree. And while the sturdy evergreen appears unmoved by the winds that perpetually rush upward from the awful chasm, the Birch shivers and trembles even as must the human visitor, and the fronds of the little oak fern, too, and the pallid blooms of

enchanter's nightshade and naked miterwort that cower, yet rejoice, beneath the trees.

Wherever it grows the Paper Birch delights in the company of conifers and in the presence of water; it loves a white and rushing stream; it loves a cold clear lake where its white limbs are reflected. Sometimes it is found in swamps and boggy meadows, and, if it must leave the neighborhood of moisture, it likes deep, rocky woods with cool soil. Fortunately it is light tolerant in youth, so comes up readily on cutover land and has replaced the Eastern White Pine and the Spruces over large parts of New England, eastern Canada, and the northern peninsula of Michigan.

Thus has Paper Birch gained ground, within historic times, and if there are fewer grand specimens than there were, time may take care of that. For the Birch, where it is found near habitations, is usually spared for its beauty. As a result it is now one of the best-loved trees of the New England landscape, and when we remember a scene there, we see Birches in it — gleaming white trunks, houses, and churches painted a cold, clean white, and pure country snow stretching white over dale and hill.

In its great range, the Paper Birch takes many forms; on the mountains of New England it is sometimes a dwarf and bushy plant, while in the rich forests it grows 60 feet high; in the virgin woods it probably attained twice that height, if old reports can be trusted. Though a botanist may quibble over differences in a leaf, all the botanical varieties add up to the same thing — a tree of incomparable grace and loveliness, identifiable at a glance by its shining, scaly bark. The only possible confusion would be with the much-cultivated European White Birch, which you will know by its pendulous "weeping" branches and by the bark that is much closer and tighter than the more readily peeling bark of our Paper Birch.

To any American of an older generation (now, alas, even canoes are being made of aluminum) there was no more blissful experience than the moment when on his first visit to the North Woods he stepped into a Birch bark canoe weighing perhaps no more than 50 pounds, but strong enough to carry twenty times as much. At the first stroke of the paddle it shot out over the lake water like a bird, so that one drew a breath of the purest ozone of happiness, for on all the waters of the world there floats no sweeter craft than this. The Indians taught our race how to strip the bark from the Birch and sew it with long slender roots of Tamarack for thread. The bark was then stretched and tied over the frame — commonly made of northern White Cedar or Arborvitæ — while the holes in the bark and the partings at the seams were caulked with resin of Pine or Balsam or Balm-of-Gilead. Other barks, and skins, were often used for canoes, but of them all Birch is the most renowned — the lightest and most beautiful, and yet so strong that the Indian trusted his life to it when he shot the rock-fanged rapids.

Birch wood furnished the Indians with snowshoe frames. The bark served him, sometimes, as a covering for the tepee or lodge; rolled into a spill, it constituted a taper or a punk stick to keep away mosquitoes. It made good paper for kindling a fire started first in punkwood of rotten Yellow Birch. A moose-calling horn of Birch bark was carried by all the red hunters in the North Woods — a straight tube about 15 inches long and 3 or 4 wide at the mouth, tied about with strips of more Birch bark.

The inner bark of Paper Birch is a favorite of the beaver, when Aspen fails. Deer and moose browse the twigs in winter; the buds are eaten by grouse. Sugar can be tapped from this Birch, as from the Maple. Thus to each inhabitant, man or beast, of the North Woods, Birch is life sustaining. Though the lumbermen in the days of the White Pine had little use for the wood itself, they were glad enough to stuff Birch bark, as a waterproof inner lining, under the Cedar shingles of their bunk houses made of Yellow Birch logs.

And, to the delight of children, the peeling bark has long been a woodland paper. But pray do not strip it from the living trees, for once the beautiful outer bark is pulled away, it never grows again. Instead, ugly black rings — which you see all too often — take its place. There is always a fallen Birch log from which you can tear sheets. For the Birch is, despite its strength, not a long-lived tree; once it is dead, decay is swift, and the white form soon topples into the old forest loam. Then the mosses gather on its fallen limbs, a pale green halo that shows how life carries on, though its forms forever change.

River Birch

Betula nigra Linnæus

OTHER NAMES: Red or Black Birch.

RANGE: From eastern Texas to Florida; north in the valley of the Mississippi River to eastern Oklahoma, eastern Kansas, eastern Iowa, southeastern Minnesota, central Wisconsin, southwestern and southern Indiana, and southern Ohio; isolated in northern Indiana; north in the Atlantic states to southern New York, and again along the lower Merrimac River in Massachusetts.

THE RIVER BIRCH RANGES FAR SOUTH of all the other Birches; others may be found by rushing streams, by cold, clear lakes; this one alone avoids such spots and grows beside the larger, slower, more silt-laden rivers of the coastal plain and piedmont, and throughout much of the course of the Mississippi and its tributaries. There it is the Birch paramount, seldom or never seen in close company with its more aristocratic relatives.

Yet all Birches are graceful, and this species, like most riparian trees, is apt to have several forks from the base, each trunk leaning outward so that a sort of indolent charm may be claimed for it. When the trunk is straight and unbranched, it may soar 80 or 90 feet on the bottomlands of the Gulf states, but northward it is usually not more than 40 or 50 feet tall. That it is a Birch is known from its thin, papery, scaly bark, which peels back after several years, to show the pink brown tints of the inner layers. The foliage in the summer gives the typical refreshing shade of all the Birches, but in autumn the leaves of this one turn only a dull yellow before they drop, late in the season.

The wood of River Birch has never enjoyed much of a reputation with lumbermen; the stems are spindling, the lumber knotty, the trees themselves scattered along tens of thousands of linear miles of rivers, never forming merchantable stands. Yet the wood has been used for woodenware and furniture, and once upon a time for ox yokes and wooden shoes. The rice planters of the Carolina coast used to employ it for hoops for their rice casks, as a substitute for Hickory. But the rice-planting aristocracy is gone, gone as are the old wood-burning river boats, gone as beaver hats and Confederate money; today the River Birch is not called on to justify itself in terms of human gain.

Yet Nature must be well content with this tree, since she has produced it in quantity. For the seeds ripen in May and June, just when the water in the rivers is high, and are borne far on the currents, until they became stranded on some muddy shore. Mud is requisite to them and they germinate in it quickly. In a few weeks the first shoots are up and ready to give a good account of themselves. The River Birch holds the banks, prevents erosion and flood and, safe from the attentions of lumbermen, it has a survival value unequaled by its more salable sister species.

CHESTNUTS

American Chestnut

Castanea dentata (Marshall) Borkhausen

RANGE: Southern Maine and Massachusetts across southern and central New York to eastern Ohio, southeastern Michigan, and southern Indiana and Illinois, south to Alabama and Mississippi.

ALL WORDS ABOUT THE AMERICAN CHESTNUT are now but an elegy for it. This once mighty tree, one of the grandest features of our sylva, has gone down like a slaughtered army before a foreign fungus disease, the chestnut blight. In the youth of a man not yet old, native Chestnut was still to be seen in glorious array, from the upper slopes of Mount Mitchell, the great forest below waving with creamy white Chestnut blossoms in the crowns of the ancient trees, so that it looked like a sea with white combers plowing across its surface. Gone forever is that day; gone is one of our most valuable timber trees, gone the beauty of its shade, the spectacle of its enormous trunks sometimes 10 to 12 feet in diameter. And gone the harvest of the nuts, that stuffed our Thanksgiving turkey or warmed our hearts and fingers at the vendor's street corner. What chestnuts we still see come to us, for the most, from Italy.

It is believed that the blight came into this country on Chinese Chestnuts (*Castanea mollissima*), which despite a high percentage of infection show, too, a degree of resistance to it. No immunity existed in our American tree. From the time the blight was first detected, in 1904 in the New York Zoological Park, it spread with a sickening rapidity. Crossing New Jersey, it entered the great Chestnut stands of Pennsylvania; that state, thoroughly alarmed, appropriated a large sum for the control of the malady, in which the federal government joined. But all in vain. Destruction of infected trees proved ineffectual; new infections broke out at distant points.

For it was discovered that the spores are carried far by wind, and the disease was already scattered so far that quarantine lines were futile. The blight (*Endothia parasitica*) penetrates the bark at cracks in the crotches of limbs and where wood-boring beetles have made lesions; it then kills the entire cambium layer and, finally, extrudes its fruiting bodies through the swollen and cracking bark, in a position to spread fresh infection on any passing breeze. At last the remotest stands of the tree, in southern Illinois, were reached. However, plantings in Wisconsin, Oregon, and California are said to be free of the disease.

It is often asked whether the little sprouts seen coming up from blight-killed trees will not perhaps show an acquired immunity. So far nothing so hopeful has been observed, and the spores of the disease are still lingering in the stumps themselves. Attempts are, however, being made, with some success, to create disease-resistant hybrids from resistant Chestnuts and ours.

But never again will those proud forests rise. Quickening the decimation, lumbermen rushed in to salvage all the sound timber, whether from dead or living trees, doomed in any case. But if a king is wholly vanished from our scene, its absence is at least less depressing than were those years when its diseased hosts and gaunt, whitening skeletons saddened the forest prospect.

Chinquapin

Castanea pumila (Linnæus) P. Miller

OTHER NAME: Chinkapin.

RANGE: From southern New Jersey to central and western Florida and west through the Gulf states to the valley of the Nueces River in Texas, ascending to 4500 feet in the southern Appalachians.

THE FIRST MENTION TO BE FOUND of the Chinquapin is in Captain John Smith's account of Virginia. But the creatures of that wilderness had known and appreciated it from time immemorial. Today it is chiefly as a wildlife crop that it can replace its vanished kinsman the Chestnut, though the sweet and abundant little nuts are sometimes to be seen in the markets of towns in our South. In that region it is useless as a timber tree, being indeed little more than a shrub, but west of the Mississippi it seems to be inspired by a new ambition and reaches heights up to 50 feet, with a diameter of 2 or 3 feet.

OAKS

Eastern White Oak

Quercus alba Linnæus

RANGE: Southern Maine to the southern peninsula of Michigan, southwestern Minnesota, eastern Iowa, and southeastern Nebraska, south to western Florida, through the Gulf states to the Brazos River of Texas and eastern Oklahoma and eastern Kansas. Rare on the southern coastal plains; ascending the southern Appalachians to 4500 feet, but becoming a bush at high altitudes.

I F OAK IS THE KING OF TREES, as tradition has it, then the Eastern White Oak, throughout its range, is the king of kings. The Tuliptree can grow taller, and the Sycamore in the days of the virgin forest had gigantic boles, but no other tree in our sylva has so great a spread. The mighty branches, themselves often 50 feet long or more, leave the trunk nearly at right angles and extend their arms benignantly above the generations of men who pass beneath them. Indeed, the fortunate possessor of an old White Oak owns a sort of second home, an outdoor mansion of shade and greenery and leafy music. So deep is the taproot of such a tree, so wide the thrust of the innumerable horizontal roots, that if one could see its whole underground system this would look like a reflection, somewhat foreshortened, of the giant above ground.

Like the detail of a cathedral, the White Oak's minor points are beauty

197

too. When the leaves unfold they clothe the tree in a veil of vivid red gradually turning pink and then silvery white. In autumn this foliage is a rich
winy color, and in its withered final state it tends to cling all winter. The
acorns germinate soon after they fall, and before the cold weather their
first little roots are in the ground — if they have not been harvested by
squirrels or birds with which they are a favorite food. They were a staple
of diet, too, with the Indians, for though a little bitter for eating out of
hand, they sweeten after boiling.

When the first New England colonists saw White Oak on the shores of
Massachusetts Bay, they recognized it gladly as a close relative of the English or Norman Oak (*Quercus robur*), which had for centuries built England's navy and merchant fleet and was a very synonym for staunchness.
But that Oak which once covered most of England had been cut and cut;
shortages were becoming evident in Queen Elizabeth's day and increased
with alarming rapidity. Cromwell, in sequestrating the Crown lands, and
those of the Church and the nobles, saw a ready revenue in leveling the
Oaks, and with them he built a great navy. But wooden ships decay faster
than Oaks can grow; the proudest ships of the line had a life expectancy of
but a few years. So the Cromwellian orgy of oaken shipbuilding was followed by forest dearth.

This offered a great chance to the American colonies. Our White Oak,
however, met with serious opposition from the British shipbuilders and

the inspection boards of the Royal Navy. Scornfully they maintained that it was weaker than their own as a structural timber, and that it was far more subject to decay. The truth of this lay simply in the haste of the cutting and carelessness of seasoning. No wood is so troublesome as Oak to season; it must be air-dried, over a long period, yet kept from exposure to sun and rain lest cracks and checks develop.

Indeed, the hastily rushed ships of English Oak were in as bad condition as those of our own Oak. Samuel Pepys describes his inspection of such a vessel in 1677 where he gathered from the boards "toadstools . . . as big as my fist." When Lord Sandwich inspected the ships at Chatham in 1771 it was necessary to shovel away the fungal filth before the timbers could be seen. Often the dry-rot never appeared on the surface but, like termites, gnawed away the interior, especially in that most vulnerable place known to sailors as the futtocks or wales — just above the water line, where the heavy guns were carried. The famous disaster of the *Royal George* in 1782 was caused when the whole bottom of the ship dropped out from dry-rot.

For all of this, the British loftily shook their heads at American White Oak as far inferior to their own. Well, if the mother country would not take our White Oak, we would build our own ships of it. The immortal frigate *Constitution* had a gun deck of solid White Oak of Massachusetts, her keel was the same wood from New Jersey, while knees of Maryland White Oak framed her keelsons. All-Oak ships became the pride of our shipbuilders; not good enough for the British Navy, they were just good enough to carry the New England sea captains around the world. Nor has White Oak entirely lost its place in the American Navy. The keels of our mine sweepers and patrol boats in World War II were still being laid in White Oak, and some of it came from Franklin D. Roosevelt's estate of Hyde Park.

On land as on the sea, this great tree gave its strength to our people. Through two centuries the pioneers built their blockhouses of its stout timbers, their bridges, barns, and mills and log cabins. For this is the best all-around hardwood in America. True, White Pine warps and checks less, Hickory is more resilient, Ironwood is stronger, and Locust more durable; but White Oak would stand second to almost all these trees in each property in which they excel, and, combining all these good qualities in a single species, it comes out in the end as the incomparable wood for nearly every purpose for which wood can be used. In a great table prepared by the Forest Service on the uses of woods, White Oak almost invariably occupies first, second, or third place under every item, except for wood pulp and plywood, tobacco pipes, artificial limbs, and airplanes. Obviously it is too hard and too valuable for the first two, too heavy for the last two, and since it develops no burls is not made into pipes.

But "pipes," in quite another sense, were some of the first objects made out of White Oak by the colonists, for to them a pipe meant a cask for wine and other liquids. Today we speak of "tight cooperage," meaning barrels that will hold liquids, as contrasted with "slack cooperage" for barrels intended to hold solids. Oak of most sorts is ideal for tight cooperage. So the pioneer people rived their barrel staves out of White Oak by hand and sent them abroad, especially to France for wine casks and to the West Indies for rum; even from the heart of the Middle West this oaken cargo went floating down the Mississippi to New Orleans for export. For generations, too, the early Americans employed great amounts of the bark in tanning. Unfortunately, the trees stripped for this purpose were taken in spring, the time of year yielding the highest tannin amounts but least favorable for logging operations, which are best performed in winter. So that the peeled logs were left exposed to decay and weathering, which, in Oak, is the opposite of seasoning. Always, too, the White Oak has been a fireplace favorite, for as a fuel it is the best all-round wood we have, weight for weight. And it is the heaviest of all our Oaks, as well as marvelously durable in contact with the soil. Indeed, its durability is taken as a standard, other woods being measured in percentages of the durability of White Oak.

As material for furniture, Oak is thus more sturdy than it is graceful. In England it was the favorite during the centuries when solid wood was employed; up to and through the Jacobean period it was uncontested. Thereafter, Walnut and Mahogany came to dispute with it, and their introduction, as well as the use of veneers, gave the cabinetmaker scope for lovelier creations, and Oak began to yield its primacy. Yet it has often returned to favor; in America we still shudder reminiscently over "the golden Oak era." Golden Oak was the name for a high varnish, laid usually on quartersawn boards. A quartersawn plank of full breadth is one which has one edge at the center of the tree, the other under the bark, and its beauty in White Oak consists in the large size and silvery brilliance of its medullary rays, which are properly seen only on this cut of the wood. When an entire room is paneled in quartered Oak, the effect is indeed striking, and it was a great favorite forty and fifty years ago in the houses of the newly rich. The trouble with the "golden Oak era," however, was not with the noble wood, but in the ostentation of the costly display, the machine-made designs of the paneling, and that flashy varnish.

At present Oak as a furniture wood is chiefly used in office desks, though White Oak flooring remains unchallenged, and properly waxed Oak paneling will never cease to hold its high place. But quartersawn Oak is not satisfactorily cut from trees under 150 years old, and, in general, dimension timbers must come from trees 100 to 300 years of age. So the supply of high-grade White Oak is running out, as the centenarian trees are cut or die.

Yet a hundred years is brief in the life of an old White Oak. There are members of this species still standing that were already tall when Columbus first raised his momentous landfall. In the Friends' Cemetery at Salem, New Jersey, there grows a White Oak that stood out as a landmark when the town was founded in 1675 and Quaker John Fenwick called the Indians together beneath its shade to make with them a treaty that, it is boasted, was never broken on either side. The whole region of the Jersey shore of the Delaware Bay is famous for its great White Oaks that line the streets of ancient towns like Salem, Mantua, Jefferson, and Mullica Hill and shade the King's Highway, which links them all to Philadelphia. The Tatum Oak at Mantua Grove was a giant said to have been 25½ feet in circumference at breast height, 87 feet tall, with a spread of branches 121 feet across. It is survived by its rival, the Hendrickson Oak of Mantua, which if not so large is not necessarily younger, for size in a tree depends in part upon the amount and closeness to the surface of the groundwater. Its base spreads out in mighty buttresses that grip the earth. Half a dozen gigantic boughs sweep out and bend to the ground, with the weight of their years. Six generations of the same family have played here, where two thousand children could probably be gathered in this patriarch's shade. The supply of Indian arrowheads discovered in the soil in which it grows seem never quite exhausted. In the probable life span of this tree have been born, have mightily wrought, and died William Penn and Benjamin Franklin, George Washington, Thomas Jefferson, Abraham Lincoln, and Woodrow Wilson, and Peter the Great, Napoleon, and Beethoven. Thrones have crumbled and new empires arisen; great ideas have been born and great pictures painted, and the world revolutionized by science and invention; and still no man can say how many centuries this Oak will endure or what nations and creeds it may outlive.

Yet there are grander Oaks than this in our country. For reasons not clear, the largest and possibly the oldest are found on the Eastern Shore of Maryland. When, two hundred years and more gone by, the first colonists came to this region of long "necks" of land between the inlet bays and creeks, they built their manor houses in great White Oak forests. And though they long ago cleared, or cut for timber, the forest itself, they were an aristocratic people who appreciated the worth of the noblest old trees, and half a dozen standing today might lay claim to being the largest White Oak in the world.

Judgment on that would depend on one's standard. But the final honors generally go to two titans. The first is the largest of the seven Oaks in the churchyard of ivy-covered St. Paul's at Fairlee, built in 1713. Twenty-four and a half feet in girth, this tree is 118 feet tall and has a spread of 127 feet. Its rival, the great Oak at Wye Mills, is a monarch of superbly symmetrical beauty with a spread of 148 feet — a dimension unequaled by any other Oak in our sylva. The Wye Oak's appearance of utmost antiquity is enhanced by great "knees" 3 or 4 feet high that surround its base.

With trees such as these, it is no wonder that Maryland has adopted the White Oak as its state tree, or that it was to the Eastern Shore that naval architects turned, when the frigate *Constitution* was to be remodeled. There they would find White Oak timbers great enough to replace the original keelsons and futtocks and compass timber that had been selected in the days of our forest abundance. Today the visitor who walks the deck of *Old Ironsides*, where she rests in honored peace in Boston Harbor, can feel an oaken-hearted strength, still sound, that is part of our American heritage.

Bur Oak

Quercus macrocarpa A. Michaux

OTHER NAME: Mossycup Oak.

RANGE: Manitoba and the Black Hills of South Dakota south to central Texas, east to southern Ohio, southwestern New Brunswick, and southern Nova Scotia, and south through New York State to Maryland, northern West Virginia, Kentucky, northwestern Tennessee, and Arkansas.

W HEN THE PIONEERS OF THE MIDDLE WEST had hacked their way through the forests of the Appalachians, they came, as they moved westward, to a new type of forest growth, something unknown in the aboriginal sylva of the Atlantic seaboard. This was the groves of wide-spaced trees, almost void of undergrowth, and carpeted with short, sweet grass. Between these trees, and under their great boughs, they drove their lumbering wagons easily; deer could be hunted through these groves on horseback; here the wind blew refreshingly free, driving away the plaguing horseflies and mosquitoes; here the ground was dry and the grass could not conceal snakes, nor were there ominous thickets to hide lurking savages. So our forefathers called these groves the Oak openings, and that is the title of one of James Fenimore Cooper's novels of primeval life in the old Northwest Territory, which now we call the Middle West.

The most characteristic tree which the settlers noted in the Oak openings was one which grows, indeed, to the eastward but never comes there to its full grandeur or its characteristic parklike vistas. They knew it as the Bur Oak because the heavily fringed cups of the acorns look almost like the burs on a Chestnut, though the cups only half cover the nut. True that other Oaks are often found in the Oak openings, or prairie groves, of the Middle West, but ecologists consider them secondary successors; they have come in after the Bur Oak has conquered the prairie for them; and they in turn make way for a climax forest of Hickory, Walnut, Ash, and Linden.

But the Bur Oak seems, from all the geological and ecological evidence which can be collected, to be the pioneer in the advance of the forest upon the prairie. For the warfare of forest and prairie, of grass and wood, is an old one; probably it was going on, in the heart of North America, before

ever the great glaciers came. Where those caps of ice rested, of course, they killed all life; when they retreated, as periodically they did, Oak and grass took up their ancient quarrel. As a Bur Oak may not reach productivity for fifty years, while the prairie grasses begin seeding themselves almost at once, it would seem that all the advantage must lie with the grass.

Yet that depends upon the climate of the interglacial periods (of which the present era is probably one), which have been alternately dry and moist. Whenever the climate tended to the dry side, the grasses advanced; in moister periods the forest advanced. Apparently a few thousand years before our time there was a dry period when prairies covered most of Illinois, but today "the prairie state," as it is called, has a forest climate. The result is that Bur Oaks have, where not actually kept back by destruction of one sort or another, advanced so rapidly, not only in Illinois, but in Wisconsin and Iowa, as to constitute a distinct agricultural problem in some localities.

Some ecologists believe that the only thing that prevented the Bur Oak from making forest states out of everything east of the Missouri was the constant firing of the region by the Indians in their hunting drives. For Bur Oak seedlings are more injured by fire than are grasses, which come back readily. Though the coming of the white man put a stop to the firing, the introduction of cattle, which eagerly browse the leaves of Oak seedlings, and whose hooves pack down the soil so that the roots have most of their air supply cut off, has often held back the spread of the Bur Oaks.

Extensive studies have been made upon the root systems of the Bur Oak, and they show that the taproot is comparatively short; like the trunk above ground, it soon gives rise to a large number of wide-spreading, horizontal primary branches, which in old systems are almost as thick as the great main lower boughs of the tree above. The primaries send off obliquely slanting secondaries in still greater numbers, and these give rise to tertiaries, which in turn send down numberless sinkers or slim roots that travel straight down. For all these thousands of sinkers there are tens of thousands of still finer rootlets called obliques, and on these are clustered the millions of fine capillary or thread-form rootlets. These capillaries may be very long, and in their search for water not only do they penetrate as widely as the widest spread of the great boughs above ground, and almost as deep as the tree is high, but others turn upward and reach nearly to the surface of the soil in order to catch all the moisture that falls from light showers but never penetrates more than a few inches of the dust. So the underground system of the Bur Oak resembles a mirror image of the mighty structure above, and it is no wonder that a tree like this is able to go deep under the roots of the prairie grasses, extensive and tough though these are, and compete with them at their own level too.

But it follows that a tree with so mighty a root system has one serious competitor which can fight it with its own weapons — and that is another Bur Oak near by. So, perforce, Bur Oaks keep a respectful distance from each other; they hold each other off, not so much by their wide-spreading branches as by the fierce competition of their root systems. And that is the explanation of the Oak openings, the wide-spaced rooms where men drew their wagons to a stop with a slow, deep "Whoa!" and resolved: Here will I build me a house; here will my children grow up.

A grand old Bur Oak suggests a house in itself — for it is often broad rather than tall, and its mighty boughs, starting straight out from the trunk at right angles, extend horizontally 50, 60, 70 feet, bending with the weight of their own mass to the very ground, so that within their circle is a hollow room, its grassy floor littered with acorns, with the sloughed-off corky bark of the boughs, with a deep bed of leaves, and the birds' nests of many a summer, and the gold of many a flicker's wing.

No child who ever played beneath a Bur Oak will forget it, and if he was brought up by the right kind of parents, they showed him all its grand, elemental beauties, and perhaps found for him old portage trees of this species, bent down by the Indians a century and more ago, in their sapling stage, to mark the canoe carries from one of the slow, historic rivers or lakes to the next. For Bur Oaks live three centuries and four or more. At Sioux City, Iowa, still stands a mighty specimen of this race, the Council Oak, which, it is believed, was already 150 years old when Lewis and Clark saw it on their way up the Missouri and there held council with the Indians. At Exira, in northern Iowa, you can see the Plow Oak, where a plow that a homesteader leaned against the tree when he went off to the Civil War has been engulfed till only its handles wait for the hands that never returned to guide the share.

Most of us who have grown up among Bur Oaks will not leave among them even so much as a plow for the coming generations to remember us by, and when we are gone the rippling fox squirrels and the jeering crows will not remember us; the big dull yellow leaves of the Bur Oaks will cover the paths of our autumns. But these same trees will see our children and our children's children, and look to them the mansions that they are.

Pin Oak

Quercus palustris Muenchhausen

RANGE: Western Massachusetts and the lower Hudson valley south to the piedmont of North Carolina and west generally to the Alleghenies, and from western Pennsylvania along both shores of Lake Erie to southern Michigan and southern Iowa, eastern Kansas, northeastern Oklahoma, northern Arkansas, and Tennessee.

THE PIN OAK TAKES ITS NAME from the great number of pinlike or short spur-form branchlets on the main branches. This is an infallible distinguishing trait of the tree when one sees it close at hand. In outline, as it stands winter-naked, the Pin Oak is remarkable for having as a rule a single, mastlike shaft of a trunk going right up through the center of the tree. Unlike most Oaks, it does not give rise to heavy horizontal branches, but to a large number of much more slender ones that arch out gracefully and then, at least in the lower half of the tree, bend down, and branch out into unusually slim and un-Oak-like, almost whip-fine branchlets. As a result of all this branching, the wood of Pin Oak is unusually full of knots, and when the lumberman cuts it at all he marks it as an inferior grade of Red Oak.

But as a standing tree this one takes a high rank, not only for its gracious manner of growth, but for the glory that comes upon it when the world turns round to autumn. The light of Indian summer passing through its foliage then is like the shaft that gleams through a ruby or a garnet. This splendor is seen to perfect advantage among the Indiana dunes along the shore of Lake Michigan, and so gorgeous are the Pin Oak's colors that one is tempted to bear away a few of its boughs. But when they are brought into the house, one wonders what one saw in them, for their glory is departed. What one saw, of course, was the generous wealth of American sunlight, blue water between the white gold of dune hills, and the purple spires of blazing-star in the little interdunal mead-ows; what one heard was the wind-torn scorn of the crows, the thunder of the surf, the hiss of the ever-lifting sand, the harsh lisp of the Pin Oak leaves themselves, as the still not unfriendly gale rattled their stiffened blades.

For an Oak, the Pin Oak is not too slow growing; it is recommended by the experts as an admirable street tree throughout the eastern United States, since it is economical of room yet generous enough of shade, free of diseases, windfirm, tall-growing, gorgeous in autumn, and elegant in winter tracery.

Valley Oak

Quercus lobata Née

OTHER NAMES: White, California White, Swamp, or Weeping Oak. Roble.

RANGE: Valleys of western and central California; at the foot of the Sierra Nevada (up to 2000 feet) from the Pit River on the north to the Tehachapi Mountains on the south; inner Coast Ranges north of San Francisco Bay and generally in the southern Coast Ranges except close to the sea, south to the valleys of the Santa Susana and Santa Monica mountains and Pasadena; also on the Channel Islands and Santa Catalina; absent from some parts of the Great Central Valley but common in others.

T O SAY THAT THE VALLEY OAK is the monarch of all the deciduous Oaks of the West is almost enough to identify it. For you take one look at an old specimen's great bole, its magnificent crown, the width and the depth of its pool of shade, and you realize that it is king in its class. True, there are more precise and botanical ways of recognizing this species. First, there is the shallow but heavily knobby cup which holds the long, slender acorn shaped like a pointed cartridge shell. There is the pale gray bark broken into small cubes; there are the deeply lobed leaves, the lobes rounded or blunt, the sinuses between them narrow but rounded, not acute, at apex. And mature trees commonly have long, almost vinelike twigs that trail in weeping sprays. These traits, taken all together, typify this great species.

In many ways — in the light green foliage, the light gray bark, the mighty spread of limbs — the Valley Oak resembles its close relative the Eastern White Oak, *Quercus alba*, greatest of Oaks in the Northeast. Only a little more distantly related is the Norman or English Oak, *Quercus robur*, king of all its clan in Europe. No wonder that the Spanish, when they settled California, thought this was indeed the Oak of their homeland, and called it *roble*. Or that Captain George Vancouver, exploring the Santa Clara Valley in 1796, thought it had been "planted with the true Old English Oak." For all three species belong to the blood-royal of the genus *Quercus*.

The name of Valley Oak was not the first applied to our tree, but it became fixed because it is so apt. For a valley tree this is. Its principal home, originally, was in the wide Sacramento Valley, near the rivers. It once clothed all of Napa Valley and the Santa Clara, on the south bay shore below San Francisco. Even far north in Mendocino County it reaches magnificent proportion, in Round Valley. In the vale of Eshom, along the north fork of the Kaweah where that stream comes singing out of the Sierra, it attains the rank of Oldest Inhabitant. The famed San Fernando and Pasadena valleys are its southernmost outposts. In the Four Creeks country of the Kaweah delta there were once 400 square miles of Valley Oak groves.

The reasons for this Oak's preference for valleys are found in what they may have to offer of deep loam and (for California) a high water table — from 10 to 20 or 40 feet below the surface. Flood plains and deltas of streams likewise favor it, for they are subject to inundations, especially the welcome spring rise which comes just when the new leaves are peeping out, pink and silky. In such a situation the Valley Oak need not fear the long, hot, arid summers of these interior valleys. Indeed, it invariably avoids the seaward slopes with their cool fogs and breezes. One mountain range between itself and the sea — as in the Santa Ynez Valley — will suffice, but that one must be there — perhaps to keep out the cold, moist breath of the ocean.

One of the outstanding characteristics of the Valley Oak groves is their open spaciousness. The trees almost invariably stand well apart from each other — held off, no doubt, by competition of their root systems in a wide search for water. Yet they are gregarious trees, almost never found out of sight of many of their fellows unless the ax and plow have intervened. They grow tolerantly with Live Oak and Sycamore, the three trees forming beautiful harmonious contrasts, like notes in a sweet chord. But more commonly Valley Oak associates only with its own kind in these spacious groves, of which Vancouver wrote with some surprise, "We entered a country I little expected to find in this region. For about twenty miles it could only be compared to a park. . . . The underwood, that had probably attended its early growth, had the appearance of having been cleared away, and had left the stately lords of the forest in complete possession of the soil, which was covered with luxuriant herbage, and diversified with pleasing eminences and valleys; which with the range of lofty rugged mountains that bounded the prospect, required only to be adorned with the neat habitations of an industrious people, to produce a scene not inferior to the most studied effect of taste in the disposal of grounds."

In the course of its naturally long life — three hundred years or more, if no accidents occur and no fatal disease supervenes — a Valley Oak changes its shape fundamentally. Four stages are described by Jepson, that lifelong student of this tree. In youth when it is but 10 to 20 feet high it owns a compact, cylindrical form, called the pole state, and this it assumes even when growing in the open with full opportunity to expand. In the Elm stage, at heights of 30 to 60 feet, a thrifty Valley Oak will have a vase-shaped crown of ascending branches while the trunk is hidden more than half way to the ground by the downsweeping of recurved branches. At this time the whole tree is very twiggy and, in consequence, densely leafy. At one hundred years of age, and for the next two hundred, a Valley Oak is in the weeping stage. That means that from the branches there trail numerous long, whiplike or vinelike branchlets which sweep almost or quite to the grass, swaying in the valley's hot summer breeze with a gracious indolence. The tree has now attained its sturdiest yet most beguiling appearance. The last stage, when winter storms and decay have wracked and broken it, has been called second youth; the tree puts out a fresh effort and a polelike growth results, with short, straightish, half-erect branches.

That specimens of great size or historic interest should occur is only natural in such a long-lived tree whose preference it is to grow where man too best flourishes. Perhaps the first to become famous, at least among English-speaking Californians, was the Forty-niner's Tree, which gave the name to the community of Big Oak Flat, a flat being, in the vocabulary of the Sierra Nevada, a high mountain valley. This tree is said to have had a diameter of 11 feet and was so sacred to the Argonauts of Forty-nine that they passed a camp ordinance to protect it. Nevertheless they themselves destroyed it, according to the story, when their mining operations caused the land to slip, carrying the tree down with it. Not far beyond this tree, at the ghost town of Second Garotte, seven men were suspended, by the neck, from the Hangman's Oak, for having stolen placer gold from the sluice boxes.

The most famous Valley Oak of all is the mammoth Hooker Oak, near Chico, California, named in honor of Sir Joseph Hooker, the director of the Royal Gardens at Kew, England. In company with Asa Gray of Harvard, he visited this tree in 1877 as the guest of its owner, General Bidwell. Hooker pronounced it the largest Oak in the world, though we know now that it is not. Yet magnificent it is as it stands 110 feet high, has a trunk approximately 8 feet in diameter, and casts a pool of shade 150 feet across. Four titanic main limbs start forth not many feet above the base; each gives rise to a score of branches big enough to be a very fair-sized tree; some of these dip at their tips to the earth. Surrounded now by a beautifully landscaped park, this mighty spirit-tree is justifiably the pride of the city.

In contrast to the grand stature of the Valley Oak is the uselessness of its wood. To the disappointment of the pioneers, it proved worthless to them, not only for boards but even for small tools; it is hard but brittle; it is heavy but weak. Its sapwood is apt to be eaten out with the Oak-root rot, and it decays rapidly in contact with soil and water, so it is not good even for fence posts. In their disgust the early pioneers called it Mush Oak.

The acorns, however, meant a great deal to the California Indians. Frémont, in his famed Second Expedition of 1844, found "an Indian village, consisting of two or three huts; we had come upon them suddenly, and the people had evidently just run off. Their huts were low and slight, made like beehives in a picture, five or six feet high, and near each was a crate, formed of interlaced branches and grass, in size and shape like a very large hogshead. Each of these contained from six to nine bushels. These were filled with the long acorns already mentioned, and in the huts were several neatly made baskets, containing quantities of the acorns roasted. They were sweet and agreeably flavored, and we supplied ourselves with about half a bushel, leaving one of our shirts, a handkerchief, and some smaller articles in exchange."

Naturally many animals beside man eat the sweet acorns — the gray squirrel, for one, and the California woodpecker. An epicure for the mast of this tree is the band-tailed pigeon, a fine game bird now growing rare. If you are fortunate you may still see a flock of these beautiful creatures as they come, banking and wheeling, incredibly swift, through the groves, uttering their hoarse cry of *hoop-a-whoo*, their wings whistling like escaping steam, and their bodies gleaming in opal hues as they rock in their headlong flight. But if no band-tails appear, you will almost certainly see another handsome denizen of the Valley Oak groves — the yellow-billed magpie, forever swooping among the trees in its jet black, snow white, and metallic green, the individuals chasing each other about like boys at play, uttering their harsh *qua* or expressing unutterable things with tails so long they wag the bird.

The Valley Oak has many foes and is losing ground before them. The worst is man, although he has no use for its timber. For the Californian farmer clearly understands that Valley Oaks grow on the most arable land, level for plow and tractor, with rich soil and high water table. So this noble old tree has been cut and burned ruthlessly to make way for wheat and fruit. The California realtor and promoter makes unerringly for Valley Oak groves when he can, and indeed such groves are fine places for human habitation, shaded in summer but open to the sun in winter. Yet something always happens to the Oaks when residences appear. Many are cut down for house sites; others have their roots cut for water and sewer mains and gas lines whose inevitable leakage poisons the roots. Wells are sunk, lowering the water table beyond the reach of the deepest roots. Streams are diverted away, their waters conducted uselessly to the sea or expended on irrigation projects at some distant point. Too often the result is that, though one sees beautiful old Valley Oaks still surviving here and there where realty development goes on apace, as in the San Fernando Valley, there is no new growth coming on, and the loss of each old tree is irreplaceable.

Throughout the season this Oak presents a gentle drama which ever-green trees do not offer — the tender haze of color when leaves and cat-kins first appear, in late spring, the beauty of the long summer shade, which is not dim and stuffy like that in a dense growth of young Redwood, Douglas Fir, and Laurel, but luminous and breezy — letting in the light but not the full heat of day. The trees hold their leaves until December and never turn any gorgeous colors, but while the bare trunks and limbs in winter stand naked, their grand, male beauty of form comes out, the bark pale against the clouds filled with the promise of rain. These Oaks are very late to leaf out, despite the precocity and warmth of Californian springs. But this is advantageous, for, the winter's rains being over and gone, says the psalmist, the flowers appear on the earth. The bare boughs have let the sunlight freely through, and the dark loam absorbs its warmth swiftly. Then the year brings forth its sweetest children, those displays of wild flowers that are the singular pride of California. Acres of lavender lupine, close as the threads of a carpet, stretch between the benignant bare Oaks, away over dale and hill, drifted with the *nievatas* ("little snows" — a sort of white forget-me-not) and burning with the orange fire of the poppy. At such a moment one can behold California as it was in its primeval inno-cence and dignity, before tractor and realtor, fool's oat and filaree altered so much.

Coast Live Oak

Quercus agrifolia Née

OTHER NAMES: Encina, California Live Oak.

RANGE: Coast Ranges of California from Sonoma County south to Baja California, Mexico, from sea level (except in extreme southern California), up to 4500 feet altitude in the mountains above Santa Barbara and Pasadena, and in the San Jacinto Mountains.

T HE SPANIARDS' NAME for the Coast Live Oak was *encina,* the word given to the evergreen Oak or Ilex of the Mediterranean world, and the word persists today as a name for streets, suburbs, homes, estates, and ranches, throughout coastal California. Indeed, the Coast Live Oak was one of the two first trees of California to be described so clearly that we can recognize them. For specimens were collected in 1791 by the Malaspina Expedition, the first and only scientific reconnaissance which the Spanish government made in California. When the exploring ship was anchored in Monterey Bay, two officers went ashore and brought back with them a branch of the Coast Live Oak and another of the Valley Oak. These were turned over to the botanists of the expedition, who subsequently published scientific descriptions of leaf, flower, and

fruit, although they had never, apparently, been ashore to see the trees themselves. So they gave no idea of the magnificent form of this species, of its abundance, or the great role that it played in the lives of the Spanish Californians. All of which goes to show that the first publication of the scientific name of a tree may be a barren thing, while the true discovery of a tree is something that comes with the years.

When in 1770 that beloved founder of California's chain of missions, Padre Junípero Serra, landed at Monterey Bay, he planted his cross under a great Live Oak close to the shore, and here he said his first mass on the Monterey peninsula and founded San Carlos Mission. Later, in order to withdraw the young Indian girls from the covetous eyes of the Spanish soldiers, he moved his mission to its present site at Carmel. But that great Oak remained in the memory of all the old Montereyans as the first Christianized spot in that part of California, and succeeding generations venerated it as their most historic tree. Already ancient when Serra preached beneath it, it died branch by branch until only its stump was left; and when even that vanished it was replaced in 1896 by a monument.

Once again the Live Oak appears in the story of good Padre Serra when, soon after the Carmel Mission was begun, he set off with Fathers Miguel Pieras and Buenaventura Sitjar to establish, 25 leagues to the south, the Mission of San Antonio de Padua, in the foothills of the Santa Lucia Mountains. In a fine grove of Oaks, Father Serra caused the goods to be unpacked; among them were the bells of the unbuilt mission. These he caused to be suspended from a Live Oak, and the sight of them so excited him that he rang them in the liveliest manner, shouting, "Hear, O Gentiles! Come! Oh, come to the holy church of God! Come, oh come, and receive the faith of Christ!"* His companions protested that there was no one to hear, yet as Serra was saying mass, a redskin "Gentile" appeared, attracted by the bells. He remained through a sermon he did not understand, left loaded with presents, and returned bringing a crowd, with gifts of Pinyon nuts for the friars. Thus was this mission founded beneath the boughs of the Oaks.

In our own time the Coast Live Oak is the American tree best known all around the world, if not known by name. For no other is so often seen in motion pictures. Sometimes it serves as Sherwood Forest for the exploits of Robin Hood, again as Bagworthy Forest in *Lorna Doone,* or it is even made to pass as the woods which the Pilgrim Fathers faced around Plymouth! In a way, Robert Louis Stevenson foresaw all this when he described the twisted trunks, the tangled growth of Live Oaks around Monterey as "woods for murderers to crawl among."

Dramatic, romantic, pictorial, and picturesque (to choose but a few possible adjectives), the Coast Live Oak certainly is. For it seldom grows tall and straight; almost inevitably its trunks lean this way or that, its long sinuous branches twist and turn, and eventually with a downsweeping

*Fr. Zephyrine Engelhardt, *San Antonio de Padua, the Mission of the Sierras,* 1929.

gesture will come, in old trees, to reach the ground. So that every Coast Live Oak is an extreme individualist, utterly unlike every other in the world, and yet the sum and total of all its many variations adds up to a composite picture of ample grace, of grace combined with strength, that make it recognizable at a glance as distinct from any other tree within its natural range.

A fine old Live Oak is a leafy mansion, a spacious house of a tree. A grove of such, dotting the plains or filling a valley, or hanging with leaning trunks upon some Coast Range hillside, is always the most lovable and livable part of any scene in California reached by the sea breezes. Whenever he can, the Californian prefers to make his home beneath an old Live Oak's shade or in a grove of Oaks. When a Californian says "the woods" he usually means an Oak woodland, or at least a hardwood growth. When he says "the forest" he commonly means dense coniferous stands, timberland, usually found in the mountains.

On headlands swept by cold sea winds, the Coast Live Oak will be sculptured by the elemental forces into fantastic forms, or its boughs or even its trunks may writhe along the ground. On steep mountainsides, these trees may cling to the canyon like a living river of green. On the gentler hills, gently the trees conform to the waving contours and slopes. Upon a plain, the trees grow taller, interlocking their branches in a natural evergreen vault. Growing singly amidst the wild oats, the Live Oak expands to its full dimensions, a great circle, and something more than hemispherical in form.

A well-grown Coast Live Oak will reach 75 feet in height, but it is not in height that this tree impresses, but rather in its spread and girth. One tree measured in the Angeles National Forest had a spread of 130 feet, with a trunk more than 12 feet in diameter, and there may be others unmeasured even more majestic in proportions. The Napa Valley, in California's vineyard country, the Santa Clara Valley, the inner slopes of the Lompoc hills, and the Ojai Valley, are especially famed for the number and grandeur of their Coast Live Oaks. It was the beauty of the Live Oaks that first made the San Fernando Valley celebrated. Fame brought hundreds of thousands of settlers, and to give them living space a large part of the Oaks have been cut down!

The wood of the Coast Live Oak is moderately strong, hard and heavy, yet it has never furnished any considerable quantity of timber to the hardwood trade, owing to the eccentric growth and shortness of the main bole and the frequent habit of branching from near the base. Furthermore, large specimens, which theoretically should furnish considerable lumber, are apt to be partially hollow, owing to the attacks of termites and dry-rot. Yet in the early days of California, the crotches were valued for ship knees and other sorts of compass timber for marine construction. In one respect the wood is almost incomparably fine, and that is for fuel. There are only a few other trees, and almost none in the West, with the heat value of a cord of seasoned Live Oak. Its logs burn with an intense and steady flame, not throwing off sparks or exploding, but forming a lasting bed of coals and giving out a sweet and subtle odor.

As a result of its high fuel value, this wood was in great demand in the days of the sailing ships, and as these came in increasing numbers after the immigration from the eastern United States began, the Spanish Californians along the coast cut back their Live Oaks ever faster, in response to the tempting prices offered by the sailing vessels. In Santa Barbara, for instance, most of the plain between the old Presidio and the Santa Ynez Mountains was originally covered with magnificent Oaks above whose tops rose the towers of the old Mission, but faster than the growth of the town went on the selling of these delicious groves for fuel wood for the ships that anchored off the harborless port. In 1855 the Council enacted an ordinance prohibiting the cutting of trees or shrubs belonging to the city. But, as much of the wooded land was privately owned, the destruction went on apace, and in 1859 the *ayuntamiento* (city council) levied a tax for the benefit of the city treasury on the countless wagonloads of wood that went creaking toward the beach. Its original Oak groves swept away, the town of Santa Barbara is now replanted with exotic trees, and the noble Oak groves persist only in Mission Canyon, Montecito, and some of the hillsides of Hope Ranch.

A similar story could be told for California towns up and down the coast — first a reckless destruction of the trees, followed by a belated appreciation of the fact that, for homesites of the highest class, no showy Palm, no lofty Eucalyptus, no golden Acacia or flowery Jacaranda can take the place of the native Oaks. Unfortunately, the practice of diverting streams at their source for use in irrigation ditches, of sinking numberless wells, which lowers the natural water table in the soil, and the laying of drainage pipes have all combined to strike literally at the very roots of the Live Oak's life. Fine old trees are dying far sooner than they should, and seedlings, which have always played against long odds, are finding their chances of survival poorer and poorer. In no other part of the United

States are human population and building increasing so rapidly as in the range of the Coast Live Oaks. So that the future of this lovely tree is dark indeed, unless it is widely realized by home owners, real estate promoters, and town councils that every Oak is a precious asset.

Chinquapin Oak

Quercus Muehlenbergii Engelmann

OTHER NAMES: Yellow, Rock, Chinkapin, or Chestnut Oak.

RANGE: Western Vermont to the neighborhood of New York City, thence southwestward through the District of Columbia to western Virginia and southward to western Florida, west through southern Ohio, southern Michigan, to southeastern parts of Minnesota and Nebraska, eastern Kansas, and eastern Oklahoma. Absent from the Delta country of Louisiana, from most of Wisconsin except the Mississippi valley and most of the southern Appalachians.

N OBODY WILL EVER KNOW how many million cords of Chinquapin Oak logs were split by the Homeric strength of our pioneering heroes into snake rail fences in the Ohio valley. Eleven feet long, mauled from the clearest, straightest timber that the aboriginal forest had to offer, these rails developed the muscle of a hardy breed of boys, and fenced in the early farms of Kentucky, Ohio, and Indiana. But the generations pass, farms are abandoned, and fences left to fall. And when, in the great days of Ohio river boating, steamships were first sent down from Pittsburgh to New Orleans, it was discovered that these old rails of Chinquapin Oak (along with many other Oak and Hickory fences, of course) made the best obtainable fuel for the devouring engines of the steamboats. So farmers came to heap them in great piles on the shore for sale to the engineers, and stops to take on these rails of seasoned, completely combustible timber were as frequent and important as ever the stops at scheduled landings where goods and passengers waited. Liquid merchandise was commonly rolled onto the boat in barrels made of this same Oak, for though its pores look large, they are admirably plugged by nature and so proof against leakage. When the railways came chuffing to take away the business of the river boats, it was on ties of this strong, durable, shock-resistant wood that the first steel tracks were laid.

Unfortunately the Chinquapin Oak delights to grow on rich soil with a high water-table, so that it has been relentlessly pushed aside by the growth of Middle Western agriculture, and not so often now does one see a trunk 3 or 4 feet thick, and practically never trees that soar up 160 feet, as they did in the primeval forest. But still the traveler down the Ohio will admire the almost snow-white bark and, on a windy day, the fluttering of this Oak's lovely foliage, each crinkly blade handsome enough in itself, but superb in mass by the marked contrast of the dark and gleaming upper surface and the flashing white of the lower. Owing to the way the leaves hang upon the stalk, they are especially likely to flutter, almost as gaily as the Aspen's. When standing by itself the Chinquapin Oak often develops an immense number of shrubby forks after a height of about 20 feet, so that it has almost the vase-like shape of the White Elm — not so graceful, perhaps, but making of it a friendly tree in the pasture or the park.

CEDARS

Alaska Cedar

Chamæcyparis nootkatensis (D. Don) Spach

OTHER NAMES: Yellow Cedar. Yellow, Nootka, Alaska, or Sitka Cypress.

RANGE: From sea level on the Islands of Prince William Sound, Alaska, up to 3000 feet altitude on the Coast Ranges of British Columbia, and south along the Cascade Range to the mountains of Siskiyou County in northern California.

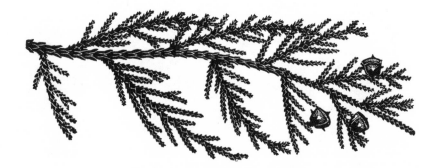

T HE ALASKA CEDAR can be one of the most beautiful yet most sorrowful of western conifers. Its long, lithe leader shoot bows its head — sometimes bent nearly double in a young tree — and its dull, dark bluish green foliage is evergreen for two years, then turns a rusty brown. The dead foliage is not shed, however, for another year, leaving the whole tree more or less tinged with the hue that, for vegetable life, is the color of mourning. The great, long lower boughs of trees grown in the open sweep deeply down, till they may touch the ground, then lift in a wide upward curve with a majestic gesture, but from the branches the twigs swing pendent, and from the very long whiplike twigs the flat sprays of foliage droop so persistently that they appear almost wilted. So the whole tree has something of a weeping habit, though not in the exaggerated form of a Weeping Willow. Rather does it look, even in summer, as if it were weighted with snows.

And indeed in the islands off the coast of British Columbia where Alaska Cedar attains its greatest size — 90 to 150 feet — the snowfall is very heavy, and so is the rainfall. Where the tree grows in mountainous situations the winds and the ice loads break it mercilessly, and it loses the beautiful symmetry seen in more protected spots and is frequently more dead than alive — one of the least attractive trees among all conifers. Or it may, near timber line, sprawl ignominiously along the ground.

The growth of the Alaska Cedar is often very slow. Two centuries may elapse before a tree reaches saw-timber size, that is, with a trunk 15 to 20 inches in diameter. Only in infrequent years, and at irregular intervals, is a good crop of seeds produced. Slipping from the cones, in the autumn gales, they glide far on their little wings, but probably the number that struggle through to success is not great.

Much of the standing timber of this tree is found in country too rough and inaccessible for lumbering, but where it can be profitably cut it is eagerly sought and exported as far as Japan. What may be the toll of the lumber industry upon this tree is not definitely known, for though the lumberman does distinguish it by name — he prefers Yellow Cedar as its title — he seldom lists it separately in statistics. The wood is certainly a fine one, probably the hardest of all trees rejoicing in the loosely given name of Cedar, and the grain straight and so regular that it takes the highest polish. It is also sweetly, resinously aromatic and highly resistant to decay; logs that have lain for decades in the forest are perfectly sound under the green winding sheet of moss.

The handsome yellow boards work up into furniture and interior finish of high quality. For boat building this is a first-class wood in decking, railing, and interior paneling. It makes a fine wood for pattern blocks. Because it is both a very light and very stiff wood (one of the rarest of combinations), and wears smoother, not rougher, with use, it was from prehistoric times the favorite material for the making of those paddles by which the Indians of the Northwest coast propelled their famous canoes of Western Red Cedar, as the Haidas, Tlingits, and Tsimshians pursued the sea otter, the sea lion, and the seal, or carried war to the very gates of Old Sitka in the days of the cruel Russian *promyshlenniks.* From its trunks they also cut their ceremonial masks, highly colored and often inlaid with copper and abalone shell to represent teeth that could be made to snap and eyes that could be made to roll — to the mingled terror and delight of beholders.

Like its relative the Port Orford Cedar, the Alaska Cedar in cultivation has produced a large number of handsome or far-fetched forms, some of them sold by nurserymen under the name of Retinospora. So this tree, one of the less-known, least domestic of all the trees of the Northwest, has made its way around the world as a garden pet, proving hardy in England and the eastern United States.

Port Orford Cedar

Chamæcyparis lawsoniana (A. Murray) Parlatore

OTHER NAMES : White or Oregon Cedar. Lawson Cypress. Ginger Pine.

RANGE : From Coos Bay, southwestern Oregon, south along the Pacific coast, ranging inland about 30 miles, to the mouth of the Klamath River, northern California; inland, also, on the Siskiyou Mountains of Oregon and California, and around the headwaters of the Sacramento River, south of Mount Shasta.

SHINING AND GRACIOUS IN YOUTH, gigantic and glorious in age, possessed of a fragrant wood of great beauty and scores of the most valuable uses, the Port Orford Cedar has but one defect with which it can be reproached: there isn't — and never has been — enough of it!

Even under aboriginal conditions it was not exactly a plentiful tree, confined as it always was to a rather small range, from Coos Bay, on the Oregon coast, south to the rugged Siskiyou Mountains of northern California, with a few stations around the head of the Sacramento River. Even then it was by no means continuous over that range, occurring only in a

spotty way. Yet sometimes the virgin growth was very dense, and the trees, towering up to 175 or even 200 feet in height, with 150 feet of the trunk clear of branches, produced sometimes as much as 100,000 board feet of high-grade lumber to the acre. Estimates place the total stand of the original growth at 4 billion board feet, which sounds like a lot until we compare it with the existing stands of other lumber trees. The Western Yellow Pine, for instance, is even today forty-five times as abundant as the entire aboriginal stand of Port Orford Cedar.

But from the first discovery of the big stands of this timber in 1855, man and fire have assaulted it relentlessly. A disastrous fire in the Coos Bay region at an early date wiped out a vast but undetermined amount. Next, sawmills were at work, and schooners were anchoring off the rocky, harborless coast to be loaded with Cedar logs carried by a high line from the cliffs to the decks.

The demand for Port Orford Cedar, as soon as it became known in eastern and foreign markets, grew swiftly and remained steady. For it is scarcely excelled in the manufacture of venetian-blind slats, mine timbers, railway ties, and millwork. Its gingerlike odor is reputed to be repellent to moths, so that it has gone into the making of clothes chests and presses. Because it is resistant to acids, it has been used for storage battery separators. Latterly it has been in demand for plywood for aircraft construction and for veneer generally. From the first it was valued in boat building; Sir Thomas Lipton ordered all his cup-challenger yachts built of Port Orford Cedar.

The wood is light in color — elegantly so — and takes well both a high polish and stains and paints. For this reason it has become a cabinet wood, which can be finished in imitation of Mahogany, Oak, and other precious woods. In its own right it early began to enjoy a reputation as a casket wood, not so much in its native land as in far-off Cathay and Nippon. Its lightness, its satiny texture when finished, its pungent odor compared by some to ginger, by some to roses, and the fact that it ranks, in contact with the soil, with the most durable of all woods, singles this Cedar out for a casket wood, and when we reflect that — according at least to a solemn tradition among small boys — a Celestial dies every time you draw a breath, one can see that the Oriental market for Port Orford Cedar would be high. Sometimes one wonders if there is not almost as much of it underground in Asia as there is above ground here.

For the mills have eaten and eaten into the limited supply, spurred on by a rising market, until today the stumpage price of this tree exceeds that of every other wood in Oregon, our greatest lumber state. Oregon coast towns such as Coquille, Marshfield, North Bend, Bandon, Parkersburg, and Port Orford itself became for a time at least booming lumber towns, which also specialized in the building of all-Cedar ships. On the streets of these settlements mingled the roistering lumberjacks, shipbuilders, dockhands, sailors from many strange ports, coal miners from the Marshfield beds, and, for many years, the inevitable pigtailed coolie whose memory is preserved only in the Chinese cemetery on Marshfield's Telegraph Hill.

Some of the above settlements have now become ghost towns, or nearly so, for they cut themselves out of all reason for existence by laying waste the Cedar without thought to the future. Others have prospered as they diversified their interests. For Bandon, once known as the prettiest town in Oregon, a special fate was reserved. It was founded by Lord George Bennet, an Irish peer, who made things more homelike, in the 1870s , by naturalizing the Irish furze or gorse, and as the majestic stands of Cedar were cleared away, it took hold in fine style on the logged-over lands and was much admired, in spite of its thorns, for its golden pealike flowers. By 1936 Bandon was a pretty beach resort at the mouth of the Coquille River surrounded by a sea of gorse, and on the hot dry night of September 26 much of the population was at the motion-picture theater seeing a film prophetically titled *Thirty-six Hours to Live*. Suddenly on the edge of town there was a flash of flame like an explosion. The tinder-dry gorse caught fire for miles around in a matter of a few moments, and a sea of flames 30 feet high rolled toward the town. Fireproof buildings burned like berry crates. The loss of life and homes was so appalling that one scarcely cares to mention what had happened to the precious resource of the Port Orford Cedar. It wiped out thousands of acres of second growth of this species and probably blasted all hopes of restocking many more acres, though it did not reach the old growth or virgin stands.

But logging, there, has proved the equal of the worst crown fires. The stand of merchantable Port Orford Cedar had sunk to 1.14 billion board feet in 1938, and in nine years of further cutting the figure has dropped to 745 million board feet. The virgin timber cannot last more than a quarter century at the present rate of cut. Second growth, what there is of it, is the only hope.

In 1938, the Forest Service set aside the Port Orford Cedar Experimental Forest, on the South Fork of the Coquille River, for purposes of regeneration and practical forestry. The tract is so situated that it will be safe from inroads of fire and logging. And well it is that this should be so. Today 69 percent of this precious timber is in private ownership, which means that its destiny is the saw mill whenever the stumpage price is attractive enough to the land owners, while 15 percent is held on the Oregon and California Railway revested grant lands managed by the Department of the Interior. Only 16 percent is in the hands of Forest Service. Very small tracts are owned as parks by the state of Oregon.

The best way to see this tree of almost legendary fame is to follow U.S. Highway 101 between Reedsport and Gold Beach, Oregon, where the Pacific comes rolling in with heavy thundering surges, pushing foam castles up the black sand of the beaches, shooting up in geysers against the isolated stack rocks, and sending its cold briny breath deep into the forest. Grand Firs, mighty Douglas Firs, Sitka Spruce, and waving Hemlocks march down from the Coast Ranges to the steep-pitched meadows — brief carpets of sunlight and flowering that end at the ocean cliffs. And here, along the roadsides and on the steep wooded hills, rises a tree that you may take at first for Western Red Cedar, so alike are the two in their flat sprays of foliage. But Western Red or Canoe Cedar (Arborvitae to the garden minded) has the foliage shining yellow green on the upper surface, dull green below. Port Orford Cedar, which is notably finer, thinner, and in every way more ferny of frond, is a dull blue green above and often flecked with a frosty whiteness below. In young trees, or trees grown in the open, the limber, zigzag branches clothe the specimen to the base. But the forest monarch, which may have lived six hundred years, will have an awesomely long, straight trunk covered with a soft, fibrous, fluted bark, and a very narrow crown of branches which droops with a grand but sorrowful gesture.

By exploring in your car up many roads — the more unpromising the better — you may find at last some limited grove of ancients, whose lonely isolation tells the story of their vanished monarchy. And you will want to cut a twig just to smell that spicy odor, one of the strongest and most lingering given out by any commercial wood — the odor that, in the old sailing schooners that bore the fresh-cut Cedar across the Pacific, grew and grew upon the sailors till they were almost mad with it.

Though always on the rare side in the wild, and growing steadily rarer, this tree, under the horticultural name of Lawson Cypress, is widespread in the gardens of the world, partly for its natural beauty, and partly for another sort that to a forester at least is more or less unnatural. For this, like all the six species of *Chamæcyparis,* is given to the production, under cultivation, of freaks, sports, and showy variations such as never exist in the wild. Eighty such have been described for Lawson Cypress — forms with silver-tipped or golden-tipped foliage, and columnar forms, sprawling forms, weeping forms, glaucous forms, blue forms, glittering forms — bearing such over-dressed Latin names as *elegantissima* and *erecta glauca.* More, this and other species of *Chamæcyparis* sometimes produce in the seedling stage abnormal needle foliage something like that of a Balsam Fir or Yew, and if offsets of these freaks are propagated, they continue to produce throughout life this abnormal showy foliage. When this is combined with, for instance, a dwarf but narrowly conical and compact habit, the ultimate in artificiality is obtained, and under the name of Retinospora (which is more gardener's Latin and not a recognized botanical genus), such plants are dearly beloved by the architect. For they look formal and expensive against the stone walls of a fashionable church or outside a city mansion. But a Port Orford Cedar springing straight and aboriginal from the wild Oregon soil is a nobler sight to anyone who loves a tree as God made it.

Canoe Cedar

Thuja plicata Donn ex D. Don*

OTHER NAMES: Giant or Western Red Cedar. Shinglewood. Arborvitae.

RANGE: Maritime Alaska (from Portage Bay south), in British Columbia on sea slopes of the Coast Ranges and inland, on the southern Selkirk and Gold mountains, up to 6000 feet altitude; in Washington on the Olympics to 4000 feet, on the west slopes of the Cascades from sea level to 4000 feet, and on the Canadian Rockies from Alberta and eastern British Columbia south to the Bitterroots of Idaho and Montana, at 2000 to 7000 feet above sea level, and south through the Coast Ranges of Oregon and the west slopes of the Cascades to Crater Lake up to 7500 feet above sea level, and in the fog belt of California (Del Norte and Humboldt counties).

O N A JUNE DAY IN 1805, near Armstead, Montana, the Lewis and Clark expedition buried the boats in which they had come, against the relentless current of the Missouri, a thousand toilsome miles and more. Now began their crossing of the continental divide, their goods packed upon the horses purchased from the Shoshones. Then they must find a navigable stream, on the westward slope where so many are unnavigable and perilous, that would carry them in boats down to the great Columbia and so to their goal, the shores of the Pacific. And near that stream, to build those boats, they must find growing a tree fit for the purpose.

To make the needed pirogue or dugout, such a tree must be of great size, big enough to carry not only men but food, trading goods, and all sorts of equipment. Its wood must be the lightest possible, for buoyancy and ease of portage around the rapids. It must, since they had but simple tools with them, be soft in texture, straight grained, with easy splitting qualities. And it must not decay in water. Lewis and Clark could not know of any such tree awaiting them, for no white man at that date knew anything of the sylva of the wilderness which we now call northern Idaho. Yet the success of the expedition depended on such a tree; already destiny had provided the passes, the Shoshones with their pack horses, and, most marvelously, the Indian girl Sacajawea, found a thousand miles from her

---

*Editor's note: Formerly *Thuja plicata* D. Don.

birthplace at the moment they needed her most, to become their loyal and dauntless guide.

And now, as the hungry and exhausted men toiled through the gigantic jackstraw timbers of Idaho's primeval forests, the captains sighted, on September 20, "an Arbor-vitae" — one they noted as "very common and grows to a great size, being from two to six feet in diameter." Next day their journal remarks that "the arbor vitae increases in size and quantity as we advance," down toward the open valleys of the Clearwater. So on the twenty-fifth William Clark, with the Nez Percé chief Twisted Hair, set out to find a promising grove of this new great tree. Near the present town of Orofino, Idaho, he located his boat timber, and here the party felled the trees whose stumps were still pointed out as late as 1900. With fire, mallet, and crude chisel, they fashioned four large pirogues and a smaller one, "to spy ahead." And on the morning of October 7, the fateful and illustrious band set out upon the last stage of the outward journey, downstream to the Pacific, borne in the great boles of the Giant Canoe Cedar, which lumbermen today call the Western Red Cedar.

Those virgin forest conditions produced in this Cedar enormous trunks such as we see today too seldom; in the early days trees were known as tall as 200 feet. But the lumbermen have left us a small race, and a specimen now regarded as a challenger is one near Lake Quinault, in Olympic National Park, which has a circumference of 62 feet and 8 inches, above the immensely greater base, all swollen and buttressed and fluted as it is. In general, trees with trunks 8 to 10 feet in diameter are considered large, in our times, while a trunk with a 3-foot diameter is mature merchantable timber, in the eyes of the lumberman. If the tree grows too old, its magnificent proportions are, for the logging foreman's purposes, too apt to be spoiled by a decayed heart inside the shell of the bark with its ruddy armor of long, twisted fibrous strips.

But the camper, the hiker, the motorist, the tourist who explores coastal British Columbia and southeastern Alaska by boat does not view the Canoe Cedar in terms of board feet. To him it is a tree of the utmost grandeur, its boughs sweeping from the narrowly conical crown nearly to the ground (for even in dense stands the lower limbs are not always self-pruned by reduced light but may be held tenaciously). Young limbs lift upward joyfully; old ones spread downward and outward with majestic benevolence. And over all glitters the lacy foliage in flat sprays that are forked and forked again, drooping parted, like the mane of a horse, from the axis of the branchlet in a gesture of strong grace.

On Vancouver Island the Canoe Cedar reaches its greatest dimensions — so gigantic, even in our day, that they place it among the greatest conifers of the world. But on the Queen Charlotte Islands, on the Olympic peninsula and all around Puget Sound, on the mainland of British Columbia and on the islands and along the fjords of southern Alaska, the Canoe Cedar is scarcely less imposing. And it was there, where the mountains fall precipitously to the sea, where the glaciers glitter on the mountain flanks, and somber forests of Hemlock, Spruce, Fir, Cypress, and Cedar march down to the very shore, that from ancient times there dwelt the Indian tribes who raised the famed totem poles, carved of trunks of the Canoe Cedar. And all the intercommunication of the villages of these tribes — the Tlingits, Haidas, and Tsimshians who were never conquered by the cruel Russians — was in canoes of Cedar. No other Indians ever exhibited such artistic skill and technical mastery in woodworking of all sorts as these, and indeed it is said that the canoe reached its highest expression among these peoples. Their family canoes were from 20 to 25 feet long, fit to transport a whole household, complete with provisions and gear and trading supplies, a load that might comprise two tons. Even longer and stronger, yet still carved from a single trunk, were the voyaging canoes, sometimes as much as 65 feet in length, bearing three masts and sails and a mainstay sail, and capable of carrying some thirty or forty people. So wondrous were these craft, so perfect in their lines, that — tradition states — models were carried away by the Yankee sailing masters of the late eighteenth century, and these furnished to the designers of the Boston and Salem clippers the lines of the fastest and fairest American ships ever moved by the wind.

Of Cedar wood these warlike people made helmets, dagger handles, bows, arrow shafts, and spear poles. Chieftains' carven batons, medicine men's rattles, and carved and painted household boxes were all fashioned from this beautiful wood that splits so easily and evenly, and takes color so well. The coast Indians built their potlatch houses (feasting halls) of Cedar uprights and stringers lashed together with bark of the same tree. Rough Cedar planks were hewn out laboriously for the sidings of the house.

But it was into their totem poles that these proud people poured their artistic genius. The Indian artist, before the white man brought him steel tools, worked with cutting edges of jadeite and shell, yet he was able to achieve anything he desired in representation. If the legends and figures to be represented were many, he had to solve the complex problem of superimposing them. He did so with ingenious skill, and so clever are his simulations that the straight beak of the raven, the curved hook of the owl's beak, the shaggy hide of the bear, the springing legs of the frog are perfectly recognizable. The totem carver worked from no preliminary model; like the Greek sculptors of old he carried the whole design in his head and attacked his materials directly with his tools. The fine marks of those tools give to the old genuine totemic wood much of its vigor and texture; only in spurious modern imitations is there a smooth surface.

Many carvers achieved great reputations, remembered long after their deaths; they traveled from village to village, accepting commissions, and their fees were so great that a family frequently ruined itself to pay a famous artist. For the totem pole was not merely a form of genealogy and heraldry; it was frequently a funereal monument and might enclose in its base the sacred ashes of ancestors. Further, it embodied what the Indian considered history — not politics and war but such matters as the origin of the world and of mankind. Humor of a sort was not lacking in some of these columns; thus if a man owed another a debt that was not collected, a special pole would be erected by the creditor to tell the world about it in mocking symbolism, and this would continue to taunt the defaulting neighbor till the debt was paid. As a form of receipt, the creditor then destroyed the pole.

The prehistoric Cedar poles were comparatively small affairs because the cost of carving a huge tree with primitive implements would have been prohibitive. Metal axes, saws, drawknives, froes, and other European implements changed all this, and in the nineteenth century the Indian artists were able to produce gigantic poles that dwarfed their villages. But this was the burst of glory before the end. The same outside influences that brought the tools of a more advanced technology brought disruption

233

and decimation to the coast Indians. Alcohol, smallpox, and venereal diseases rotted the magnificent physique of these great peoples; a taste for the white man's luxuries caused a neglect of their tribal arts. And education under the missionaries turned many earnest red souls against the ancestral religion. They began to pull down and destroy their totemic columns, or to turn out debased and insincere imitations, colored gaudily with modern commercial paints, for the tourist trade. Whole villages were abandoned when families sought employment in the white man's settlements, and under the tremendous rainfall of the coastal area, the poles began to molder away, just as the very memory of the carving art and the knowledge of its religious symbolism faded in the Indians' minds. One hundred and twenty-five poles were counted, in 1916, by a visitor to the deserted village of Tuxekan, and fewer than half were sufficiently preserved to be worth moving.

Then the Forest Service began to undertake the restoration of the vanishing art. Aged men who had been apprentices to master carvers in boyhood were found and set to work; their assistants were teenaged Indian boys who showed a marvelous aptitude for learning, though they had never handled a stone adz before. For only the primitive tools were used, only the original dyes, derived from native roots, berries, ferns, clays, and ores. The ancient legends were again collected, the ruined models pieced together and studied, and finally Saxman Totem Park was established near Ketchikan, Alaska, where more than fifty reproductions of authentic poles preserve in Cedar wood the art and history of the gifted coast tribes.

And much of the life of those tribes, from their beginning, was braided with the life of the Canoe Cedar. The fiber of its inner bark furnished them with their chief textile and cordage materials — sufficient indeed for everything in their lives. Their blankets and clothing were composed of twisted twine or cord of Cedar bark fiber for the warp, while the woof was worsted spun from the wool of the mountain goat and dyed with brown, yellow, black, and white, to make superb totemic patterns. Woven hats of Cedar bark fiber, shawls and girdles of the same material added to the costumes of men and women. Rope was regularly made from Cedar bark and provided (in default of nails or, rather, superior to any nails) the lashings that joined pieces of wood in all sorts of construction. Cordage of Cedar bark made the dip nets and drag nets of these great fishermen, and their women wove it into bags and baskets for every use.

The white man has found so many uses of his own for the Western Red

Cedar as to place it among the six premier coniferous woods of North America, and probably among the dozen greatest timber trees of the world in quantity cut, while in the more intangible matter of quality it is equally high. The only serious defect of Red Cedar is that it is not strong enough for heavy usage, but for house construction it is quite sufficient. It has a beautiful soft, close, straight-grained texture, making it a joy to work with the plane, and finishes to a satiny smooth surface. It takes and holds enamels, paints, and stains with the half-dozen best of lumbers and has superior gluing qualities for the production of laminated wood. A natural preservative oil in the heartwood makes it immune to decay to an unexcelled degree, without the use of artificial preservatives. It is thus superfluous to paint Cedar to preserve it from rot, for even under severe climatic conditions it does not deteriorate when left in a natural state. The coloring is extremely attractive, the almost pure white sapwood contrasting beautifully with the dark reddish brown to yellowish heartwood. When weathered by the elements, Red Cedar turns to a driftwood gray.

In the Pacific Northwest, this is a favorite wood for home building, and indeed it is exported to every state in the Union, partly on account of its freedom from the pitch that makes Pine such a "hot" wood to live with, and so inflammable, and partly because it is among the lightest of all lumber when dried, and hence inexpensive to ship by rail. For mountain cabins, motor lodges, and the like, knotty Cedar makes a handsome rustic interior finish, but more elegant effects are produced by clear lumber. The rich yet cheerful and varied color, the exquisite surface, the attractive figures of its flat-grain finish make it as charming a panel wood for bedroom, dining room, or library as one could ask. As siding for the exterior of the house, as molding, door, and window stock, its popularity is immense, and thus it has frequently taken the place of the old Eastern White Pine in the construction of frame houses. One of its attractive properties in home building is its insulating qualities when used for shingles, roof boards, subflooring, siding, and sheathing; it tends to keep the house cool in summer and warm in winter.

The famed durability of Western Red Cedar makes it a wood of the first class for flumes and mud sills and tanks, for barn boards and feed platforms, greenhouse wood, hotbeds, and nursery equipment in general — all of which are constantly exposed to changing weathers, to water, soil, and all the seeds of decay. Beehives are often built of Red Cedar, and silo doors, fence posts, well curbing, and stop gates. Because of its lightness and resistance to water decay, Red Cedar is claimed, by its promoters, as the world's foremost material for boat construction, from the college team's racing shells to the millionaire's pleasure cruiser.

Everyone knows something about the heartwood of this magnificent tree — whether he knows it by name or not, he has tested its weight or, rather, its lightness; he has seen its characteristic dark ruddy color and smelled its delicious odor; he has fingered its soft, coarse grain, its ready splitting properties and has often harkened to its characteristic pitch and timbre — when raindrops play upon it. For it is the leading shingle material of the United States, probably of the world. In America, 80 percent of all shingles are made of Western Red Cedar. The large size of Red Cedar shingles, their freedom from knots, their fine straight grain make them incomparable. On the score of durability they are equally satisfactory. On San Juan Island in Puget Sound, the roof of a house built in 1856 was covered with Red Cedar shingles which were still intact in 1916.

The introduction of the shingle-sawing machine has speeded production and correspondingly reduced the price, turning out the excellent commercial thin-tipped, thick-butted shingle in lengths of 16, 18, and 24 inches, ½ inch thick at the butt, and 4 inches wide or more as desired. Shingles are sold in bundles of about 250, and four bundles are enough to cover 100 square feet. An ingenious machine buncher speeds the process of modern production still further, and a good "shingle weaver" can pack eighty thousand a day. But hand-riven shakes, such as our ancestors knew, have never gone completely out of fashion, and, if you can afford them, they give a roof an individual and handwrought appearance that is not to be expected of any machine-made product.

The Northwest shake maker is a very specialized artisan, almost an artist. His tools are ax, saw, and froe or splitting blade, and his raw materials are usually salvaged from logging operations — old ones more than new, because old-time loggers were more wasteful and left more good wood and high stumps. Usually the shake maker builds himself a cabin in the midst of the big-butted stumps, and there he is likely (since he generally is an old man) to find enough shingle wood to work on the rest of his life. If he has a family, his sons help, and their wives and sisters tie the shakes into bundles. First, logs are sawn and then split into bolts of a size easy to handle and are trucked to the shed where the work can go on under all weathers. The shake maker's implement, the froe, is perhaps the only hand tool that has not been changed through the centuries from the original model. It is a blade 14 to 20 inches long, and 3 inches wide, the butt end terminating in a metal ring or eye through which passes a wooden handle. The bolt of wood to be split is stood on end on a block, the froe is placed a half-inch from the edge of the bolt, and then the handle of the froe, which is held firm in the right hand, is struck a blow on the butt by a club of Vine Maple, held in the left hand. The blade bites into the Cedar and a shake is neatly split off along the grain. Rough defects are then trimmed off, usually by womenfolk. Then, when he has a truckfull of shakes, the artisan drives to the local lumber yard and sells for cash. With it he buys a twist of strong chewing tobacco, a supply of black-eyed peas, some kitchenware and fixins for his wife, and then returns happily to his stumps and froe, content in his life, which is that of a specialist who earns little, perhaps, but is not replaceable by more ambitious men.

Incense Cedar
Calocedrus decurrens (Torrey) Florin*

OTHER NAMES: White, Bastard, or California Post Cedar.

RANGE: Both east and west slopes of the Cascade Range in Oregon, from the foothills to 6600 feet, and south through the Sierra Nevada, and Coast Ranges of California (3000 to 9700 feet) to the Sierra San Pedro Mártir in Baja California. Also in Washoe County, Nevada.

MANY A PERSON WHO COMES to the Sierra Nevada looking for his first sight of the Giant Sequoia, or California Bigtree, is likely to think he has seen one when he first beholds the Incense Cedar. For it has a ruddy, thick, and deeply furrowed bark, a ponderous and heavily buttressed and fluted trunk, and a lofty carriage such as we have learned, from pictures and descriptions, to associate with the mighty Sequoia. More, both trees have scaly leaves that closely overlap upon the twigs. But much as the two trees resemble each other, and closely as they are related, they must not, need not, be confused.

*Editor's note: Formerly *Libocedrus decurrens* Torrey.

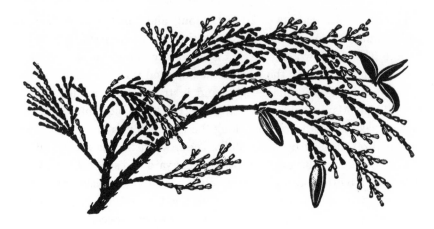

In the first place, the Bigtree is seldom found below 4000 feet above sea level. The Incense Cedar is found all the way down to the western foothills of the Sierra Nevada — with the Gray Pines in the old Gold Rush country. Nor does it form groves, as Bigtrees do, but occurs scattered among the Pines. The bark is a rich, bright cinnamon red, not a reddish brown like the Sequoia's. Thick though it is, the bark is much less massive than that of its gigantic brother; it is more stringy, less spongy; its furrows are far narrower and its ridges too. An Incense Cedar may live a thousand years, exceptionally, and grow to be 150 feet high, but never will it endure three thousand winters, or tower up 300 feet. Once you have seen a genuine Giant Sequoia, you will never again mistake an Incense Cedar for it.

The comparison, of course, is all against the Incense Cedar, when it comes to majesty and hoary age. But it is not fair to compare anything with a Sequoia, which is a god among trees. Judged by ordinary mortal standards, Incense Cedar is a splendid species, with its flat sprays of foliage which reflect the clear Sierra sunlight, its colorful trunks, its limber boughs full of grace. In youth it forms a strictly tapered crown from the broad base to the slender spirelike top, the lower branches sweeping downward in ample curves, the topmost ascending sharply to form a feathery tip. The years and the centuries change the grace of youth for a craggy strength, with irregular big boughs starting out at right angles from the trunk and then sending forth, as if from bent elbows, short ascending branches. The crown becomes broken — perhaps even dead at the tip — but only gains in picturesqueness thereby. Of the "plumes" of an Incense Cedar's foliage, John Muir says: "No waving fern-frond in shady dell is more unreservedly beautiful in form and texture, or half so inspiring in color and spicy fragrance. In its prime, the whole tree is thatched with them, so that they shed off rain and snow like a roof, making fine mansions for storm-bound birds and mountaineers."*

"In the fall," writes Mary Tresidder,† "the edges of the flat sprays are picked out with the immature green pollen buds, like the old-fashioned scalloped edges of embroidery we used to do. Then in December these pollen cones ripen and shed their golden pollen, and many of the local inhabitants have attacks of hay fever and long for the first storm to settle the pollen dust." The little pale green female flowers appear on the tips of last season's growth. Then, in the late summer, the flowers having been fertilized, the slim cylindrical cones hang gracefully from the tips of the branchlets, each scale enclosing one or two tiny seeds that go sailing away on the September winds. Highly tolerant of shade or sun, the seedlings spring up abundantly. In spite of fire dangers and dry-rot, a prevalent disease, this species seems able to stay on top of any perils and hardships in its life, for it is holding its own well, at least in the national forests and parks. On the floor of the Yosemite Valley it is, with Yellow Pine, a dominant species, whose hosts, at once so virile and so smiling, shine in every prospect. Even to remember them, from afar, is to see again the wind-blown tresses of Bridalveil Fall, to hear the clamor, half harsh, half sweet, of the jays, smell the tang of the dry exciting air, the incense-laden breath of this lovely tree.

Abundant though this Cedar is on federal lands, it has, on privately owned holdings, been exploited for almost a century, though never lumbered separately but only in connection with general cutting of conifers. The remaining stand is estimated at 9.7 billion board feet. During the war years from 1940 to 1943 the cut reached a peak of 30 million board feet a year. From the durable wood are turned out door and window frames, because of its lightness and the quiescence of the wood once it is well seasoned; it is cut for cedar chests on account of its odor, for shingles and railway ties because of its great durability. And, from the earliest settlement of the Great Central Valley of California, it has been employed for fence posts in large quantity. Unfortunately the post industry rejects the creamy sapwood, which may constitute more than half the woody cylinder, leaving it to waste and rot, for only the long-lived heartwood is acceptable to the trade.

When the commercial supply of pencil wood from Eastern Red Cedar

*The Mountains of California.
†The Sierra Nevada.

came to an end, half a century ago, it was to the Incense Cedar that the pencil makers principally turned. The western tree has all the needed properties for a good pencil wood; it is soft but not too splitty and can be sharpened in any direction with equal ease. Voracious though the demand for pencils, the Incense Cedar can probably stand up under the assault. The actual lumbering operations are on a small scale. Pencil trees are usually selected and felled singly by farmers and other landowners. The log is then cut into sizes that are later reduced to pencil blocks 7¼ inches long, ³⁄₁₆ of an inch thick and 2⅝ inches wide. From this, seven pencils of standard size can be struck out at the factory where the blocks are surfaced and grooved on one side, the graphite leads then inserted in the grooves between two blocks, and the pair glued together. Then the blocks are slit between the grooves and turned, polished, and painted as desired.

Monterey Cypress

Cupressus macrocarpa Hartweg ex Gordon*

RANGE: Known in native growth only on the sea coast at Carmel, California, in two groves, at Cypress Point and Point Lobos. Widespread in cultivation.

THE MOST SPECTACULAR BEAUTY on all the coast of California is the rocky, forest-clad shore that winds between Monterey and Point Lobos, including Pebble Beach, Cypress Point, and Carmel. To the south rise the grand Santa Lucia Mountains, bearing their Redwoods and Firs and plunging in fearsome cliffs into the sea. To the north, Monterey Bay curves gracefully off to the misty Santa Clara coast. Now the fogs roll in dramatically, pouring through the forest aisles like wraiths hurrying to Judgment, while the foghorns blow a raucous Gabriel trump, the buoys toll as if for drowned mariners, the surf thunders hollowly, and the bellowing of the sea lions on their island rocks is a savage Cerberus barking. And now the fog lifts, the sun bursts out on silken blue sea and curdy rollers, the pungency of pine and sage is steeped from the hillsides, the white-crowned sparrows' *sirr-sweet-see* rises drowsily where they sway upon grass stalk and golden poppy. Soft and ancient sound the bells of

*Editor's note: Formerly *Cupressus macrocarpa* Hartweg.

weathered old Carmel Mission where lies buried Padre Junípero Serra, the first of white men to love this spot and plant the Cross upon its shores.

In this romantic setting, and only here — always within half a mile of high tide, and along a few winding miles of shoreline — grows natively the Monterey Cypress, perhaps the rarest, certainly the most fantastic tree of North America. This species is in fact confined to two groves, the one at Cypress Point north of Carmel, and the other at Point Lobos State Park, just south of it. The number of individual trees in them has been rather precisely estimated by Harry Ashland Green who found (in 1929) that there were 7850 trees in the main grove at Cypress Point and 2700 in the strip of shoreline along the Seventeen Mile Drive through Pebble Beach.* The other grove at Point Lobos is much smaller and contains far fewer trees. Yet from these two stands have descended all the specimens, running into untold numbers, which are now grown in Europe, Australia, New Zealand, and South America, as well as up and down the coast of California in every garden and city park, and on many a ranch where this tree forms, with its intricate growth and adaptability to pruning, a solid windbreak to protect the precious citrus crop.

But a Monterey Cypress cultivated away from its spray-bitten native cliffs is but a tamed thing, fast growing, obedient to the gardener's will, and handsome, though not superior to other Cypresses. It is indeed so far from the bewitched forms of the wild tree as not to be recognized as the same species by anyone but a specialist. For it is the sea wind and the salt spray and the close, colonial habit of a Cypress wood's growth that account for all these fantasies in form comparable only with the tortured

*Madroño 1:197–98, 1929.

shapes of trees at timber line, or with that style in Japanese gardening by
which trees, after years of being deliberately pot-bound, bud-nipped, and
otherwise mistreated, take on a gnomish and perverse distortion. But,
however bizarre, the native Monterey Cypresses have no appearance of
unnaturalness, for Nature shows her hand in every contortion of the
twisted and incredibly stunted and thickened or flattened trunks, in the
sinuous, flattened buttresses that spring from the base of the trunks and

snake their way down the sea cliffs, in the long arching of the lower limbs, in the massed intricacy of the twigs, in the sculpturing of the flat-topped crown, which may be ten and twenty times as wide as it is high. Sometimes it is also tilted, like a great hat worn aslant; if the stem leans over the cliff toward the sea, the crown will usually lean backward toward the sward of the rocky shore or mesa. If the wind is too constant, and the brine too abundant, the trunk may sprawl along the ground, and the branches and their foliage lie as a mat to leeward. Often many will grow together thus, crouching with their backs to the lash of the salt winds but presenting landward an impenetrable natural hedge.

A result of the excessive growth of the tree on one side is the development of heavy, fluted, swollen, and asymmetrical butts. Asymmetrical is a weak word, indeed, to describe the contours of such boles. When these specimens have been felled, the outlines of their cross sections look like pieces from a jigsaw puzzle, and the annual growth rings are compressed here, expanded there, until they become illegible as indicators of the age of the trees.

Little indeed is known of their ages, but what can be determined scientifically does not substantiate any claim to antiquity like the Sequoias'. Two centuries is perhaps the average, three extreme. It is rather the hard lives that they have lived which have aged the Cypresses early, for those specimens growing farthest from the sea approach most nearly the appearance of the lusty normal forms of the cultivated examples, with symmetrical outlines and a straight central leader.

The appearance of utmost eld which is seen among the seaside fantastics is increased by the long trailing beards of dripping gray "moss" — really a lichen, *Ramalina reticulata* — which clothe almost all the old specimens. Forever stirring in the sea wind, they waver not like healthy foliage but with the listless despair of cobwebs. The *Ramalina* is indeed an enemy of the Cypresses, for it smothers its foliage and, always gaining headway, eventually kills the tree without actually parasitizing it, but by a sort of suffocation. It is, however, valuable to the bird life of the Cypress groves. Not only does it provide shelter, but the majority of nests are composed of this gray green and mournful growth — the bush tit's pendent, ball-shaped nest, and the homes of the Hutton vireo and the tuneful linnet.

On many of the trees, particularly those at the tip of Point Lobos, a mysterious ruddy or orange glow lights up the tip of the branches. At sunset it would be mistaken for the natural color of the sun's last rays. But it is there at all hours. Approach the twigs closely and you find that they seem infested with a sort of rusty, cobwebby, dry, felted, fungoid mass. This is no natural part of the tree but a living organism and, like the beards of lichen, a perching not a parasitic plant. Strangest of all, this is a filamentous alga with the odd faculty of being able to grow out of water, although the air is so saturated with wind-borne spray and prolonged fogs that its humidity is high indeed. Technically this alga, *Trentepohlia*, belongs to the great class of the green algae, but its green pigments are masked by a red orange layer which functions, perhaps, as a reserve food store supplemental to starch. So abundant is *Trentepohlia* on the trees that its color may locally dominate the landscape — the only case, maybe, where anything so lowly as an alga does so.

A dead Cypress lasts as long as a live one or nearly so, for its wood is remarkably resistant to decay, and when dead the tree is, if possible, more picturesque than when living; its bark sloughs off, the foliage browns and drops from the twigs; these too are torn away; then the sea winds and the sunlight scour the great bole and boughs to a bonelike whiteness, and so the ghostly thing remains standing, a gesticulating skeleton. More birds are seen on dead cypresses than on living, for a leafless tree forms a favorite lookout for flycatchers, woodpeckers, and hawks. Sometimes gulls rest upon them too.

Under the Cypresses it is always strangely dim and damp; the footfall is hushed by the bed of needles accumulated through centuries, a moist, not a dry bed, for this is the belt of almost daily fogs. Very few birds save the hermit thrush forage down there, and humans, as they wander, are apt to fall silent in some awe. Then the sound of the surf, the bellowing of the sea lions, and the chittering of pigeon guillemots invade the hush of the groves; and the glimpses of the blue and breathing ocean, the swift angelic flight of terns and gulls, seen through the aisles and boughs, are like the bright outside world framed by a window slit in the dimness and damp of some ancient building.

Little wonder that the Monterey Cypress has accumulated legends about it. If they had arisen in medieval Europe, they would take a turn to the supernatural; but in our times and in this location they drift into the pseudoscientific. Some will have it that these are Cedars of Lebanon, and were brought hither by the Franciscan Fathers when the Carmel Mission was founded. Others, perhaps confounding the Cypress with the Cryptomerias so common in Oriental temple grounds, would prefer to believe that they were carried here across the Pacific by Buddhist monks who came, presumably, by way of the wonderful land of Mu!

The truth of it is that the first European scientists to see our trees recognized them immediately as a new and distinctive species. In June 1846, just when the American flag was being raised for the first time on the soil of California, a young botanist, Karl Theodore Hartweg, in the employ of the London Horticultural Society, set out from Monterey for a botanical ramble over Huckleberry Hill, having decided that the disturbed political conditions between Mexicans and Americans made it unsafe to botanize far from his quarters. His footsteps led him to the Cypress groves. "Here I found . . . *Cupressus macrocarpa* . . . attaining a height of 60 feet, and a stem of 9 feet in circumference, with far-spreading branches, flat at the top like a full-grown Cedar of Lebanon which it closely resembles at a distance." This is the first valid botanical naming of our tree, yet several years before Hartweg's arrival, the Monterey region had been botanized by such great collectors as Archibald Menzies, David Douglas, and Thomas Nuttall. How could they have missed the most striking tree of the region? Perhaps they collected specimens which were lost or misplaced, yet they do not even mention the Cypress in their diaries and correspondence.

In cultivation this tree is easily germinated from seed. It sprouts in the open nursery bed within two or three weeks, and the seedlings shoot up fast as weeds. For many years they have been sold at nurseries at ten to fifteen cents each, and as a result the symmetrical but somber and rather uniform shape of the cultivated tree has sometimes been repeated to triteness. Yet most of the land surface of this world can never have the Monterey Cypress. For it retains this much of its maritime heritage: that out of the reach of damp sea winds it will not thrive. Even in central California it lives only a few years, then pines away for lack of the very winds that flog it till it writhes into forms that might, as Robert Louis Stevenson said of them, "figure without change in a circle of the nether hell as Dante pictured it."*

---

*"The Old Pacific Capital," in his *Travels and Essays.*

ELMS

White Elm

Ulmus americana Linnæus

OTHER NAMES: American, River, Water, or Soft Elm.

RANGE: From southwestern Newfoundland to Manitoba, south to central Florida and central Texas, west to central Oklahoma and the extreme western parts of Nebraska and the Dakotas. Absent from mountain systems and high land, and in much of Oklahoma and Texas confined largely to riverbanks, extending on stream courses far out on the prairies.

WHY ARE THERE TREES," asks Walt Whitman, "I never walk under but large and melodious thoughts descend upon me?" The answer, any New Englander would tell him, is that those trees must have been White Elms. Wherever this tree grows, whether as a native or cultivated beyond its aboriginal range, it is fairly sure to constitute itself Chief Inhabitant for miles around. It must have done so centuries before Thoreau climbed Poplar Hill in an autumn dusk to pick out unseen homes of his neighbors (whom he declares so much less estimable than their trees) by the high domes of the "imbrowned" Elms, and the "hundred smokes" of the village chimneys twirling peacefully up through their noble crowns. For, long before the white men came, Elms were council trees for Indian tribes, later the meeting place for treaty-making

between whites and reds, and then the favorite house site of the first settlers, who spared Elms when they razed all other trees.

So an Elm can scarcely grow to old age without collecting rich human
associations around it. In this respect it has but two rivals in all the sylva
of North America — the White Oak of the northern states and the Live
Oak in the South. But a survey of all the historic trees of our country
shows that among them Elms outnumber each of these Oaks nearly two
to one. Summing up hundreds of accounts of such, one finds that in almost all cases it is the tree that makes some man or some event remembered. If you want to be recalled for something that you do, you will be
well advised to do it under an Elm — a great Elm, for such a tree outlives
the generations of men; the burning issues of today are the ashes of tomorrow, but a noble Elm is a verity that does not change with time. And
though Elms too are mortal, great ones are remembered as long after they
are gone as are great men. "On this spot stood once an Elm —" so begins
many a marker, many a sentence in a book of local history, as one would
say, "Here was born a man," "Here died a king."

This tree, so often a living monument, takes on several forms; there is
what is called the Oak form, with heavy, more or less horizontal branches,
and there is a "weeping" form and a "feathered" form; but typically the
White Elm is vase shaped. In this, the most beloved of all its outlines, the
main trunk separates at 15 to 30 feet above ground into several almost
equal branches. At first these diverge slightly and gradually, but at a
height of about 50 to 70 feet they begin to sweep boldly outward so that
they form a great dome on the periphery of which the branches arch and
the branchlets droop. Thus a great old Elm appears like a fountain of vegetation — the trunk as the primary jet gushing upward and forking as it
rises, then the jets again forking, the forks spreading out and falling as
if by gravity in a hundred branchlet streams that become a thousand
streamlet twigs and a million drops of spattering foliage.

So, because of its fundamental architectural form, this is the ideal
street tree, for its branches meet across the road in a vaulted arch that
permits the passage of the highest vehicles. As a dooryard tree, it hangs
above the roof like a blessing — clean of branches under the crown but
shading the roof like a second air chamber above it. On a college campus a
colonnade of Elms is a living stoa; the ancient Elms of Yale are sacrosanct
in its deepest-rooted traditions, yet not more so than in colleges all across
the country. The very way that the leaves hang accounts for the special
quality of Elm shade. A big old specimen will have about a million leaves,

or an acre of leaf surface, and will cast a pool of shadow a hundred feet in diameter. But, though umbraculate in shape, an Elm is fortunately not too perfect a parasol in function. The leaves hang more or less all in one plane on the bough, and they make a pattern roughly like a lattice. Hence the dappling of shadow and light that is full half the charm of many a fine old facade in Portsmouth and Portland, New Haven, Newburyport, and Salem, on Pleasant Street in Marblehead, on Brattle Street in Cambridge. Within an old room, the play of light and shade from Elm leaves is like music without sound, a dance without dancers.

"What makes a first-class elm?" asked Holmes in *The Autocrat of the Breakfast Table,* and answered: "Why, size in the first place, chiefly. Anything over twenty feet of clear girth, five feet above the ground, and with a spread of branches a hundred feet across, may claim that title, according to my scale." Holmes mentions only six first-class New England Elms known to him, nor does he speak of the Elm of Cambridge Common under which, it is fondly told, George Washington took command of the Continental Army. This Elm, long a shattered wreck, died in the 1920s, and before the souvenir hunters had carried it quite away its rings were counted by an acknowledged expert. Alas for legend, it was found that this particular tree would have been little more than a sapling at the time of the siege of Boston. So, if Washington really stood under it, that third day of July, 1775, he must have picked it just because it was so small and young; he must have wished to give it a good start in life, to endow it with a legacy entailing his illustrious name. For Washington is perhaps the only man who ever added stature to an Elm.

Holmes makes no mention of Connecticut Elms, yet there are no New England villages so beautifully shaded by this species as Fairfield and Litchfield, Woodstock and Windsor, Woodbury and Wethersfield. The Great Elm, at the last-named, is 102 feet high, with a spread of branches of about 150 feet, is 41 feet about at breast height (the correct place for measuring the girth of an Elm, by the way), and its age today should be 190 years. The Whipping Post Elm at Litchfield was used as a place of chastisement as late as 1815; today no culprit's arms could be tied around its doughty girth. When Sarah Saltonstall came from New London to be the bride of David Buck of Wethersfield, she intended to bring, after an old Connecticut custom, a bridal tree to plant, but ice on the river prevented the transportation of any gift except herself. Next spring she encountered an Indian bearing an Elm sapling in his hand, and after a pow-wow in sign language, secured it in exchange for a quart of rum. Perhaps

more impressive than the fame and stature of Sarah's Elm is the mystery
of how a church-going lady would have a quart of rum about her!

The Markham Elm at Avon, New York, is said to be almost 50 feet in
girth and about 654 years old, which leaves the New England Elms rather
in the shade! Nor are all the historic Elms found east of the Hudson;
monarch among them was the Penn Treaty Elm that stood at Shack-
amaxon; here it was that William Penn made what was probably the only
absolutely upright treaty ever offered the red man, certainly the only one
scrupulously honored on both sides for as long as fifty years. This Elm
blew down in a storm on March 3, 1810, but scions and grandscions of
this monument to integrity are scattered all over Penn's Woods.

George Washington's diary shows that he was constantly searching
the bottomlands along the Potomac for wild Elms to transplant to the
grounds of Mount Vernon. Today four of those set out by his hand still
stand, the largest of them on the Bowling Green. But more venerable still
is the Elm that young Mr. Washington, the surveyor, set out as the merest
switch of a sapling at what is now Berkeley Springs, West Virginia, to
mark the southern boundary of the land grant of Lord Fairfax. Elms and
George Washington came naturally together throughout his life — at Valley Forge, at Brandywine, in the churchyard at Alexandria where he wor-
shiped, in the streets of Fredericksburg that he knew from boyhood.

There are so many Elms in Lincoln's life that it would be impossible to
speak of them all even by name — the Elm above his mother's grave in Indiana, the Elms on the White House lawn that must have known his sor-
rows, and best of all, perhaps, the Lincoln memorial tree at Atchison,
Kansas, where the vast crowd that had gathered to hear him, and could
not be accommodated inside the little church, sat under the shade while
Lincoln spoke by the open window.

The great Elm of Boonesborough, in Kentucky, is gone now — indeed
Boonesborough itself is nothing today but a cornfield, a patch of wood,
and a lovely bit of stream. So wondrous was this tree they called it the Di-
vine Elm; it stood at the heart of this ghostliest of ghost towns, with a turf
of wild white clover making a carpet beneath it right to the mighty roots.
On that sward gathered on May 23, 1775, the first legislature of Kentucky.
See them there — Harrod of Harrodsburg, in his coonskin cap, cradling
his long rifle, and Richard Henderson in his scarlet coat and powdered
wig, Squire Boone and Daniel Boone and Calloway, the old fox — heroes
of our Homeric days, who were founding a new state, in the American

way. Transylvania they called it then — Kentucky, the Great Meadow, "beyond the woods."

In Missouri still stands the Justice Tree, an Elm where the aged Boone, as syndic of the Femme Osage district, dispensed the law to his consenting neighbors. At Le Claire, Iowa, the citizens still honor and protect the Green Tree, an Elm of enormous spread which was the "green hotel" of travelers and rivermen in the days of Mark Twain's boyhood. They say that Buffalo Bill played beneath this tree when he was a child. More importantly, the Green Tree is still the natural meeting place for all the folk of this old river town. When a railroad obtained a right-of-way through Le Claire, along the riverbank, its citizens stoutly refused to let it pass unless it routed its way around the Green Tree.

There are many Le Claires scattered over this country — little towns that worship big Elms, and all of them but prove the Elm does not belong to New England alone, not even to the national capital, although Washington is the most Elm-planted of all our cities.

The love of Elms goes naturally with the settling of a countryside, and belongs to the period that comes after the first fierce encounter of the pioneers with the wilderness. For the early settlers took, perforce, a utilitarian view of trees — they were a sign of good land or of bad, they filled a need or they were useless. Even today the pioneer psychology sometimes persists when the White Elm is mentioned. "They are the most useless piece of vegetation in our forests," one Iowan can still complain. "They cannot be used for firewood because they cannot be split. The wood cannot be burned because it is full of water. It cannot be used for posts because it rots in a short time. It can be sawed into lumber but it warps and twists into corkscrews and gives the building where it is used an unpleasant odor for years."*

But from simpler days to these of competitive lumbering, Elm has been of service. Country folk have long made ox whips by peeling the bark and braiding its long, supple, and stinging strength. The Indians fashioned canoes of the bark, and ropes. And the defects of White Elm are also its virtues. For it is at once a strong wood and supple. Technicians say that its modulous of rupture is 12,158 pounds per cubic inch, which, in simpler language, means that a weight of that amount will just suffice to break a White Elm stick 2⅝ inches square resting on supports 1 foot apart. For

*C. A. Sheffield, *Atlantic Monthly*, October 1948.

these reasons Elm, from pioneer times, has been used for the hubs of heavy wagons, where it resists all the pressure and friction that can be brought to bear on it. Large amounts are employed in agricultural implements and sporting goods, in shipbuilding and heavy-duty flooring, and wherever shock resistance is essential. It is a leading wood for barrel staves and hoop poles. It holds screws better than almost any other wood and so is valuable for boxes and crates. It makes ideal chopping bowls, and the more the housewife scours her woodenware of Elm, the whiter it shines. No wonder that the cut of White Elm in 1946 was some 200 million board feet, most of it from Ohio and Wisconsin.

The lumberman's ideal of an Elm is somewhat different from the property owner's. The lumberman was delighted to find, in the Middle West of half a century and more gone by, a type of Elm growth that he prized for its straight, long, clean, columnar trunks, out of which boards could be sawed for 50 feet without encountering a branch. Such trees, of course, lack the fountainlike or vaselike form of the beloved street and dooryard tree. Yet they were forest kings. In the early days of lumbering in Michigan, the White Elms, according to the testimony of their chronicler Henry H. Gibson,* were as lofty and straight and shapely as Tuliptrees. One splendid specimen, located near Jefferson, Pennsylvania, was 140 feet high, 5 feet in diameter at breast height, and had, though a forest-grown individual, a crown with a spread of 67 feet across. At the sawmill (for that, of course, is where this giant went as soon as it was discovered), it sawed out at 8820 board feet of lumber. There are no such timber Elms left, in Pennsylvania or anywhere else, nor will they grow again unless the American people vanish from the lands they have conquered, and the wilderness reclaims its own.

This is not to say that the Elm, in some of its forms, cannot reproduce itself abundantly. By taking refuge on the riverbanks and in the narrow bottomlands of small streams where the farmer does not pass the plow, the Elm is secure along thousands of winding miles, in the company of Willow and Cottonwood and Sycamore. Its reproductive capacities are immense. Sometimes the little waferlike fruits are almost ripe by the time the leaves begin to shoot, in early spring. Then every puff of wind carries them away on their gliderlike wings by the thousands, and he who looks up may see the tiny air fleets flashing in the sunlight as they sail above the roof tops of the village. The seeds germinate readily, with a high percent-

*Gibson and Maxwell, *American Forest Trees.*

age of viability, and the seedlings come up in shady sites and sunny, well able to compete with most sorts of natural vegetation.

By all these tokens, White Elm should be one of the most promising of trees for natural reforestation, able to hold its own even with man, since it can play skillfully upon his sentiments. But the Elm has long had serious pests and is prey, like human flesh, to many ills. The worst of them all is a new disease, or rather a combination, as we now know, of an insect pest which is also a carrier of a fungus disease. Their joint inroads are so swift and so full of menace for every White Elm in the country that, though this is not a book which makes any pretense at dealing with the pathology of trees, it is unavoidable to close these pages on the Elm without some account of the great tree's battle for its existence.

For the White Elm has proved shockingly susceptible to a fungus called *Ophiostoma ulmi** that was first noticed some years ago in Europe where it was ravaging the Elms which helped to hold the dykes of Holland and, no respecter even of majesty, had attacked the magnificent row of English Elms which line the long approach to Windsor Castle. Our quarantine authorities thought they had every avenue of entry blocked against the Dutch Elm disease. Yet it broke out in the heart of the country, in Ohio in 1930. Converging at once upon the local outbreak, sanitary forces exterminated it; but in 1933, 3800 diseased Elms were found in New Jersey and 23 in Connecticut, across the Hudson. Every year brought more alarming reports of spreading malady, and it was evident that, carefully though all living Elm stock was inspected at the ports of entry, *Ophiostoma ulmi,* all unseen, was some way coming over here in lethal doses.

The locus of infection was found at last in logs of English Elm, which we imported wholesale for the manufacture of veneer. For some of the European Elms produce abnormal lumpy growths on the trunk, called burls, which when sliced by the veneer knives reveal fancy figures that unhappily pleased the public taste here. These logs were swarming with the Elm bark beetle (*Scolytus multistriatus*) who, disgustingly healthy himself, is the carrier of the disease. And since once it has gained entry within an Elm, nothing can be done save to fell and burn the tree, the war for the Elms has concentrated attack on the bark beetle.

If the beetle is present, you may find in the tree's crotches a lot of rust-colored frass, and also "shotgun holes" made where the larvae have emerged through the bark. Under the bark will be seen the characteristic

---

Editor's note: Formerly *Graphium ulmi.*

"engraving" of centipedelike form — the broad galleries of the larvae. The presence of the fungus may be known by the shepherd's-crook curvature of the twigs, by the yellowing and falling of foliage even in spring and early summer, and in late summer and winter by the persistence of dead leaves at the tips of the branches. If you cut open the twig of an Elm diseased with this fungus, a cross section will show brown streaks and discolored rings in the wood. Since all these symptoms are imitated by other maladies of the Elm, the layman should send doubtful specimens to his State Department of Agriculture for expert identification.

Cork Elm

Ulmus thomasii Sargent

OTHER NAMES: Rock, Hickory, Corkbark, or Cliff Elm.

RANGE: Southwestern Quebec and southern Ontario, west through Michigan and northern Wisconsin to the southern half of Minnesota, south to Vermont, western New York, northern New Jersey, Kentucky, Indiana, northern Illinois, Missouri, northeastern Kansas, Nebraska, and Iowa.

ROCKY SLOPES AND THE BLUFFS of rivers, dry gravelly uplands, and heavy clay soils are the habitat of this fine tree, which sometimes rises 80 or 100 feet tall, the trunk clear of branches in the forest for 60 feet, and attaining as much as 3 feet in diameter. If not so graceful as its close relative the White Elm, the Cork Elm is manyfold more valuable as a timber tree.

At an early date British contractors for the shipbuilding firms overseas began to appreciate this tree, which grows plentifully in southern Ontario and southern Michigan. The finest specimens and the largest stands occurred there, and large cuts were made at a time when no other Michigan hardwoods were equally appreciated, and exported through Canada to Britain. There the lumber was received with high acclaim, for even Hickory scarcely surpasses Cork Elm in toughness. With its interlaced fibers, it is almost impossible to split — and splitting was a serious consideration in the days of wooden battleships and sailing vessels. Under water it is particularly durable. Tradition states (but there are no definite figures to prove or disprove it) that the finest stands of Cork Elm were long ago cleared out of the country, and, as it is a slow-growing tree and the country that it chooses to occupy is forever being cleared of its forest, we have never seen a second growth of it comparable with the virgin stands.

Axmen of the old North Woods often preferred ax handles of Cork Elm to any other. In the early days of the automobile industry in Michigan, when much wood was going into car construction, large quantities of Cork Elm were used for hubs and spokes and in other places which had to take great strain. During the era when most kitchen furniture, including refrigerators, was wooden, this was a favorite, not only because it stood up under heavy usage, but because no matter how discolored the wood became, vigorous scrubbing with brush, soap, and water would always whiten it. Although Cork Elm is not usually listed as a furniture wood, great quantities have gone into furniture, as the hard core or stock on which more fragile and elegant woods are veneered. It is used in veneer form itself, not for the visible exterior, since it has no beauty of grain, but in the form of plywood — sheet after sheet glued together, to form boxes or the frames of trunks, which are then covered by leather, cloth, or metal. Because of its stiffness, it has been used for a long time for flour barrels. To one rough usage, however, this stouthearted tree has never been put, surely. And that is a split rail fence; the steel edge of an ax would turn, the Ash handle break, before a sound log of Cork Elm would permit itself to be mauled.

Wahoo

Ulmus alata A. Michaux

OTHER NAMES: Winged, Mountain, Witch, Red, or Small-leaved Elm.

RANGE: Central Florida west to southern Texas, north on the coastal plain to southeastern Virginia, and in the Mississippi valley to central Missouri, southern Indiana, and Kentucky.

THE CURIOUS NAME OF WAHOO is said to come from the Creek Indian language where the original word was *Uhawhu*. And what did it mean? What else but this very tree, the Wahoo! Or so the dictionaries tell us, though there have been those who trace this name to the Yahoos in *Gulliver's Travels*, and others think it derives from the hoot of an owl!

Next to its name, the most curious feature of this tree, of course, is the corky wings which beset the twigs. The wings begin to form on the twigs during the second year, and when the twigs are still small, perhaps only a quarter of an inch thick, the wings have already attained their breadth of half an inch on each side of the twig; however, as the twig enlarges the wings do not increase in proportion. Usually the lowest branches, and those nearest the trunk, are most heavily furnished with wings; sometimes no twigs on the tree display this distinguishing mark. Since the Cork Elm also has winged twigs, the difference between the two trees will be important for identification in the field. The wings of the present species are half an inch or more broad, while the Cork Elm has generally narrower wings. In the Wahoo the wings form two continuous lines opposite each other on the twig, interrupted only at the nodes, where a leaf or secondary twig emerges; in the Cork Elm there are usually three or four wings of much less continuous occurrence.

On dry, gravelly upland or sandstone, the Wahoo is usually a short and straggly tree, often an understory species as in the heavy timber of the Great Smokies, but on the borders of swamps, on banks of streams, and in bottomlands occasionally inundated by rising rivers, it may reach 80 or 100 feet with a trunk as much as 3 feet in diameter. Such trees are usually found west of the Mississippi. In Texas, where the heaviest cut is taken, the wood is used for table legs, tool handles, and hubs of wheels; the inner bark has been made into rope for fastening the covers of cotton bales. In many a town in the lower Mississippi valley Wahoo makes a fine street tree, for under such conditions it develops the broad umbrellalike crown of the White Elm, with branches arching gracefully and meeting above the center of the street.

Tuliptree

Liriodendron tulipifera Linnæus

OTHER NAMES: Tulip, Yellow, or White Poplar. Popple. Canoewood. Whitewood.

RANGE: From northern Florida to Rhode Island and central and western Massachusetts, and west through central and southern New York, the southern peninsula of Ontario, southern Michigan, to the Indiana dunes of Lake Michigan, southern Illinois, eastern Arkansas, and northern Louisiana. Ascends in the Appalachians to 5000 feet altitude.

T HIS TREE OF STATELY BEAUTY and immense practical use has a bewildering handful of folk names. The lumberman calls it Yellow Poplar or just plain Poplar, though of course it is no sort of a Poplar at all. However, to him Tulipwood means a tropical cabinet wood, so to do business with him one must use his terms. Country people call this wood Poplar too or, more easily, Popple, or Tulip Poplar, sometimes shortened to Tulip. Canoewood is heard in Tennessee. In pioneer days it was called Whitewood, and architects in New England sometimes specify it by this name for interior finish. The foresters prefer Tuliptree, and with reason, since this name brings to mind the glory of this species in spring, when its flowers, erect on every bough, hold the sunshine in their cups, setting the whole giant tree alight.

This is the king of the Magnolia family, the tallest hardwood tree in North America. In the southern Appalachians, where it is the most commercially valuable species, it attains its most superb dimensions, up to 200 feet tall, with a trunk 8 to 10 feet in diameter, clear of branches — in sound, old, forest-grown trees — for the first 80 or 100 feet. Its crown is then (as in its youth) narrowly pyramidal, giving a soldierly pride to the tree and an impression of swift upsurgence in growth. Under field conditions it takes a different form; the trees of the famous "Poplar walk" at Nomini Hall in Westmoreland County, Virginia, are known to be over two hundred years old, and in these centuries their limbs have attained a magnificent weight and sweep, while their trunks measure as much as 20 feet in girth, at breast height. The great mansion is gone; the sandy road which leads to this place is a remote by-path; the trees alone remain as monument to the Carter family. Beneath them passed the color and the vigor of a once baronial life, inimitably recorded by Philip Vickers Fithian in his journal. Frequently the young tutor speaks of strolling in the double avenue of these trees, which must have been noble even then and which today are giants of longevity, speaking, themselves, in many-leaved, elegiac voices, of how mayfly were the bright and vanished humans they knew.

But, despite the splendor of its dimensions, there is nothing overwhelming about the Tuliptree, but rather something joyous in its springing straightness, in the candlelike blaze of its sunlit flowers, in the fresh green of its leaves, which, being more or less pendulous on long slender stalks, are forever turning and rustling in the slightest breeze; this gives the tree an air of liveliness lightening its grandeur. So even a very ancient Tuliptree has no look of eld about it, for not only does it make a swift growth in youth, but in maturity it maintains itself marvelously free of decay.

This look of vitality comes partly from the vivid palette from which the Tuliptree is colored. The flowers, which give it this name, are yellow or orange at base, a light greenish shade above. Almost as brilliant are the leaves when they first appear, a glossy, sunshiny pale green; they deepen in tint in summer and, in autumn, turn a rich, rejoicing gold. Even in winter the tree is still not unadorned, for the axis of the cone remains, candelabrum fashion, erect on the bare twig when all the seeds have fallen. No wonder that in the gardens of France and England this is one of the most popular of all American species.

The date at which it reached Europe is a very early one, at least 1687, when it was first described from a tree growing then in a Leyden garden. Certainly this is a species which the colonists would remark, and it must have been sent back to Europe many times in the early days. In America it was described enthusiastically by the rare cultivated traveler, and to the American himself proved picturesquely useful. As the eighteenth century opens, John Lawson, Surveyor-General of North Carolina, reports a Tuliptree "wherein a lusty Man had his Bed and Household Furniture, and lived in it till his labour got him a more fashionable Mansion." More commonly, the pioneer made a fine canoe of this straight-growing tree, hollowing out a single log to extreme thinness, for the wood is easy to work and one of the lightest in the forest. Such a canoe 60 feet long did Daniel Boone make, when his fortunes were low, and into it he piled his family and his gear and sailed away down the Ohio into Spanish territory, away from an ingrate Kentucky.

The pioneer sometimes built his house, too, of Tuliptree logs, and he lined his well with it, since it imparts no taste to water. That same quality makes it today an appreciated crate for perishable food stuffs. Light in color and weight, taking the shipper's stencil well, it is used in immense quantities for boxes, and even more goes into millwork. For though a hardwood, Poplar, as the lumberman calls it, is softer than any softwood in North America except Western White Pine and Alpine Fir. It is also one of the very lightest of our woods, hence easy to float in rafts on the river. Since so much of its bulk is in air, it is valuable as an insulating material, against sound as well as heat and cold. Though fairly flexible and tough, it is not strong as a beam or column, yet it takes paint excellently and holds up well as an outside finish.

Indeed, White Pine and so-called Poplar, regarded as standing timber, floating logs, boards at the mill, and lumber on the market destined to certain uses, are strikingly alike. Poplar has never engendered the wealth that Pine has, nor had so spectacular a history, but the drain upon it has been long and great. In the beginning of settlement it went down under the ax in sheer destruction, for it was taken as a sign of good soil and simply felled to clear a field. So, like the Beech, it was widely dispossessed of its primeval holdings. Then, two decades after the Civil War, when railroads penetrated the southern Appalachians, and the great hardwood resources of these mountains were first tapped, Poplar was the prize of extensive selective logging. Only centenarian trees of great size were felled; those under 30 inches in diameter at the stump end would not have been cut, and only perfectly clear logs, containing upward of 400 board feet, were accepted at the mill in the 1880s. By 1905 the mills were beginning to be glad to get Poplar 14 inches at the stump end, which sawed out with 100 board feet clear. Today the portable sawmill is absorbing what is, for Poplar, almost sapling growth — logs 9 and 10 inches thick. Even the very young trees are now unfortunately cut, for pulp, since by the soda process Poplar can be made into high-grade book paper.

Sweet Gum

Liquidambar styraciflua Linnæus

OTHER NAMES: Red or Star-leaved Gum. Gumtree. Liquidamber. Alligatorwood.

RANGE: From western Connecticut and Long Island to the southern parts of Ohio, Indiana, Illinois, and southeastern Missouri, and south to central Florida, eastern Texas, and southeastern Oklahoma. Ascends to 4000 feet in the Appalachians. Occurs in Mexico in the mountains of Veracruz, Puebla, Hidalgo, Oaxaca, and Chiapas, and in Guatemala.

O UT OF A BIZARRE AND DRAMATIC MOMENT of history comes, like a puff of pungent smoke, the first reference to this American tree. It is written by a witness of the ceremonies between Cortez and Montezuma, and he says, of the Emperor: "After he had dined, they presented to him three little canes highly ornamented, containing liquid-amber, mixed with an herb they call tobacco, and when he had sufficiently viewed and heard the singers, dancers, and buffoons, he took a little of the smoke of one of these canes."

This remarkable author and soldier, Don Bernal Díaz del Castillo, who accompanied Cortés in 1519 on the conquest of Mexico and became its most celebrated historian, published his account (here translated by Keating) in 1632. He must have recognized the burning liquidamber (in

spite of its being called by the Aztecs *xochiocotzoquahuitl!*) by its odor, since, though no *Liquidambar* is native to Europe, the gum of an Asiatic species was well known in the pharmacopeias of western civilization and was prized as an incense in Christian churches and Indian temples. The plant which produced it, however, was for a long time quite unknown to science, and the gum arrived mysteriously in the markets of Constantinople either as a resin floating in water and sewed up in goatskin bags, or as a bark in camel's-hair bags. Retailed over Europe at advanced prices, it was valued both in perfumery and incense and in the treatment of diphtheria and gonorrhea. Ultimately Europe learned that the gum was derived from *Liquidambar orientalis*, which grows in the mountains of southern Anatolia, Turkey, and was gathered by wandering Turcomans.

The American species, which produces a like resin, was described to Europe by Francisco Hernandez, the first great herbalist of Mexico, who dwelt in that country from 1571 to 1575. He speaks of it aptly as having leaves "almost like those of a maple," and a resin of which the "nature is hot in the third order, and dry, and added to tobacco, it strengthens the head, belly, and heart, induces sleep, and alleviates pains in the head that are caused by colds. Alone, it dissipates humors, relieves pains, and cures eruptions of the skin. . . . It relieves wind in the stomach and dissipates tumors beyond belief."*

This account of the learned, if credulous, Hernandez did not see print until about 1651. Yet over twenty years earlier the Sweet Gum tree, as most Americans call it, had been recognized — for the first time on the soil of the present United States — by Alvar Núñez Cabeza de Vaca. This

---

*Translated in Paul Standley's *Trees and Shrubs of Mexico*.

bold, Christian, and observant adventurer was a member of one of the most desperate of the Spanish expeditions into the New World, and so it was he found himself in 1528 near the present Appalachicola, Florida. "The country," says he, "where we came on shore to this town and region of Apalachen is for the most part level, the ground of sandy and stiff earth. Throughout are immense trees and open woods, in which are walnut,* laurel† and another tree called liquid-amber, cedars,‡ savins,§ evergreen oaks, pines, red oaks and palmitos** like those of Spain." Now this account was apparently published for the first time in 1542, long after Cabeza de Vaca had returned home after shipwreck, Indian captivity, near starvation in the wilderness, and further incredible hardships. A man must have a keen eye and mind to recollect so clearly a tree he had seen in a distant place long ago, and still more astonishing is it that he knew it when he saw it, for he could only have recognized it by its gummy exudation.

Yet this Sweet Gum is a noble tree that might well impress anyone new to the sight of it. And the sight is a common one, for it grows along any fence row in piedmont Virginia, beside any country road of the Carolinas, in any field abandoned by agriculture and growing up to Scrub Pine and Dogwood. It comes up in company, in these upland sites, with Sassafras and Red Cedar and may be known by its beautiful star-shaped leaves. Their upper surface has a starlike glister, but unlike most shining leaves, those of the Sweet Gum are not dark at maturity but a light, gay yellow green. Crushed in the fingers, they give out a cleanly fragrance; on the tongue they have a tart taste. Foliage so odd and yet so attractive would make any tree conspicuous.

But even when the leaves have turned a deep winy crimson and fallen, Sweet Gum is striking by reason of the broad corky wings on the twig. True, one might confuse them with those of some of the Elms, but the fruiting heads of woody spiny balls, hanging all winter on the slim stalks after the winged seeds have escaped, are unique among all American trees. In the eastern states and on uplands, the Sweet Gum is often a small tree, sturdy rather than graceful, 20 to 40 feet tall. In the deep gumbo soils of the Mississippi Valley, in the swamps of Missouri's Tiwappatty

*Probably White Hickory.
†Probably Magnolia.
‡Probably Bald Cypress.
§Red Cedar.
**Scrub Palmetto.

Bottom, Sweet Gum becomes a giant, up to 140 feet high, with a trunk 5 feet thick.

There is something about Sweet Gum that looks like a living fossil, like a member of some family more abundant in another and far different sylva than ours, and that is exactly the case. Today there are three extant species of *Liquidambar* — one in Formosa and one in Turkey, beside our own. Such a disparate distribution bespeaks a long story of spread over the planet, then a history of tragic extinctions. Twenty extinct species are known, the oldest found in the Upper Eocene rocks of Greenland, in an age when that continent had a subtropical climate, some 55 million years ago. Later fossils turned up in Italy, Siberia, and Colorado, and in great numbers in the Miocene lake beds of Switzerland. From the Pleistocene or Glacial Period, we distinguish Sweet Gum leaves in much the same regions the living species are found in today — as in Formosa and North Carolina.

To the lumberman the heartwood of this tree is Red Gum, and the sapwood, which is marketed separately as if it were a different wood, he calls Sap Gum. Country folk refer to it simply as Gum tree, and to furniture salesmen the wood is plain Gum, or Gum wood, which is confusingly ambiguous, since many trees are called so. In the pharmaceutical trade the name for the exudate of this tree is liquidamber, or copalm balm, or, incorrectly, storax. The gum, which is considered identical in its properties with the oriental gum, flows from the tree in the form of bitter-tasting but sweet-smelling balsamic liquid. It is then semitransparent and yellowish brown, but on exposure to the air it hardens into a rosinlike and darker solid. From pioneer times it was used in the South for the treatment of sores and skin troubles, for a chewing gum, and for catarrh, and in the treatment of dysentery was much favored by doctors in the Confederate armies.

However, in the years that followed the Civil War, American copalm sank into insignificance, for Oriental storax could easily undersell it. During the First World War, interest in the native gum revived, only to languish again. In the Second World War, with Formosa (whence it had been coming chiefly) completely cut off, it became definitely important as a needed base of salves, adhesives, perfuming powders, soaps, and tobacco flavoring, just as in the days of Montezuma. Clarke County, Alabama, which had retained from the First World War a memory of the technique of tapping the trees, became the center of the industry.

The operation is reported by a local agent to yield ½ to 1 pound of the resin from a tree each year, with the amount greatest from trees with the most green leaf surface. When the leaves are fully spread in the orchards in spring, the trees are expertly peeled, and the gum slowly gathers as an exudation, to be scraped off after some days. Then it is heated — carefully, since it is highly inflammable — strained, and canned. A tree will produce like this for three to five years, and the young and healthy ones then grow new bark and can later be cut for lumber.

Not strong enough for a structural timber, the wood of Sweet Gum has only recently come into the place its beauty deserves. For though the very thick white sapwood is rather featureless, the pink or ruddy heartwood, which develops in trees over sixty or seventy years old, may sometimes show handsome figures on the quartersawn cut. All the wood is capable of taking a high polish and can be stained to look like even nobler woods. Thus it happens that the lumber often leaves this country as Red Gum, is received in England as "Satin-Walnut" (forsooth!), and after various transmogrifying rites have been performed upon it, may return to America as a Mahogany, Rosewood, or Circassian Walnut antique. The bands of distinctly darker wood in natural figured quartersawn Gum especially lend themselves to substitution as Circassian Walnut.

Obviously, everything about Red Gum points to its use as a cabinet wood. But only in the last half-century has it risen from the most despised position in the list of hardwoods to second place among them, inferior only to Oak in the amount cut in this country, far outstripping Birch and Maple. With an annual cut of something like 690 million board feet a year, Red and Sap Gum (which are only one species) show a higher cut than any other species of deciduous hardwood. The cut is wholly in the southern states, with Louisiana and Mississippi far out in the lead.

One reason for this new popularity is the conquest, by technological processes, of some of the difficulties inherent in the wood of Sweet Gum when seasoning. The sapwood dries easily enough, but the heartwood warps badly and has a tendency to stain. Through the use of modern scientific drying methods, Sweet Gum's seasoning difficulties have been largely overcome, so, although at first considered fit only for crates and boxes, the wood of Sweet Gum now shows its best face in the veneer of furniture and promises a fine commercial future.

MAGNOLIAS

Cucumbertree

Magnolia acuminata (Linnæus) Linnæus*

OTHER NAME: Indian-bitter.

RANGE: From western New York to upper Georgia and northern parts of Alabama and Mississippi, throughout Arkansas to eastern Oklahoma, extreme southern Missouri, southeastern Illinois, southern Indiana, and southeastern Kentucky. Not found above 5000 feet in the southern Appalachians.

I N THE RICH MOUNTAIN FORESTS of the Carolinas and Tennessee, known as the cove hardwoods, flourishes this tree with the primitive flowers and the curious fruits that give it its name. Sixty to 90 feet tall, with a trunk 3 to 4 feet thick, this Magnolia makes a beautifully symmetrical, pyramidal tree, the middle and upper branches ascending sharply, the lower downsweeping. Its greenish flowers are less lovely than others in its genus, but the "cucumbers" are notable, greenish at first, but as they ripen appearing dark red or scarlet. It is the seeds upon the fruit that take on this color, set as they are upon the surface like scanty grains of corn on a cob. They are not winged, neither are they palatable to any creatures of the forest, so that no means of dispersal seems provided to them. Furthermore, even when they are ripe the fruit seems reluctant to

*Editor's note: Formerly *Magnolia acuminata* Linnæus.

let them go, for instead of falling free they drop each on a small thread from 1 to 3 inches long and hang dangling there, as if uncertain of their fate.

Despite this awkward machinery of distribution, increased by the fact that half the flowers are apt to remain sterile, the Cucumbertree flourishes, not only in its mountain fastnesses but in parks and in city streets, for it has been popular in cultivation since the day of its discovery. This was in 1736, when John Clayton, Virginia's early botanist, found it; a few years later John Bartram sent the first plants to his patron Lord Petre, who grew them at his estate of Thorndon Hall in Essex, then considered the finest garden in England. In this era, toward the turn of the century, collectors in England and France became avid to obtain American Magnolias, a genus wholly new to Europe. Thus were these trees prominent among the treasures sought by François Michaux in our virgin wilderness, and he records the care he lavished on keeping their delicate seeds viable by putting them into fresh moss, constantly renewed throughout his travels. In July 1802, on the banks of the Juniata River in Pennsylvania, he makes a dry observation on the Cucumbertree: "The inhabitants of the remotest parts of Pennsylvania and Virginia and even the western countries, pick the cones when green, to infuse in whiskey, which gives it a pleasant bitter. This bitter is very much esteemed in this country as a preventative against intermittent fevers, but I have my doubts whether it would be so generally used if it had the same qualities when mixed with water."

It is said, too, that the pioneer people extracted the bitterness from the cucumberlike green cones and ate them, but the art, such as it was, seems to be quite lost. More enduring and profitable is the use of the wood, which in its properties so closely resembles that of its relative the Tuliptree that it is sold as "Poplar," though lumbermen know the difference and so do some of its buyers. Thus it is probably cut on a much greater scale than the scanty statistics under its own name would show, for it serves well for boxes, crates, slack cooperage, furniture cores, and interior finish of houses.

Umbrellatree

Magnolia tripetala (Linnæus) Linnæus*

OTHER NAME: Elkwood.

RANGE: Southeastern Pennsylvania to the coast of North Carolina and south to southern Alabama and southwest to southern Ohio, middle parts of Kentucky and Tennessee, and northeastern Mississippi. Also in central Arkansas and southeastern Oklahoma.

A S YOU TRAMP OR MOTOR beside the roaring streams of Great Smoky Mountains National Park in May, the Umbrellatree, with its big, creamy white flowers, repeats itself over and over, until the forest — made up of the most magnificent hardwoods of the North American continent — seems populated by a troop of wood nymphs.

Though so showy a tree in flower, the Umbrellatree is usually a straggling understory species, 30 to 40 feet high in the Great Smokies, where it attains its maximum, and often much less, with numerous shrubby stems from the base. The branches, commonly irregularly developed, are contorted or wide spreading nearly at right angles with the stem. In autumn the foliage takes on no beautiful colors. It turns suddenly brown at the touch of frost and soon drops, but in summer the great, filmy, pale green

*Editor's note: Formerly *Magnolia tripetala* Linnæus.

leaves, clustered umbrella fashion at the end of the stem, seem the very embodiment of the Appalachian forests' spirit, as they shine through the underwood, or stream on the fresh breeze that seems perpetually to sweep down the long valleys. Distance undoubtedly lends some enchantment to the flowers, for when one actually drinks of the odor in the deep chalice, it is strong and, to many persons, disagreeable.

But reproach this species as one will for its minor failings, it is still a beauty, and naturally it was introduced at an early date in the gardens of Europe, where the Magnolias of America created such a sensation in the eighteenth century. This species was first described by Mark Catesby in his *Natural History of Carolina*, published in 1743, but he must have seen it years earlier, when in 1712 this English naturalist first came to Virginia to visit his relatives and was so delighted that he remained for seven years.

Not the least of the charms of the Umbrellatree is its elusiveness, for it is by no means always present within the external boundaries of its range; in many areas it is lacking altogether, and over others it is distinctly a rare species. On the coastal plain it seeks the margins of the great swamps and the shade of lofty Swamp Chestnut Oak, Scarlet Maple, and Gum tree; in the mountains it loves the shady side of a deep gorge, and, with its roots buried in rich cool loam, it sends its stems to overtop banked masses of Rhododendron.

Mountain Magnolia

Magnolia fraseri Walter

OTHER NAMES: Fraser Magnolia. Ear-leaved Cucumbertree.

RANGE: From southwestern Virginia to the high country of Georgia, and from northeastern Kentucky to Alabama. Ascends to 4000 feet altitude.

IN THE COVES of the southern Appalachians, cooled by the breezes set astir by ever-falling water and fresh with fern and saxifrage, this lovely tree is most at home, its flowers shining forth serenely as water lilies floating in the forest green. Its leaves are borne all at the ends of the branches, which gives the Mountain Magnolia a wilder and more careless look than the cultivated species familiar in the garden. Indeed, it has proved too tender for gardens as far north as Massachusetts and is happiest in the rich, humid soils to which it is native. There it rises some 18 to

30 feet in height, in many stems from one source, its "crooked wreathing branches arising and subdividing from the main stem without order or uniformity, until their extremities turn upwards, producing a very large rosaceous, perfectly white double or polypetalous flower, which is of a most fragrant scent."

So it was described by the lucky naturalist who discovered it, William Bartram, the first American botanist who ever explored the southern Appalachians. On the headwaters of the Keowee in the mountains of South Carolina he found it, in that morning of exploration when this land was young and half its wealth unnamed. The month was May, the year that in which a young nation was to declare independence, but the happy naturalist was far from any human struggle but the toil up the mountains. When he had crossed "a delightful river" and climbed "swelling turfy ridges, varied with groves of stately forest trees, then again more steep grassy hill sides," he rested at last on what he conceived to be the highest ridge of the "Cherokee mountains," which he named Mount Magnolia, in honor of the new and lovely species he had found here so abundant and in such "a high degree of perfection." There is but one first recognition, in science, one Adamite moment of discovery, but over and over those who climb those gentle mountains in the spring can share old William Bartram's pleasure when they come upon this flowering tree.

Its history, indeed, may be said to antedate by eons a May day in Revolutionary times. For Mountain Magnolia is a descendant of one of the oldest (excepting the conifers) of all trees; systematists used to believe it was certainly the most primitive of them all, and many are coming back to that view. Its antiquity is visible in its flower structure, which is primitive, and so is that of the fruit and of the wood. And Magnolia fossils are found, to a total of perhaps twenty-three species, in the lower Cretaceous rocks, which would place them as far back as any trees we have save the conifers. At that time the genus was represented from western Greenland to Texas and Nebraska. In the Middle Cretaceous there are fossil Magnolias from Vancouver, Portugal, and Moravia, and in the Late Cretaceous from Tennessee and Wyoming.

From the Eocene come twelve known species of Magnolia, from Spitzbergen to Alaska, Tennessee, and Louisiana, and all over the Rocky Mountain and Pacific coast states, as well as central Europe. The Oligocene has yielded only eight species, mostly from Italy, the Miocene sixteen from Europe and North America, while the Pliocene, which is almost never represented by American fossils of any sort, showed eleven species in Europe and Pacific Asia. The Pleistocene glaciation wiped Magnolia out of Europe and our western states, leaving eastern Asia and eastern North America in possession of the surviving species. Like similar locations in far China and Japan, the wild sweet glens of the Appalachians keep for us a flora of strangely ancient lineage, and Mountain Magnolia is one of the loveliest plants in it that have come down to us, by the winding ways of evolution, from an unimaginable antiquity.

Sassafras

Sassafras albidum (Nuttall) Nees

OTHER NAMES: Saxifraxtree. Sassafac. Aguetree.

RANGE: From southern Maine through southern Vermont and southern Ontario, central Michigan, northern Indiana, northern Illinois, and southeastern Iowa to eastern Kansas and Oklahoma, south to central Florida and the valley of the Brazos River in Texas; ascending in the southern Appalachians to 4000 feet altitude.

A GAINST THE INDIAN SUMMER SKY, a tree lifts up its hands and testifies to glory, the glory of a blue October day. Yellow or orange, or blood orange, or sometimes softest salmon pink, or blotched with bright vermilion, the leaves of the Sassafras prove that not all autumnal splendor is confined to the northern forests. Deep into the South, along the snake-rail fences, beside the soft wood roads, in old fields where the rusty brook sedge is giving way to the return of forest, the Sassafras carries its splendid banners to vie with the scarlet Black Gum and the yellow Sweet Gum and other trees of which the New Englander may hardly have heard. The deep blue fruits on thick bright red stalks complete a color effect in fall which few trees anywhere surpass.

In spring the leafing out is late — later at least than the inconspicuous pale gold flowers that bloom on the naked wood. But once they burst their buds, the heavy glossy leaves form swiftly. On old boughs they are simple in outline — boat shaped and rather small; but on young trees and vigorous new growth they grow large and take on their characteristic mitten shape — with one "thumb" lobe and a larger terminal lobe. Or they may have three terminal lobes, the middle one a little longer, a strong vein running through each lobe. Such a blade is almost unique in our flora and could be mistaken for nothing else save perhaps the leaf of our wild Mulberry. But the Mulberry's mitten-shaped leaves are thin, dull, dark green, harsh above, and many toothed. The Sassafras blade is thick, waxy glossy and yellow green above while chalky white below, and it has no teeth on the margin. More, the Sassafras leaves, when chewed, at once set up a mucilaginous slime in the mouth, like that of Slippery Elm twigs, which country children love to taste; the hot and thirsty botanist, as well, has been known to resort to chewing Sassafras to promote salivation, when no water was to be found on his dusty tramps.

In the North, Sassafras is usually a small tree. Yet in the South it may reach 80 feet, with a trunk 6 feet thick and stout branches leaving the trunk at right angles to form a strong rather than a graceful outline. On the Lake Michigan dunes of Indiana, Sassafras growing out of pure shifting sand may be a mere shrub, its stems only limber green canes. In northern Illinois the Sassafras seems to be gaining ground, much as is the Red Cedar, and is present now in places from which it was unreported by the first botanical explorers. Because its bright blue fruits are eagerly eaten by birds and the seeds carried and then voided, and because the Sassafras does best not in forest country but in lands opened up by agriculture, it seems destined to continue to increase its range, while so many other trees are losing ground.

Its role in American folklore and early exploration is unique. About it have clung fantastic hopes and promises of gain, and superstitions that have not yet wholly departed. The wood, which has less shrinkage in drying than any other hardwood (10 percent), is not only durable, so that it appealed to the pioneer for fences and is still esteemed for small boats, but its odor was reputed to drive away bedbugs; hence many bedsteads were made of it, in a more innocent age and the more innocent states of Arkansas and Mississippi. Negro cabin floors in Louisiana were often laid in Sassafras for the same reason. In Kentucky, where soap is still sometimes a home product, it is often supposed that the kettle must be stirred with a Sassafras stick to make a good quality of soap. In West Virginia it is believed that Sassafras hen roosts keep out chicken lice.

But it has been the bark on the roots of the tree, yielding an oil once prized beyond all reason, that gave the Sassafras its fame. As a demulcent and emollient, oil of Sassafras has never completely ceased to be of some importance in the manufacture of soaps and perfumes; it disguises the bad taste of some medicines and may perhaps still be employed in the flavoring of candy. At one time, however, especially in Virginia, roots were grubbed out by the ton for the production of this essence, thereby clearing cutover land for the farmer and at the same time yielding a paying harvest. But the old belief in Sassafras as a tonic that would prolong life has yielded place to acceptance of radio advertisers' claims for vitamins to do the same, and it is probable that Sassafras at the moment is at an all-time low in its chequered career.

Yet no other American tree was ever exalted by such imaginary virtues, in expectation, as Sassafras or has fallen so far in esteem. Its reputation was launched upon the world in 1574 by Nicholas Monardes, "physician of Seville," in his work on the resources of the West Indies (translated into the English by Frampton), with the delightful title *Joyfull Newes Out of the Newe Founde Worlde*. And these are some of his glad tidings:

"From the Florida, which is the firme Lande of our Occidentall Indias, Hying in xxv degrees, thei bryng a woodd and roote of a tree that groweth in those partes, of great vertues, and great excellencies, that thei heale there with greevous and variable deseases.

"It may be three yeres paste, that I had knowledge of this Tree, and a French manne whiche had been in those partes, shewed me a peece of it, and told me merveiles of his vertues. . . . After that the French menne were destroied,* our Spaniards did beginne to waxe sicke, as the Frenche menne had dooen, and some whiche did remaine of them, did shew it to our Spaniardes, and how theei had cured them selves with the water of this merveilous Tree, and the manner which thei had in the usyng of it, shewed to them by the Indians, who used to cur theim selves therewith, when thei were sicke of any grief . . . and it did in theim greate effectes, that it is almoste incredible. . . .

"The name of this Tree, as the Indians dooeth name it, is called *Pauame*, and the Frenche menn doeth call it Sassafras."

Monardes goes on to say that Sassafras is a sovereign remedy for "Quotidian Agewes [malaria], large importunate fevers . . . it comforteth the liver and the Stomacke . . . it dooeth make fatte . . . doth cause lust to meate." It is also good for "Tertian Agewes, griefes of the breast caused of cold humours, griefes of the head," for "them that bee lame and creepelles and them that are not able to goe."

Such a panacea as this was certain to raise high hopes in the Europe of that day, when almost no disease was correctly understood in either its origin or its treatment, so that credulity might mount untrammeled. It was the easier to believe in a cure-all that came from the New World and had never failed — because it had never been tried except by the Indians. Indeed, the early Spanish, French, Portuguese, Dutch, and English were as gullible about "Indian medicine" as the Americans of a later date. The great value of Sassafras to the red men (aside from the undoubtedly soothing effect that the mucilaginous properties of its sap would have on raw mucous membranes) was doubtless in its aromatic nature. A plant with a strong pleasant smell was supposed to ward off evil, and evil, rather than bacteria, is believed still, among the Chinese, Indians, and certain American sects, to be the real cause of sickness.

This conception of the curative, since evil-dispelling, nature of an odor is very ancient; it goes back to Egyptian and druidical ceremonies and was strongly believed in by Europeans during the bubonic plague, when doctors wore great nose-beaks filled with spices; indeed, it survived to our own times in the only recently abandoned theory of fumigation. The

---

*Reference is to the attack by the Spanish of St. Augustine, Florida, upon the French Huguenot colony at Port Royal, South Carolina, when the French, after surrendering, were coldly butchered by the Spanish.

American Indians believed, above all, in the efficacy of tobacco smoke, and it was as a curative that tobacco was first introduced into Europe; Catherine de' Medici took tobacco for a cold in the head! Such then is the background, the psychological preparation, which greeted the first arrivals of Sassafras in Europe. It rated with the spices of Ormuz and Araby as a precious substance.

Impatient to secure adequate supplies of it, the English charged their early explorers to search for it. Thus when Philip Amadas and Arthur Barlowe dropped anchor in Pimlico Sound, North Carolina, in 1584, they immediately began the search for Sassafras. In 1602 Bartholomew Gosnold was sent out to explore what is now the coast of New England for the marvelous tree, for the price of Sassafras in England had risen to £336 sterling the ton. Then in 1603 the merchants of Bristol, urged thereto by Richard Hakluyt, the celebrated historian and anthologist of early exploration, formed a company to send to Virginia for the sole purpose of gathering Sassafras. They sailed in two vessels "plentifully victualled for eight monethes, and furnished with slight Merchandizes thought fit to trade with the people of the Countrey, as Hats of divers colours, greene, blue and yellow, apparell of coarse Kersie and Canvasse readie made, Stockings and Shooes, Axes, Hatchets, Hookes, Knives, Sizzers, Hammers, Nailes, Chissels, Fishhookes, Bels, Beades, Bugles, Looking-glasses, Thimbles, Pinnes, Needles, Threed and such like."

After a long voyage they reached land, probably in the neighborhood of what is now Old Orchard, Maine. Meeting with no Sassafras there, they continued southward, always hunting for it, and first encountered it on the Connecticut shore of Long Island Sound. Here they spent a month filling the hold of the bark with Sassafras and then sent her home to England "to give some contentment to the Adventurers," that is, satisfy the stockholders. The remaining company continued to cut Sassafras and load it into the larger ship, but either this aroused the jealousy of the Indians or the redskins decided the foreigners had stayed long enough. Several surprise attacks were made, ambushes were laid, and treachery attempted, but the stout banging of a brass "Peece" (cannon) and the fear inspired in the natives by two mastiffs belonging to the Bristol men drove off the Indians, and a fair wind brought the Sassafras cutters away at last in safety to Bristol and, we hope, returned great profit to the gentlemen "Adventurers."

Sassafras was one of the first exports sent by Captain John Smith from the Jamestown colony, and as late as 1610 it was still demanded from Virginia, like tribute, as a condition of the charter of the colony. But soon it began to share the fate of other panaceas. It wasn't curing all the ailments it was claimed to cure. A disillusioned public lost its faith in Sassafras — but not in panaceas! So, through the years, Sassafras as a medicament sank to the position of a tonic to "purify the blood" — a continuation, of course, of the notion that our ailments originate in some inner evil. Thus for generations it was administered, in connection with black cherry and various other unpleasant ingredients, to pioneer children as the dreaded "spring tonic." Older people left out the unpleasant ingredients and simply sipped Sassafras tea.

Even that placid custom is becoming a part of the past — that long American past in which the Sassafras tree shone boldly forth, just as today when it is only a bright reminder of the time when everything here was wonderful and new.

POPLARS

Western Trembling Aspen

Populus tremuloides Michaux*

OTHER NAMES: Quaking Aspen. Quaking or Aspen Poplar. Popple.

RANGE: In Alaska north in the Yukon Valley to the latitude of the Arctic Circle, south slopes of the Endicott Mountains (to 2000 feet), west nearly to the Bering Sea and south to the inland side of the Coast Range and to its seaward side at Cook Inlet, Kenai Mountains, base of the Alaskan peninsula. In Yukon Territory and British Columbia west to the inland slopes of the Pacific Coast Range and noted on Klondike, Stewart, Liard, Stikine and other rivers. East to the high plains of Saskatchewan, the western parts of the Dakotas and Nebraska, and south in the Rockies to the mountains of western Texas, southern Arizona and the northern parts of Nevada, and California, to the northern Coast Ranges.

THE TREMBLING ASPEN is the most widespread tree of North America, ranging from Atlantic to Pacific across Canada, and in the western United States it extends, at increasingly higher altitudes as one goes south, through all the great mountain systems to Mexico. But, a small tree in the eastern provinces and states, it can never mean — there where it is but one of hundreds of hardwoods — what it does here in the West. For here it is actually a finer tree, up to 90 feet tall in some fa-

*Editor's note: Formerly *Populus tremuloides* Michaux variety *aurea* (Tidestrom) Daniels.

282

vored localities; in many regions of the Far North, it is the only hardwood to break the somber monotony of the vast coniferous forests. In the Rockies, it grows in the very spots most sought by the vacationing camper — in the high, dry, cool places, commonly close to clean, rushing water. It is apt to form open, sunny groves, where the snow or the night damps and chill do not linger, and the breeze sweeps away the insects. Sweet, dry grass carpets the floors of these groves, flecked with the blue of lupine and wild flax, of larkspur, columbine, and monkshood (where else are there so many blue wild flowers as in the Rockies?). Where the deer bound, where the trout rise, where your horse stops to slather a drink from icy water while the sun is warm on the back of your neck, where every breath you draw is exhilaration — that is where the Aspens grow.

The least observant city dweller quickly notices Aspens and learns to identify them on sight. Their boles, except at the roughened, darkened base of very old trunks, are smooth as flesh and chalky white just tinged with green. Unlike the bark of the Birch, Aspen bark never peels in thin layers but is always compact and thick. Aspens resemble their relatives the Poplars and Cottonwoods, but those have very sticky buds, while Aspen buds are only slightly resinous. So there is no other tree in the West that can be confused with Trembling Aspen.

And above all there is the tremble that gives them their name. Father De Smet, the early missionary to the Northwest, relates that the *coureurs du bois* had a superstition that this tree furnished the wood of the Cross, since when it has never ceased to quake. If you prefer to look for a scientific reason, there is one: the leaves of the Aspen are hinged upon leafstalks longer than the blade and flattened contrary to the plane of the blade, with the result that the leafstalk acts as a pivot and the foliage cannot but go into a panic whispering every time the slightest breeze flows down the canyon. Cottonwoods and Poplars, too, rustle their leaves, but not all of them have that right-angle pivot of blade and stalk. And with a little experience one can distinguish, even without seeing the tree, the light, soft rustle of Aspen leaves from the coarser rustling of the heavy-leaved Cottonwoods. As Aspen foliage moves it twinkles brilliantly, for each shiny surface acts like a little mirror to flash sunlight in your eyes.

The color of Aspen foliage, too, is distinctive — in spring and summer a pale green, compared to the Cottonwood's darker green, in autumn the clearest shining gold in contrast to the dull butter yellow of Cottonwood. So you can pick out from afar the zones of Aspen, or its clumps, and groves, and the long riverlike streaks where it seems to pour from the edge of a plateau like the north rim of the Grand Canyon, down the draws and gulches. And as if it wished to be seen to the utmost advantage, it is commonly found chattering and displaying its vivacity, its white limbs and green or golden mane of foliage, against the dark unmoved conifers. Engelmann and Blue Spruces, White and Alpine Firs, Douglas Fir and Lodgepole Pine are its constant companions in the Rockies, and in the Far North it associates with somber White and Black Spruce.

In all the West there is no tree with such brilliant autumnal foliage. This might seem to be faint praise, since the West is lacking in the great range of color seen in the East; but the West is so rich in the gold of the Aspen's coin-shaped leaves that it can afford to forget what it lacks of copper and bronze. And western Aspens are more brilliant than the same tree in the East, for the dry, crystalline atmosphere lets the sunlight through them like a clear, sustained blast on angelic trumpets. The foliage shines for miles; thus as you cross the deserts in October, still hot and sere, you can see the gold band of Aspens in the sky, where they top the mountain peaks. But better it is to ride some horse trail up into the meadows where the Mormons graze their sheep in summer, or walk an old lumber road through the Aspens in fall, and let the golden glory rain tranquilly down around you.

As you go, you may notice on the usually smooth bark of the Aspens curious deep pits and long slashes. These are made by the claws of bears who stretch up to their fullest height to achieve them. And to see just how high that sometimes is may make you take a quick look over your shoulder. Yet if the slashes are bordered by a rim of black, corky scar tissue, then those marks were made long ago. If Bruin passed this way recently there will be no black borders; the green cambium layer may show under the bark, or the sapwood, freshly exposed and white, will be moist still. Opinions differ as to the motives behind this ursine writing on the Aspen's inviting page of bark. Some think bears sharpen their claws in this way, and others, on the contrary, that bears intentionally so dull their claws. Many believe that old bears mark up the trees as a proclamation of foraging or courting rights in a certain bailiwick and that rival bears, seeing how high the marks reach, can tell whether they dare issue a challenge.

The animals which eat Aspen buds or bark make a long list. It is an important food of the snowshoe hare and the moose; black bears, cottontail rabbits, porcupine, and deer include Aspen in their menus. Grouse feed on it abundantly at certain seasons and so does the boomer or mountain beaver (which is not really a beaver but a forest pest related to rats). Sheep, goats, and cattle are so fond of Aspen shoots and sprouts that where they are allowed to browse heavily, little Aspen reproduction takes place. In the days when elk were abundant in Colorado they sometimes killed whole groves of small Aspen by overbrowsing.

But the real Aspen worshiper is the true beaver. The inner bark, though bitter as quinine to our palates, is his favorite food, preferred to that of Cottonwoods, Willows, or Alders. Every sensible beaver lays up large stores of Aspen cuttings for his winter supply, anchored to the bottom of the pond by mud. Since it grows so handily by streams, Aspen is also the commonest tree cut down by those chisel teeth, for the making of the dam that will back the stream up into a moat where he can set his lodge. Tree-falling by beavers is more industrious than clever, but once the tree is down the beavers show endless ingenuity in snaking and skidding the poles to the stream; if necessary, canals are dug by these little lumbermen, and the Aspen logs are then driven, as loggers say, to the pond. In time the pond may silt up; the beavers then leave, but on the new-made ground the Aspens spring up quickly.

In the first forty years of the nineteenth century, beaver fur was at a premium, for every gentleman in Europe and the eastern United States had to have a beaver hat. So it was beaver, more than any other fur-bearing animal, that brought the white man and the half-breed or *coureur des bois* as the first explorers of the West, long before the days of the cowboys, before the gold rushes, before the Indian wars. And wherever those hardy "Mountain Men" and Hudson's Bay Company's employees went, they looked out for Aspen, for it was beaver sign. The best method of trapping the beaver was to breach a hole in the beaver's dam, set an Aspen stick in the break, and attach the stick to a trap. The beaver, swimming out to repair the dam, instinctively seized the Aspen stick; the trap fell on his leg and carried the little flat-tail down under water where he drowned. And it was commonly in the delicious Aspen groves that, annually, the Mountain Men appointed their rendezvous; there they brought their beaver pelts and, while waiting for the St. Louis supply train, would trade with the Indians for beaver and girls. Around the campfires of Aspen logs you could have seen, in that far-off Homeric age of the West, the weather-seamed faces of Jim Bridger, Kit Carson, "Brokenhand" Fitzpatrick, Jedediah Smith, Bent, Beckwith, St. Vrain, the Sublettes, Bonneville and Ashley and Vanderburgh. It is natural, therefore, that all the early accounts of western exploration mention the Aspen, over and again, and always with love for the beauty of its groves.

Aspen flowers bloom in earliest spring, their mouse gray buds bursting from the shining chestnut scales. By the time the first delicate haze of foliage puts out, about a month later, the wind-pollinated flowers have turned to fruits, and the minute seeds, in immense quantities, float away on their coating of fluffy down. Sometimes this will accumulate in the corner of a corral to the depth of several feet, and the air may be filled for a while with millions of these shining argosies. Streams backed up by a log jam or beaver dam may have the surface covered with a thick cottony layer. Of course only the female trees bear seed, and many of these have a high degree of infertility, so that it is but a fraction of the Aspens in a region which do all the work.

Many of the seeds, too, are abortive — without a viable embryo. All are very short-lived. An Aspen seed must sprout almost as soon as it finds lodgment or it will not grow at all. And in the dry springtimes of many portions of the West, the climatic conditions are hostile to such an event; there Aspen reproduction is largely from root sprouting or suckers. Aspen is very susceptible to fire damage at all stages of its growth, but if the trees are killed by crown fires, the roots will soon send up a host of suckers which actually make faster growth than the shoots of seedlings. They are, however, shorter-lived, and if an Aspen is forced to sucker repeatedly, owing to crown fires, its suckers grow progressively feebler. Seedlings, having the vitality that comes with sexual reproduction, are naturally strong but very susceptible to ground fires.

Harmful though fire is to Aspen, it is also the chief factor in the abundant success of Aspens over large areas. For Aspens do far better than most of their competitors in the intense sunlight of the tract cleared by fire; their seeds thrive in mineral soil such as may be laid bare by a humus-destroying ground fire. Thousands of seedlings spring up on burned-over and logged-over lands, and, though only a fraction will survive, they will form those groves which make such excellent nurseries for other trees. As if designed to be nurse trees, Aspens, after a precocious burst of speed, begin to flag after fifty years or so — just when other trees, slower to get started, begin their period of greatest growth. In the next half-century Aspens are likely to be shaded out by their competitors, and, their life expectancies being in any case short (one hundred years or exceptionally two hundred), they often give way to conifers, their good work done. In the Far North, though, and high on the Rockies, where the harsh climatic conditions bear more heavily on other trees, the hardy Aspens may form permanent stands.

The wood of Trembling Aspen will never be of value to the lumberman; it is not strong enough for structural purposes, its grain is commonly twisted and cannot be dependably seasoned; more, by the time most Aspens have reached saw-log size they are already infected by heart-rot fungi, species of *Fames*. But whole logs of Aspen have been cut for log cabins; the Mormon pioneers made furniture of it in Utah, and its white wood recommended it for the kitchen utensils of their wives. But, though weak in many senses, it is also tough, like Willow — tougher far than most Pine; so from early times it has been used for barn floors and fence posts, corral posts and siding, and the stalls of horses, for it stands up against the kicking and gnawing of horses without splintering. It is used for snake rail fences and has been extensively cut for mine props; the poles have even been pressed into service to carry telephone wires.

And Aspen wood has certain qualities that recommend it above all other woods. Its peculiar shredding properties make it ideal for excelsior, extensively used in the West for packing watermelons, avocadoes, and cantaloupes, as padding for furniture and coffin cushions, and as an absorbent or filter in air-conditioning units for cars. Aspen excelsior is in great demand for wallboard, making a good soundproof and insulating product with the appearance of compact "shredded wheat."

The fibers of Aspen wood are too short to make a strong paper, but when mixed with the stronger Spruce pulp they are ideal for book and magazine papers, for the wood is inexpensive to start with, cheap to log and peel, and easy to bleach and to size so that the paper will take printer's ink.

Pulpwood logging begins in early spring because at this season, when the sap runs, the bark is easy to peel. When the peeling season is over, the logs are cut into 4-foot lengths and hauled or sledded to the railroad. If they are to be driven downstream, the intact logs are usually floated with Spruce, since green Aspen is likely to sink. Large mills, using the soda process, produce about a ton of paper an hour. A cord of Aspen bolts will yield about 1000 pounds of pulp.

Despised once as the veriest weed of a tree, Popple, as the pulp loggers prefer to call it, has sprung up on lands logged over for more valuable timber trees in such abundance that many erstwhile deflated lumber boom towns are returning to prosperity. And when Popple is cut over it may, under good conditions, reproduce itself, quite unaided, within fifty years. So what seems a shallow-rooted, short-lived tree, driven like a vagabond from site to site as other species crowd upon it, may prove to have as much value, in the aggregate, as many a species of more solid reputation. All this — and charm as well!

Balsam Poplar

Populus balsamifera Linnæus

OTHER NAMES: Tacamahac. Balm-of-Gilead. Bam. Rough-barked Poplar.

RANGE: Nova Scotia, Newfoundland, and Labrador to Hudson Bay, the valley of the Mackenzie, and Alaska, south to Idaho, Colorado, the Black Hills, the Turtle Mountains, and northwestern Nebraska. Minnesota (except the corn belt), central parts of Wisconsin and Michigan, and to northern New England. Of scattered occurrence throughout New York State.

THOSE WHO HAVE VENTURED BEYOND the great North Woods, out on the arctic prairies, where all the rivers fall into the polar sea or Hudson Bay, tell us of the surprising beauty of the isolated groves of Balsam Poplar there. How fair it must look then is something we can hardly realize when we encounter this species in the United States, for even when it is a fine tree, as in northern Michigan, it is still a forest tree, crowded upon by others, its best points rivaled by the similarities of its own close relatives the Aspens, and its claims to kingship contested by

Birch and Maple, Beech and Pine. But up there, far to the north, the Balsam Poplar accompanies the lonely canoeman all the way, like a friend. In the endless monotony of horizontal scenery, it may tower up to heights of 100 feet, such as it never attains in the southern part of its range. And, forever twinkling its bright foliage and shaking it in the breeze, it makes music where otherwise all were silence. It gives fuel and shade where none could be expected. The foliage is like a cloak with a lining of another color, the upper leaf surface brilliant and cleanly, contrasted with the white or rusty lower surface. When the wind turns all the blades over, they flash silvery, and then, the breeze failing, the tree once more assumes its dark green and lustrous habit.

Balsam Poplar delights to grow upon low and repeatedly inundated bottomlands — riverbanks and sandbars, borders of bogs and swamps. So streams like the Athabasca, the Peace, and the Mackenzie, as they eat at their banks or change their course in flood, are continually sweeping down great trunks of the Balsam Poplar on their turbulent floods, to bleach upon their estuaries and the unvisited shores of the arctic sea.

A fast-growing tree, whose trunk may attain 6 or 7 feet in diameter, this species, like so many other Poplars, acts as a nurse tree, preparing the way for the seedlings of Spruce. But as the Spruce grows tall it creates about itself and on the forest floor a dark, cold environment, completely hostile to the future seedlings of the sun-loving Balsam Poplar. So it is driven away by the brood that it nurtured, and on its far-flying wings the seed must seek a new home.

The forester's name for this tree is Balsam Poplar, but to the pulp loggers of the North Woods it is Balm-of-Gilead (though the horticulturist means by that a variety mentioned below). Sometimes the loggers call it

Balsam, which is confusing to say the least, or, again, they may designate it simply as Bam — a corruption, presumably, of Balm. Yet when it goes to market this wood usually loses identity in the general designation of Popple, and so the cut of this particular species cannot always be distinguished statistically on the ledgers of the wood-using industries.

A wood so quick growing, so abundant on otherwise useless logged-over and burned-over lands and so soft among hardwoods is nearly ideal for pulp, especially in the manufacture of magazine stock. Slim poles of young growth will do as well as large old trees, where pulp is the only consideration, and if the stand is cut over frequently it tends to keep on reproducing itself instead of giving way, at length, to Spruce.

The lumberman too has an interest in Balsam Poplar but prefers large trees, which yield broad clear planks. Though so soft and weak a wood, Balsam Poplar is remarkably tough in proportion to its light weight. This makes it valuable for boxes and crates, and for cutting into thin veneers for berry baskets. It is not even despised by the furniture manufacturers, as a core for costlier surfaces.

There is a variety of the Balsam Poplar, called by horticulturists the Balm-of-Gilead — botanists call it variety *candicans* (Aiton) A. Gray* — which some think is a wild or natural hybrid between the Balsam Poplar and what other parent who can say? Nor does anyone seem to know where this offspring originated. Some say, or rather guess, it was in a European nursery, and others that Siberia is the birthplace of Balm-of-Gilead Poplar; they insist that it is never seen far from cultivation in this country, and so it must be an exotic tree which has naturalized itself. But the distinguished horticulturist Liberty Hyde Bailey thought that it was native in early days in Michigan, where he grew up, and formed extensive groves which were felled in the whirlwind destruction of Michigan's forest resources. Balm-of-Gilead differs from Balsam Poplar in that the blades of the leaves are much darker on the upper surface — darkest of all Poplars' — and downy or hairy on the lower surface; also the leaf is broader and more heart shaped, with coarser teeth. The leafstalks are downy, not smooth. And instead of forming a tall, more or less conical crown, Balm-of-Gilead has a much broader, more open head; so one may designate it as a broad shade tree, not a towering giant of the wilderness. It has the same general range as the true Balsam Poplar but is much more erratic in its occurrence.

Editor's note: Now *Populus balsamifera* subsp. *balsamifera* Linnæus.

An ointment is, or used to be, made of the clear gum of the buds, hence the name of the tree. Bees are said to smell this gum from afar and to gather it on their thighs, later to employ it in sealing up the crevices of their hives. The name for the gum among the bee masters is "bee glue," and in consequence of its now widely recognized use in the honey business the tree is often planted near apiaries.

Frémont Cottonwood

Populus fremontii S. Watson

OTHER NAME: White Cottonwood.

RANGE: From the Sacramento Valley and inner Coast Ranges of northern California, south through the central and southern Coast Ranges and the water holes and streams of the Mohave Desert to northern Baja California; also in southern (rarely in northern) Arizona and southwestern New Mexico to the Sierra Madre of Sonora and Chihuahua; also in western Nevada and southwestern Utah.

THE FRÉMONT COTTONWOOD is a true Cottonwood, for it belongs to the section of the genus *Populus* having, generally, leaves as broad as or broader than long, triangular in shape, and usually with a truncate base and a translucent margin, while the leafstalks are flattened in a way that keeps the foliage spinning in every light breeze. More, Cottonwoods, which are typically trees of riverbanks and water holes, are inclined to fork near the base into several equal trunks; as a result, all will be outward leaning, and the crown of foliage will be very broad, casting a wide pool of shade in summer. So, sign of water in the arid lands, fuel in an unwooded country, shade where shade is needed most, Cottonwoods are mentioned more often than any other vegetation in the literature of early exploration in the open Far West.

Most of the pioneers, though men of epic courage and ability, were not botanists, and to them any Cottonwood was just a Cottonwood. But John Charles Frémont, whose courage was seriously impugned by those who traveled with him, who proved his incompetence as a soldier and governor, who was styled "The Pathfinder" but seldom found a path in all the West not already known to traders, trappers, and Indians, was quite a genuine scientist. He was an excellent topographer, geologist, and mathematician, a good linguist, and a very fair botanist. Carefully he wrote up every night, by the flickering campfires that must soon be extinguished for fear of Indian attack, his notes on the vegetation. And on the night of January 6, 1844, near Pyramid Lake in present-day Nevada, he made the first note of the tree that was to bear his name:

"Taking with me . . . [Kit] Carson, I made a thorough exploration of the neighboring valleys and found in a ravine in the bordering mountains a good camping place where was water in springs and a sufficient quantity of grass for a night. Overshadowing the springs were some trees of the sweet cottonwood, which, after a long interval of absence, we saw again with pleasure, regarding them as harbingers of a better country. To us they were eloquent of green prairies and buffalo." The reference to "sweet" Cottonwood is not an adjective of endearment, but a recognition that these trees had an inner bark palatable to his mounts. Certain other species of *Populus* — for instance the Balsam Poplars — have bitter bark, and these Frémont habitually calls by the French Canadian name of *liard amère*.

On April 10, being then in the San Joaquin Valley of California, Frémont writes again: "Turning a few miles up toward the mountains, we found a good encampment on a pretty stream hidden among the hills and handsomely timbered with large cottonwoods (*populus*, differing from any in Michaux's Sylva). The seed vessels of this tree were now just about bursting." From this we may assume that Frémont traveled with the heavy three-volume *Sylva* of François André Michaux, illustrated with

Redouté's beautiful plates, and had the habit of making comparisons between that early classic and any specimens he met.

Leaving the San Joaquin Valley, Frémont set out on the Mohave desert to look for the reputed river of "San Buenaventura" and he struck it in the neighborhood of present-day Victorville, California. "The morning of the 22d of April was clear and bright and a snowy peak [San Antonio —"Old Baldy"] to the southward shone out high and sharply defined. . . . We travelled down the right bank of . . . a clear bold stream, 60 feet wide, and several feet deep. . . . It is well wooded . . . with willows and the beautiful green of the sweet cotton-woods. As we followed along its course the river, instead of growing constantly larger, gradually dwindled away, as it was absorbed by the sand." So much for the stream (now called the Mohave River), which was supposed to flow from California to the Mississippi! But if Frémont had disproved the existence of a great river, he had discovered a great Cottonwood — *the* Cottonwood of all Arizona and southern California — Frémont's Cottonwood.

Growing from 50 to 100 feet high, with diameters of 1½ to 4 feet through the bole, this is an astonishingly large tree to find in such arid country. However, the spots it chooses are not in themselves truly arid, for it succeeds only along permanent streams and around water holes. Where the streams are intermittent, it ventures for a while, but usually gives up.

When you stand on the rim of the Grand Canyon, the line of green that you see at the very bottom is made up of Frémont Cottonwoods, and this species follows the mighty river to its great, muddy delta where it empties into the lonely Gulf of California. There this riparian tree is forever being swept into the stream as the braided channels shift and eat at their banks. But forever the tree comes back, undismayed and determined.

Throughout the year Frémont Cottonwood maintains a changing drama of beauty; in earliest spring the catkins ripen on the naked wood, and the bees collecting pollen may make an uproar among the male flowers. When these fall, they litter for a brief while the pools, the cattle trough, and the streets of the western towns where they are so much planted. But the female catkins, of course, remain on the trees till the necklacelike strings of pods burst open and the seeds on their fluffy down float away. Then once again the litter is deep — a sort of snow that flies through the air in spring all around the ranches, the rivers, the towns, catching in the window screens, drifting in the corners of the corrals, and giving a sort of wild autumnal air to the days that are really lengthening and growing steadily warmer.

In the meantime the leaves have come out, and for a while they shine a brilliant, pale, cleanly green that gradually darkens and becomes glittering. Then, if not stripped away by the tussock moth, they spread their great pools of shade. And with every hot summer wind there comes from the dense crowns a mocking sound as of rushing water — a sudden gushing forth of some secret spring, that stops again as suddenly as it began, when the dry wind fails.

In fall the leaves turn yellow — not a beautiful translucent gold like Aspen's, but still very welcome in desert lands that else would scarcely know autumn hues at all. About this time the buzzards begin to gather in great flocks in the Cottonwoods, stretching their naked necks and heads, silently, somberly congregating before their migratory flights. Early in the autumn mornings they unlimber their great black wings and soar up in circles to scout all the desert for its toll of dead.

Then when winter comes, and sunlight is needed for the traveler, the Cottonwoods stand naked. But their upper bark shines whitely against the winter skies, and the twigs, long before spring, begin to glow with a fresh pale yellow tint. And now show forth the tufts of sickly green mistletoe that parasitizes the Cottonwoods even to the extent, sometimes, of killing them.

The tree's own twigs are forever competing with each other and killing their brothers. So there is a perpetual self-pruning going on in a Frémont Cottonwood's crown, with a corresponding litter beneath the trees. These bits make ideal kindling for the campfire of the old "desert rat," and he gathers them while he turns his burro out to graze on the *cienaga* cactus and to drink at the water hole.

The Mohave Indians once had their own uses for this tree, in the days when they painted themselves with ocher, clay, charcoal, and oil. For the women's skirts (their only garments, which did not even reach their knees) consisted, behind, of a mass of strips of the inner bark of Cottonwood hung from a string passing around the hips, while the front was made gay with twisted cords of vegetable fiber dyed in various colors.

To the Spanish pioneers this tree was the *alamo*, and most of the cities of northern Mexico are planted, at least around the inevitable plaza, with double rows of it; under its gracious shade at dusk walk the girls in couples and threes, in one direction, while the boys circulate in the other, with comments and glances exchanged in this grand right-and-left. Commonly the Mexicans and the Spanish-speaking people of the southwestern states pollard the Cottonwoods each year, in order to obtain a perpetual supply of fuel, and this gives their trees an odd, squat look. We gringos usually prefer trees to assume their natural shapes, but to the Latin peoples a tree exists to serve man, *por Dios,* and is often made to serve him by being bent to his will quite out of its primitive shape.

Eastern Cottonwood
Populus deltoides W. Bartram ex Marshall*

OTHER NAMES: Big or Yellow Cottonwood. Carolina or Necklace Poplar. Cottontree. Whitewood.

RANGE: Throughout the Ohio valley to western Pennsylvania, the Mississippi valley (except northern Wisconsin and Minnesota), up the Missouri and its tributaries to about the 102nd meridian west, on the inner coastal plain and lower piedmont from Texas to Connecticut, up the Connecticut valley to Vermont and the shores of Lake Champlain, along the shores of southern Lakes Michigan and Erie, the north shore of Lake Ontario, and the upper St. Lawrence.

O N THE ATLANTIC SEABOARD the Cottonwood is just a tree among many trees, and few of the colonists, it would seem, held it in much honor. But as the pioneers of later times came out of the Oak openings of the Middle West and faced the heat of the prairies, the Cottonwood groves around the sloughs, so tall you could see them for miles across the waste, offered sweet shade and even on the hottest, driest day reminded you, by the sound of their rustling leaves, of lake waters coolly lapping. On the other side of the Missouri, men found that the Cottonwood withstood the blizzard and drought. Poor though its wood might be, it gave the prairie pioneers their fences and corncribs, their cabins and stables, their ox yokes and saddletrees, and even their coffins. Though the

Editor's note: Formerly *Populus deltoides* W. Bartram.

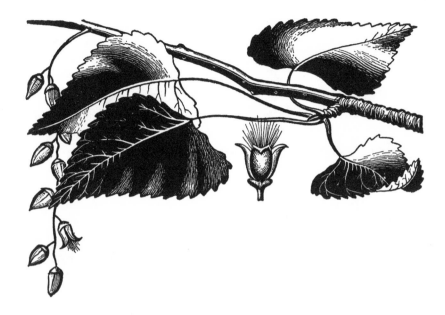

wood checks and warps badly in seasoning, many a primitive church or
first hotel or school was run up out of green Cottonwood.

Nor could the lumber industry despise a tree which might be 150 feet
tall and 6 to 8 feet in diameter, with 50 or 60 feet of the bole clean of
branches under the crown. The wood, for all its faults, is as stiff as White
Oak, yet weighs no more than White Pine. For decades it was made into
every kind of crate and box from packing for the heaviest pianos to the lining of cigar boxes. It was cut for excelsior, poles, posts, barrel staves, iron-
ing boards, and trunks. But in this century its production has steadily
fallen off, for the fine, straight, forest-grown trees have been felled. Left
are the trees that grow in the open, by the banks of streams, on the shores
of midwestern lakes, the muddy beaches and crumbling bluffs of the Missouri, the front-line dunes of Lake Michigan. Such trees usually fork from
near the base into two to six trunks, making a crotch ideal for children's
play, but anything save what the lumberman desires.

The life of a Cottonwood is short; at seventy-five years of age it is already old, the heartwood eaten away by decay, and the hollow becomes
the home of the high-holder, the red-headed woodpecker, and the sap-
sucker, perhaps, too, of owls, bluebirds, and starlings. A Cottonwood 125
years old is probably exceptional. Yet, in compensation, it grows faster
than any other of our trees — 4 or 5 feet a year. In fifteen years a Cotton-

wood may be 60 feet high and in fifty years have a trunk 2 yards in diameter. A height of 125 feet is usually the limit, but only death halts the broadening of the crown, which may cast a pool of restless shade and light as broad as the tree is high.

The Cottonwood presents, through the seasons, a drama of changing appearance. In late winter the bark of the boughs and twigs begins to brighten and thus announces the rising of the sap. So the Cottonwoods shine across the prairie, serene and cheerful, just at the season when the snow is dingy, the vegetation sodden and colorless, the atmosphere heavy with damp.

Early in spring the catkins appear on the naked wood and may drop, three weeks later, so heavily into the sloughs that they cover the water, the male bright yellow, the female a rich carmine. Cottonwoods shed immense amounts of pollen and cause hay fever in a few persons. Not until the flowers are falling do the leaves begin to shoot, coppery at first and strikingly handsome. Then in midspring the seed pods burst, and the downy seeds are loosed in great quantities upon the wind, reminding one of thistle down and milkweed down in fall, so that the spring is touched with a wild autumnal quality wherever there are Cottonwood groves and in all the midwestern towns where this tree is planted. And all summer long there is the constant motion of the leaves, heavier and coarser than the music of Aspen foliage, a sound like a sudden gush of water that as quickly stops, like the rustle of heavy skirts, like distant pattering applause.

About the last week in August, in the latitude of Chicago, the leaves on some individuals, particularly those in dry soil, begin to turn yellow, but leaf by leaf — not all at once — and to drop, leaving the tree naked in September. Around sloughs these trees stay green much longer. When the slough, too, goes dry in autumn, the leaves fall and the drying marl is found littered not only with the leaves but with quantities of punky twigs, for the Cottonwood is forever pruning itself of dead wood and is, indeed, forever dying even while it continues its phenomenally rapid growth. Yet though so short-lived, so swift to decay, the Cottonwood, when cut back, sprouts with great vigor. So that, after all, though its years are numbered, youth may return to it over and over.

Desert Palm

Washingtonia filifera (L. Linden) H. Wendland*

OTHER NAMES: California Fan, Arizona, Washington, Fanleaf, or Overcoat Palm. Wild Date.

RANGE: Bases of the desert (eastern) side of the San Jacinto Mountains of Riverside County, California (Palm Canyon, Palm Springs), and base of the southeastern end of the San Bernardinos (Twentynine Palms), south irregularly in the desert canyons of eastern San Diego County to Baja California and Sonora; also in mountain canyons just above Yuma, Arizona.

O N ITS MANY MERITS, the Washington or California Fan Palm has made its way around the gardens of this world wherever a Palm can be grown, and under glass in colder climes. In Hawaii and Algeria it is now so familiar in the landscape of cultivated districts as to seem like a native. Indeed, in Hawaii it has received a thoroughly native-sounding name, the Hula Palm, in allusion to its skirtlike thatch of dead leaves hanging beneath the crown of living ones, like the grass skirt of a Polynesian dancer. The same appellation has been applied to it in Florida, where it is now a familiar garden and street tree. On the Riviera it is highly prized. No other Palm indigenous in this country has proved so

*Editor's note: Formerly *Washingtonia filifera* Wendland.

popular in cultivation. Yet in the wild it has always been a rare species within the borders of the United States. Until Palm Springs (which takes its name from this tree) became a winter resort, in the second decade of this century, few indeed, except bands of Indians and old "desert rats" or wandering prospectors, had ever seen it growing natively, with an artless dignity, a wild, desertic fitness, that it never wholly possesses in the flashy horticulture of subtropical cities.

The chosen habitat of the Desert Palm, as it is called where it is native, is, though so restricted, one of the grandest on the continent. For this tree inhabits the canyons at the foot of the eastern or desert side of the Coast Ranges in Riverside and San Diego counties. From elevations of over 11,000 feet, in the San Jacinto Mountains, where Lodgepole Pines stand all winter amid glittering snows, the surface of the planet here drops abruptly for two vertical miles to the floor of the intensely desertic Coachella Valley. Portions of this chasm lie below sea level, as if a great block of the earth had slipped out of place and sunk deep. And this indeed is probably the case; the Gulf of California, our American Red Sea, is doubtless but a portion of the same deep planetary crack, now filled with ocean water; and fossil oyster beds and old shorelines around the Coachella Valley show that in former geologic times the Gulf was here, or there was at least a landlocked salt lake, a sort of Dead Sea, of which the enameled blue of the Salton Sea is a recent manifestation.

Around the shores of this vanished sea are dotted the scattered colonies of our Palm. They are found at the baylike bases of the canyons, between the waterless capes of the San Jacintos' buttressing ridges. They cling to last water holes in the Little San Bernardino Mountains, which enclose the Coachella Valley to the east. All the way down the inner face of the Coast Ranges to the Mexican boundary and beyond, into lower California, colonies of Palms cluster wherever there are mountain walls to give them shade, for part of the day, from the fierce desert sun, and springs or streams or the least slow seepage to nourish their deep, far-traveling roots. A few of these groves, near the popular resorts, are visited yearly now by many thousands of people, but most of them are still little accessible. In profound desert loneliness they catch, each morning as the planet rolls eastward, the first fierce rays of the sun, spilling it in swords of light from the ribs and fingerlike lobes of their fronds. Each year they produce, all unseen, their great compound bunches of creamy flowers, and ripen their black cherries, and drop their horny seeds. They have no company but the trade rats and lizards that scuttle under the thatch of dead leaves around the stem, and the liquid raptures of the canyon wren who nests behind the thatch, or the rolling whistle of orioles that hang their nests from under the living fan fronds upon threads made of the long fibers of the leaves themselves.

Yet though so rare a tree, the Washington Palm was early discovered by Europeans. On March 29, 1769, the Franciscan Father Juan Crespi, chronicler of the Portola expedition, observed it 30 miles north-north-west of Vallicola, Baja California, near the future site of Mission San Fernando. He speaks of camping here, after a desolate *jornada,* under the grateful shade of a grove of fine Palms, and since Washingtonias are the only Palms growing there, no doubt can be entertained of their identity. On May of the same year, the immortal Padre Junípero Serra mentions Palms at the same spot. So, contrary to widely received opinion in California, the "Mission Fathers" (Franciscans) did not bring the Palm here from the Holy Land, or from Spain.

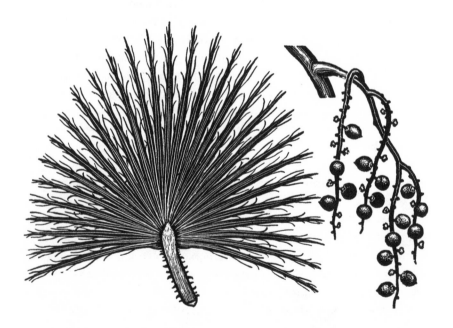

In 1848 Colonel William Hemsley Emory, "Bold Emory" as his fellow West Pointers named him, soldier, explorer, engineer, and astronomer, brought the Mexican Boundary Survey party safely across the terrible wastes of then-unknown desert roamed over by Indian hostiles. At last the sun-scorched, saddle-sore, and foot-sore party, parched with thirst, saw from the Little San Bernardinos the towering, barren rock wall of the San Jacintos, and as they crawled across the Coachella Valley toward the mouth of Carrizo Creek Canyon, at a spot then called the Ojo Grande spring, they descried a shady grove that was not, after all, another mirage. "Here," says Emory in his *Reconnaissance*, "on November 29, several scattered objects were seen projected against the cliffs and hailed by the Florida campaigners, some of whom were along, as old friends. They were cabbage trees and marked the locale of a spring and small patch of grass."

We know now that these trees were not the Cabbage Palms (*Sabal palmetto*) of Florida, but our own Desert Palms, the only members of this great tropical family native to the western United States. And we know, too, that the Ojo Grande spring of Emory's day is now no less than Palm Springs, one of the glossiest pleasure resorts in the world, where motion picture stars come to acquire a desert tan.

Only ten minutes' automobile ride from Palm Springs lies Palm Canyon, the largest of all the groves of Desert Palm in California, and perhaps in the world. Your car mounts a steep hill, to the parking area, and there below you lies a narrow watered canyon where thousands of these trees go trooping up the winding defile of the mountain. One sees there trees of every size, seedlings and young trees, and old patriarchs whose 70 feet or more of unbranched height is only dwarfed by the towering mountain backdrop of this setting. One sees erect trees, and trees picturesquely canted at all angles. In the desert sunlight the fronds flash proudly. They stir in the canyon draft with a soft lisp and clash. And, deeply cut as the leaf blades are, into palmate lobes like the fingers of the hand, the narrow, flexible segments move separately and seem to twinkle glittering, beckoning digits. The long marginal filaments, streaming and curling in the wind, add the final touch of airy grace.

By moonlight these trees are especially magical — Palms indeed seem meant for the moon and warm winds — and then this desertic portion of the planet, its barren features unsoftened by water, seems indeed like some lunar landscape, save for the proud difference of the Desert Palms, waving life's green banners. Travelers who have been among them during one of the desert's rare but violent summer storms speak of the stiff whistling of the thrashing, living fronds, the hollow drumming of the driven rain upon the armor of dead leaves.

Like other Palms, and unlike the conifers and hardwoods, these desert trees have peculiarities that account for their strange ways and habits, almost topsy-turvy to the rules that apply to growth in other trees. Growth, for instance, is all by the great terminal bud. If this be killed — as when the Indians cut it out and roast it — the whole tree will die as surely as a man with his head cut off. This bud gives off all the leaves that the tree will ever bear in the course of its life, and looking down on top of a Palm from the mountainsides, one sees leaves in all stages of development, the innermost the youngest, the middle the full-grown, and the outermost beginning to fade and finally hang, head downward, against the stem. For this Palm does not cast its leaves when they die but retains them tenaciously as a dry persistent coat of armor about the stem. Indeed, if not burned or cut away, this shard may enclose the trunk right to the ground like a trouser leg or pantalette. When seen thus in cultivation, our Palm is apt to look dingy and unkempt in contrast to the polished formality of city parks and estates of the rich, wherefore gardeners sometimes cut away the dead, reflexed foliage. But this leaves the tree looking skinned and top-heavy, and, having lost its chief distinction, it now owns no superiority over other and more gracile Palms.

Yet in the wild this thatch has a look of tightness and dignity, and its weathered colors harmonize naturally with the desert's tints. The Indians used sometimes to burn off the leaves in the belief (perhaps not unfounded) that a heavier crop of the sweet edible berries would result. The fire permanently blackens the stem but does not otherwise injure the tree, for Palms have no true bark to lose, no all-vital cambium layer under their rind to be killed. And indeed a fire-seared Desert Palm has a picturesqueness of its own, in the wild, and speaks of the days when it was to the wandering bands of desert tribes what the Date Palm means to the Arabs and Bedouins. For where it grew it was a sign of water and herbage. Its berries and buds or hearts-of-palm fed the hungry; its seeds were ground into a flour. The leaves were used to thatch the Indian's shelters, and the threads from the foliage served to bind the cordage of the women's baskets. A band of Indians who found a good Palm grove had no reason to hunt further for a settlement site, and even today the famous Palm Canyon grove serves the Agua Caliente Indians on whose reservation it stands, for at the gateway an Indian collects a coin from you for his tribe.

It is possible that the Indians sometimes planted this species beyond its primitive range. For instance, the grove at Twentynine Palms, on the Mojave Desert, is not only out of the seemingly normal range of the species, but it is associated with so many archaeological remains that one suspects strongly that this is a plantation rather than a natural grove. Certainly it is a strangely magnetic one, what is left of it, inevitably drawing the visitor to the little oasis where, amid Cottonwoods and Mesquite, these northernmost representatives of the species stand.

Everyone who visits the grove at Twentynine Palms remarks a grave, a small mound ringed about, like a child's play place, with white quartz stones and honored only with a nameless wooden cross. Here is buried a young girl, who was being brought out on the desert for her health, by her mother, a poor woman hoping to reach the Virginia Dale mines to serve as a cook. When the young spirit left the body, February 10, 1903, the woman turned to the Palms as the only beautiful things in all that waste where she could bear to leave her child. Two old desert rats dug the grave and made a narrow coffin; they and an Indian band sang such songs as they knew or thought appropriate; a Bible was produced from somewhere and "an educated mining man" read from it. Then the desert earth was thrown upon the box. For many years the Indians and prospectors laid wild flowers on Mary Whalen's grave. Now only the old Palms could remember how long the woman looked back at them as she was led away.

HAWTHORNS

Flat-Topped Hawthorn

Cratægus punctata Jacquin

OTHER NAME: Dotted Haw.

RANGE: Montreal and west through Ontario and southern Michigan to southern Wisconsin, southeastern Minnesota, central Iowa, northern Illinois, northern and eastern Indiana, and south through western New England and New York to Delaware, and along the Appalachians to northern Georgia at high altitudes.

FROM MONTREAL almost throughout the Great Lakes basin and the upper Mississippi valley, the North American continent is covered by a vast geological stratum known as the Niagara limestone, giving rise above it to particularly fertile, deep, dark soils. So this was a region which, when it was not already prairie, was soon stripped of its primeval forests to make way for a rich agriculture, as well as the great industrial population naturally centered along the Great Lakes. As the overshadowing virgin woods were cut down, there emerged from them a little understory tree which may not have been especially important before the coming of the white man. But today the Flat-topped Hawthorn, over all this area, is frequently the commonest species of its genus, and not seldom is this the dominant tree. It is certainly so in many sections around

Niagara Falls, southern Ontario, northern Illinois, and southern Wisconsin.

Flat-topped Hawthorn may grow 20 or 30 feet high, with a trunk as much as a foot in diameter but under field conditions is usually 18 to 20 feet tall, and its long, almost horizontally spreading or gradually ascending branches give it a broadly flat-topped appearance which is unmistakable in the landscape, resembling little else in our sylva and reminding one, rather, of those Thorn trees (Acacias) which one sees in pictures of the savannas of central Africa, usually with a herd of giraffes browsing among them.

But central North America, too, has its thorn forest, though even ecological botanists often neglect to point it out. For around all the great Oak and Hickory groves of the Chicago area, for instance, there is always a ring of thorny trees of smaller stature than the members of the true groves. This thorn forest consists in Crab Apple, wild Plums, cultivated Pears and Apples which have gone back to the wild and developed thorniness, in thorny English Buckthorn which has become naturalized, brambles, and predominantly, the many kinds of Hawthorn. The two leading Hawthorns there are the dome-shaped Red Haw (*Cratægus mollis*) and the present species.

No tree is more active than this in invading the prairie. Its pioneers may be seen far out ahead of the groves of other trees, those nearest the groves grown full size, and so on, in descending steps, until on the farthest periphery of the encroaching woodland there are hundreds of little seedlings only a few inches high. And if no stately giraffes are seen browsing upon them, dairy cows do so abundantly, despite the armory of thorns.

The flowers are very late in blooming — not till well into June in the latitude of Chicago — and the fruits do not ripen until late October and even then are not edible. They are sour, hard, and gummy to the palate, up to the moment when they suddenly become dry, soft, mealy, and tasteless. But animals are less demanding than we, and the birds and rodents devour the fruits abundantly in the spring, after the little pomes have been frostbitten and rain soaked. This seems to be Nature's form of cookery, bringing the fruits to the taste of animal epicures all in good time. It is likely that a process of afterripening goes on with the seeds of this species, just as described for the Red Haw.

The same birds love to nest among the Flat-topped Hawthorns as those mentioned for the Red Haw, and the same fox squirrels hop among the boughs, and pine mice burrow about the roots, devouring the bark. The stems of this species are apparently the favorite for the apple borer, a beetle whose larva gives great trouble to orchardists. It makes gall-like swellings in the stems of this tree and these thus become a permanent locus of infection for Apples. In fact, the apple grower has a long list of just grievances against this Hawthorn, so long and grave that the lover of our native trees prefers to forget it, and to remember, rather, that this little tree is one of the most picturesque in all our sylva, striking at all times of the year but especially so in autumn when the heavy crops of fruit are on the tree and the leaves are turning bronze, gradually becoming clear gold, or sometimes deep claret red.

A closely related species, the Sandhill or Foothill Thorn (*Cratægus collina* Chapman),* is distinguished by the fact that its fruit is spherical or nearly so instead of being short-oblong, and that the stalks of the fruit and flower clusters are densely woolly. It ranges through the southern Appalachians from Virginia to Georgia and central Alabama above 2500 feet.

Editor's note: Now considered identical to *Cratægus punctata* Jacquin.

Red Haw

Cratægus mollis Scheele*

OTHER NAMES: Downy Hawthorn. Thorn Apple.

RANGE: Northern Ohio and southwestern Ontario to northern Missouri, eastern South Dakota, eastern parts of Nebraska and Kansas, and south to central Tennessee.

ALMOST EVERYONE who ever had a midwestern childhood knows about Red Haws. Their tiny apples may be eaten without stint by experimental small boys, from the moment they ripen in early September until the last of them has fallen in late October, and little girls may string them into necklaces, a jewelry better than rubies, since it can be devoured at any time. The Red Haw — Thorn Apple is usually the farmer's name for the tree itself — which has its seeds distributed by all fruit-eating birds and every little wild rodent, comes springing up joyfully along the fence rows and especially in the Oak openings between the tolerant Bur Oaks. Like them it spreads relentlessly out from the woodland upon the prairies, being another forerunner of the encroaching forest itself, forever at war with the great grasslands. When fully grown, a Red Haw may be 40 feet high and 60 feet broad, and its wide-spreading limbs may reach out so far that they rest their tips upon the ground, making a great ball-shaped mass inside of which the farm child finds a roomy house, where she can play at her woman duties.

The leaves burst their buds in midspring, and two weeks later flowering begins when the leaves are half grown, continuing in fine style for a fortnight more. Toward the end of summer the fruit is just beginning to turn a dull crimson with a purplish bloom, and at that time the Hawthorn thickets take on their colorful appearance, which reaches a height in the first and second weeks of autumn, when these trees may be loaded from top to bottom with clusters of bright red fruits. These then begin to fall swiftly; there are none left by the end of the month. During the dropping of the fruit, the leaves have begun to turn color, generally yellow or orange or a coppery hue, rarely dark red or purplish. Leaf fall is apt to be swift,

*Editor's note: Formerly *Cratægus mollis* (Torrey & Gray) Scheele.

309

and soon the trees stand quite naked, the bright harvest of pomes scattered in a circle beneath the boughs.

Here they generally lie all winter, for apparently animals prefer them after they have been softened, though children like to eat them from the tree. With respect to their edible quality, they are variable just as apples are. Some are rather dry and tasteless, and others hard and sour. But no apples could be finer than the best specimens of this species, which lack only in size. So Hawthorn fruits are often preserved by farm wives.

A curious circumstance in the germination of this species, and perhaps other kinds of *Cratægus,* is the phenomenon known as afterripening. It appears that the seeds are not capable of germinating till a high degree of acidity has developed in the embryo. This increase in acidity seems to be aided by low temperatures, so that it is likely that the ripening of the seed goes on upon or in the ground during the winter. The same effect can be produced by removing the seed coat and immersing the kernel in a weak acid solution. Gardeners report that seeds of native species of Hawthorn commonly do not germinate for two or three years; but whether this is true of the same plants under wild conditions is not certain. Apple seeds, too, exhibit afterripening; it may be said of their seeds that they are "green" or immature when they fall from the tree in the fruit. Apples are more successfully reproduced from the seed by planting outdoors in the winter than by trying to sprout them in the greenhouse with high temperatures. It is the same with this Hawthorn, and it would seem that it simply cannot sprout without a cold winter.

The Red Haw is host to a large number of little creatures. The song sparrow, mourning dove, indigo bunting, yellow warbler, and goldfinch nest, feed, and sing in the Hawthorn groves all summer long. Cattle browse the foliage eagerly, as high as they can reach, and often trim back the young trees severely into a sort of uncouth rustic topiary. The haws are a favorite food of squirrels, and field mice devour and store the seeds. The seeds themselves are digested by the field mice, not voided, but probably many a cache is forgotten or never reclaimed by its little miser, and eventually some seeds in it sprout. Sometimes a tree is completely stripped of its fruits by animals before they are even wholly ripe, causing chagrin to the botanist who may have marked that very tree and collected its flowers and waited patiently for months to collect it in fruit.

It is under the Hawthorn that the pine mouse often passes his obscure life in tunnels around the roots, on the bark of which he nibbles all winter underground. The round-headed apple borer is a longhorn beetle whose larvae work in the base of the trunk in large groups, pushing their telltale sawdust piles out of their burrows. The larvae of the tineid moth (*Ornix cratægifolia*) misspend their youth in rolling up the edges of the leaves; leaf-miners, burrowing in the tissues, write little cabalistic letters there, and gallflies make cockscomb galls on the leaves and globular galls on the midribs.

Under the dense shade cast by these old Red Haws grow happily some of the sweetest and most familiar wildflowers of the Middle West — the tall bluebell, the white snakeroot, touch-me-not, sweet cicely, and the nodding waterleaf. So each Red Haw tree and each grove of Thorn Apples is a little world in itself, and in all the world there is nothing precisely like it — quaint, yet subtle and self-contained.

Joshuatree

Yucca brevifolia Engelmann

OTHER NAMES : Yuccatree. Yucca Palm. Yucca Cactus. Tree or Joshua Yucca. Joshua.

RANGE : Irregularly scattered on the higher gravel slopes skirting the deserts of California, southern Nevada, southwesternmost Utah, and eastern Arizona, and at the bases or on the talus slopes of various desert mountains and in mountain passes, usually between 2000 and 6500 feet above sea level.

T RADITION HAS IT that the Mormons gave the Joshuatree its name. Certain it is that in 1857 Brigham Young, wishing to concentrate the power of the Latter-day Saints in Utah, summoned a Mormon colony from San Bernardino, California, to join him. They left by way of the Cajon Pass, and just on the other side of it, as they made their way down toward the Mojave River, they passed through one of the most impressive Joshua forests in the country, near present-day Victorville. We can still see what they must have beheld — a wide-spaced grove, running far as the eye can see to north and south, of the strangest tree in North America. From a distance, indeed, a Joshua looks more like the blasted skeleton of a tree which had grown all awry, for it spreads abroad no shade-giving foliage. On close inspection it is found that leaves there are, but they appear to have been hurled by a sword-thrower into the short

trunks and branches. And what leaves — a desert gray green, rigid as a dagger, with as sharp a point, and with formidable sawtoothed edges! Around the older parts of the stem and trunk the dead foliage is reflexed as a sort of palmlike thatch.

But if these trees gave no shade to the desert-crossing Mormons, they were at least full of expression. For the thick rigid branches come out at right angles to the trunks and are often bent again, as if at the elbows. So the trees seemed to the Mormons to be gesticulating, as if to wave them on their way, and the shaggy, hoary leaves added the look of some bearded Old Testament prophet. More, the Saints kept encountering these groves as they went, for this Yucca, though so erratically distributed, does recur at certain altitudes through the Mojave, and in the deserts of southern-most Nevada and southwesternmost Utah. Thus the Saints' fancy grew to a sort of mystical certainty that this gesturing prophetic tree was leading them to the promised land of Deseret, and, filled as Mormon pioneers were with biblical imagery, they named it the Joshuatree.

There are some who love it from the moment they first behold it, sil-houetted, perhaps, against some desert sunset sky, with the snows of far-off peaks still flashing their signals, and the twilight filled with the last cry of the day birds — the ash-throated flycatchers and plaintive Say phoebes — while nighthawks sweep the skies with pointed wings and the burrow-ing owls begin to pipe from their holes in the sand. At such a moment the Joshuas lose their gauntness and take on a spiritual quality. With every day that you stay among them they come to seem friendlier and the one right tree in their place. When you set off again across the treeless spaces of the great Mojave, you greet each rare recurrence of these great Yuccas as a Bedouin greets a palm grove.

But for others the first sight of this vegetation is abhorrent and the strangeness never wears off. Thus Captain John C. Frémont, the first Eng-lish-speaking traveler who ever (so far as written record goes) noticed them, found these Yuccas, with "their stiff and ungraceful forms . . . the most repulsive tree in the vegetable kingdom." True that Frémont had just come out of the San Joaquin Valley, in the days when it was still one vast meadow of wild flowers, still laced with streams from the Sierra snows and dotted with parklike groves of Oaks. Then as, crossing the Tehachapi Pass, he descended upon the vast, sere wastes of the Mojave, the sense of contrast was brutal. Yet the year was at the spring, and even he admitted that the desert too had its beauties; streaks of purple sand verbena, orange poppy, and blue gilia carpeted the Yucca groves, and his troop galloped swiftly through the air heady with perfume.

Most of Frémont's botanical collections on this, his second expedition, were lost when a mule bearing his specimens fell down a cliff into a river. No scientist sighted the Yucca forests again for ten years, when the War Department sent out reconnaissance expeditions to survey railway routes to the Pacific. The party which explored the route later taken by the Santa Fe, under two young Army officers (later to become famous), Lieutenants Whipple and Ives, reached the Victorville Yucca forests in March 1854, and the surgeon-botanist of the expedition, Dr. John Bigelow, collected specimens still without flowers. Not until 1871 did the flowers become known to science.

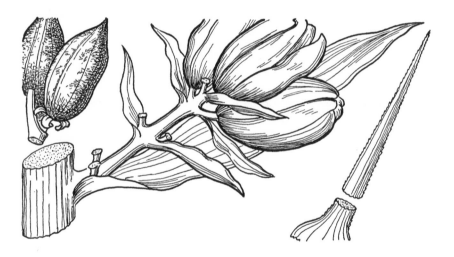

And what strange blossoms! They belong to the lily family but have the texture of creamy leather, breathing forth an odor like that of mushrooms. Flowering is most irregular; there is a little every spring, but there come "Yucca years," when all the trees of a given region will, for unexplained reasons, bloom heavily at once. Quite as curious are the fruits, the size of an ostrich egg, with a rind half dry and capsular, half berrylike and spongy. Once they are ripe, they drop quickly and, light as they are, may roll and tumble before the desert winds, shaking out seeds as they go.

The young shoot of a Joshua is a simple unbranched affair, making very slow growth, and very reluctant about producing its first bloom. But when flowering does occur at the tip, the terminal bud thereafter dies; then the first branch puts forth, a few feet below the point of flowering, and when this branch has flowered the same thing takes place again; so the Yucca forks, and forks again, dichotomously, and thus comes naturally by its gesticulating appearance. But the fantastic asymmetry is due in part to the loss of branches by self-pruning. In time the branches may be so many and so far from the stem that they weigh the main boughs down, and at last the branchlets point to the ground and may finally touch the desert sands. No one knows how old a Joshua may live to grow, and desert enthusiasts sometimes claim thousands of years, knowing they cannot easily be disproved since a Yucca does not, any more than a Palm does, produce concentric annual rings of wood. But one can distinguish the infancy, youth, middle life, and old age of these trees by the amount of the branching. Patriarchs may have a hundred branchlets and develop a trunk 4 feet in diameter, and heights up to 40 feet are known.

Under the desert sands there is a corresponding root development. Roots both grow down vertically and spread horizontally in the search for moisture, and underground runners send up the many sprouts one sees about vigorous trees. The ultimate rootlets are red, and from them the desert Indians used to obtain a dye for their patterned baskets. There is, however, no great taproot or powerful cordage of roots to anchor this top-heavy vegetable in the soft, shifting sand. As a result, one sees a great many down trees, toppled over in some desert gale.

Like Palms, Joshuatrees have no solid cylinder of wood. As the pith — always a juvenile tissue — tends to disappear with the years, the stems are apt to become hollow. But this is not to say that there is no woody tissue; there are bundles of wood fiber around the hollow center, just as in a bamboo stem. These suffice to give the tree an efficient structural system, for the hollow cylinder, as engineers know, is stronger in proportion to its weight than a solid one. For this reason Joshua wood has been used for surgical splints, since it is at once light and strong, and even for the posts of desert pioneers' houses. At one time paper was made of the fiber, and a pulp mill was started in Los Angeles. Several eastern and British newspapers bought up some of the paper stock, but fortunately it proved of poor quality. For it would not have taken long to destroy almost the entire stand of this rare tree, once serious pulp-logging operations started.

The distribution of the Joshuatree is erratic; there are many areas where one would expect it yet does not find it; and where it is found the next nearest grove may be a hundred miles away. All this suggests that it is a species once more widespread which has endured many losses and is lucky to survive at all. In general it occurs only where there is enough rainfall, or rather enough runoff from regions with 10 to 15 inches of annual precipitation, to support its thirsty roots and the water requirements of its ponderous stems and branches. The snows of the San Bernardino and the San Gabriel mountains, melting in spring, course briefly down in freshets to the foothills where the Joshuas grow in a zone of their own below that of Oneleaf Pinyon and Juniper, but above that of the treeless wastes of creosote-bush, and here and east of the little San Bernardinos and in Antelope Valley are found the only extensive forests of the Tree Yucca. But small groves recur in passes and on the benches of what are known as the "lost ranges" of the mountainous Mojave desert.

In a region such as the Mojave, which has frequently only one species of tree, it is not surprising that that tree should be a center of life for much of the fauna. So in Joshua branches and trunks, the red-shafted flicker and the cactus woodpecker drill holes for their nests. After these are abandoned they may be taken up by screech owls, bluebirds, Bewick wrens, titmice, and ash-throated flycatchers. With the long fibers of the leaves, the Scott oriole suspends its nests from the branches of the Joshuatrees. Wood rats often climb the trees to gnaw off the spiny leaves with which to make their nests impregnable.

One animal there is which seldom leaves the shelter of the Joshuas for any cause — the desert night lizard, a species of *Xantusia*. It lives under the thatch of dead leaves, in cracks of the rind, and inside decayed and fallen branches — for Joshuas are forever dropping their boughs. Because of its nocturnal habits, and because confined to the Yucca trees, it was formerly thought to be a very rare animal; at least it was rare in collections. But the California herpetologist Van Denburgh has found that every fourth or fifth tree examined yielded from one to four specimens of this little saurian. He reports that when exposed to the light it turns a pallid color, in keeping with the desert, but shows no inclination to escape by running down holes in the sand, preferring to return only to the patriarchal shelter of the Yucca. In the dark it quickly turns dark again, like a chameleon.

Extinct now is a mammal which, like the lizard, was closely bound in its life history to the Joshuatree. This is the giant ground sloth, *Nototherium*, whose remains — skeletons, desiccated hides and hair, and even the fossilized dung — were discovered in 1930 in Gypsum Cave near Las Vegas, Nevada. Analysis of the dung showed that it consisted of 80 percent, by volumetric measurement, of Joshua leaves, readily identified by their sawtoothed edges. At the present time Joshuas are as extinct as the ground sloth in the neighborhood of Gypsum Cave and only grow 3000 feet higher up. This, too, seems proof that the Joshua once inhabited a greater range, either in Glacial times or in Recent times just following the Pleistocene.

But of all the creatures linked with the Mojave's Joshuas, the most famous is the Yucca moth, *Pronuba* (*Tegeticula,* by the latest nomenclature). Its life history was discovered by that celebrated early American entomologist Charles Valentine Riley. With his old-fashioned lantern Riley watched the strange rites of the *Pronuba* and found that the female lays her eggs in the ovaries. But it is essential that the ovules should be fertilized, if a ripe supply of fruit tissue is to be at hand for her larvae. And, as if she understood the principles of pollination, she gathers loads of pollen and crams them down on the stigma — the female receptive organ of the flower. Thousands of species of insects pollinate flowers, lured there by the odor, and myriad are the floral mechanisms for catching or lifting off the pollen brushed on the insect bodies. But there is no other known instance of an insect which seems to pollinate the flowers deliberately. Say if you like that her act is some sort of reflex and not the product of forethoughtfulness like that of a human intellect. But what stimulates the reflex to such an elaborate and careful ritual? More, the Yucca flowers appear dependent on the *Pronuba* moth for fertilization. Probably no other insect visits them. A more complete symbiosis between a flower and animal could not be found.

With time, a belated appreciation of the strange beauty of the Yucca forests has come to the public, and, as resorts and guest ranches multiply on the western edge of the Mojave, they are commonly located in Joshua groves, and the trees are protected and individually valued for their fantastic qualities. The federal government in 1936 established Joshua Tree National Monument, containing 1344 square miles of desert and Yucca forest, a region so wild that it still retains some of its aboriginal fauna, which includes the desert bighorn sheep and the mule deer. You reach it most easily from Twentynine Palms, where the monument headquarters are located. But the roads are still few and sandy, and subject to sudden washouts from summer thunderstorms. Unfortunately there are many enclaves of privately owned land within the periphery of the monument — tracts that might be sold at any time that the desert's mineral wealth attracted the attention of mining interests. The status of a national monument is quite different from that of a national park, which cannot be exploited unless an act of Congress actually alienates the land from park status; but a monument can be opened up to commercial development at the discretion of the secretary of the interior. As to the wonderful Joshua groves in Antelope Valley, where Frémont rode so long ago, they are at the present time entirely in private hands, and neither the state of California nor the rich county of Los Angeles has seen fit as yet to take a step toward preserving them, beyond evincing a willingness to accept them as a gift.

Wild Black Cherry

Prunus serotina Ehrhart

OTHER NAMES: Rum or Whiskey Cherry.

RANGE: From Nova Scotia to the north shore of Lake Superior and the eastern parts of the Dakotas, Kansas, Nebraska, and Oklahoma, and into central Texas; south to central Florida.

I N THE FOREST THIS, the tallest of all Cherries and the most precious cabinet wood in the rose family, may rise to a noble 100 feet in height, with a trunk clear of branches for 30 feet and attaining 4 or 5 feet in diameter, the small horizontal branches forming a narrow oblong head. In the days when our woods were rich with such fine old Cherry trees, the Appalachian pioneers invented a drink called cherry bounce; juice pressed from the fruits was infused in brandy or rum to make a cordial which, though bitter, was in high favor among the old-time mountaineers. Bears were plentiful then in the Appalachians, and the ripening of the cherry crop was a signal for an ursine congregation. The cubs of the year learned to climb trees by following their mothers up them, to reap the wild cherry harvest. "Cherry bears" were considered especially mettlesome and best left strictly alone.

Still today it is claimed that even the cultivated cherry does not have

320

more juice than this one, and the ripe fruit is sometimes employed as a flavoring for alcoholic liqueurs. The bitter aromatic bark has a distinct odor of bitter almond or hydrocyanic (prussic) acid, which is also found in the leaves. As an astringent, the medicinal properties of the bark are even today in use for cough medicines, expectorants, and the treatment of sore throat.

But it is for its beautiful smooth-grained wood that this Cherry has found highest favor. As long ago as 1820, a traveler on the Ohio writes, "When we reached Brown's Island, five miles from the Wabash, and four from Shawneetown, the wind obliged us to anchor on the left side, close to three large flat boats, loaded with flour, bacon, whiskey, tobacco, horses, and pine and cherry planks, for the Orleans market."* It thus appears that sawn Cherry was transported from Henderson, Kentucky, all the way to New Orleans, and the presumption is that the price was even then fairly high, and esteem for the wood great, to justify such a long haul.

So from pioneer times, Cherry has grown steadily rarer. The assault upon it was twofold, just as in the case of Beech, Tuliptree, and Sycamore, in that the land on which Wild Black Cherry grew being counted the best agricultural soil, the trees were disposed of as fast as possible, even to the extent of girdling magnificent virgin growth, or burning it down, while at the same time there was a constant culling out of all the finest specimens for the sawmills. In the days of wooden Pullmans, wooden streetcars, and

---

*John Woods, *English Prairie in the Illinois Country.*

fine carriage making, Cherry was of the utmost importance. It is astonishing to remember that only fifty years ago a city could order a whole fleet of streetcars paneled in superb Cherry, when today boards of such dimensions might not be obtainable at the price of Rosewood or Ebony.

Indeed, by the close of the nineteenth century, hardwood buyers were cruising the country in a tree-to-tree search for Cherry of fine dimensions. They were so successful that dimension timber is now harder than ever to find. True, the tree is prolific, and birds devour the fruits and so scatter the seeds over the countryside, with the result that large numbers are coming up along the roadsides where the seeds are voided by the birds perching on the telephone wires and fences. But these field-grown specimens are limby, knotty, and short trunked. Only under forest conditions are Wild Black Cherries forced by competition into splendidly tall, straight growth producing saw timber. For this reason alone has Cherry sunk to twenty-eighth place among native trees, in the amount cut, and ranks at the bottom of the native cabinet woods.

Yet its virtues as such are many. Though it is weak — weaker than Black Willow — when used as a beam, it is fairly hard, and furthermore it is very smooth grained, takes a handsome finish, shrinks but little in seasoning, and warps not at all after it is seasoned, no matter what the temperature and moisture changes in the air. True that it rarely develops a fancy figure, but compensating for that is the splendid way the tree grows under forest conditions, producing wonderfully knot-free, clean, broad planks. Thus it is that Cherry came to rank second in cost only to Black Walnut, as the finest cabinet wood of temperate North America.

Cherry wood, fresh cut, is not at all cherry colored. While its pinkish tone will darken somewhat with age, stains and varnishes are commonly used to give it a "Mahogany red," which is itself, of course, not the natural hue of fresh Mahogany wood. Indeed, Mahogany and Cherry in their natural state are much alike in tone, and when both are finished off with a deep stain they are difficult to tell apart. The readiest distinguishing mark is that a smoothly cut end surface of Mahogany shows pores visible without a magnifying glass; in Cherry the pores are not visible without a magnifying glass. However, where only a veneer of these woods is used on a core of a less noble cabinet wood, these points of difference are not available. Hence, in the days when Cherry was cheaper, it used to be possible to substitute Cherry for Mahogany in a way to baffle experts. But Cherry has been so severely overcut that it is sometimes almost as expensive as Mahogany, and in its turn Cherry is imitated by skillful staining of Black Birch!

As it would no longer pay anyone to imitate Mahogany with Cherry, it will not lead us into temptation to describe the method by which it was done: "A well-known and perfect method of making cherry look like mahogany is to have the wood rubbed with diluted nitric acid, which prepares it for the materials subsequently to be applied; afterwards, to a filtered mixture of an ounce and a half of dragon's-blood dissolved in a pint of spirit of wine, is added one-third that quantity of carbonate of soda, the whole constituting a very thin liquid which is applied to the wood with a soft brush. This process is repeated at short intervals until the wood assumes the external appearance of mahogany."*

The greatest use of Cherry at the present time is for showcases, counters, and bars, closely followed by weighing apparatus, on account of its ability to "stay put" under all conditions, never throwing the metal fittings out of alignment; for the same reason it is almost always the wood used for spirit levels and is exclusively sought for the backs of electrotypes in the printing arts. The fourth most important use of cherry is planing-mill work such as paneling and interior finish. After that there is a sharp drop to much lower figures, in board feet, to furniture, which comes in fifth place; next, scientific and other precision instruments; then handles; then backs of hairbrushes; then musical instruments (actions for organs); and the list virtually ends with caskets. If many woods outrank Cherry for this last purpose, in number of board feet cut, this does not mean that most of them are better but rather that the cost of Cherry is now so high. The perfect joinery possible with such a stable wood, and the satiny smoothness with which the lid of a Cherry casket can be made to glide in the groove of the box, all recommend it highly. It is related that the immortal Daniel Boone made himself several Cherry caskets and used occasionally to sleep in them, in his old age, but gave up all but his last to needy corpses.

---

*Gibson and Maxwell, *American Forest Trees.*

Redbud

Cercis canadensis Linnæus

OTHER NAME: Judastree.

RANGE: Southern Connecticut and New York west through extreme southern Ontario and southern Michigan, northern Illinois to southern Iowa and eastern Nebraska, south to the Gulf of Mexico and northeastern Mexico.

TREE-PLANTING MR. GEORGE WASHINGTON of Mount Vernon confided many times to his diary that he had transplanted Redbuds from the woods to his garden, and when they filled the land with their flowering, he liked to tell us, in his unsentimental way, of the lovely sight. For Redbud blooms in the first fine weather — in February in the far South, in May at its farthest north, generally about the same time as the Peach trees and when the Wild Plums are clothing themselves in shining white. But Redbud flowers, which bloom on the naked twig, are neither Peach pink nor Plum white, nor red like the clay soils of the piedmont country that they love; they are a striking purplish pink or magenta. And though this is not a color which blends well with most gardens, it is one of which Nature seems to be particularly fond in the flora of eastern North America. When the Redbud flowers, the still leafless deciduous woods display its charms down every vista; it shines in the somber little groves of Scrub Pine; it troops up the foothills of the Appalachians; it steps delicately down toward swampy ground in the coastal plain, flaunts its charms beside the red clay wood roads and along the old rail fences of the piedmont. Inconspicuous in summer and winter, Redbud shows us in spring how common it is. It is notable that wherever Redbud, Dogwood, and Mountain Laurel grow, the local population believes that it has the finest display of these trees in the world. The people of eastern Texas will sincerely urge Virginians to come to the Lone Star State if they really want to see Redbud!

Once the Redbud has put out its leaves, and the flowers have faded, and all the woods are leafing out, Redbud is forgotten till in autumn the foliage turns a clear bright yellow. When the tree stands winter-naked, the pods persist on the boughs almost till spring. Yet even in summer the Redbud is a gracious little thing, with its heart-shaped, softly shining foliage. In general this is but an understory tree, never over 40 feet tall, and elbowing out little room for itself. For these reasons, and for the precocity of its blooms, Redbud is a favorite garden tree for the small property.

A passage in John Lawson's *History of North Carolina*, published in 1708, speaks of salads made of the blossoms, and in Mexico the flowers are still fried and eaten as a great delicacy. As a result of its presence in Mexico, the Redbud was first distinguished and described by Francisco Hernandez, author of the *Historia de las Plantas de Nueva España* (1571–

75). Who sent the first specimens from America we do not know, but it was described in 1696 by the herbalist Leonard Plukenet, so that it is likely that his correspondent, John Banister the Virginia missionary, was the first to send Redbud to England.

Judastree is the older but more foreign name for this tree. It is sometimes transferred to our American species from the related plant of the Mediterranean zone (*Cercis siliquastrum*), which was called Judastree in accordance with an old belief that it was the wood on which Judas Iscariot hanged himself. Wherefore its flowers, stated in the myth to have been formerly white, turned red either with shame or blood. But the name Redbud was already in use in North Carolina by 1700, for it is thus that John Lawson spoke of it. George Washington and Thomas Jefferson called it Redbud too, and that should be good enough for any American.

Oregon Alder

Alnus rubra Bongard

OTHER NAME: Red Alder.

RANGE: From Yakut Bay, Alaska, south along the coast and on the islands and Coast Range of Alaska and British Columbia through western Washington and Oregon, and along the coast of northern California.

EVERY TROUT AND SALMON FISHERMAN of the Northwest coast, surely, knows the Oregon Alder. For from Alaska to the Redwood belt of California it overleans, with its flickering, beechen shade, almost every trout pool, laving its roots in the clear, cool water. And since it grows most abundantly near the sea it is sure to be found on almost all the salmon runs, where the great king salmon comes up from the ocean to find the fresh waters where it was born, there to spawn and there to die. More, the true Chinook angler will have his catch cooked over this Alder's coals, just as the epicure of hams insists on Hickory smoke to flavor them.

True, there are other creek-side Alders of tree size, but this species is known at once by its concave-convex leaves, the margins somewhat curled under, and by the markedly paler undersides of the blades. When forest wind or ocean breeze sweeps through the boughs, the undersides flash silvery, like some Willows'. And always there is the reflection on the under-

sides of this Alder's light canopy, of water, running, or wind-whipped, or troubled into concentric ripples where a big fish has plopped — crawling silvery ring on ring of light, like music of which the sound is inaudible, only the nimble rhythm running on.

Everywhere that it grows this tree is associated with water, whether plunging mountain streams, or the mouth of a creek wandering to the sea, or the stagnant swamp behind some long lagoon sheltered from the tumbling, hoarse-voiced open water by a gleaming sandspit. In such a location grows what is perhaps the most beautiful grove of this tree on all the coast; you see it from the shores of Tomales Bay, in Marin County, California, as you drive along State Highway 1. On the other side of the long narrow bay, over on the Point Reyes peninsula, these Alders grow for miles, their pale trunks shining almost white as some Birch's, out of the inner gloom of the dark wood, gracefully leaning or picturesquely contorted, clear of branches nearly to the top where their domes of foliage interlock, crown with crown, to form a high canopy. One longs to walk in these groves, but distance lends them their greatest enchantment. The ground where they grow is boggy, the groves are trackless, the air is stagnant and full of mosquitoes; best to admire them from across the water and pass on.

It is in the Puget Sound region that this Alder attains its greatest height — 100 to 120 feet, with boles 1 to 3 feet thick — a very respectable tree even in the company of the great Brown Birch, the Black Cottonwood, the Douglas Firs, and the Grand Firs with which it associates. But even when the trees are only 30 and 40 feet high they never lose their feminine charm, with that pale bark, those gracile stems commonly growing in sisterly groups and leaning picturesquely away from each other.

The bark is the loveliest feature of the tree. It is, in youth, a soft grayish white, quite as pleasing as any Aspen's or Beech's bark and almost as lovely as a Birch's, though it never peels. As the trees grow older, irregular low lumpy growths appear on the boles; these are generally blackish. And the very rainy or foggy climate of this Alder's range induces long lines of dark green moss to grow, especially on the north and west. The resultant mottling of colors is exquisitely subtle and harmonious. One could not ask for a lovelier sylvan presence than this.

Lumbermen prefer to call this the Red Alder — a most misleading name to the student in the field, for no Alder has so white a bark. But scratch that bark with your penknife and you will find that inside it is a rich red. The wood, too, turns reddish brown on exposure to the air or, if cut in autumn, a pale golden yellow. This is no disadvantage, however, for most of the cut Alder is destined to be stained darker, in imitation of Walnut and Mahogany. It is a hardwood of many fine qualities; if properly seasoned and stored it does not warp or check appreciably in any plane. Though it has no fancy figure, it sometimes shows fine pith-ray flecks, similar to the clash of quartered Oak. The wood is highly shock-resistant and in the position of a beam or post is not too far behind Douglas Fir in strength. For high-grade veneer panels it is the equal of Yellow Poplar and Basswood, and for turned parts of furniture better than Red Gum. It takes paint, enamel, glue, and nails well, and its only fault is that it decays so rapidly in contact with the weather and the soil.

Formerly Red Alder was considered by lumbermen fit only for fuel (it is a good one), but the Northwest furniture companies began less than fifty years ago to realize that they need not import eastern hardwoods for all of their work, and today more Red Alder is cut than any other Northwest hardwood, including trees with such famous reputations as Oak, Birch, Maple, and Poplar. It is sometimes used as a three-ply or five-ply laminated wood, but in general it is manufactured into medium and cheap grades of furniture — that is, the sort made of solid, not veneered wood, such as kitchen chairs. The total amount of demand for such furniture is high, even if the styles are utilitarian and the prices low. Dozens of other uses are found for Red Alder, from ladder rungs to the inner soles of sports shoes.

The expanding business in Red Alder is limited only, but importantly, by the limited amount — perhaps only some 2 billion board feet, with the cut 23 million a year. Red Alder logging is not a business which can be profitably carried on as a continuous operation. And indeed most mills that saw and plane it do not lumber it. Lumbering is done by thousands of small operators, mostly ranchers who turn to logging for a few months in the slack season, selecting trees on their own lands and hauling them to market.

The greatest value of the Oregon Alder is not as lumber but as a species that moves in swiftly on burned-over lands. Owing to the abundance and lightness of its seeds and their high viability, it reproduces well and grows swiftly, enriching the soil and providing shelter from sun and wind for other trees. Then, in fifty to eighty years, old age begins to overtake this short-lived nurse tree, and the valuable softwood timber trees outstrip and at last replace it.

LOCUSTS

Sweet Locust

Gleditsia triacanthos Linnæus

OTHER NAMES: Thorny, Honey, or Black Locust. Thorny or Three-thorned Acacia. Honeyshucks.

RANGE: Central New York and eastern Pennsylvania to northern Florida, west through southern Ontario, Michigan, and Wisconsin to southeastern Minnesota and eastern South Dakota, and along the Gulf of Mexico to eastern Texas, with its western limits in Nebraska and Oklahoma. Extensively planted, and the exact limits of its natural range difficult to determine.

DOWN IN FLORIDA THIS TREE is still sometimes called by the obsolete name of Confederate Pintree, because its formidable spines were used to pin together the tattered uniforms of the Southern hosts in the war of the Blue and the Gray. Honeyshucks is the name used in some parts of Virginia, and very appropriate it is on account of the sweet pods eagerly eaten by cattle and sometimes by nibbling country boys. True that Honey Locust is the name given it almost throughout our horticultural, botanical, and forestry literature, but as country people usually apply Honey Locust to *Robinia pseudoacacia* (q.v.) because of its showy as well as fragrant flowers, both trees lay nearly equal claim to this as a name. Thus the best thing to do, in the interests of clarity, is to apply

331

it to neither, since both have other, and usually different, titles. The word Locust, of course, is a transposition to a New World tree of an Old World name. When Saint John went into the wilderness he lived on "honey and locusts," says the Bible, and by a later transposition the name of the noisy insect became attached to the rattling, edible pods of Carob (*Ceratonia siliqua*), often called St. John's bread.

Not unnaturally, a sweet-tasting pod on an American tree received the name of Locust. The pods are eagerly eaten by cattle when they can find them on the ground, though it is not easy for the animals to browse them from the thorny branches, and thus the tree is spreading far in its range, as the voided seeds are distributed by the cattle from pasture to pasture. In such open places, the ponderous trunk of this tree soon forks with many erect secondary trunks. The gradually spreading limbs and branchlets tend to droop at the tips, while the crown is generally open and rather flat topped — a habit rare in a lofty tree. And Sweet Locust, on the rich bottomlands of southern Illinois, is said to grow 140 feet high, or it did, at least, in the days of forest virginity. A tree in Dayton, Ohio, has a spread of more than 100 feet in diameter, with a girth of nearly 15 feet.

Although sometimes the stout trunk of the Sweet Locust is devoid of thorns, other specimens are beset by a horrendous armory of long, triple-branched thorns that may be a foot long, and are sharp as bayonets. Not even when closely pressed by dogs, it is said, will a squirrel attempt to climb such a tree. While the thorns of the Black Locust are superficial and easily picked off, those of the Sweet Locust arise from the wood and cannot by any means be pulled out. At first they are bright green, then bright red, and when mature a rich chestnut brown that shines as if it had been polished. In the days when the southern mountain folk had to use the natural resources at hand, they employed these thorns in carding wool and for pinning up the mouths of wool sacks.

Even the twigs may bear thorns, especially the lower ones and those on little trees, though some trees are prickly to the very top. Sometimes the thorns bear leaves, proving that they are modified branches. This is a slow tree to leaf; long after other citizens of the forest are clothed in foliage, the fiercely thorny, dark-barked Honeyshucks stands naked and secretive, as if refusing to yield to the persuasions of spring. At last the tender, airy, feathery foliage begins to appear, which early in autumn turns clear yellow, then falls, leaving the tree bare for another six months.

Bare save for the strange fruit. In late summer one begins to notice the clusters of hanging flat pods, a foot or more long. Gradually twisting and contorting (for some time without opening), they remain on the tree most of the winter, where one can hear them rattle dismally in the wind. At last they fall, before spring.

The wood can boast a remarkable durability — 80 to 100 percent of that of White Oak. A knot-free or thorn-free board, where one can be found, ranks second in strength under pressure as a beam only to Black Locust, among all our trees. Far less than Black Locust is this tree attacked by borers; in fact, it seems entirely repellent to them. Yet with all these stalwart qualities, which should place it with Hickory, Ash, White Oak, and Black Locust as a heavy-duty lumber, Sweet Locust is rarely cut and has even been sent to market as Sycamore! Some say that it is weakened by the trunk thorns, others report that it is considered too coarse for any but the roughest uses. True that it makes excellent railway ties and fence posts, on account of its durability, but many a wood can now be creosoted and preserved against decay, which makes this virtue less precious. A kind of antique honor remains to the wood of Sweet Locust from the fact that, before they adopted firearms, the proud and intelligent Cherokees of Tennessee chose to make their bows of it.

Water Locust

Gleditsia aquatica Marshall

RANGE: From south-central Florida to the coastal plain of South Carolina along the Gulf Coast to the Brazos River, Texas. Northward in the Mississippi basin to central parts of Kentucky and Tennessee, and southern and west-central Illinois and extreme southern Indiana.

O NE OF THE FEATURES of the North American sylva which most profoundly impressed foreign travelers, like Prince Maximilian of Wied, Nuttall, the two Michaux, and even the earliest *conquistadores* like DeSoto and Cabeza de Vaca, was the solemn grandeur of the forests which inhabited the land regularly inundated by the annual floodwaters of the Mississippi and its great tributaries. On such low-lying land where the spring floods stood long in numberless sloughs and bayous and oxbow lakes, grew the Cypress, the cane, the Sycamore, Bottom Hickory, Sweet Gum, Black Gum, Swamp Cottonwood, and the present species, the Water Locust. It formed an understory tree beneath the towering Cypresses and yet was 50 or 60 feet high, and sometimes made up densely thorny groves. The short trunk usually divides a few feet from the ground into stout, spreading, and contorted branches to form a wide, irregular, flat-topped head, something like the Mesquite of Texas. The spines can be formidable indeed — simple or triple-branched and half an inch thick at base, clothing sometimes the entire tree. Such was not a vegetable with which the pioneers cared to try force, as they threaded their way through the ancient timber of the primeval bottoms.

The flowers do not appear until the leaves have completely grown, in May or June; the fruit is fully ripe in August. At almost all times during the summer one may see a handsome glossy red growth of new foliage putting out. The Water Locust would not be a bad-looking tree in cultivation, but its demand for a high water table will probably confine it forever to the kingdom of the water moccasin and the no less deadly malarial mosquito.

A fine polish is taken by the wood of Water Locust, and it should make an excellent cabinet wood, but when lumbermen cut it at all they never seem to send it to market under its own specific name, so that it is impossible to say how much of it is ever used. Farmers in the region where it grows have, because Water Locust is so durable in contact with soil, made fence posts of it for more than a century.

Black Locust

Robinia pseudoacacia Linnæus

OTHER NAMES: Yellow, White, Red, Green, Post, or Honey Locust. False or Bastard Acacia.

RANGE: Originally, perhaps, only in the southern Appalachians, Virginia, the lower Ohio valley, and the Ozarks, at present naturalized as an escape from cultivation over most of the eastern United States, sometimes in the western states and Europe.

WHEN IN 1607 THE FIRST ENGLISHMEN to make a permanent settlement in the future United States of America landed upon a little island in the James River, Virginia, moored their ships to some great trees leaning over the bank, and faced the forest wilderness of the New World, there wasn't an axman or carpenter in this well-dressed shipload of fortune hunters, younger sons of prominent families, and ne'er-do-wells. Yet there have been illustrators and historians who represent them as building log cabins (no mean feat!) for their first habitations. Here, however, is the testimony, as to the first homes of these Virginians, by Mark Catesby, the British naturalist who visited Virginia only a century after the founding of Jamestown:

"Being obliged to run up with all the expedition possible such little houses as might serve them to dwell in, till they could find leisure to build larger and more convenient ones, they erected each of their little hovels on four only of these trees (the Locust-tree of Virginia), pitched into the ground to support the four corners; many of these posts are yet standing, and not only the parts underground, but likewise those above, still perfectly sound."

These words attest to two significant points — the great durability of Locust wood in contact with the soil, and the lack of any notion of log cabins. That form of domestic architecture did not exist in Britain, and these colonists had presumably not only never seen a log cabin but never even heard of one. For the log cabin was brought to us by the early Swedish colonists of Delaware, many decades later, and formed no part of the archi-

tecture of Jamestown, Plymouth, or most of the earliest European settlements on the Atlantic coast. Those early colonists first lived, as Mark
Catesby says, in "hovels," and when they had time to make themselves
houses they laboriously hewed out and tongued and tenoned the structural beams and covered them with clapboards.

Apparently the name of Locust for this species was given it first in
Jamestown, for we have the evidence of William Strachey in his *Historie
of Travaile into Virginia Britannia* (1610), which tells us of "a kynd of low
tree, which beares a cod like to the peas, but nothing so big; we take yt to
be locust." By this he meant that the Jamestowners supposed it to be the
Old World Locust tree (*Ceratonia siliqua*) of the Mediterranean zone, the
Carob, or St. John's bread. Obviously Strachey and the others had never
seen St. John's bread, but the name of Locust has stuck to our tree. There
is no substitute for it except by calling on another analogy, as the English
do, and titling it False Acacia. But country people today, almost everywhere in the northern states, call this tree Honey Locust because of the
sweet breath of the blossoms. Yet the botanical and horticultural works all
try to confine the name Honey Locust to the Sweet Locust *Gleditsia
tricanthos*. This confusion, which has persisted a century or so and promises to continue, is best circumvented here by designating our tree as the
Black Locust, a name in good standing with the foresters.

Under any name, this tree is impressive, when it grows to a soldierly 80
feet, the trunk 3 or 4 feet thick and the topmost branches often spreading
the ferny foliage high above the surrounding trees. When the Locust
flowers, in late spring, its pendant spikes of honey-sweet blossoms look as
though some white wistaria had climbed in the stalwart tree and let down
fragrant tassels of bloom.

Among the Locust's numerous familiar charms, most famous is the so-
called sleep of the leaves. At nightfall the leaflets droop on their stalklets,
so that the whole leaf seems to be folding up for the night. Physiologists
assure us that the mechanism of this "sleep" is the loss of cell turgidity or
sap pressure in the little secondary stalks that bear each leaflet. Because
some minds require that all things in Nature shall serve some useful purpose, as from a human point of view we understand usefulness, it has
been asserted that the sleep of the Black Locust's leaves is a habit that has
been acquired as a means of avoiding too great loss of moisture. But this
can scarcely be so, since the leaves fold at night when the moisture content of the air normally rises and its warmth diminishes. In the heat of the

day, when the leaves should be in the greatest danger of withering, they are fully expanded. So the "sleep" has not yet been explained in purposive terms.

It is not certain when Black Locust was first introduced into Europe. Either Jean Robin, herbalist to Henry IV of France, or his son Vespasien grew seeds of this tree and sent them between 1601 and 1636, presumably from Louisiana. At any rate, the generic name *Robinia* does honor to these Robins. Toward the end of the eighteenth century in Europe the growing of Black Locust became a rage. No other American tree has so extensive a foreign literature. Senator de Neufchâteau, in 1803, published a 315-page book extolling its virtues and explaining its cultivation to the French. William Cobbett, famous English publicist, anti-Jacobin, politician, rural economist, having fled to America, took to growing Black Locust, between 1817 and 1819, on his farm on Long Island where there was then a vogue for the culture of this tree, the hope being to supply the British Navy with treenails. For the Locust nails of many an old-time vessel were stronger than the strongest hulls, and far longer-lived; the British gave as one excuse for their defeat on Lake Champlain, in the War of 1812, the superiority of Locust in our hastily built fleet.

But Cobbett made America too hot to hold him, by libeling the famous Dr. Rush for having allegedly killed George Washington by malpractice, so he returned to England with a quantity of Black Locust seed — and the corpse of Thomas Paine. This he had dug up from its neglected grave in New Rochelle, intending to inter it in a splendid monument, to atone for his former attacks on the author of *The Rights of Man*. The monument was never erected; on Cobbett's death, the coffin was auctioned off to a furniture dealer, and the renowned corpse inside was lost to history!

But Cobbett, if he failed to inter Paine nobly, did wonders keeping alive the popularity of Black Locust. His panegyric on this tree in his widely read *Woodlands* (1825) aroused sanguine hopes. To satisfy the demand he himself had created, Cobbett imported immense quantities of seeds from America and sold over a million plants. Even this did not suffice, and he exhausted the London nurseries to satisfy the clamor of his customers.

"The evidence of Cobbett's activity is very marked in the gardens around London and all other cities and towns throughout Great Britain. ... British-grown Acacia has been used occasionally in old furniture, and will compare favorably with satinwood for such work. Exposure to light and air improves the colour, and it is often mistaken for the latter wood. The burrs [burls], cut into veneer, although lighter in colour, compare favorably with Amboyna. On more than one estate the owners have planted Acacia trees for more than three generations for estate work, and have always refused to sell any as they have recognized the value of the timber for estate purposes."*

Long before Cobbett's day our pioneer ancestors learned that no other wood in America has more high qualities than the Locust's. In the first place, almost the entire woody cylinder of the trunk is heartwood, always the strongest part of a tree. It is the seventh hardest in all our sylva, and, as to strength in the position of a beam, Locust is the strongest in North America outside the tropics. It is the stiffest of all our woods, exceeding Hickory by 40 percent. Of all important hardwoods, Black Locust shrinks least in drying, losing only 10 percent in volume though 20 percent in weight. It is the most durable of all our hardwoods; taking White Oak as the standard of 100 percent, Black Locust has a durability of 250 percent. The wood takes such a high polish as to appear varnished. The fuel value of Black Locust is higher than that of any other American tree, exceeding even Hickory and Oak, being almost the equal, per cord at 20 percent moisture content, of a ton of anthracite coal.

Yet with all these splendid qualities Black Locust is not even mentioned in the usual lumbering statistics. The chief reason is that the Locust borer beetle (*Cyllene robiniæ*†) is so ruinous in many regions that Black Locust is too seldom found in sound condition. In North America, but not in Europe, the infection is all but universal, and no measures of control have had any effect. Locust boards are therefore almost unknown, and the only common use has been for fence posts, railway ties, and small articles such as rake teeth, tool handles, ladder rungs, and (in the days when such things were in common use) buggy hubs and policemen's clubs.

Not until 1936 did botanists get around to describing, as a distinct variety (variety *rectissima* Raber‡), a form of the Black Locust known as Shipmast Locust, which farmers of New York State and New Jersey and estate owners of Long Island had, for a hundred years or more, recognized by its distinguishing points and superior qualities. The Shipmast Locust takes its name from the fact that the main stem grows straight up through the branches, without forking till near the top, like the mast of a ship, or like

*A. L. Howard, *Trees in Britain*, 1946.
†*Editor's note:* Now *Megacyllene robiniæ.*
‡*Editor's note:* Now considered identical with the species.

the stem of a Spruce. The lateral branches are few in number, and after leaving the main stem they rise upward at a sharp angle of 60 degrees to 90 degrees with the main axis. Commonly the lateral branches do not taper out to the end in the gradual and uniform manner of most trees, but instead they narrow down abruptly, somewhat in the manner of Japanese dwarf trees. Especially in winter is the Japanese look of the trees apparent. The shipmast habit and the short branches are found not only in close groves of these trees but even where the Shipmast Locust is growing alone on a lawn with all the space it needs to develop.

In the common Black Locust the bark, though deeply furrowed, has the horizontal lines of the furrows broken by many "cross checks," but on the Shipmast Locust there are none such and the massively heavy bark is very deeply furrowed, the ridges straight or somewhat twisted and standing out like the muscles of a Titan's leg, reminding one in its grain of the bark of the California Redwood save for the gray color. Flowering in the Shipmast Locust is comparatively sparse, and the calyx is usually green or yellowish green, not reddish or reddish brown as in the common Locust. Futhermore, the pistils seem too commonly infertile so that seed is scarce. Although there is no difference in the microscopic structure of the wood, the Shipmast produces a yellowish, not a reddish brown heartwood. But most important of all, the wood of Shipmast Locust, in the neighborhood of New York, endures much longer in contact with the soil than that of the common sort, which ordinarily lasts fifteen years, while a surveyors' stake of Shipmast Locust, dated 1881 and dug up in 1942, was found to be in perfect condition.

Apparently Shipmast Locust is never found apart from cultivation; with its almost total lack of seeds, this could hardly be otherwise, and it appears that for generations a small but knowing group in the Hudson valley and on Long Island have been propagating this valuable tree.

Those who know it well call it sometimes the Old-fashioned and sometimes Yellow Locust. Where this variety originated and when is not known, but it is most abundant in the oldest-settled parts of Long Island. To take a single example, the great Shipmast Locusts still standing at Roslyn, on the grounds of Washington Tavern, the former residence of the old Dutch family of the Bogarts, are mentioned in an article in *The Long Island Farmer* for March 6, 1879, and stated then to have been planted about 1700 and probably introduced by Captain John Sands of Sands' Point. They were enormous and ancient trees in 1791, according to the memoirs of a member of the family.

The Shipmast Locust may not be as beautiful as a lawn specimen, but as a timber tree it is distinctly more valuable and less subject to borers than the typical Black Locust. If ever we come to our senses and start planting and growing our valuable hardwoods instead of cutting them down faster than they can be replaced, Shipmast Locust might well be one of the first varieties on which to concentrate.

The discovery of a possible ancestral form of the mysterious Shipmast Locust was announced in 1948 by the federal Department of Agriculture, as a result of a prolonged investigation by Dr. Henry H. Hopp of the Bureau of Plant Research in the quest of a beetle-free strain of Locust having the qualities of fine saw timber. In Randolph County, West Virginia, Dr. Hopp discovered scattered stands of tall, straight Black Locust, the finest quality in the country, producing trunks of arrowy straightness, free of branches for 50 feet or more. These trees are highly resistant to the attacks of borers, and yet, unlike the Shipmast Locust, they seed heavily under forest conditions. Seeds are now being propagated by the Conservation Commission of West Virginia and will be distributed for afforestation purposes. This strain is said to possess properties that make it particularly advantageous for mine props, millions of which are used in the state's great coal-mining industry.

Rose-Flowering Locust

Robinia viscosa Ventenat

OTHER NAME: Clammy Locust.

RANGE: Mountains of Pennsylvania south on the Appalachians to Alabama.

THE DISCOVERER of this little tree (which is sometimes 20 feet high) was the first great American nature writer, William Bartram, whose classic *Travels*, first published in Philadelphia in 1791, was a favorite of Wordsworth and Coleridge, profoundly influencing them with its description of pure wilderness, so that the Lake Poets dreamed at one time of removing in a body to found a Poets' Perfect State on the

banks of the Susquehana (choosen for its poetic name). Of Bartram's book, Carlyle wrote to Emerson that "all American libraries ought to provide themselves with that kind of books and keep them as a future *biblical* article."

William Bartram, himself the son of a famous botanist, old John Bartram of Philadelphia, was the first plantsman who ever collected in the southern Appalachians, and many were the trees which he, first of all white men, beheld. Often without guides, quite at ease even in the midst of the hostile Cherokees in the summer of 1776, William Bartram gives us this picture of Blue Ridge scenery on the day when he first collected the Rose-flowering Locust:

"My next flight was up a very high peak, to the top of the Occonne Mountain, where I rested; and turning about found that I was now in a very elevated situation, from whence I enjoyed a view inexpressibly magnificent and comprehensive. The mountainous wilderness which I had lately traversed, down to the region of Augusta, appearing regularly undulated as the great ocean after a tempest; the undulations gradually depressing, yet perfectly regular, as the squama of fish, or imbrications of tile on a roof; the nearest ground to me of a perfect full green; next more glaucous; and lastly almost blue as the ether with which the most distant curve of the mountains seemed to be blended."

Of the little tree itself he says: "This beautiful flowering tree rose twenty to thirty feet high, with a crooked leaning trunk; the branches spread greatly, and wreathing about, some almost touching the ground;

however there appears a singular pleasing wildness and freedom in its manner of growth; the slender subdivisions of the branches terminate with heavy compound panicles of rose or pink coloured flowers, and amidst a wreath of beautiful pinnated leaves."

In 1790 André Michaux collected the Rose-flowering Locust in the same region (the mountains of South Carolina) and introduced it into his acclimation garden at Ten Mile Station near Charleston. Thence the plants were sent to Michaux's son François in Paris, and the first plantation of which we know in Europe was made from descendants of these plants by Louis Guillaume Lemonnier in his garden near Montreuil. Then, from the time of the elder Michaux for nearly a century, Rose-flowering Locust disappeared from scientific ken. It became a lost tree even as was John Bartram's famed Franklinia, and Michaux's own little flower, Shortia. Not until 1882, or ninety-seven years after it was first found, was the Rose-flowering Locust rediscovered, on Buzzard's Ridge near Highlands, North Carolina, by the distinguished Baltimore collector, bibliophile, and philanthropist John Donnell Smith.

Presumably the wood of this tree would be valuable if ever the trunks grew large enough, in view of its strength and hardness, but a species so outstandingly pretty in flower need neither toil nor spin. It does, however, have high value because of its extensive creeping roots and the many sucker shoots it sends out; these make an excellent binder of soil on railroad and highway embankments and road cuts. At the same time, it beautifies the raw spots it thus covers, so that this plant has come into great vogue all over the country. It is now escaped from cultivation northward to Nova Scotia and Wisconsin and extensively on the piedmont of Carolina.

In midspring the flowers appear, and though the blossoms have no odor, they make up for this in size and in grace of form and above all in color; the flesh-tinted strains are not so pleasing to some eyes, but the rich rose-hued are unsurpassed in depth and warmth. So brilliant and large are they that they quite transform the roadsides where they are planted, and when encountered in their native wilds they look like garden flowers bred by the most premeditated art; it seems at first hard to believe that they had already attained to such positively showy perfection when first discovered so long ago by Bartram.

Yellowwood

Cladrastis lutea (F. Michaux) K. Koch

OTHER NAMES: Virgilia. Yellow Locust. Yellow Ash. Gopherwood.

RANGE: Rare and local in extreme southwestern North Carolina and eastern and central Tennessee, northeastern Georgia, western Alabama, Kentucky, and very rarely in central Indiana. Reported from Missouri, Arkansas, and Oklahoma, but not certainly as a native.

A N ICY RAIN was falling — a rain that presently turned to blinding snow — and the roaring creeks of Tennessee were rising fast, on the last day of February 1796 when André Michaux stopped his horse, somewhere in the lonely woods 12 miles from Fort Blount, to examine a curious tree. True, the leaves must have been off it then; it stood winter-naked, but with its smooth silvery gray bark shining like some wood nymph through the drear forest. With his experienced plantsman's eye, this wandering Frenchman, whose romantic life included adventures in Persia, Mesopotamia, and the Trans-Caspian regions and had even embraced curing the daughter of the Shah of a mysterious malady, now added to his long list of first discoveries of American tree species what is one of the rarest trees of eastern North America. For the Yellowwood has a most restricted range, and even within the described limits of that range it is often a distinctly rare tree. But André Michaux, that cold

and nasty day in 1796, was recognizing by his native flair something neither he nor many other white men had ever seen — the only American species of this strange genus which is best represented in the mountains of China and Japan.

The plantsman remained over at Fort Blount seeking an opportunity to pull young shoots of his new tree, but the ground was so covered with snow that he was unable to get any. A young officer stationed at the fort obligingly cut down some trees for him, and from them Michaux was able to gather seeds. He also cut off some of the roots of the felled trees to replant in his acclimation garden near Charleston, South Carolina. Thence he would one day send them, with his Magnolias and Rhododendrons and so many other of his American discoveries, to France. But no happy fate awaited them there; it is said that Queen Marie Antoinette dispatched a large part of Michaux's collection, which was sent to Versailles (since he was a royal botanist), to her father, the Emperor of Austria, after which all trace of them is lost. Others were banished to Marly, that simple little country place which the kings of France had established to get away from the fatigues, splendors, and lack of privacy at Versailles (which had also started out as a simple country place). But Marly soon came to rival Versailles in cost and splendor, though it was never popular, and there Michaux's collection of living trees from America probably shared the fate of the whole of Marly's ostentatious, overreaching scheme, since almost from the first Marly was neglected, especially the planting. Later, François Michaux, the son, when he was in Nashville, gathered seeds of Yellowwood, and it is told that their descendants grow still in the Tuileries gardens in Paris.

The elder Michaux's own life was to be thrown away, when he left

America, on the far-off island of Madagascar, but of his fate and that of his trees he could know nothing now, as he sat down to write to Territorial Governor Blount an account of his discovery, with the information that the inner bark of the roots yielded a dye which he thought must be valuable.

And so the pioneer Tennesseeans came to learn. They reduced the roots to chips with the ax; the women then boiled the chips, and the yellow coloring matter was thus extracted. Many a yellow stripe in a piece of old-time homespun must have been dyed by this lovely tree, before synthetic dyes became cheap at the stores.

Yellowwood soon attracted the attention of the menfolk as well. Its lightness, combined with unusual strength, and the beautiful pale wood which takes so high a polish, made a unique gunstock, for in those days mountaineers were accustomed to buy the metal fittings and barrels from the gunsmith and blacksmith, but it was each man's pride to whittle out his own stock. If only Yellowwood did not habitually fork from near the base into several thin stems, no one of which would repay the cost of felling it, in terms of board feet, this would be a superb cabinet wood. But then, if Yellowwood were a merchantable tree it would long ago have grown rarer than it is.

Fortunately its lovely appearance, with that mottled bark, the graceful fronds of foliage, the milk white spikes of drooping flowers like wistaria, and the clear sunset gold of the leaves in fall, have all combined to make this tree a favorite in cultivation. Not, to be sure, as the hardy Black Locust is popular — with the millions — but among the knowing who choose trees for their refinement and rarity.

SUMACS

Staghorn Sumac

Rhus hirta (Linnæus) Sudworth*

OTHER NAMES: Velvet, Virginia, or American Sumac. Vinegar-tree.

RANGE: From the Maritime Provinces and Quebec to Minnesota, south to Maryland, Virginia, West Virginia, northern Kentucky, northern Indiana, and Illinois to northeastern Iowa, and in the mountains to North Carolina.

THE RICHLY VELVETY, thick, branching twigs, so like the antlers of a stag when they are "in the velvet," have given this handsome little tree the first part of its popular name. The second half, which is spelled, according to your taste, Sumach, Summaque, Shumac, Shumack, and probably with even more variation, is said to derive from the Arabic title for another species (*Rhus coriaria*) of the Mediterranean zone, which is *simmâk* according to some, and *summaq* if you follow Webster. Still others there are who insist that the word is simply a corruption of "shoe-make," in reference to the tree's properties useful in tanning fine leather. The name *typhina* is an allusion to the supposed medical virtues of the plant, applied in the past by country folk in the treatment of typhoid fever. As for the name *Rhus*, you may — if you are one of the happy quibblers who enjoy such innocent detection — trace it all the way

*Editor's note: Formerly *Rhus typhina* Linnæus.

347

back to ancient Greece, where the great botanist Diocorides had a word for it.

There is a Danish proverb that says "a dear child has many names," and certainly the varied titles of this tree and its relatives show the interest in which they have been held through the ages. Yet there is nothing in Europe to compare with the American Sumac, and of all the Sumacs of the New World, the Staghorn is the most striking. In autumn gorgeous, often mottled, shades of orange, crimson, or purple may be seen on the same tree, and with them other leaves which have not yet turned but keep a deep green on the upper surface and a silvery underside. No wonder this tree caught the eye of some of our very first colonists, who must have sent it back to Europe in the sixteenth century; at least, it was described by Caspar Bauhin, the celebrated physician and botanist of Basle, Switzerland, in 1596, in a work whose modest little title was *Pinax Theatri Botanicorum seu Index in Theophrasti, Diocoridis, Plinii, et botanicorum qui a sicula scripserunt opera.*

Sumac is one of the chief plants to give to our Indian summer scene a sort of mellow savagery, a colorful wilderness character like that of a "good Injun" in a childhood storybook. It was, indeed, a part of the redskin's peace pipe. For the leaf of the tobacco plant was seldom smoked by him unadulterated; to him a "smoke" was understood to be a blend of cured leaves among which Sumac was a most important ingredient. For our own folk, in the days when our land was young, the plant had a friendly place in daily life. A cooling drink like lemonade was made out of the fruits, whose acidulous hairs contribute a pleasant sour taste. The country people of the Appalachians, especially in Maryland and the Virginias, used to bring Sumac to the tanneries, for its leaves and twigs are rich in tannin; the finest grades of leather, at one time, were cured with Sumac.

With synthetics and progress those simple uses are over. But still in summer, unchanged, the Staghorn Sumac lifts its immense panicles of vivid flowers among the great frondlike pinnate leaves, and still in autumn the brilliant fruits, the most variously brilliant foliage, shout out their color to the dying year. Flaunting orange, war-paint vermilion, buttery yellow, or sometimes angry purple may be seen all together on a single tree. More, it commonly happens that half of a compound leaf, or even half of a leaflet may retain its rich, deep, shining green, in calm contrast to the flaming autumnal hues. And at all times the lower surface of the foliage keeps its pallid, glaucous cast that, when early frost has brushed it, turns silver. Probably no tree in the country, perhaps in the world, may exhibit so many and such contrasting shades and tints, such frosty coolness with its fire.

Poison Sumac
Toxicodendron vernix (Linnæus) Kuntze*

OTHER NAMES: Poison Dogwood. Poison Elder. Poison Ash. Poisontree. Poisonwood. Thunderwood.

RANGE: Florida to central Maine, southern Vermont, the southern tip of Ontario, throughout Ohio and Indiana, southern Michigan, northern Illinois, to Wisconsin and Minnesota, and in the South west through Mississippi and Louisiana to eastern Texas; largely absent from the Mississippi basin except as listed above.

EVERY AMERICAN CHILD, unless he has been confined exclusively to city life, has been taught to recognize poison ivy by means of the old ditty: Leaflets three, quickly flee. He knows that poison

*Editor's note: Formerly *Rhus vernix* Linnæus.

ivy is either a climbing vine or a sprawling shrub, found in fence rows, woods, and thickets. And once he has learned to recognize the plant and has had, perhaps, some painful experience with touching it, he is on the watch for it. But the ditty does not describe Poison Sumac, tree-sized relative of poison ivy, as witness this testimony of a well-known tree student:

"I had been botanizing in some bottom lands of Mad River on an October afternoon and had been successful in finding several rarities; as I turned to leave the swampy ground, I noticed a tall shrub with most exquisitely colored leaves; I worked my way carefully over the soft muck and, on reaching the bush, found that it was new to me. I cut off several shoots, some with their clusters of beautiful red-purple leaves and others with a few whitish berries, intending to look up the little tree in my books when I reached home. I put the branches with my other specimens into a long box, tied it securely and hastened . . . home. . . . I eagerly took up the unknown specimen and again admired the lovely, glossy red and purple leaves with their brilliant crimson stalks set on a twig of soft, creamy gray — an unusually charming complex of colors. Having no flowers to help me identify this lovely thing, I began to trace it down in the leaf-key of Sargent's *Trees of North America;* I had almost reached the end of this long analytical key when my eye fell upon the line leading to the genus *Rhus* and then came the shocking realization that I had been playing with fire — my beautiful little tree was the Poison Sumach!"*

Poison Sumac resembles poison ivy distinctly in flower and in fruit, but fruit and flower are both small and have each their passing season. Much

*William B. Werthner, *Some American Trees.*

350

of the time Poison Sumac would only remind one, by its foliage, of the common and harmless sorts of Sumac. But no innocent Sumac grows in swamps, like the poison kind. The harmless species have erect, dense, and many-branched clusters of fruits covered with greenish or reddish or rusty, velvety hairs. The fruit of the poisonous species is of a dead, unhealthy-looking waxen whiteness, or yellow like old ivory. Unfortunately there is just enough resemblance to the berries of mistletoe to deceive some persons, and it is well to remember that true mistletoe is a little shrub with greenish twigs which grows perched upon the branches of high trees. The gorgeous coloration of the autumnal leaves of Poison Sumac, too, tempts the fingers. It is best to recall that the "good" Sumacs have, most of them, finely toothed leaves while the "bad" kind show only a few low scallops on the margins.

There is general agreement that the sap of this species is the most intense and virulent of all contact poisons in the American sylva, save only the tropical Poisontree of Florida. The poisonous principle in the sap is an amber red, clear, sticky resin; it floats in water and is not a volatile substance; hence its particles cannot float on the air and give susceptible persons dermatitis without contact, as is often supposed. The pollen, for instance, may be rubbed on the skin, or swallowed, with no injurious effect, and even the bark, plant hairs, and surface of uninjured leaves, though intensely poisonous, may be rubbed on the skins of susceptible persons, providing that the tissue is not broken. For it is only the sap that is poisonous, and it is secreted by special poison canals which are found in the bast of the stem, in the veins of the leaves, and around the seed in the fruit. A new set of canals forms with each spring and autumn growth of the wood, each separate canal being surrounded by secretory cells which pour their poison into the canals; even the flowers have them, and the slightest injury to the plant sends the sap pouring out.

Iron chloride salts in a solution of alcohol is the easiest remedy to apply, once poisoning has set in. This is essentially the formula of the common "D.D.D." of the drugstores. Calamine lotion is also good. Where the case is serious and widespread, physicians often bandage the lesions with sugar of lead. The Public Health Service has recently announced a vanishing-cream preventive, which can be rubbed invisibly on the hands and face and is supposed to impart immunity to persons going into the woods. Many country folk have long believed that the best treatment is to swallow some of the leaves. This sounds dangerous indeed, and perhaps no physician would recommend it; yet on the principle of "a hair of the dog that bit you," modern medicine has also tried the "shock treatment": the poisonous oleoresin is given in gelatine capsules which are swallowed, and the skin thereafter is said to be desensitized to the poisoning, just as in the case of the treatment of many other allergies.

When the poisonous sap flows from an injured part of the plant, it soon hardens on exposure to the atmosphere into a sort of black varnish and has indeed been used in the preparation of a durable and shiny varnish similar to that obtained from the Lacquertree (*Toxicodendron vernici-fluum**). Japanese lacquer workers, it has been reported, are often the victims of constant poisoning, though tradition has it that immunity is acquired — after the first seven years! All over the main island of Japan and in some districts of Kiushu and Shikoku the Lacquertree is cultivated, and in the valley of Tadami-gawa whole villages of lacquer workers are embowered in groves of this beautiful venomous tree. Why there has never arisen a lacquer industry based upon our probably equally valuable Poison Sumac, no American needs to be told.

But many will ask, perhaps, if the world would not be a better place without so toxic a tree in it. Undoubtedly this were so, if the ideal were a world in which all of Nature should be sweet and refined, harmless and useful, parklike and tame. But Nature is not thus — certainly not American Nature, certainly not the aboriginal wilderness. And it is in the bogs and swamps, so hostile to human encroachment, that wilderness still lingers close to the city, the village, and the farmhouse. If one longs for the Nature of strange and far-off places, where curious vegetation waves its fronds, if one would like to see the "deadly Upas Tree" of travelers' tales — one does not have to cross the sea. As strange, as poisonous, as beautiful a tree as anything the tropics have to show grows down there in the old swamp, with the chain fern, the sphagnum moss, and the Black Gum.

**Editor's note*: Formerly *Rhus vernicifera*.

MAPLES

Sugar Maple

Acer saccharum Marshall

OTHER NAMES: Hard or Rock Maple. Sugartree.

RANGE: Maritime Provinces and eastern Quebec west north of the Great Lakes to Minnesota, and south to New Jersey and Pennsylvania and along the mountains to Georgia, west through Tennessee, Kentucky, Illinois, and northern Missouri to central Iowa and Minnesota.

THE MOST MAGNIFICENT DISPLAY of color in all the kingdom of plants is the autumnal foliage of the trees of North America. Over them all, over the clear light of the Aspens and Mountain Ash, over the leaping flames of Sumac and the hell-fire flickerings of poison ivy, over the war paint of the many Oaks, rise the colors of one tree — the Sugar Maple — in the shout of a great army. Clearest yellow, richest crimson, tumultuous scarlet, or brilliant orange — the yellow pigments shining through the overpainting of the red — the foliage of Sugar Maple at once outdoes and unifies the rest. It is like the mighty, marching melody that rides upon the crest of some symphonic weltering sea and, with its crying song, gives meaning to all the calculated dissonance of the orchestra.

There is no properly planted New England village without its Sugar Maples. They march up the hill to the old white meetinghouse and down

from the high school, where the youngsters troop home laughing in the golden dusk. The falling glory lights upon the shoulders of the postman, swirls after the children on roller skates, drifts through the windows of a passing bus to drop like largesse in the laps of the passengers. On a street where great Maples arch, letting down their shining benediction, people seem to walk as if they had already gone to glory.

Outside the town, where the cold pure ponds gaze skyward and the white crooked brooks run whispering their sesquipedalian Indian names, the Maple leaves slant drifting down to the water; there they will sink like galleons with painted sails, or spin away and away on voyages of chance that end on some little reef of feldspar and hornblende and winking mica schist. Up in the hills the hunter and his russet setter stride unharmed through these falling tongues of Maple fire, that flicker in the tingling air and leap against the elemental blue of the sky where the wind is tearing crow calls to tatters.

As a street tree, Sugar Maple is surpassed in form adapted to traffic only by the White Elm; and it is far less demanding of water, less injured by disturbance to its roots when pipes and drains are laid. But it suffers from city smoke and industrial gases; that is what keeps it a village tree, a tree of old colonial towns. On the lawn it develops, from its egg shape in youth, a benignant length of the lower limbs which is ideal for the play of children. The fine tracery of the tree in winter stands revealed in all its mingled strength and elegance. In spring the greenish yellow flowers appear at the same time that the leaves begin to open like a baby's hand. The full spread of its foliage in summer gives what is perhaps the deepest, coolest shade granted by any of our northern trees. Not until fall do the "keys," the winged fruits, mature. When they drop at last, they go spinning away, joined like Siamese twins, on their veiny, insectlike wings, with a gyroscope's motion.

Under forest conditions, Sugar Maple may grow to 120 feet, with a 3- or 4-foot trunk clear of branches half the way — a cylinder of nearly knot-free wood almost unrivaled among our hardwoods. It is immensely strong and durable, especially the whitish sapwood called by the lumberman Hard Maple; a marble floor in a Philadelphia store wore out before a Hard Maple flooring laid there at the same time. Few are the standard commercial uses for lumber where Hard Maple does not figure, either at the top of the list or high on it. Tough and resistant to shock, it becomes smoother, not rougher, with much usage — as you will notice if you look at an old-fashioned rolling pin.

And Sugar Maple can produce some notable fancy grains. There was a day that might be called the Bird's-eye Maple Era. Some of us were young then and may have believed it when we were told that the figure in the best bedroom set was made by woodpeckers. But woodpeckers work over a trunk in a straight line, and that is not how bird's-eye is found in Maple. It is due, say some botanists, to the presence of hundreds of bark-bound buds; others believe the effect is produced by fungal growths; in either case, when the saw passes through these, on a tangential plane, the dainty effect is seen on the cut surface. Familiar to all is the figure displayed by curly Maple, for it is the wood used for the backs of fine fiddles. Produced by dips in the fibers, it gives a striped effect that the violin makers insist upon procuring, rare though the figure is. In the age when an American made his own gunstocks, curly Maple was his favorite.

But even the featureless, straight-grain wood has been in demand for furniture since the earliest cabinetmakers of New England plied their tools. Today it is more popular than ever, in designs good, bad, or indifferent. The cut of Sugar Maple is probably in the neighborhood of 480 million board feet a year. In Vermont, where the New England hurricane of 1939 downed an estimated million Maples, only the increasing farm abandonment keeps the young sugar bush growth ahead of the saw, in the state that is, above all others, famous for its maple sugar production. For the pressure for Maple logs at sawmills has forced the price up, of recent years, as high as thirty dollars a thousand feet. When that happens, even Vermont farmers stare hard at their grand old Sugartrees and begin to do a little figuring in their hard heads. Maple sugar extraction costs have been steadily rising. Why not sell the trees for their stumpage value — five or six dollars when the market is high? The lumber companies will even come in and cut the trees for you and hand you cash. So the last sweet sap oozes from the bleeding stump when spring comes vainly back.

Plant physiologists tell us that the very glory of the Maple's autumnal leaves is due in part to the sweetness of this sap, no less than to the acidity of New England soils, the dryness and sharpness of her swift autumns. That sweetness amounts in the Sugar Maple to 2 percent or even 6 percent of the sap. But of course the yield of sap varies much with the method of tapping, the size of the tree, and the given season. Yet from 5 to 40 gallons of sap may be drawn yearly from each tree. As it takes about 32 gallons of sap to yield 1 gallon of syrup or 4¼ pounds of sugar, the yield of a tree in a season (nine to fifty-seven days at the end of winter) will be 1 to 7 pounds per tree; the average would be 3 pounds.*

As early as 1663, the great English chemist, Robert Boyle, told the learned world of Europe that "There is in some parts of New England a kind of tree . . . whose juice that weeps out of its incisions, if it be permitted slowly to exhale away the superfluous moisture, doth congeal into a sweet and saccharin substance, and the like was confirmed to me by the agent of the great and populous colony of Massachusetts."

The early colonists, both English and French, learned the art of sugaring, of course, from the red man for whom maple sugar was the only sweet. The Indians had their sugar camps, just as the white man, though it was usually, no doubt, the women who did the work. Their method was to slash a gash in the tree, when the sap was rising, and insert a hollow reed stem or a spile of hollow Sumac twig or a funnel of bark. The sap was then allowed to pour from the spile into a bark bowl or bucket or a gourd shell, and this in turn was emptied into a large vessel of Elm bark or a tree trunk hollowed out to form a trough. Having no metal vessels to endure direct contact with the fire, the Indians let the sap freeze and took off the ice from time to time (thus, in effect, concentrating the syrup), or they boiled it by dropping hot stones in the sap troughs. Some of the hot syrup might then be poured out on the snow for the children, who ate it as a sort of candy. But for future use the sugar was stored in bark boxes. Often on the frontier "barks of sugar" were bartered from the Indians by the pioneers. Maple sugar formed a sauce for much Indian cookery, especially (however odd it seems to us) with meats.

Captain John Smith is merely the first of a host of explorers who men-

*Figures from James B. McNair, *Sugar and Sugar-making,* Field Museum of Natural History, Chicago, 1927.

tion sugar making by the Indians. In no time at all the colonists had adopted maple sugar enthusiastically into their diet. It was the opinion of the famous Congregationalist the Reverend Samuel Hopkins of Waterbury that, of all sugars, that from the Maple was the most wholesome. And modern medical opinion is inclined to bear him out. For maple sugar is the only sweet except honey which contains the bone-building phosphates that cause calcium retention. It has therefore been used in the dietetic treatment of rachitic and tubercular children. It has even been asserted by doctors that certain New England farmers and their families could do twice or three times the work performed by others because of maple sugar in their diet.

The wise in these matters say that certain Maples yield more and better sugar, precisely as Apple trees give each their own special apples. The age of the trees, the particular season, the nature of the soil, the general climatic conditions play their part. That grove is best, some say, which stands on a slope with a south exposure, in sandy soil; heavy soils and north exposures make a cloudier syrup with a coarser flavor. Yet one might add that sugar is best which is most quickly reduced from sap to syrup, and with the cleanest equipment.

The Vermont farmer of today may make his own maple sugar into cakes and sell it on the roadside or by mail order direct to the customer. Or he may dispose of it to producers of maple syrup, maple cream, maple flavoring, and confections. The destiny of some maple sugar is to be blended with corn syrup or even (*horribile dictu*) molasses. Sizable amounts of maple sugar have been absorbed by the tobacco business, for flavoring the Virginian weed. The wholesale dealers scatter barrels in January at the country stores of Vermont; the farmer picks them up, fills them, is paid (none too well, he says), in cash at the store, and the filled drums are then retrieved by the wholesalers. On most farms today tractors have replaced the picturesque oxen or horse teams pulling the filled drums over the snow on sledges, and on some farms mechanical efficiency in the sugar bushes has banished hand-emptied buckets by introducing aluminum-painted lead pipes that run from the tree downhill to the evaporator!

Silver Maple

Acer saccharinum Linnæus

OTHER NAMES: Soft, White, River, Water, Creek, or Swamp Maple.

RANGE: Western New Brunswick and southern Quebec to northwestern Florida, west through southern Ontario, Michigan, northern Wisconsin, and Minnesota to southeastern South Dakota, and in the south to Louisiana (where rare), eastern Oklahoma, Kansas, and Nebraska.

WHEN THE TRAVELER FIRST LOOKS out of his train window in the Ohio valley he will, if he has any eye for trees, see a magnificent Maple with short columnar trunk and long branches which, at least in the lower half of the tree, sweep grandly down toward the ground, then lift again near the tip in a gesture of airy grace. In the upper half of the tree the branches are apt to be ascending, so that the outline, especially in winter, is somewhat pagodalike. Fine old specimens — and the Ohio valley is the place to see them — impart to every stream and bank where they grow, to every big red Hooiser barn and little white farmhouse, to all the village streets and the long straight roads where they have been planted, an air at once of dignity and lively grace, a combination rare in a tree as in a human.

All our best and most beloved species in the northern sylva present a drama throughout the year, and the Silver Maple has a leading role in every act. In winter the fine, flaky, gray bark of the trunks shines almost silvery; the elegant downsweeping of the boughs, the graceful upturning of the twigs seem etched by the strokes of the finest engraving tool, and as one tramps the woods of the Middle West, perhaps through some chill morning mist, the Silver Maples take solid shape more slowly than the more ponderous trees; there is always something wraithlike about them at such a time.

The snow has usually not departed when the first twigs high over head begin to brighten, and the shy apetalous flowers, too high above one's eyes to see clearly at all, bloom in an upper atmosphere, chill and beeless, so that one wonders how they are ever going to set fruit. Yet the fruits, daintly meshed as dragonflies' wings, are already twirling from the twigs when the leaves, themselves distinctly precocious, put forth from the buds, so silvery white at first that they are often mistaken for flowers. As the leaves uncrumple from the constrictions of the bud, the fruits go spinning away on those odd wings in the last fury of some spring gust.

In summer the full beauty of the Silver Maple's leaf expands; very deeply lobed, each pointed lobe again deeply jagged with coarse teeth and these again finely fringed with smaller ones, the Silver Maple's blade is what nurserymen call a cut-leaved type; in other species, as in European White Birch and even English Elm, cut-leaved strains are usually sports or freaks for which there is a demand among the sort of tree planters for whom Nature is seldom good enough but must be prettified. But the Silver Maple comes by such charms naturally. The mighty tree has the strength to wear them without being made effeminate.

Like some of the Poplars, the Silver Maple suspends its leaves on very long, somewhat flattened stalks, so that every breath of wind is sure to set the foliage to spinning, or fling it over. Then the contrast in the hues of the two surfaces is seen to greatest advantage; when composed, the tree seems clothed in dark green foliage (which, however, is filmy and delicately poised; never heavy). In the next moment the whole of one bough, or one half side of the whole tree, will suddenly turn silver, as the blades are reversed and show their under sides. Then, the summer breeze having sighed away, the tree regains its green composure, and again one hears that rolling, fluting whistle from the blue jays in the orchard, carrying piracy to the blue summer airs. But when begin those day-long gales that are destined to blow summer quite away, the Silver Maples along every stream are whipped into continuous whitecaps, threshing and seething and flashing their silver in more torment than delight.

The Silver Maple lacks the autumnal splendors of the Red and Black and Sugar and Mountain Maples, for the orange and scarlet tints are quite absent. It turns only a pale clear yellow. But the blades are likely to retain their silver undersurface even then. So that the greenback leaf of yesterday becomes a bank note — redeemable only on such banks as the Muskingum, the Thornapple, the Sangamon, the Scioto and Miami, the Rock and the Fox and the Kentucky, in the silver of hoarfrost and the gold of Indian-summer noons.

A tree with so many charms has naturally been planted far beyond its natural range, and everywhere within it. In the South, where it is rare as a native tree, it is common as a street tree. In the West, even in southern California where deciduous trees usually find little favor, it is a favorite, for it cannot grow without lending grace to any spot; it makes a railroad station look like a home, and adds a century to the appearance of a village street. It is the fastest growing of all our Maples, one of the fastest among all trees suitable to our climate, be they native or exotic. It is as charming in its childhood as in age, and in its youth goes through no awkward stage.

Yet landscape architects have little good to say of it. They complain of the insect pests that attack it, and of its comparatively short life, as well as the breakage of its brittle and too-long boughs under wind and ice damage. They urge that it be planted, if at all, in the full knowledge that its quickly achieved effects will not last long, and that more permanent if slower plantings be started at the same time. It may be that we should always listen to cautious and sensible people and not allow ourselves to think too highly of a tree that will perhaps only live three times as long as we do.

François Michaux found that, in his day, the midwestern farmers tapped the Silver Maple for its sugar and got a much finer grade than is yielded by the Sugar Maple. Unfortunately the amount of flow is too small to compete commercially with that of the more abundantly yielding species.

Lumbermen have so far cut comparatively little Silver Maple; they say that a small proportion of the wood that goes to market simply as "Maple" is cut from this tree, especially in the South, but it has little reputation of its own and goes for the most plebeian of uses. It is, however, a wood with many fine qualities, except for its tendency to split, and should the supply of Sugar Maple become much more sharply curtailed, perhaps the industry will begin to stare at this tree with speculative gaze.

Red Maple

Acer rubrum Linnæus

OTHER NAMES : Swamp, or Scarlet Maple.

RANGE : Maritime Provinces and eastern Quebec, west through the Upper Great Lakes region to southern Manitoba and Minnesota, south to Florida and west to central Texas, central Oklahoma, central and southern Missouri, and Illinois.

A T ALL SEASONS OF YEAR the Red Maple has something red about it. In winter the buds are red, growing a brilliant scarlet as winter ends, the snow begins to creep away and the ponds to brim with chill water and trilling frog music. They are so bright, in fact, that if one takes an airplane flight anywhere across the immense natural range of this tree (the most widespread of all our Maples), one can pick out — as far below as the color can be detected — the Red Maples, by the promise of spring in their tops, for no other tree quite equals them at this season in quality or intensity of color. The flowers too are generally red, sometimes yellow, and, minute though they are, they stand out brilliantly because they bloom upon the naked wood before ever the leaves appear. This may be as late as May; around Washington, D.C., February brings the Red Maple to bloom; down on the Gulf Coast, January or even December may call the flowers forth. The most conspicuous feature of the showier male flowers is the long scarlet stamens; the petals and sepals scarcely count at all. Unlike the Sugar Maple, which does not bear its fruit until August, the Red Maple's "keys," twirl on their slim stalks a month after flowering and while the leaves are still very small. These early leaves have a positively autumnal brilliance — scarlet or crimson — as they unfold from their fanwise crumpling in the bud. Even in summer the leafstalks are very red. And in autumn the foliage turns crimson or winy red and is second in splendor only to the Sugar Maple.

The Red Maple loves swamps and river flood plains and low woods where spring pools form from the melting snow or the overflowing streams. When Red Maple grows up into the hills and even ascends the Appalachians, it likes deep ravines, the shady side of cliffs and high mountain coves. With its cool, deep, yet not oppressive umbrage, and its elegant leaves, it ranks wherever it is found with the first choice of our finest shade trees.

In height, it may attain 100 or even 120 feet, especially in swampy situations, with a trunk 3 or 4 feet thick. The branches tend to be upright, so they form a narrow head, those near the halfway mark of the tree being generally the longest; thus the outline is rather diamond shaped when the tree is growing in the open, with a short trunk. Though slower growing than the Silver Maple, and more demanding of water than the Sugar Maple, this species is yet a fine street and lawn tree, with columnar trunks of a beautiful, almost Beech-like bark, and a generous pool of filmy shade.

If Red Maple were as valuable a timber tree as Hard Maple, it would, with its immense range and abundance, be a national resource of the first class, but the wood is only three-fourths as strong and yet weighs almost as much. It is said that Red Maple is sometimes sold as Hard Maple, sometimes as Soft Maple, but never goes to market under its own name. It is made into box veneer, interior finish, flooring, kitchenware, clothes hangers, and clothespins. Curly and wavy grains occasionally occur, and some bird's-eye grain is also found. Sugar may be drawn from Red Maple, though in smaller quantities than from Sugar Maple. Our pioneer ancestors made ink by adding sulfate of iron (copperas) to the tannin extracted from Red Maple bark. If, instead, alum was added, a cinnamon-colored dye was produced; the use of both alum and sulfate of iron with the bark extract produced a black dye. The Indians seem to have had still other uses for this tree. John Josselyn in *New-Englands Rarities Discovered* (1672) wrote: "The Natives draw an Oyl, taking the rottenest Maple Wood, which being burnt to ashes, they make a Lye therewith, wherein they boyl their white Oak-Acorns until the Oyl swim on the top in great quantities."

Peter Kalm, Linnaeus's greatest student, who visited America in 1750, especially in the old Swedish settlements in Delaware and Pennsylvania, records of this tree and of his countrymen, that "out of its wood they make plates, spinning wheels, spools, feet for chairs and beds, and many other kinds of turnery. With the bark they dye both worsted and linen, giving it a dark blue color. For this purpose it is first boiled in water, and some copperas, such as the hat makers and the shoemakers commonly use, is added before the stuff (which is to be dyed) is put into the boiler."

The Carolina Maple (variety *tridens* Wood*) is strikingly different from the true Red Maple in foliage, but not in flowers or fruit. The bark is remarkably smooth even on old trunks, reminding one of Beech boles. The leaves are thicker, almost leathery, a darker green and shining above, and coated below with a heavy bloom and with persistent cottony tufts in the axils of the main nerves which are very prominent beneath. In autumn the foliage commonly turns yellow, not crimson.

The lobes of the leaves are usually three, rarely five, and rather broad, the two lateral ones somewhat divergent, with wide-angled sinuses between them. The teeth are not nearly so close or numerous as in the true Red Maple, except near the base, and are not especially sharp or fine. The Carolina Maple, confined to a somewhat more southerly range, is still included, in its distribution, within the wide range of the true Red Maple and cannot be considered a separate species but only a variety of it.

Box Elder

Acer negundo Linnæus

OTHER NAMES: Ash-leaved or Manitoba Maple. Sugar Ash.

RANGE: From central Texas north to southern Manitoba, western and southern New England, west through southern Ontario to British Columbia and eastern Washington State, Nevada, and Arizona, south to Florida, Texas, and northern Mexico. Also in central and southern California.

THE BOX ELDER PROBABLY TAKES its name from its elderlike leaves and its white wood like that of Box. The foliage would make one think of some sort of cut-leaf Ash. Yet this tree's nearest relatives are undoubtedly the Maples, as is shown by its flowers, pendent on

*Editor's note: Now *Acer rubrum* var. *trilobum* Torrey & Gray ex K. Koch.

long stalks in early spring, and its autumnal crop of fruits, the typical double samara of the Maples.

In the states east of the Missouri, Box Elder is not considered a tree of any importance in the wild; it is simply one of the common trees of riverbanks, especially of slow and muddy streams, never associated with clear, cool rushing water; there it mingles with Willows, Cottonwoods, and Sycamores, most of which far outclass it in size and beauty and in the affections of eastern people. In cultivation it does rather better; the biggest Box Elder of record is one grown at White Plains, New York, having a spread of 102 feet, a height of 75 feet, and a circumference around the trunk at breast height of 19 feet, 11 inches — a very fine shade tree by any standard. At one time Box Elder was extensively planted, indeed much overplanted, by persons seeking a quick and cheap effect for mushrooming midwestern communities. But though it does soon begin to give a respectable amount of shade, it is a short-lived tree; its weak wood, worthless except for fuel, undistinguished in color and grain, all too easily splits when violated by wind and sleet storms; its leaves, in the eastern states, generally turn crisp and brown in fall, without ever assuming any of the beautiful autumnal tints of the Maples. Thus, in every respect, Box Elder in the East seems but a poor relation of the aristocratic Maples. Says the Kansas State Board of Agriculture in a bulletin on trees of that state: "There is no excuse for planting this tree." Yet excuses might be found, not the least of them that many people appreciate its resistance to heat, cold, drought, and ceaseless winds that would soon kill species with more exalted reputations. And even in winter it has its charms, with those smooth bright green twigs that bear, so precociously, in early spring the curious flowers.

But in the West, on the Great Plains and the southwestern deserts, in the hot interior valleys of California, any shade begins to look good — especially the wide-spreading, cool shade of a filmy-leaved deciduous tree like this one. The deciduous habit is valuable, of course, as admitting light and any warmth there is in the winter months, while providing a parasol in summer. No wonder that the Box Elder's name is pronounced gratefully wherever, in the West, it grows beside some watering spot for cattle, or at the ranch-house door, or along the roads and highways, in the school playground, or on the small-town street.

More, the Box Elder in its western varieties, especially in Colorado, New Mexico, Utah, and Arizona, sometimes takes on a particularly lovely form. Probably this is indefinable, and partly subjective, or associated with the beauty of the surroundings. But its charms are real where in some of the gorges of the Colorado Rockies, for instance, the commonly sprawling habits of this tree seem corrected by the strictures of the sheer canyon walls and the competition of other trees, till the Box Elders stand straight and graceful as eastern forest-grown hardwoods, and the breezes that sweep above the dashing water set the frondose foliage to dancing in a way one never sees beside the lazy rivers of the lowlands.

In the West, Box Elder often takes on beautiful autumnal tints. In Arizona it is sometimes a rich red, almost worthy of one of the true Maples. A soft light yellow is not uncommon, and occasionally in some of the darker, moister canyons, or when closely pressed upon by conifers, Box Elder in Colorado will assume the very palest of translucent yellows, or almost a white, when, after an autumn rain, the sunlight steals through the foliage. Later you will see Box Elder leaves drifting into the trout pools of the mountain streams, piling up upon some rocky reef, swirling away like doomed galleons on the current.

Most easterners would never imagine that Box Elder yields a sweet sap, like Maple syrup. Yet it does. The sugar is fine grained and white but is not so sweet as that of the Sugar Maple, and more is required to make the same quantity of sugar. However, writes Melvin Randolph Gilmore, "This tree was used also for sugar making by all the tribes [of the Missouri River basin]. The Dakota and Omaha and probably the other tribes used box-elder wood to make charcoal for ceremonial painting of the person and for tattooing. Previous information as to the making of sugar from sap of this tree pertained, among the Pawnee and Omaha, only to times now many years in the past; but it has been found that among some tribes sugar is still made from this source. In September, 1916, the writer found a grove of trees on the Standing Rock Reservation in North Dakota, of which every tree of any considerable size showed scars of tapping which had been done the previous spring in sugar making."*

*Bureau of American Ethnology, "Uses of Plants by the Indians of the Missouri River Region," *Thirty-third Annual Report, 1911–1912,* 1919.

Christmas Holly

Ilex opaca Aiton

OTHER NAMES: American, Prickly, or Evergreen Holly.

RANGE: St. Augustine and Charlotte Harbor, Florida, north near the coast to Quincy, Massachusetts, and up the Mississippi valley to southeastern Missouri, and to the lower slopes of the southern Appalachians, west to Arkansas and southeastern Texas; in Kentucky only in the mountains, but common in Tennessee up to 3000 feet altitude.

N O ONE NEEDS A DESCRIPTION of the appearance of the Christmas Holly's leaves and berries. But so relentless has been the attack upon the female trees in fruit that only far from cities is the Holly a common tree. Low altitudes are its favorite habitat, yet it does not grow on wet ground. Sometimes it is scattered in with Pines, Magnolias, Hickory, Sweet Gum, and Sassafras; again, the traveler in the South may find himself in a beautiful little forest of pure Holly. With its inescapable associations of the great festival, such a grove seems all dressed up for Christmas — at any time of year! Down south the Holly sometimes grows 100 feet tall with a trunk 4 feet thick, but in the circumscription of this book it is a little tree, densely pyramidal in shape, with a short trunk about 2 feet in diameter, at best, and only 20 to 40 feet high.

Though sometimes the prickles are lacking on the margins of the leaves, Holly is still the only tree within the area embraced by this book, except in the southern Appalachians, which is at once broadleaved and evergreen. All our other evergreens, of course, are needleleaved. The broadleaved evergreen habit is characteristic of tropical trees, yet we associate Holly in our minds with cold and snow.

The problem of conservation of the Christmas Holly from destruction will never be settled until the public stops buying more than it needs, and the law begins to police the market. For the real problem is that too much of the Holly on the market is simply stripped from the trees by professional pickers who violate the property rights of the owners of the woods. True that the owner has a legal right to sell all the Holly he wants, but in many cases the owner is never consulted by the vandals who relieve him of his property. If boughs of Holly are to be removed, they should be sawed, but ordinarily they are torn off, thus opening the way to disease and death. The Wild Flower Preservation Society recommends that Christmas Holly, when purchased, be shellacked. This will preserve it from decay, and in that way the same Holly can be used year after year, just like Christmas-tree ornaments, lights, and other fittings, thus aiding in conservation.

A study of all the colonial gardens of Virginia shows that Holly was a favorite in most of them, for, slow though its growth, Holly deserves a place of the first honor wherever the climate permits. The number of entries in George Washington's diary concerning the Christmas Holly is surprisingly large. It seems that the master of Mount Vernon was devoted to this tree. For Holly has exactly that formal elegance which we should expect to please the taste of George Washington. In one year he tells of transplanting many little Hollies from the woods. In another he confesses to his diary (what so many gardeners are unwilling to confess even to themselves) that his experiment was a complete failure; all the Hollies had died. On a March day Washington notes "received a Swan, 4 wild Geese, and 2 Barrels of Holly Berries (in Sand) from my brother John." These he sowed on the seventh of April, in the South Semicircle in the rear of the mansion; but he was still delighted, on March 28, 1786, to receive from Colonel "Lighthorse Harry" Lee of "Stratford" (father of Robert E. Lee) a number of small Holly trees boxed with earth, and these he set out with his great Holly planting in the South Semicircle. Today thirteen of the Hollies which Washington planted still stand.

As a valuable cabinet wood, Christmas Holly has never been appreciated by the buying public, although the wood technicians and some lumbermen understand its value. Harder even than Black Locust, almost as hard as Dogwood, Holly is yet only in the medium-heavy class. Its texture is so uniform throughout the woody cylinder that its growth lines are practically indistinguishable in the greenish white wood; this is due perhaps to the fact that Holly is primarily a sapwood tree. Such a hard, pale, even-grained wood is ideal for taking dyes. Practically all the white and black inlaid lines in musical instruments and furniture and much of the colored wood in marquetry are Holly. Modern styles in elaborate furniture sometimes call for the use of bizarre shades impossible to find in natural wood; Holly fills in these lacks by obligingly taking any sort of stain or dye. It is unexcelled for taking enamel finishes. Sliced one-sixtieth to one-sixteenth inch thick, it makes an ideal veneer. Because it is so hard, it can be used for all sorts of turnery, knife handles, and, dyed black, for black piano keys. Engravers, because of its whiteness and even texture, demand it in art work; more nearly than any other American wood, it approaches ivory in color. It is fortunate that it yields so little lumber that it is not heavily cut, since the depredations of the Christmas-green pickers take toll enough.

SYCAMORES

Sycamore

Platanus occidentalis Linnæus

OTHER NAMES: Buttonwood. Buttonball-tree. Plane. Planetree. White-wood. Water Beech. Virginia Maple.

RANGE: Rare and local, but apparently indigenous, in Maine; thence west at low altitudes across southern New Hampshire and Vermont, New York, southern Ontario, Michigan, in Wisconsin north to the lower Wisconsin River, southern Iowa, eastern Nebraska, and Kansas, south to central parts of Texas, Mississippi, and Alabama and to the Gulf states.

B Y THE BEAUTIFUL BRIGHT SMOOTH BARK, the Sycamore is known as far off as the color can be descried; it shines through the tops of the forest even in the depth of summer when the leafy crowns are heaviest. In winter against a stormy sky it looks wonderfully living, amidst all the appearances of lifelessness in other deciduous trees. Yet seen as a snag in the Mississippi, with the bleaching timbers of some wreck piled on it, the white bark looks deader than any other dead tree can look, with the gleam to it of picked bones. In the woods, the trunk looks patterned with sunshine. The cause of this is that constantly, as the swift growth of the wood goes on, the bark keeps sloughing off in thin plates and irregular patches. On close inspection, one usually sees three different colors of bark; the outer light gray and the inner variously pale

370

tan, greenish, or chalky white, but the impression at a slight distance is that of an exquisitely mottled tree, as if dappled with green shade and pale sunlight.

Thus the beauty lies in the body of the tree itself, rather than in its adornments of flowers or foliage; the latter turns but a pale dull yellow in autumn, becoming brown or browning directly, while the flowers do not catch the eye of any but the observant admirer of trees. Yet they produce the curious fruits that have given the tree the name of Buttonwood — hanging balls that persist on the tree over winter and then break up into fluff, when the fruitlets are borne away upon the down and the seeds thus widely distributed both by wind and water.

It is on the borders of rivers and lakes, and in rich bottomlands, that the Sycamore takes happy root. With the Black Willow it marches beside the Father of Waters; along the Ohio River it was the outstanding river-bank tree of the primeval forest, unsurpassed in picturesque grandeur and in the cooling depth and mighty spread of its shade. Wide groves of it covered the rich bottomlands, as far as the eye could see up and down the stream, while upon some bend or promontory of the river, or on some island in its flood, stood forth here and there a Sycamore so gigantic in its girth that the marveling traveler wrote of it half doubting he would be believed. For the Sycamore is, in girth of trunk, the largest deciduous hardwood of North America, and in those early days there were indeed giants in the earth.

To the pioneer the sight of it was welcome, since in general its presence and enormous growth were correctly taken to denote rich soil. However, from its predilection for low grounds, where malaria also was harbored, it often worried the early prospector for lands; well might it be a warning, he felt, of ague, chills, and fever. He dreaded, too, its proximity because of the down that grows on the underside of the leaves; to his mind it was this, producing a constant though imperceptible irritation of the lungs, that brought consumption to any rash enough to live beneath it. Though we smile at this, we may find some reason in this distrust of the abundant deciduous hairs upon the leaves, for being at once very light and sharp, they float long in the air and undoubtedly some people are allergic to them.

But in a sturdier day hay fever was the least of a man's problems, and the Sycamore answered many practical ones. Though not strong in the position of a beam or column, and with little resistance to decay, its wood is hard, fairly tough, and almost impossible to split. So the pioneer cut trunks of great dimension into cross sections which he then bored through the center, to make primitive solid wheels for his ox cart. If the trunk were hollow, as it often was, he sawed it in lengths of three to four feet, nailed a bottom in it, and so had a stout hogshead for grain. As time went on, and American civilization evolved into the sophistication of barber poles and wooden washing machines and lard pails, Sycamore was a favorite for such things. The very broad panels that could be sawed out of Sycamore recommended it for use in Pullman cars — in the days of wooden Pullmans. Stereoscopes used to use immense amounts of Sycamore wood in the days when Americans used immense amounts of stereoscopes! Slats of the ubiquitous Saratoga trunks were commonly of Sycamore, and formerly piano and organ cases and phonograph boxes employed this light-hued wood. Today, though it is used for crates and boxes and in some furniture manufacture, the place you are most likely to see it is at the butcher's, since it can be endlessly hacked without splitting.

So on the block ends a noble once undisputed in the virgin Ohio valley forests! It had great fame, and it had great friends. André Michaux wrote of a Sycamore growing on a little island in the Ohio "the circumference of which, five feet from the surface of the earth . . . was forty feet four inches, which makes about thirteen feet in diameter. . . . Twenty years prior to my travels, George Washington had measured this same tree, and had found it nearly of the same dimensions." And Michaux's own son, François, coming after him in 1802, found an Ohio Sycamore which beat his father's record, "the trunk of which was swelled to an amazing size; we measured it four feet beyond the surface of the soil, and found it forty-seven feet in circumference. By its external appearance no one could tell that the tree was hollow; however, I assured myself it was by striking it in several places with a billet." Most Sycamores over one hundred years old are hollow at the heart, which of course does not prevent the tree from continuing to expand through the years. So it was that pioneers often stabled a horse, cow, or pig in a hollow Sycamore, and sometimes a whole family took shelter in such a hospitable giant, until the log cabin could be raised.

Long before there were any chimneys to send up a twirl of smoke in lonely clearings, these hollow Sycamores were home to the chimney swift — "swallow," as the pioneers often called it. On an evening of July, not far from Louisville, Kentucky, there came to such a tree John James Audubon. "The sun was going down behind the Silver Hills," he remembers, "the evening was beautiful; thousands of Swallows were flying closely above me, and three or four at a time were pitching into the hole, like bees hurrying into their hive. I remained, my head leaning on the tree, listening to the roaring noise made within by the birds as they settled and arranged themselves, until it was quite dark, when I left. . . .

"Next morning I rose early enough to reach the place long before the least appearance of daylight, and placed my head against the tree. All was silent within. I remained in that posture probably twenty minutes, when suddenly I thought the great tree was giving way, and coming down upon me. Instinctively I sprang from it, but when I looked up to it again, what was my astonishment to see it standing as firm as ever. The Swallows were now pouring out in a black continued stream. I ran back to my post, and I listened in amazement to the noise within, which I could compare to nothing else than the sound of a large wheel revolving under a powerful stream. It was yet dusky, so that I could hardly see the hour on my watch, but I estimated the time which they took in getting out at more than thirty minutes. After their departure, no noise was heard within, and they dispersed in every direction with the quickness of thought."

Not only swallows (swifts, more exactly) loved the Sycamore, but a now-vanished bird of the primeval woods. The men of Long's great expedition to the Rockies noted, as they passed through, that "the fruit of the sycamore is the favorite food of the paroquet, and large flocks of these gaily-plumaged birds constantly enliven the gloomy forests of Ohio." The Carolina paroquet, only member of the parrot family native in the United States, is extinct now, and so are the gigantic Sycamores of the virgin forest. Long ago the great trees were cut down recklessly, to clear the land, to feed the sawmill; the merest shadows of their great dimensions are all that we see today. But nothing of our past is wholly lost that still is treasured in the American saga.

Western Sycamore

Platanus racemosa Nuttall

OTHER NAMES: Buttonwood. Buttonball-tree. Planetree.

RANGE: Banks of streams in the Great Central Valley of California and canyons of the Coast Ranges from Monterey south to Baja California; also in the western foothills of the Sierra Nevada; ascending the southern slopes of the San Bernardino Mountains to 4000 feet. The variety *wrightii*, here included, ranges through central Arizona south into Mexico and east to southern New Mexico.

H ERE IS A TREE that might have been created as the friend of mankind. Out of all the western sylva, the forests vast and somber, the ranked species in their cohorts, each with its boast of economic value, this one stands apart. For it grows singly or in little groves in the interior valleys, along the sandy washes, the upside-down rivers of the desert, in the cool of the canyon walls, more needed where you find it than valuable if felled, sawn, dressed, and exported. With its intimately leaning trunks it seems, even in the wild, to be preformed for bending above the roof tree that will come to it. The quality of its shade — broad but filmy leaved (more like some eastern hardwood's) — is never so dense as to be stuffy; ever the breeze moves under the boughs, and any stir of air, in the warm habitats it chooses, even the rangeland's or the wheat field's, is better than none. So the white-faced Herefords stand or lie for hours in the long burning summers beneath the Sycamores.

Whether this tree throws shadow of palmate leaf and zigzag twig upon the stone of a canyon's walls or on doorstep and lintel, that scrawl is like a loved and familiar handwriting to the westerner. And that marbled bark, forever sloughing off in irregular mottled flakes of brown, tan, green, gray, and off-white is a detritus not so rubbishy as comfortably homelike.

Certainly there is a pleasant quality about the shade cast by this, the outstanding shade tree of the Southwest. For one thing, the leaves are not glittering on the upper surface — a great relief in the hard-leaved evergreen woodlands of the desert and southern California where so many leaves are blades turned against the tired eyeballs. Sycamore leaves have at most a soft shine to them, when the down wears off, and the undersides

remain permanently coated in rusty or gray woolly hairs so that when the breeze spins the blades over they gleam silvery but cool. More, the shade, though so ample in summer, is taken down by Nature in the short period of winter in the Southwest, allowing all the warmth and light in the sky to penetrate to soil or roof. Unlike the conifers, the Sycamore does not hold the cold but scouts it.

All species of *Platanus* have as their outstanding beauty their massive trunks and mottled, smooth bark. The species *Platanus orientalis*, native from southern Europe to India, was thousands of years ago a favorite shade tree; it was planted in the Greek schoolyards just as Elms are the traditional academic trees of America, because its boughs were so wide, its shade so good, its trunks so like stout marble columns. Or perhaps, rather, the school came to the tree, at least the informal assemblies of Plato did so; under the tree that he called *platanos* (whence French, *platanier*, and English, "Plane") he paced with his following, discoursing of his republic.

Call it Plane, or Sycamore, or Buttonwood, or *aliso* as the Spanish-speaking pioneers of the Southwest did, our western *Platanus* cannot help falling into picturesque attitudes, and a Sycamore that looks regular, like a forest-grown type of tree, is a rarity. When growing on stream banks the tree is almost certain to lean, sprawl, or fork deeply, oftenest in a V-shape. But a trunk with a J-shape is common too, even well back from water, in the dry ranchland grass, for there is something slouching about most bottomland Sycamores. Indeed, some pasture specimens never stand up at all but may be seen lying down on their backs, as it were, in a meadow, sending up vertical branches all from one side, like a horse scratching his back on the ground and kicking up his legs! But in general the trees on rich alluvial lands that, however, stand well up and away from the actual stream or gully bank, have very straight but short trunks clear of branches. As times goes on, this rapid-growing tree will thicken the base of the trunk into a great barrel-shaped affair, without pruning many of its lower branches, so that the true trunk ends abruptly in a perfect jet of trunklike branches, and these, in turn gracefully arching, may sweep low at the tips. This is the grandest, most lovable form of the tree, and it may perhaps be called the normal form.

In general, the Western Sycamore is about 40 or 50 feet high when mature, but specimens up to 80 feet are known, with trunks 5 feet in diameter. What must have been one of the biggest Sycamores in existence still stands, a truncated wreck, on Milpas Street, in Santa Barbara. Though a quarter of a mile inland from the beach, it was once so lofty that, in the days when this city had no harbor and yet could be satisfactorily reached only by boat, a lantern was hung from this great tree's topmost boughs on stormy nights. Captain George Nidever, an old sailing master, reported that it was the mariners' custom to sight their course, by day, by this tree. That custom began back in 1800; today the tree is still alive though its top has been broken by storms and its great boughs were cut off some years ago to relieve their strain upon the hollow heart. In one respect only is it the tree it once was — in girth; it now measures 11 feet 11 inches around at breast height.

Whitish woolly hairs on the undersides of the leaves are deciduous and so a nuisance to some persons. For several weeks they drift on the atmosphere, setting up an acute inflammation of the mucous membranes of sensitive noses. This is the only drawback to such a fine tree, unless we add the brittleness of the living wood. "Of its want of tenacity," said Dr. J. S. Newberry, surgeon-botanist of the Army reconnaissance that surveyed in 1855 for a railway from San Francisco to the Columbia River, "we had a striking illustration when we encamped under the tree. . . . Our beds were spread on the ground under its branches, nearly touching each other. During the evening — a fresh breeze blowing, but not a high wind — we were warned by a cracking overhead that danger was impending, and had just time to 'stand from under' when a branch about eight inches in diameter came crashing down directly where we had been lying."

The Sycamore's greatest moment of beauty comes to it in earliest spring or at the end of winter. For then the flowers bloom upon the crooked, golden-fuzzy twigs. The heads of the male flowers are no bigger than peas and filled with long-haired scales, so that they seem like little greenish or yellow chenille balls. The female heads are the showy ones, the size of big marbles, with deep and bright brown and remarkably long and thread-thin styles bristling out all over them. Simultaneously the leaves begin to unfold, like opening hands; all covered with golden down the palmate blades shine in the sunlight as if rimed with a glow. Then in summer when the foliage is full but fresh, the female heads ripen into fruit, each tiny seedlike nutlet deeply imbedded in a tuft of silken gray hairs. In winter these break up like so many dandelion heads blowing, and so the nutlets go gliding away on the wind to some other canyon or pasture.

The Arizona and New Mexican specimens differ so markedly in leaf that they have been described as a separate form, variety *wrightii* (Watson) Benson.* It has deeply five- to seven-lobed leaves, with slender and elongate lobes and the bases deeply heart shaped. This is a more beautiful foliage than the Californian, but as there are only leaf differences, the desert trees are not quite distinct enough for a separate species.

The Sycamore is the largest desert tree of Arizona, growing up to 80 feet in height. Sycamore Canyon is but one of the many places where one can see the Arizona variety, but it is certainly the most romantic, and still, because of the rugged nature of the country, little visited. It lies for some 25 miles in the deep-cut bed of Sycamore Creek, which flows into the Verde River in the Coconino National Forest. Indian caves are still found in it, and once, according to local legend, it was a hideout of badmen and renegade Indians. Today the great Sycamores throw their shadows on the canyon walls in peace. One specimen measures 17 feet in circumference, perhaps the doughtiest hardwood tree in the Southwest.

Many birds love the desert Sycamore. The red-tailed hawk will commonly nest in it and will perch all day in its groves on the lookout, sallying forth with its cry of *killee, killee!* Because Sycamores are so often hollow,

---

Editor's note: Now classified as the species *Platanus wrightii* S. Watson, the Arizona Sycamore.

Gila and Lewis and Arizona woodpeckers all delight to nest in it. And if ever you find yourself down on the border, in the Chiricahua and Huachuca mountains, in summer, watch for a tiny comet of a bird with bronzy green back, metallic purple cap, and emerald green gorget. That will be the rare Rivioli hummingbird, up from Central America, who commonly nests in the canyon Sycamores, at 5000 to 7000 feet altitude, and sometimes lines its babies' cradle with down of the swinging fruit balls plucked from the tree.

Tupelo

Nyssa sylvatica Marshall

OTHER NAMES: Sour or Black Gum. Pepperidge.

RANGE: In typical form from western Maine to northern Florida, west to Lake Champlain, the north shore of Lake Erie, southern Michigan, the south shore of Lake Michigan, northern Missouri, extreme northeastern Texas, and probably adjacent Oklahoma. Most abundant on the coastal plain of the North Atlantic states and in the Ohio valley, rare in the southeastern states and the southern Appalachians.

WHEN, TO THE AMUSEMENT OF CREOLE SOCIETY, the tall and emaciated General Andrew Jackson leaped beside the short and immensely fat Mrs. Jackson, at a ball held after the battle of New Orleans, it was to the jig tune of "Possum Up De Gum Tree." The possum, we may suppose, goes up the Gum tree in fall to get the fruit — or perhaps is merely treed there by hounds — but that does not make it clear why this species is called a Gum. Nowhere on the American continent has anyone ever expressed from this dry and disobliging vegetable one fluid ounce of any sort of gum. Yet lumbermen and foresters insist on the name. The title of Pepperidge seems derived, by far-fetched analogy, from an old English word for the barberry bush. As for Tupelo, applied to this species in New England, it is said to come from the Creek language, *eto* meaning "tree" and *opelwv* "swamp." Tupelo is thus our paleface attempt to speak Creek, and bad as that would sound to General Jackson's proud enemies, the "Red Sticks," it might do nicely if it were not strongly objected in Dixie that Tupelo should be reserved for another tree. Perhaps the open-minded bystander will approve, for once, the Latin binomial. *Nyssa* has a lovely sound, as it should, since it was the name of a water nymph in classical mythology; *sylvatica*, of course, means that it is of the forest.

Growing in swampy woods throughout its wide range, this water nymph of the forest has, in the full tide of summer, an almost tropical look about its glossy, leathery leaves. One would think they were evergreen. But in the fall, the foliage turns a gorgeous deep burgundy color. Frequently one-half of the leaf retains its lustrous summer green intact, adding to the effect by contrast. After the leaves have fallen, the handsome blue drupes swing a while until the robins get them; then the female trees stand as barren as the male, and the Black Gums are revealed in all their rigid nakedness. For the ponderous trunk rises more or less a mast, giving off short, scraggly branches, as stiffly as the main stem of a conifer. When spring comes back to the swamp, the leaf buds very early take on much the same vivid color as the autumnal foliage and are more beautiful by far than the inconspicuous flowers that bloom as the young leaves are thrusting out.

The Black Gum grows about 60 feet tall, at the most, and frequently never attains over 30 feet. Decay sets in early, as time is measured by tree growth, and death often starts at the top of the tree and works downward. At first these dead tops help to identify the tree, in a not very complimentary fashion, but, when the tops keep breaking off, the tree actually grows shorter as it grows older — perhaps the only case of a tree which commonly does so.

Usually the decay attacks the heartwood first, so that hollow trees are common. When the country folk in the South find such a tree, they cut it down and saw it into short sections. These are then stood up on boxes, with a board laid over the top, for beehives. Hence the time-honored name of "bee gums" for hives. Longer sections are often arranged as traps for rabbits and laid in the woods; the hunter calls these "rabbit gums."

To the Black Gum, as a timber tree, the pioneers said anathema with every abhorrence. For its fibers are not only interbraided but cross-woven. It is as easy to split across as lengthwise — that is, it can't be done at all, even with wedge and sledge. As our ancestors were a nation of rail splitters, they left the Black Gum pretty well alone. More, in contact with the soil its wood decays quickly, which is unusual in a swamp tree. Though it yielded to the saw, it warped and shrank so, before the days of dry kilns, that it was considered just too worthless for a self-respecting lumberman to fight into boards.

But precisely because nothing can split it, Black Gum was worked into the handles of heavy-duty tools. It carried the head of the maul and took up the shock of the blow that split other, nobler timbers into rails. Quartersawn and stained it makes a good imitation of Mahogany, but if it will never be a fine cabinet wood in its own right, yet it has borne the tremendous strains of the rollers over which the great cables in mine shafts are dragged by the steam donkeys. It has been used for gunstocks and pistol grips. As a veneer for berry crates it has the advantage over the usual deal of being unbreakable. It is in favor for scaffolding and chopping bowls, for the wooden parts of agricultural machinery, and the floors of factories which receive the hardest usage.

The Yellow Gum or Upland Tupelo is simply a variety of this species, variety *caroliniana* (Poiret) Fernald.* It differs on the technical grounds of having thinner, less glossy leaflets, with rather long tips, the undersurface persistently somewhat downy and covered with minute warty excrescences easily seen under an ordinary hand lens. The young twigs are brit-

Editor's note: Now considered to be identical with the species.

tle, not limber. Yellow Gum is not a swamp tree, like Black Gum, but an inhabitant of dry land, hills, and the coves of the southern Appalachians which it ascends to 3500 feet. There it grows up to 90 or 100 feet tall, much taller than the Black Gum. The range is not perfectly known but appears to be from Philadelphia to Detroit, south to the mountains of South Carolina and in the Ohio valley; it is widely distributed in Tennessee and Arkansas and reaches eastern Texas and northern Mississippi.

"Pioneers," says Charles C. Deam, state forester of Indiana,* "have always insisted that there were two kinds of black gum. They distinguish them by their splitting qualities. The form very difficult to split was known as the black gum, and the form that 'split like poplar' was known as yellow gum. The bark of the variety much resembles that of the tulip tree and the branches are usually ascending." Much Yellow Gum lumber has undoubtedly been sent to market as Yellow Poplar. This variety therefore belongs in the category of genuine timber trees and has none of the disadvantages, yet none of the advantages, of the refractory old Black Gum.

*The Flora of Indiana, 1940.

Osage Orange

Maclura pomifera (Rafinesque) Schneider

OTHER NAMES: Bois d'Arc. Bowdark. Bowwood. Mock Orange. Osage. Prairie Hedgeplant. Yellowwood. Hedge Apple.

RANGE: Native in southeastern Oklahoma, southwestern Arkansas, northwestern Louisiana, and eastern, south-central, and western Texas. Widely naturalized from cultivation in the eastern and southern states.

I N PAST GEOLOGIC TIME there were many species of *Maclura;* now there is only this one,* in all the world, so that *Maclura* is today a monotypic (one-species) genus, in the Breadfruit family. Even this one is now greatly restricted in its native home, for in interglacial times it seems to have grown, to judge from fossils, as far north and east as Ontario; today it is confined to the southern states west of the Mississippi. Or it was, when first discovered by scientists; it is now abundantly grown for its many fine qualities far beyond its original home and has become widely naturalized east of the Mississippi and in the Missouri Valley. As a native plant it enters the circumscriptions of this book in trans-Pecos Texas, notably at Bois d'Arc Spring, in Big Bend National Park.

*Editor's note: Currently, a second species, *Maclura tinctoria*, is recognized and found in Central and South America.

The name of Osage Orange derives from the big, green, spherical and heavy fruits — rather larger than any orange, and with the mammillate surfaces quite different in texture and in color. Yet the comparison has survived all the onslaughts of common sense; and the word Osage, at least, was once appropriate since it was among the Osage Indians of Arkansas and Missouri that this tree became famous as a wood for bows, so strong it is — stronger than White Oak — and tough, tough as Hickory. The early French explorers of the Mississippi Valley named it *bois d'arc*, meaning "bow wood," and this is sometimes corrupted to Bow-dark.

For a bow wood, Osage Orange is in first or second rank with archers, among all native trees. It is by many considered more reliable than Yew, and the beauty of its grain, often stained in the heartwood with red, makes it the pride of fanciers. It takes time for a bow, like a violin, to become sweet and mellow, it seems, for one amateur, A. E. Andrews, tells us concerning a bow in his collection: "One osage bow was blood-streaked when worked down so green that the sap oozed out on the scrapers. In seven months that bow was made, seasoning as it formed. In four years the blood-shots disappeared and the bow gained in strength of draw. At four to five years it seemed at its strongest and its color was brown. At the age of ten, it still shoots with a clean, quick, mellow smoothness."*

The reputation of the Osage's own bow wood spread widely among the Plains Indians. Prince Maximilian of Wied-Neuwied found that the Montana Blackfeet had prized bows of Osage Orange, which they obtained by barter. The Kiowas too appreciated it. A band of them seen by Lieutenant Whipple on September 8, 1853, on the Llano Estacado "carried superb bows of bois d'arc, ornamented with brass nails, silver plates, and wampum beads. The arrows were about 28 inches in length, with steel points and tinted feather trimmings. The quiver and belt, of wolfskin, were wrought with beads."†

John Bradbury, the Scottish traveler on our Great Plains, tells us that the price among the Arikara Indians of a bow made from this wood was, in 1810, a horse and a blanket — a very high charge indeed, but as the Arikaras had no Osage growing in the treeless country, Bow-wood was to them a precious timber. "Many of the war clubs," Bradbury adds, "are made of the same kind of wood, and have the blade of a knife, or some sharp instrument, fastened at the end, and projecting from four to six inches, forming a right angle with the club." Not a weapon to be treated with contempt!

Because of its great strength, Osage wood early proved one of the finest for railway ties, and nothing but its scarcity prevents it from being widely used for that purpose still. "In 1873 we procured from Texas," Bernet Landreth wrote in 1893 to Professor Sargent, "some railroad ties of Osage Orange, and had them set out in the road-bed of the New York division of the Pennsylvania Railroad alongside of oak, chestnut, and catalpa. The soft woods were all torn out in two or three years, but the Osage Orange, after twenty-one years, is still in place, after having been turned several times, and still as good as the first year."‡ Pavement blocks were formerly extensively made of Osage Orange, and it was in high demand for wheel stock. The first chuck wagon ever built, according to a well-founded tradition, was that invented by Charles Goodnight, the most famous Texan cattleman, and it was built of seasoned *bois d'arc*, in order to withstand the terrible usage of bumping over the far-flung Goodnight empire that covered much of the Panhandle in early days.

*"Wood for Archers," *American Forests*, October 1940.
†*Pacific Railway Reports.*
‡Charles Sprague Sargent, *Silva of North America.*

The fame of the Osage Orange spread gradually from the early *voyageurs* of the lower Mississippi Valley, who knew it well, to the English-speaking pioneers. It was first mentioned, in our language, in President Jefferson's message to Congress (1806), quoting from an account of it by two British explorers who had seen it two years before at the post of the Washita, Arkansas. They alluded to its probable value as a hedge plant. When that excellent botanist and ornithologist Thomas Nuttall found it a few years later growing luxuriantly on rich bottomlands of the Red River, he named it in honor of his friend William Maclure, geologist, librarian, and philanthropist of the famed little town of New Harmony, Indiana.

At an early date, in the nineteenth century, Osage Orange began to be cultivated in the southern states as a natural hedge plant. For this it has every qualification, with its ability to grow thickset, as gardeners say, with its scattered thorns, its hardiness in drought, heat, and wind, its zigzag branchlets, and the way that it keeps its lower branches all the way to the ground. It is easily propagated from seed, sprouting the first year and growing very rapidly. Yet it never grows so tall as to turn the hedge into a shade-casting wall harmful to crops. It meets the old demand that a hedge plant shall be "horse high, bull strong, and pig tight."

When the midwestern prairies were first settled, and before the coming of barbed wire in the 1870s, the only method of fencing, in such a way as to hold stock, was by a pale of long wooden stakes — far too costly for any but small enclosures; and without fencing the settlers were forced to form broken and scattered settlements on the margins of groves and streams, treating the fertile prairies as common pasturage. Social organization, under such conditions, was kept to a primitive level, until the Osage Orange was first introduced in the fifties, into the Middle West by the efforts of John A. Wright, editor of the *Prairie Farmer,* and his friend Professor Jonathan B. Turner, who stumped the country for human betterment in general, Osage Orange in particular. The interesting story is told in detail in Lloyd Lewis's *John Wright, Prophet of the Prairies.* There is space here only to relate that thousands of miles were planted, in a few decades, to Hedgeplant, as these proponents called it, and to this day, especially in Missouri, one sees endless fields still hedged by this strange, glittering tree, producing a compartmental landscape almost like that of parts of Normandy and England. But many farmers are now grubbing out their picturesque and historic old Osage hedges. When they do so they are also destroying valuable cover without which game birds like bobwhite are left at the mercy of hunter and dog and hawk, and thus soon destroyed.

True, there are severe criticisms of Osage; it is not a gracious tree; it sends out, unless carefully tended, long sprawling shoots that render it shapeless and unsightly. The foliage is very tardy, not appearing until mid-May in the latitude of Chicago, and the unattractive flowers, which bloom in June and July, are wind pollinated and cause some hay fever; large quantities of pollen are on the air at flowering time wherever the tree is grown.

The leaves, very late in autumn, turn a clear, beautiful, shining yellow. The fruits are eaten by black-tailed deer in Texas, and devoured in the Middle West by fox squirrels, who carry them up in the trees and then drop them, allowing them to smash open. Crossbills are also said to peck the seeds out of the great fleshy green fruit. Recently it was announced by Professor George M. Toffel, chemist at the University of Alabama, that a single Osage Orange in a room will drive away cockroaches, apparently by its Cedar-like aroma. A distillate, which was even stronger smelling, was found to be quite as effective as the fresh fruit in its pest-repellent qualities.

American Linden

Tilia americana Linnæus

OTHER NAMES: Common Basswood. Bass. Lin. Lime. Limetree. White-wood.

RANGE: New Brunswick and southern Quebec to the eastern shore of Lake Superior and west to the Assiniboine River of Manitoba and the central parts of the Dakotas and Nebraska, south to northern Missouri, central Illinois, Indiana, eastern Kentucky, West Virginia, the District of Columbia, and Delaware.

W HEN THE SHADE BEGINS to be heavy and the midges fill the woods, and when the western sky is a curtain of black nimbus slashed by the jagged scimitar of lightning, when the wood thrush seldom sings except after rain and instead the rain crow, our American cuckoo, stutters his weary, descending song — an odor steals upon the moist and heavy air, unbelievably sweet and penetrating.

It is an odor that comes from no bed of stocks, no honeysuckle. More piercing, yet less drugging, than orange blossoms, it is wafted, sometimes as much as a mile, from the flowers of the Linden. All odors have evocative associations to those who know them well — wild grape, wild Crab, wild rose, and honeysuckle. The odor of the Lindens in bloom brings back to many of us the soaring wail of the treetoads, the first fireflies in the dusk, the banging of June beetles on the window screens, the limpness of the flags at Fourth of July, and all that is a boy's-eye view of those languorous first days of vacation from school.

As a wild tree, this Linden, or Basswood as lumbermen and farmers call it, grows sometimes as much as 130 feet tall, with a trunk 3 or 4 feet thick, forming a broadly round-topped crown with short, often pendulous branches. It flourishes in low woods, in company with White Elm, White Ash, and Cottonwood; formerly it often formed nearly pure groves in some spots. Today, though much reduced within its natural range, it is common in cultivation as a street and lawn tree. There it has rivals in a number of Lindens of European origin, including many hybrids. Some of these are preferred for their pretty little leaves and their profusion of flowers. But none of them equals the American Linden in splendid stature — a tree completely benignant and well worthy of planting beside the door, to shade the roof with its lovely crown. The great heart-shaped leaves, though not so prettified as those of some exotic species, cast a deep cool shade. Rather unusually, it is the undersides of the leaves that are shiny, not the upper surface. When the cold wind that just precedes the advance of a summer thunderstorm rushes through the Lindens, the blades are flung over and shine unearthly bright against the black advancing skies.

Bees, when the Lindens bloom, forsake all others and cleave only unto these flowers. The honey that they make of Linden nectar is white in color, with a rather strong flavor, but regarded as of high quality. Though to the shortness of the blooming period, about three weeks, is added the drawback that abundant honeyflows can be depended on only two or three years out of every five, yet when an unusually heavy flow comes, it yields enormous quantities.

As a timber tree, this Basswood belongs to a special class of woods which, though without a beautiful figure, and soft and very light and weak in the position of a beam, have their own sort of value. For the reason that it is so light, Basswood is used for crates and boxes and the core of chair stock that is to be veneered with fine cabinet woods, for toys and drawer sides, window sashes, picture frames, and musical instruments. It is familiar to us all as the wood in which comb honey is framed, as the household or dressmaker's yardstick, and on the backs of picture puzzles. Because it is cheap and still fairly abundant, it is coming to be important in paper-pulp manufacture. Basswood collectively (lumbermen make no distinction between this and other species recognized by foresters) ranks fourteenth in the cut of American woods, just after Hickory and ahead of such a sturdy hardwood as Ash.

The inner bark of Basswood yields some of the longest and toughest fibers in our native flora. It was stripped by the Indians in spring, and thongs prepared from it without further processing. Good rope, however, was made from it by retting — keeping the bark under water for about a month, until the soft tissues should rot away, leaving the somewhat slippery fibrous tissue. Or sometimes the bark was pounded, or simmered in wood ashes in a kettle. Long strips of rope or string were then twisted to form cordage, which the Indians used to insist was softer on the hands when wet than the white man's hempen fibers and not so liable to kink. Thread of Basswood bark was used to stitch together the mats made of cattail leaves, and the bark, perhaps because of its mucilaginous qualities, was used to bind up the warrior's wounds. Some of the Iroquois' masks were carved in the sapwood on the living tree, and then split off from the trunk and hollowed out from behind.

California Laurel

Umbellularia californica (Hooker & Arnott) Nuttall

OTHER NAMES: Oregon Myrtle. Spicetree. California or Green Baytree. California Olive. Mountain Laurel. California Sassafras. Pepperwood.

RANGE: Southwestern Oregon (South Fork of the Umpqua, Coos County, and in the Coast Ranges and Siskiyou Mountains) south through the Coast Ranges of California to northern Baja California, and on the west slopes of the Sierra Nevada from 1200 to 4000 feet altitude.

THE MANY FOLK NAMES OF THIS TREE tell a tale of the vivid impression it has made on the generations that have known it. To the Oregonians it is Oregon Myrtle, to the Californians it is California Laurel; though not strictly speaking either a Myrtle or a Laurel, it is at least in the Laurel family and, like the classic Laurel or Bay (*Laurus nobilis*) with which ancient victors and poets were crowned, it has a spicily aromatic and evergreen leaf. Hence the name of Green Baytree, Spicetree, and Pepperwood. The little dark fruits are shaped like an olive; so it has been called California Olive.

Grand old trees have the noble stature of Oaks and are surmised to be two and three hundred years old. Young trees have all the elegant, formal charm of the true Laurel or Bay. The leaves are dark as some Magnolia's, yet graceful as a Willow's.

And always there is that pervading aroma, something like the true Baytree's, but much stronger, with a slight admixture of camphor and something peppery. One becomes aware of it after a few moments in a thick Laurel grove or under a great specimen, and the odor grows more, not less, insistent as you stay with it. Crush a leaf lightly and you will pronounce it delicious; but do not inhale it too much, for it may cause violent sneezing, even headache and dizziness.

If you travel south along the Pacific's shore you meet the green Baytree first in Oregon, keeping company with other hardwoods like the streamside Alders and Maples, becoming more and more abundant and beautiful. Indeed, it takes on there a special shape, seldom seen in California; at least along the highways, though not on the rich bottomlands, it is a low tree with a short trunk, but broadened in crown to an almost globular mass. It looks then remarkably like some of the great old Box trees one sees in colonial gardens of Virginia, and so regular is its form that it is hard to believe it has not been clipped to an artificial perfection. A particularly lovely grove of such is Myrtle-wood Lane — some twenty miles of trees along Oregon State Highway 42, between Coquille and Myrtle Point. One would think they must have been planted here, when in fact the road is new, the trees are old. To preserve this species, Oregon has established a state park, the Maria Jackson Grove, on Brummet Creek, 26 miles from Myrtle Point, an area of 84 acres containing Myrtles of all shapes.

And almost everywhere along the roadsides of southwestern Oregon you see Myrtlewood for sale — platters and bowls, gavels and trays and cigarette boxes fashioned of it. Very light brown with lighter and darker streaks, or a lovely pale gray, Myrtlewood, when cut from burls, is of fancy and fanciful grain. Unfortunately too many of the objects offered for sale are in the souvenir class. The lumber has been cut for shipbuilding, interior finish, furniture, and the jaws, bits, cleats, and crosstrees of small boats. Formerly, at least, a volatile oil — limpid and straw colored, with an odor resembling that of nutmeg and cardamom — was distilled from the wood and leaves and used hopefully in the treatment of catarrh and nervous headache, colic, diarrhea, and even meningitis. As a pharmaceutical product it seems not to be on the market at present.

Oregon's Myrtle becomes California Laurel as soon as you cross the state boundary. Now it assumes many other forms, as it adapts itself variously to growth upon sea bluffs forever swept by salt-laden winds, or in the profound shade of mighty Redwoods and Douglas Firs, in the sun-scorched chaparral, on the open hills or in the depths of canyons. The typical woodland form is that of a tree taller (40 to 70 feet) than broad, with erect or ascending branches. In this form it resembles that of most forest-grown trees, and thus you see it in among Redwoods. In well-watered canyons, as on the slopes of Mount Tamalpais, dense jungles of Laurel form a dwarf forest, their boughs deeply covered with lichen and moss to make what children call a fairy-tale wood. There is also the pendulous form, seen only here and there, in isolated lofty trees whose branchlets drip in almost vinelike sprays. The thicket form is one where all the trees are of the same height and almost flat topped, as if clipped off by pruning. Even when this form is found growing on the steep sides of a hill or canyon, the tops of the trees are apt to form an almost level expanse, for the trees higher up are mere shrubs, while lower trees may be 40 feet high. The wind, of course, is the sculptor of such groves — fast and constant breezes such as blow in from the ocean through the mouth of Tomales Bay, Marin County, California, modeling the trees of famed Laurel Hill. Where briny gales forever blow, as on Pacific bluffs, the Laurel becomes prostrate, crowding into any hollows it can find, and streaming along the ground like a green river. In the chaparral a dwarf form is found, as intricate and twiggy as every other tree that grows there. Where old, large specimens have been cut down, great numbers of shoots sprout up, a perfect fountain of many-jetted tree-life, bushy and luxuriant.

Great specimens are still numerous, despite the fact that in the pioneer days of agriculture the old and noble trees were as ruthlessly felled and grubbed out by the roots as the younger ones, in order to take over the soil for crops. In almost all parts of its range — in scores of California counties — the Laurel has specimens of unusual size and age, locally famous and often the object of deep affection. In the town of San Leandro there stands at 624 Lewelling Road a dooryard tree which is 70 feet high, has a crown 85 feet across, and a trunk 28 feet and 4 inches in girth. But its great tablelike base is 49 feet in circumference. At 8 feet from the ground it gives off five gigantic forks, the largest of them, in itself, 14 feet in circumference. Old inhabitants say that it was once a much larger tree than now in its old age, and that it was an Indian meeting place. Old Spanish coins have been found buried under it, or so runs the local legend, and this is not impossible, for the present town was all once the property of José Joaquín Estudillo whose rancho was one of the finest in Alta California, famous for its white cattle. Squatters in the 1850s tried to drive the Estudillos from their land and for some time the family was in danger of its lives as well as its fortunes; perhaps the coins were buried here then. At one period there was a great hollow in the base of the trunk, and in it a little girl had her playhouse. The bark has now grown completely over it.

On the old San Marcos Road near Santa Barbara grows another great Laurel; above its immensely swollen butt, the trunk is 23 feet in circumference. The total height is 82 feet, and it casts a pool of shade 104 feet across. In many respects this is the finest specimen which has been precisely measured in all its parts — a temple of a tree, breathing aromatic incense.

The little umbel of greenish white flowers passes almost unnoticed when the blossoms appear in spring. But the foliage is at all times conspicuous, as freshly gleaming on the dark upper surface as if sparkling with dew, the undersides beautifully pale. The new growth of foliage pushes off the old leaves, which turn, a leaf here and there, a soft butter yellow no matter at what season, but there is never a time when all the tree is golden nor when it stands all bare. Indeed, few trees cast so deep and constant a shade as this one, and when you get a mixture of bushy young Laurel with densely growing Redwoods or broadleaved Alders and Maples, the darkness of the underwood is amazing. No eastern woods and none in Europe are so astonishingly dim. The light, for some unexplained reason, is often a golden brown like that in the backgrounds of the old Dutch masters, and in the intense umbrage only a few lush wood ferns are content to grow.

DOGWOODS

Flowering Dogwood

Cornus florida Linnæus

OTHER NAME: Virginia Dogwood.

RANGE: Extreme southern Maine and southern Vermont across southern New York, the southern tip of Ontario, southern Michigan, and northern Illinois to the southeastern half of Missouri, eastern Oklahoma, and Texas south to the Gulf of Mexico.

STEPPING DELICATELY out of the dark woods, the startling loveliness of Dogwood in bloom makes each tree seem a presence, calling forth an exclamation of praise, a moment of worship from our eyes. On the almost naked branches the blossoms shine forth like stars, and these blossoms are borne in long flat sprays of bloom along the boughs, turning their pure faces up toward the sky with a suggestion of the most classical traditions of flower arrangement. It is a botanist's quibble to point out that the four white "petals" are not petals indeed but bracts; by any name, they make a clear and pleasing design, in detail as in mass. And the little tree bears them with a royal grace, tier upon snowy tier, the slim trunk often leaning slightly from the hillside, as though to offer its burden of blossom, princesslike, to the spring world.

But it makes no great demands on its environment. It is well suited to comparatively dry soils; it comes up quickly after fire; it shines through

sterile Pine woods and troops along the fence rows that divide field and pasture, and along every country roadside, where the birds have voided the seeds. It steals out of the neighboring woods to invade the clearing left by loggers, or the field abandoned by farmers. It goes, too, climbing high in the mountains, and lights up the somber coves; by stream banks its white branches or, in fall, its scarlet berries gleam as brightly as the waters.

Man's hand has widened this wide distribution. The Flowering Dogwood is the state tree of Virginia, and the noblest of Virginians have cherished it. George Washington was an inveterate planter of Dogwood. On his birthday in 1785, he noted in his diary that he had removed some from the woods to a Mount Vernon shrubbery, and speaks on March first of that year of planting "a circle of Dogwood with a red bud in the Middle, close to the old Cherry near the South Garden House." Thomas Jefferson loved it too, and planted it in "the open ground on the west" of his house at Monticello. An especially prized variety has pink blooms.

Lovely as it is, Dogwood stoops also to be useful. The wood has an extremely high resistance to sudden shock, ahead even of Persimmon and inferior only to Hickory. For that reason Dogwood has long been a favorite for the heads of golf sticks and for the handles of chisels, since they can be hammered on the ends without "brooming," that is, splitting and mushrooming out. The same virtue makes it useful for mauls, mallet heads, and wedges. Small pulleys, and spindles too, of Dogwood are strong and light and serviceable in the textile industry. Knitting needles and sledge runners are made of it because it wears smoother with use, and in the old days its fine properties made it a favorite for distaffs, spindles, hog yokes, hay forks, barrel hoops, hubs of small wheels, machinery bearings, and rake teeth. Still the jeweler prefers Dogwood sticks for cleaning out deepseated lenses, since they do not scratch the glass.

But fully 90 percent of the Dogwood cut in the nineteenth century has gone to the making of shuttles in the textile industry. When the shuttle was thrown from hand to hand by the weaving woman, almost any wood might do, but with the invention of mechanical looms, where the shuttle is hurled at top speed, carrying the weft thread, the shuttle is in continual contact with the threads of the warp. So a wood must be used which will not crack under continuous strain and will wear smoother, not rougher, with use. Walnut wears smoother, but is too weak. Hickory is stronger, but wears rough with usage. Dogwood is ideal. Yet it did not come into much use while Turkish Boxwood was plentiful. Then, about 1865, the roller-skating craze began to absorb the market for Box, and Dogwood came to the fore. Cut in the South, it was manufactured and used in New England or exported as logs from the southern seaports to Britain, France, Germany, Italy, and Switzerland. Soon it was found cheaper to ship the manufactured article, and most Dogwood shuttles are now made in small but numerous mills in the South.

Dogwood is lumbered where it can be found in the virgin forest because the longest, straightest, knot-free trunks are grown there. It is also felled by the farmers at the time they are cutting their woodlots in winter for fuel, and sold, a few sticks at a time, or traded at the local general store, which then piles the wood on sidings for the trip to the mill. Commonly, then, Dogwood is sold by the cord, because of its small dimensions and high prices. At the mill it is seasoned with great care, halved into flitches, quartered, then cut out into rectangular blocks roughly parallel to the annual growth rings. Highly skilled labor is required, for the buyers demand absolutely perfect, defect-free shuttles and unfortunately insist on the pure white sapwood, though the heartwood is no whit inferior, nor is there danger of splitting where heartwood and sapwood meet.

The cut of commercially valuable Dogwood is far in excess of the annual growth rate. Formerly Dogwood was uprooted or bucked down by tractors in the lumbering operations amid the great pineries of the Gulf states. Owing to the high price for the fine kind of Dogwood grown under Yellow Pine, it is now sold off to contractors and removed before logging of the Pines begins. True that Dogwood is on the increase in abandoned fields, among second growth of Virginia Scrub Pine, along fence rows and roadsides; but such open-grown trees retain their lower boughs, and superior though they are in beauty, they are too short and knotty for the block mills. At present the greatest stand of merchantable Dogwood is in Arkansas, and when the virgin timber there is seriously reduced, the future supply has a far from bright outlook.

Certain obsolete uses of Dogwood make picturesque footnotes to our history. The aromatic bark, above all the inner bark of the root, has marked bitter and astringent properties; the alkaloid cornin or cornic acid is the active principle. The Indians used it as a remedy for malaria; the pioneers improved on this by steeping the Dogwood bark in whiskey and imbibing this when they had "the shakes" and the "ague." When the blockade of the southern ports by the U.S. Navy, from 1861 to 1865, caused a shortage of quinine in the Confederacy, Dogwood bark was used like "Peruvian bark." And farther back in our fading past, certain Indians derived from the roots a scarlet dye for coloring porcupine quills and bald eagle feathers.

Today our modern savages destroy the tree chiefly for the sprays of its pure white bloom. Around Washington, D.C., the threat to the tree was so merciless that the Wild Flower Preservation Society waged a long battle to save it from local extinction. Their method was simple and immensely effective. They placed posters on the fronts of the city's streetcars, urging the public to save Dogwood by refusing to cut or buy any. As a result, the sales of Dogwood on the streets, where it had been commonly vended, on the roadsides, in florists' shops and markets has fallen off so severely that merchants have stopped buying it. And this prompt and effective conservation has been achieved without the tedious and imperfect method of passing a law; that powerful legislature, public opinion, was called upon to utter the decree.

Pacific Dogwood

Cornus nuttallii Audubon ex Torrey & Gray*

OTHER NAMES : California, Nuttall, or Flowering Dogwood.

RANGE : Vancouver Island and the Puget Sound region generally, south through western Washington and Oregon, along the Coast Ranges of California to the San Bernardino Mountains and south to the mountains of San Diego County, and on the western slopes of the Sierra Nevada.

A	S YOU MOTOR UP, IN MAY, through the solemn coniferous woods to Sequoia National Park, the forest aisles are lighted by drifts of shining bloom — the Dogwood, holding out its still nearly leafless and naked branches that are yet clothed, as fair as any bride, in shining white. Each bloom is like a great white star, and each bough is fairly snowed under beneath the gleaming flakes, and each little tree becomes an artful drift of blossoming whiteness. In the forests around Puget Sound the Dogwood is even more striking; the trees are

*Editor's note: Formerly *Cornus nuttallii* Audubon.

taller and more abundant; and by contrast with the glistening, joyous little Dogwood, the aisles of the coniferous woods are even more somber.

David Douglas was the first botanist to observe this tree, but he made an error in botanical judgment that was rare for so perspicacious a plantsman; he mistook it for eastern Dogwood, so that he did not bother to send seeds to England. It differs, though, in having the white bracts (which are often mistaken for petals) not notched and green tipped, but wholly white and rounded out; where the eastern tree, *Cornus florida,* has regularly only four bracts, this one has four to six, commonly five, to make a five-pointed "star" whose perfection surpasses that of even the eastern species.

The first scientist to recognize this as a new species was Thomas Nuttall, the botanist who, with Dr. John K. Townsend, a Philadelphia ornithologist, joined the second Wyeth Expedition to the Northwest, and Nuttall tells us of his first sight of this enchanting tree which he saw then in fruit when it is almost as brilliant as in flower: "On arriving, toward the close of September, in 1834, at Fort Vancouver, I hastened again on shore to examine the productions of the forests of the Far West; and nothing so surprised me as the magnificent appearance of some fine trees of this beautiful Cornus. Some of them growing in the rich lands near the fort were not less than fifty to seventy feet in height with large . . . *lucid* green leaves, which, taken with the *smooth* trunks and unusually-large clusters of crimson berries, led me, at first glance, to believe that I beheld some new Magnolia, until the flower buds, already advanced for the coming season, proved our plant to be a Cornus, allied, in fact, to the *Florida,* but with the flowers or colored involucres nearly six inches in diameter! These appeared in all their splendor, in May of the following year, of a pure white with a faint tinge of blush. . . . Though the berries are somewhat bitter they are still, in autumn, the favorite food of the Band-Tailed Pigeon."*

It was at Fort Vancouver that the ornithologist Townsend, as a physician, responded to a call of the Cowlitz Indians, in whose lodges two children lay sick with intermittent fever. "My stock of quinine being exhausted," he notes in his journal, "I determined to substitute an extract of the bark of the Dogwood (*Cornus Nuttallii*) and taking one of the parents into the wood with his blanket, I soon chipped off a plentiful supply, returned, boiled it down in his own kettle, and completed the preparation in his lodge, with most of the Indians standing by and staring at me to comprehend the process. This was exactly what I wished, and as I proceeded, I took some pains to explain the whole matter to them in order that they might at a future time be enabled to make use of a really valuable medicine which grows abundantly everywhere throughout the country. . . . I administered to each of the children about a scruple of the extract per day. The second day they escaped the paroxysm, and on the third were entirely well."†

Cornus nuttallii was named by John James Audubon. One does not think of the great bird painter as a botanist, but he was Nuttall's friend, and the specimens of the band-tailed pigeon which he received through Dr. Townsend suggested to him, when he came to figure them, in his *Birds of America,* the thought of including their food plant, the Dogwood. He has represented them — the bird and tree together — in Plate 367, and in his *Ornithological Biography* he gives a complete description of the plant, "a superb species of Dogwood, discovered by our learned friend Thomas Nuttall, Esq., when on his march towards the shores of the Pacific Ocean, and which I have graced with his name!"

North American Sylva.
†Narrative of a Journey Across the Rocky Mountains to the Columbia River, 1839.

ASHES

White Ash

Fraxinus americana Linnæus

OTHER NAMES: American, Biltmore, or Cane Ash.

RANGE: Nova Scotia to southern Quebec, south to northern Florida, northern Louisiana, and northeastern Texas, west to Minnesota, and eastern parts of Nebraska, Kansas, and Oklahoma. Absent from the Gaspé peninsula, the north shore of Lake Superior, the higher Appalachians, and usually from the neighborhood of the South Atlantic and Gulf coasts.

EVERY AMERICAN BOY knows a great deal about White Ash wood. He knows the color of its yellowish white sapwood and the pale brown grain of the annual growth layers in it. He knows the weight of White Ash not in terms of pounds per cubic foot but by the more immediate and unforgettable sensation of having lifted and swung a piece of it, of standard size. He even knows its precise resonance and pitch, the ringing *tock* of it when struck. For it is of White Ash, and of White Ash only, that good baseball bats are made. Ash is the commonest wood for the frames of tennis racquets, for swing seats, for hockey sticks, for polo mallets, and for playground equipment. The reasons why it is the favorite wood for sporting goods are found in its fundamental properties; it is tough, too tough to break under much strain, but pliant, and just pliant

enough, not too much so. It can be bent into desired shapes and worked with comparative ease, yet it is hard. Despite its great strength, Ash is comparatively light. At least, true White Ash is so. A number of other botanical species, the Green Ash, the Blue Ash, for instance, go to market as White Ash; they are not quite the equals of true White Ash in all its virtues, but they are nearer to them than any other woods, and the lumberman may be allowed his broad general classification.

True that White Ash is not as strong as the best Hickory, and so it is not used for the handles of tools that, like hammers, are to be violently struck. But Hickory is a much heavier and more expensive wood. Ash is ideal for the tools of most garden and agricultural implements. It is used in preference to all others for the D-handles of spades and shovels. The list of the uses of White Ash would take up many pages. It goes into both church pews and the floors of bowling alleys, into rods for sucker pumps, and oars and keels of small boats, into butter-tub staves, and garden and porch furniture, into airplanes and farm wagons — everywhere that strength and lightness must be combined. White Ash has occasional fancy grains — the curly figure such as is seen in fiddleback Maple and the step figure so popular in Walnut; special beauty in these is brought out by quartersawing, and it is used as veneers in the cabinetmaker's art. But plain-sawn Ash is still a very fine wood, if you can admire the honest, functional beauty of the growth layers of a tree that grows straight and at a regular pace. Ash furniture, especially in modern styles with much plain surface and geometrical and functional lines, if given a light stain or a very thin coat of paint in a gray or almost neutral green color, will cause the most casual observer to exclaim over its beauty and ask what wood that is.

The uses of White Ash are, on the whole, so specialized that when it is cut it is not usually stored in the general hardwood lumber yard but is shipped on to a few companies that buy and sell little else. Actually the amount of White Ash, the country over, is not great. The largest part of it is not found today in virgin forests or in dense stands anywhere; it is mostly growing in the farmer's woodlot, which may be anywhere in an area of a million square miles, in any state east of the Mississippi and several beyond it. Yet normally the quantity of White Ash in the woodlot will not be more than 4 percent of the total stand of timber. Fortunately very large and ancient trees are not required for most of the uses to which Ash is put. On the contrary, the toughest, strongest, soundest White Ash, with the greatest proportion of the pale sapwood that retail buyers prefer, is cut from the fast-growing, comparatively young trees of second growth, such as commonly constitute most of the woodlots of the eastern states. Fortunately, too, the chief Ash-using industries require quality, not quantity of board feet.

Many of our valuable hardwoods are extremely difficult to propagate or to manage for timber production. In the case of White Oak, for instance, where dimension timbers are required from a very slow-growing tree, one would have to lay plans to harvest a merchantable crop 150 years from now. Not so with White Ash. With a little forest management the present seedling crop could be increased and hurried to a stand that is mature, from a lumberman's viewpoint. For what a White Ash chiefly needs is room and light. Its seedlings may be fairly numerous in the woods, but suppressed by shade from more umbrageous trees; a seedling only a foot high may be fifteen years old and have developed an extensive root system, if growing in deep shade. If the forest crown is thinned, these seedlings, with their highly developed root system, will shoot up with surprising speed, producing more valuable timber than those White Ashes of the virgin forest that used to live three hundred years and grow 175 feet tall, with a trunk 5 feet or more in diameter. Most such are vanished, anyway, and today we call a White Ash with half those dimensions a splendid specimen, as indeed it is. When an old White Ash is felled, it sprouts very freely from the stump, the more so if the stump is cut low. Growth of these sprout trees, too, is very rapid, for the old root system is all there to draw water, while the growth from the long-suppressed buds seems to release a green fountain of refreshed energy.

The chosen site of White Ash is a deep, rich, sweet loam, with abundance of ground water but good drainage. It is at its best in the zone of the broadleaved deciduous trees of the cool temperate regions, in the company of Beech, Birch, Maple, and Basswood, as in the high coves of the Appalachians. In the prairie groves of Illinois, where the rainfall is lower and the evaporation is higher, White Ash takes to low, but not saturated, ground and associates with White Elm, American Linden, Cottonwood, and Hackberry. In New England and New York it is found on rocky upland soils with Oaks but is never so tall a tree there as on the deep loams of the Middle West.

When a White Ash is young it has a narrow head. But with age the boughs widen until the crown is broader than long, if the tree is growing in the open without too severe competition, and a great pool of shade results. The foliage tends to cluster on the outside of the tree, so that when you stand beside the bole and look up, you see through easily to the sky, and can observe what business the birds are at — the nuthatches gleaning the bark with soundless thrift, the woodpeckers drilling at the trunks with red heads moving so fast they are a blur, and high overhead the hawks waiting-on in noble style and whistling their shrill war cry. As it is not too umbrageous a tree, so too the shade of White Ash is further lightened by the softly shining, almost silvery undersides of the foliage, so that to stand and look up under it is to see a misty whiteness, while, viewed from outside, the foliage is richly dark and gleaming.

When a White Ash grows old, it is apt to bear great horizontal arms, wondrously strong and springy, from which swings may be safely hung. If it is late in leafing out in spring, yet the flowers, on the naked wood, are (to those who have eyes for such things) very striking, with their clusters of black anthers and purple stigmas. No tree makes less litter beneath it — only those neat little winged fruits on the female trees, that plummet soundlessly down and spear the grass. In fall, White Ash is the most versatile colorist of all our woods. Some trees may stand, like transfixed angels, shining in a light of heavenly gold; others may robe themselves in royal purple. But the bronze and mauve tints that are the rarest in our autumn displays are the specialty of the White Ash.

How many thousand-thousand of untold White Ash trees are the respected companions of our doorways, kindliest trees in the clearing beyond the cabin? No one can say. But this is a tree whose grave and lofty character makes it a lifetime friend. White Ash has no easy, pretty charms like Dogwood and Redbud; it makes no overdramatic gestures like Weeping Willow and Lombardy Poplar. It has never been seen through sentimental eyes, like the Elm and the White Birch. Strong, tall, cleanly, benignant, the Ash tree with self-respecting surety waits, until you have sufficiently admired all the more obvious beauties of the forest, for you to discover at last its unadorned greatness.

Charles Darwin once wrote to his friend Asa Gray, the great Harvard botanist, asking him what plant might be considered to top the list of the vegetable kingdom in its long story of evolution from a pond scum to a flower. Englishmen are known to have "hearts of oak," and Darwin wondered if the apex of plant evolution might not be an Oak. But Gray replied that the plant kingdom has no single culminating species. Botanists believe that the two great evolutionary lines in the seed plants do culminate in, respectively, the Orchid Family and the Composite Family. Neither of them, however, has anything that could properly be called a tree. Yet this much one may say, that so far as concerns the trees of northeastern North America, the White Ash is Nature's last word.

That is not to say that the Ash is "higher" than other trees, for the whole concept of "higher" and "lower" species is unscientific; there are only older types and more recent types. It is a long way, in pages and species and perhaps in geologic time, from the very old type of the White Pine to the newer one of the White Ash. But one is not a finer tree than the other, nor better adapted to its environment. And the same would be true of all the intermediate species. Each has its place; each is, or it was in the days of virgin innocence, adjusted to its environment and held with its neighbors in a precise ecologic balance. All are equal in the sight of an impartial Nature. All are fellow citizens of the grand American sylva.

Black Ash

Fraxinus nigra Marshall

OTHER NAMES: Hoop, Basket, Brown, Swamp, or Water Ash.

RANGE: Western Newfoundland, Anticosti Island, and Quebec to Manitoba, North Dakota, and Iowa, south to the Ohio River valley, northern Virginia, northern Delaware, central New Jersey, and western Connecticut.

THERE ARE A NUMBER of fairly good reasons why this should be called the Black Ash. The shiny blue black winter buds, for one, the very dark green of the foliage too, perhaps, and the dark heartwood, which frequently in this species occupies almost the entire woody cylinder of the trunk, even in comparatively young trees.

Deep cold swamps are the favorite site of this most northerly of all Ashes, in the company of Tamarack, Black Spruce, and Arborvitæ in the North Woods. On drier soil in the north it keeps company with Hemlock, Balsam, Hard Maple, and Yellow Birch; farther south, it lines the stream banks, with Elm, Soft Maple, and Willow. No fine stands of Black Ash are known south of Pennsylvania and Ohio. Seldom now do we see specimens 90 feet tall with trunks 20 inches through, as in the virgin North Woods, but at all times the Black Ash may be known by its strikingly slim figure. The slender branches are almost upright and form a narrow head, making a remarkably gracile outline for an Ash. When the odd flowers appear on the naked wood in spring, they are not without their loveliness. Very late, the leaves at last appear. Handsome for their brief season of greenery, they turn at the first hint of the northern fall a rusty brown, with none of the subtlety of White Ash coloration. Then they drop all at once, so that for perhaps eight months, in the Canadian clime, the Black Ash is bare.

This is the tree that George Washington, surveyor of his own land claims on the Kanawha and Ohio rivers, always called "hoop tree" in his notes. Those were the days when surveyors notched "witness trees," instead of setting up stone or metal boundary markers — two hacks of the hatchet for a corner, three for a line or pointer — and the young surveyor called it hoop tree for the same good reason for which it is called Basket Ash. For the wood of Black Ash, which lacks the proverbial strength and shock-resisting qualities of some of its sister species, has certain properties they do not possess. Among them is its capacity for splitting easily into very thin yet remarkably tough pieces. The springwood — that is, the portion of the annual growth ring that is laid down in the spring months when water and sap are abundant and growth is fast — is made up almost entirely of large pores, with precious little wood fiber between them, so that it is largely air spaces. As a result, billets of Black Ash are easily separated into thin strips, the line of cleavage following the springwood's weakness. The Indians, with some vigorous beating, thus separated long strips of tough summerwood, just as they did with the Arborvitæ, and of the splints made fish baskets. The white man turned this property into account for the making of woven chair bottoms and barrel hoops. A dozen minor uses are known for this tree, from washboards to church pews, but though the form of the trunk in a fine old tree is the lumberman's delight, rising straight and thick as a granite column, it has never been a great commercial timber tree.

When a great old Black Ash grows in a swamp, it sends out aggressive roots everywhere. No other tree has a chance in close proximity and prolonged competition with a Black Ash. As a result of long occupation by Black Ashes, however, swamps become shallower, by filling up with decay and muck, and finally become almost dry ground. Time then for ecological succession by another association of trees adapted to low ground but not standing water; then the short-lived Black Ash has to give way to Elm and Linden and Red Maple.

Trees growing in supersaturated and oxygen-deficient conditions are especially likely to develop burls. Black Ash burls as big as washtubs sometimes develop on the trunks of old swamp-grown trees. They seem to owe their origin to the stifling of adventitious buds inside the wood, buds that are thwarted yet send out shoots that branch like stunted little trees, and though hopelessly bound by the wood, they braid and distort it in every direction, as well as bulging out the trunk in great bark-covered tumescences. Veneers of Black Ash burl look like contour maps of mountainous country, like displays of the aurora borealis, like a dark and riffling tide sweeping over clear white sands. Curly Ash, as lumbermen call the burl grains, is cut as veneer and sold to cabinetmakers who esteem it as perhaps the most beautiful of all American woods.

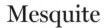

Mesquite

Prosopis juliflora (Swartz) De Candolle

OTHER NAMES: Western Honey Locust. Honeypod. Honey or Velvet Mesquite. Algarobo. Albarroba. Algaroba-tree. Texas Ironwood.

RANGE: Northern Mexico north to the low deserts of California, southern Nevada, and southwesternmost Utah, throughout the deserts of Arizona and New Mexico, and the arid parts of Texas and western Oklahoma, reaching southern Kansas and western Louisiana. Also on the island of Jamaica, south through Central America to Venezuela.

O F ALL THE GOLD SEEKERS who were misguided into Death Valley in 1849, the most pathetic was the Bennett-Manly party. For it was accompanied by the wives and children of this group of midwesterners. And the frailty of these hostages to fortune caused their menfolk to tarry beside the springs, hoping that strength would return to the emaciated bodies. Yet the longer they waited, the hotter grew the season, and the lower ran their food supplies. Eventually they escaped, after terrible hardships. But, all along, their sufferings could have been greatly lightened had they known enough to eat the sweet, nutritious pods which were swinging on the Mesquite trees right over their heads. The trees they knew were perhaps the very ones that still stand around the water hole that is known now, after this unhappy party, as Bennett Wells. But these

courageous greenhorns — these corn-and-beef-fed farmers, these small-townsmen whose food came out of barrels, sacks, and boxes — how could they guess that the Lord had appointed any manna in the valley and shadow of death?

Their ignorance was more pathetic than that of the eastern tourist who, looking from the train window at the miles of Mesquite *bosque* between San Antonio and Uvalde, Texas, exclaimed that never had he seen such extensive Peach orchards. Texans slapped their thighs in glee as they told him what this growth really is and taught him, no doubt, to pronounce it "mez-*keet*"* — for Texans decide these things for us. But indeed there is a remarkable resemblance in a Mesquite to a Peach, with its very short trunk, the deep V-shaped forks of its branches, its many twigs, and low stature. Or when a Mesquite grows old it may come to look more like some ancient Apple tree, bent with years of bearing till its twigs grow knotty and its overborne boughs sweep downward at the ends. But on a second look the traveler sees there is something wrong with these "orchards." Those tough stems perversely twisted, those crooked twigs, those thorns set upon black and warty bases — they belong to no sweet Peach, no friendly Apple.

But do not compare this tree to such as grow by man's husbanding hand. Judge it rather by its peers, by all the thorn-set, hard-bitten desert flora. Then Mesquite appears as an astonishingly tall, umbrageous, and thrifty growth. For, where you would not think that any sort of tree could exist, in such arid soil, such flaming heat, or in the depths of the Grand Canyon with its raging floods, the Mesquite, when it comes to leaf, is a blessing on the earth that bears it.

Spring comes to the Mesquite first as a sudden rush of green to the twigs whose arthritic fingers seem to grow limber now; at this time the twigs are palatable browse to deer and cattle. Then the leaf buds burst, and the foliage, at first an ethereal green, spreads over the thorny crown like a halo; swiftly each *bosque* catches the green fire, as the twice-compound leaves expand their ferny, frondose grace.

In spring, too, flowers appear for the first time — for there are two blooming seasons: April, after the winter rains, and again in June and July, continuing intermittently till fall. The flowers, really in the Mimosa family but looking like yellow catkins, do not make the magnificent dis-

*From *mizquitl*, the Nahuatl Indian word for this tree, by way of Spanish *mesquite*.

play of such desert trees as the Palo Verde and the Ironwood, but they are delightfully fragrant, gently perfuming all the stern desert's airs. Bees come to them by the millions, especially in the honey-raising districts of west Texas. Mesquite honey is clear amber in color and of good if not the highest quality.

In the lives of many Southwest Indian tribes, Mesquite was the most important of all trees. The Papago house was commonly built of it. Four to nine forked Mesquite posts made the pillars, and through the forks were laid light poles or horizontal stringers of Mesquite. Next, light slender rods of Saguaro were laid from pole to pole as a roofing. Then around the central core slender Mesquite poles were set in a circle, as siding, but standing about four feet from the posts. The tips were then bent over and tied to the horizontals with strips of soapweed (*Yucca glauca*) fiber. Thus was formed the skeleton of the dome-shaped hogan. Then the ribs or siding of Mesquite were bound to each other with withes of the ocotillo bush, to make a sort of lath.

"Kickball" was a Papago game, played with spheres of Mesquite wood, though how even an Indian toe could stand up to it is a matter of amazement. Paddles of Mesquite — one for the bottom, like a butter paddle, one for the sides, like a cleaver — were used to shape pottery. Cradle boards of Mesquite roots in the form of an elongated arch, shaped papooses. A snag of sharpened Mesquite was used as a plow from the coming of the Spanish to the coming of steel shares.

But it is the fruits — locustlike pods — that make this tree a blessing. Every Southwest Indian tribe within its range made ample use of the pods, which could be eaten out of hand, or boiled, or stored in the ground, or even fermented to make a mild alcoholic drink. The handsome mottled seeds have always been of the highest importance as an Indian food, from our deserts all the way to South America, serving for flour for cakes and mush. As feed for horses, Mesquite pods were considered so valuable in the days when the United States Cavalry was out after Apaches, that the Army paid three cents a pound in New Mexico for Mesquite beans.

From the first introduction of livestock into the Southwest, the *algaroba*, as the Spanish-speaking pioneers called it, was of recognized importance as browse. Not that the foliage is often touched, but the pods, which contain 25 to 30 percent grape sugar, are more than palatable to stock — they are devoured. Cattle reach as high for them as they can, or horn them down rather than risk tender muzzles among the thorns. Bulls sometimes batter off whole branches for their dehorned cows. Goats climb lightly into the Mesquite boughs, venturing far out to devour pods, leaves, and twigs. Perhaps they even digest the thorns! At any rate it takes a goat but a short time to browse the toughest, driest, wiriest Mesquite to death.

Over much of its range, Mesquite is but a shrub, the underground stems sending up many small shoots, and these frequently branched right at the point where they leave the ground. But this is a species which passes the ill-defined border between tree and shrub, and throughout its range Mesquite is also arboreous, commonly 15 to 20 feet in height, often much more. "Old Geronimo" is a gigantic Mesquite on the grounds of the Santa Cruz Valley School, near Tumacacori, Arizona, with a trunk 14 feet and 11½ inches in circumference, that seems — to judge from its pollarded condition — to have furnished firewood and fence posts for over two hundred years. On the same grounds stands another Mesquite 40 feet in height. The biological survey of Death Valley, made by the Department of Agriculture in 1891, found between Bennett Wells and Mesquite a specimen about 30 feet high, with a spread of branches 75 by 90 feet — quite a pool of shade for the hottest and most ill-reputed spot in all the annals of the desert!

The "Jail Tree," at the corner of Tegner and Center streets in Wickenburg, Arizona, is a historic Mesquite to which badmen and suspects were chained, in lieu of any calaboose in the early days. To serve a sentence under its shade was perhaps more merciful than being locked in any jail the hell-raising frontiers would have provided.

Like the swallows in the Southwest, the Mesquite has a way of associating itself with ruins, such as the Tumacacori Mission near Nogales, Arizona, and Fort Richardson near Jacksboro, Texas. One of the most moving spots in Arizona is Fort Lowell, built of adobe in 1873 and then far outside the pueblo of Tucson with its temptations. Fine streets divided the company buildings, set with Mesquite and Mulberry trees; there were green lawns, and the deep verandahs, vine-clad and olla-hung, formed outdoor living rooms. Then there were balls and dress parades; visitors were lavishly entertained, and splendid cavalry mounts waited in the stables. Today all but a little is a crumbling ruin. For with the end of the Apache wars in 1886 the fort was abandoned, and with every succeeding year fierce sun and rain and wind have done their work. Gone are the lawns, the flowers, the Mulberries, and the adobe arches are fallen. But everywhere the triumphant Mesquite invades, like the jungle tree it is, thrusting up through the very floors, rooting in crannies of the walls, aiding the tooth of the elements in the process of dissolution.

The good points of Mesquite are almost endless. It exudes a gum that was well known to the Indians, who chewed it, used it for wounds and sores as gum Arabic is employed in the Old World, mended pottery with it, and obtained from it a black dye. As early as 1871, more than 12,000 pounds of the gum were gathered in one Texas county alone and sent east for use in the preparation of gumdrops and mucilage. Several hundred pounds are exported annually to Australia, for what purpose is not known. The bark is useful in tanning and dyeing. The wood, almost as hard and beautifully colored as Mahogany and taking a high polish, would be precious cabinet wood if only the trees grew larger, the trunks taller and straighter. Even so it has served for years as a highly valuable fence post and corral stockade material, cheap to cut, and lasting in contact with the soil for years. The Navaho bow was made of the tough wood, and Mesquite beams were placed in that aboriginal apartment building, the Casa Grande, near Coolidge, Arizona. The Texas pioneers used Mesquite almost exclusively for the hubs and spokes of wagon wheels.

Though trunks and branches are used for fuel, the favorite part is the underground stems, erroneously called roots. These are still excavated for fuel wood where labor is cheap enough, and in the old days of exploration, survey parties were dependent on Mesquite "root" for warmth and cooking. It burns with an intense heat, but very slowly and down to a long-lasting bed of coals, so that blacksmiths always preferred it to any other wood.

Water and grass and Mesquite, Mesquite, grass, and water — over and over, they are theme of the early Southwest travelers' prayers and thanks, till we feel as though we could still see the campfires of these courageous pioneer parties and smell again the sweet incense of the burning Mesquite "root" — an odor as haunting as that of Pinyon.

Finally, the Mesquite is valuable because its great root system holds the banks of the dry stream courses and the washes of the southwestern streams down, which, after summer thunderstorms, rush flash floods of water. And the root system of the Mesquite is a wondrous and a fearsome thing. Its branches may penetrate 50 or 60 feet to tap the deep veins of ground water that underlie much of our deserts. But they also come right up under the soil surface, to catch every possible drop of the light winter rains, and they spread laterally in a great circle. So the Mesquite is prepared to adapt itself to the benefits of the most passing shower and yet survive the most prolonged periods of drought.

With all these wonderful qualities, Mesquite is yet the most feared and hated tree that grows, a menace that is every year extending its ravages, spreading desolation where once was wealth. In fifty years it has crossed Texas from the west and south, where it was always native, to southeastern Colorado and right over Oklahoma to southwestern Kansas — one of the most spectacular biological phenomena of this country. It is now beginning to become naturalized in Louisiana and Missouri and will probably not be stopped by anything except the isotherm of prolonged freezing. Carried to the Philippines in the days of the Manila treasure galleons, Mesquite is now firmly established there and, more recently, in the Hawaiian archipelago where it flourishes up to 60 feet in height. It has invaded the Bahamas from the West Indies, and is on the loose in South Africa, Australia, India, and Persia, where it was doubtless at first introduced only as a promising cultivated tree but soon found itself able to elbow its way into the native plant cover and displace it.

How could all this come about, when the tree had for ages been a well-behaved species sticking closely to streams, washes, bottomlands, arroyos, and desert wells and springs? It seems that the cattle, devouring the fruits, void the seeds, often undigested and quite viable, on the upland range grasses. However, the Mesquite seedlings could not compete in the closed community of the range grasses but for the factor — reluctantly admitted or hotly denied by most stockmen — of overgrazing. In short, the rangelands were already broken down, ecologically, before the Mesquite began its jungle march. True, once established on grassland, Mesquite becomes covillain in the plot by shading out the grass and competing for soil moisture. So the vicious circle is closed. As a result, in the last few decades Texas has lost 37 million acres to noxious brush of which Mesquite is the chief factor. Along U.S. Highway 281, between Mineral Wells and Wichita Falls, the Texans — many of Norwegian, Polish, German, and Austrian descent — wage a constant warfare against the greedy trees that are always encroaching on their farms and ranches. Where the highway passes Gap Mountain, it is constantly being menaced by the thorny trees.

In Arizona in 1906, scientists could state that they saw no indications of danger from the increase in Mesquite; by 1936 the stockmen, so scornful of government interference, were begging their government for aid. The Mesquite jungles, stockmen found, were so extensive that cattle had to be hunted through them for days. The thorns are an agony to the cowboy and his horse.

Many methods of control were attempted. The first and most obvious one was to cut the Mesquites down. But since most of the stems are underground, this amounted to nothing better than lopping off the branches above ground. And, because Mesquite crown-sprouts, where one stem had been before, there were now twenty in its place. If you didn't cut it down, then the Mesquite increased by seeds. Gasoline blowtorches were used, but though the flame did wound the tree, a wounded Mesquite is something like a wounded tiger — if not so quick in its reactions. Next, poison injected through the wounds was tried. But even that didn't suffice.

In the end it was found best in Arizona to cut the tree down to the stump, then poison the stump with sodium arsenate applied from an engineer's oil can fitted with a small pump operated by the thumb. The cost of the poison and that kind of labor is low; more, the felled trunks sold for enough as fence posts or fuel to pay off the cost of cutting and poisoning. And land cleared of Mesquite yields still further profit. For instance, it has been found that native uncleared Mesquite brush near Kingsville, Texas, will carry only one cow to every 25 to 30 acres, while cleared brushland will carry two.

Stockmen generally believe, however, that it will always be well to allow Mesquite to occupy some of their bottomlands. The value of the tree for fence posts and fuel, the browse and shade it affords to livestock are worth more than the same type of land would be if it were all range grass. So Mesquite is something more than a tree; it is almost an elemental force, comparable to fire — too valuable to extinguish completely and too dangerous to trust unwatched.

BUCKEYES

Sweet Buckeye

Æsculus flava Aiton*

OTHER NAME: Big Buckeye.

RANGE: From the mountains of southwestern Pennsylvania south along the Blue Ridge to extreme northern parts of Georgia and Alabama, thence west to northern Mississippi, northwestern Louisiana, northeastern Texas, and eastern Oklahoma, and north to extreme southern Illinois, Indiana, and Ohio.

COUNTRY FOLK HAVE NAMED THIS TREE for its big shiny brown seed which, with the large pale scar upon it, has looked to them like the eye of a deer. They are seeds pleasing to look at and satisfying to hold, but there is poison in them, as there is in the young shoot leaves. Pigs, horses, and cattle — even children who were tempted by the seeds — have been repeatedly reported as poisoned by them, with symptoms of inflammation of the mucous membranes, vomiting, stupor, twitching, and paralysis. The glucoside aesculin is one, at least, of the poisonous elements involved.

Yet with this bitter principle removed, the very starchy seeds are both

---

**Editor's note:* Formerly *Æsculus octandra* Marshall.

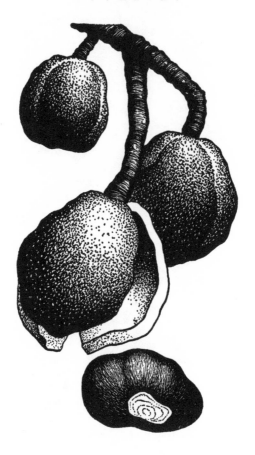

edible and nourishing. "The Indians roasted the nuts among hot stones, thus loosening the shells, peeled and mashed them, and then leached the meal with water for several days."* Thus there was left to them a highly nutritious meal. The very presence of the poison, however, serves to make the seed useful in another way; bookbinders prefer above others a paste made of its starch since it is not eaten by the insect enemies of books.

The tree that bears this tempting and dangerous seed is a beautiful thing in the forest, growing sometimes 90 feet high, with a trunk up to 3 feet thick. The big, branched clusters of bloom which appear in late spring, when the leaves are half grown, light up the whole tree with their yellow petals; in autumn too the tree glows again, when the foliage turns clear yellow.

*Fernald and Kinsey, *Edible Wild Plants of Eastern North America.*

But in the lumberyard Buckeye is rated so low it scarcely dares to pass under its own name. Softest of all the woods in our sylva, including even the so-called softwoods, it is also the weakest of them, nor does it resist decay. It has an ill odor when green, shrinks more than any other wood (50 percent of weight in drying), and though it does not warp excessively, holds nails well, and works easily, it is surprising that it is even at the bottom of the list of the thirty-five leading timbers of the United States. Most of it goes, naturally enough, for crates and boxes, since its lightness lessens the cost of shipping merchandise in it. Commonly Buckeye is graded and sold in the lumberyard as sapwood of Tuliptree — not with intent to defraud but because most lumbermen see no difference.

A superb variety of this tree with rose red or purple flowers was first discovered, near the mouth of the Cheat River in what is now West Virginia, by none other than George Washington. It was on the occasion of his visit in 1784 to Colonel Morgan of Morgantown (where now the University of West Virginia is located) to confer with him on the possibilities of an inland waterway or land route to the Ohio (for Washington, founder of the Union, was ever fearful that the lands beyond the Alleghenies might lose touch with the country and break off from it unless communications were improved). Probably these trees were noted by the tree-loving general on some of his own lands; his holdings in the Ohio basin were great. At any rate, he collected seeds and planted them the following year at Mount Vernon, where four of them may still be seen in the Serpentine. For many years they were thought to be the only known examples of this splendid flowering tree, but careful search has now shown that wild specimens still occur in Ohio, Tennessee, West Virginia, and presumably, eastern Kentucky and southwestern Virginia.

Ohio Buckeye

Æsculus glabra Willdenow

OTHER NAMES: Fetid or Stinking Buckeye.

RANGE: Western Pennsylvania on the west slopes of the Alleghenies to northern Alabama, and west to northeastern Kansas, southeastern Nebraska, and central and southern Iowa.

OHIO, THE BUCKEYE STATE by its own account, has adopted this sprawling shrub or small tree, which rarely reaches as much as 70 feet in height with a trunk 2 feet in diameter, for its floral emblem. But Americans seldom take their emblems seriously, and there is a bit of crude pioneer humor in the choice of the Stinking Buckeye, as it is called on account of the nauseating odor of the bruised bark. Probably much capital has been made of this by Ohio's neighbors, but the retort might be made that the wolverine is a thoroughly disgusting animal, and the sucker an ugly and not too tasty fish, and so the score be paid off with Michigan and Illinois, respectively.

But the Buckeye has its hour. As soon as the first warmth comes stealing up from the south, its great buds begin to swell, the inner scales thrusting aside the outer brownish ones and showing a lovely greenish tint with an inner surface of deep rose. Then, like the petals of some large flower, the scales fold back and the first frail young leaves and the flower buds themselves push outward. At first each leaflet is folded, fanwise; looking almost like green grapes, the crowded clusters of flower buds emerge from among the five-fingered little leaves. If the good weather keeps up, the leaves fairly rush into full foliage while, all about, the Hickories and Oaks, the Locusts and Ashes remain closed in winter's steely secrecy. Soon the flowers, borne stiffly in open clusters at the ends of the upturned clumsy twigs, make their appearance, the color of pale spring sunshine. In early summer the prickly pods split into three valves, and from them drop the big seeds, shining and dark brown, rather like the gleaming coat of a fine horse, and beautified by that large pale scar that is seen on each one.

Many an Ohioan in the old days probably carried a Buckeye in his pocket to ward off rheumatism, and at one time, at least, an extract of the bark was used as a stimulant of the cerebrospinal system. Bark and fruits are both poisonous, though it is probable that, as in the other species of this genus, the poison is driven off the seeds by boiling, and the starchy meat would become edible. The seeds, which look too large, surely, for any but the clumsiest method of distribution, are so light that doubtless spring floods carry them along, leaving them on many a Middle West stream bank when the water subsides. Squirrels are not known to eat them, and it is doubtful if any bird tackles this bitter fruit. The poisonous qualities of the fruit are counted by some farmers as a distinct menace to their cattle, and in certain localities an unremitting warfare is waged against this strange tree.

Because the wood is so light it has been much used for artificial limbs, the more especially as it does not readily split. Buckeye logs in short sections used to be hollowed out and cut into troughs, especially for catching maple sap. Pioneer babies of the Middle West were rocked in cradles hollowed out of a thick Buckeye log, and it is related that the first settlers used to make summer hats from Buckeye shavings.

"The farmers would take a straight Buckeye limb 4 to 6 inches in diameter, 15 to 18 inches long and plane off fine shavings. They would then drive 5 or 6 pins through a board about ⅛ of an inch apart, the points coming about a quarter of an inch above the surface of the board, and the shavings, while being drawn over the pins, would be divided into proper width for plaiting. A hat made in this way would wear for a long time."*

*John F. Edgar, *Pioneer Life in Dayton.*

California Buckeye

Æsculus californica (Spach) Nuttall

OTHER NAME: Horse Chestnut.

RANGE: Foothills and valleys of the California Coast Ranges from Mendocino County south to San Luis Obispo County, and on the lower western slopes (up to 5000 feet) of the Sierra Nevada from the region of Mount Shasta in the north all the way to the Tehachapi Pass in the south and Antelope Valley and the Canada de las Uvas near Fort Tejon.

THIS ODDLY BEAUTIFUL LITTLE TREE is an inhabitant of the Coast Ranges of central California and the dry foothills of the central Sierra Nevada, where the forty-niners were the first English-speaking Americans to know it well. They gave it — for its great, green pear-shaped pods — the name (perhaps derisive) of "California Pear." It is also, of course, a Horse Chestnut, generally speaking, and that too is possibly derisive, for the big glossy seeds do indeed look like chestnuts and look deceptively appetizing, but in fact are inedible and even poisonous unless properly cooked. The name of Buckeye is apt, though; well might one say that the seeds are like the great melting brown orbs of the deer.

And, under all names, this is an oddly lovely little tree. One sees it in abundance on the famed Skyline Drive that goes looping over the high grassy knobs which cap the Coast Ranges just south of San Francisco, and in the shelters and hollows of the highlands, forever swept by the sea winds, of western Marin County just north of the Golden Gate. Probably the biggest and oldest specimens are to be seen on the Alder flats of the Point Reyes peninsula near Inverness, but there are fine groves of it along the lower course of the Kaweah River where that stream descends from the Sierra Nevada into the burning San Joaquin Valley.

Amid all the somber needleleaved evergreens of central California, and the glittering broadleaved evergreens, the Buckeye makes a striking contrast. Barren of leaves for one-half of the year, like certain eastern hardwoods, the pale gray and crooked boughs are refreshing and always full of individual character, for no two Buckeyes are anything alike. Each is contorted in its own way. In general the outline of the tree is that of a low, broad dome, but wherever the sea winds reach it, they sculpture it or clip

it with a sort of wild topiary, or force it to conform to the hollow of the hill where the tree seems to crouch in refuge.

A Buckeye 40 feet tall is unusually high, but that is not for lack of years. It is popularly said that it takes a Buckeye one hundred years to mature, and that it lives at least another hundred without making much growth except the slow and subtle increase in thickness of trunk and boughs. Frequently, where conditions are arid, it never attains more than 12 feet in height and takes on the many-stemmed form of a shrub.

Unfortunately, most Californians do not appreciate the Buckeye as a domestic tree; the saying goes that you should never have one unless you like to rake leaves. The dropping of the big seeds — horse chestnuts — and the still bigger green pods seems to annoy intensely those who want their Nature tidied like a drawing room, and some have the dooryard Buckeye hewn down and think they have made the world a better place.

Yet this is one of the most beautiful of western hardwoods, not only in its shining nakedness — which lasts from late summer to February — but in spring when the refreshing pale green of the quaint, compound leaves is first seen, and in early summer when the trees are covered with thousands of fragrant or rosy blossoms in great candelabralike spires, till in autumn the curious pods hang from the boughs and, breaking open, let loose the seeds. Poisonous to cattle and humans, these seeds were yet a staple in the diet of the California Indians. For, by leaching out the poisonous principle with boiling water, the Indians obtained an innocuous sweet starch of which a nutritious flour was made. The nectar of the flowers, however, has been charged with poisoning bees.

In autumn the leaves turn a dull sear brown, without any particular glory, yet picturesque to the last. The wood, though it has no reputation in the lumber business, is very long lasting, even in contact with the soil, and hence makes a fine fence-post material that has been appreciated for a century in the foothill ranching country where it delights to grow.

Sourwood

Oxydendrum arboreum (Linnæus) De Candolle

OTHER NAMES: Sorreltree. Sour Gum. Arrowwood. Lily-of-the-valley-tree.

RANGE: Southwestern Pennsylvania to the coast of Virginia and of North Carolina, south to western Florida and eastern Louisiana, west to southern Ohio, extreme southern parts of Indiana and Illinois, western Kentucky and Tennessee. Ascending the southern Appalachians to 3500 feet.

THE GLITTERING LEAVES OF THE SOURWOOD, wondrously fresh-looking and spirited, have completed their growth long before the flowers appear, yet so handsome are the great bouquets of bloom at the ends of the branches that they are not put out of countenance by the splendid foliage, but looking like hundreds of little lilies-of-the-valley, they sway and dance in the warm, friendly wind of late June and early July. In case you have not looked up and seen them, you may soon be made aware of them by the roar of the bees gone nectar-mad at their lips.

When autumn comes, the foliage turns a gorgeous scarlet or orange or crimson, doubly welcome because the Sourwood in general grows outside the range of the Sugar Maple and the Aspen and takes their place in the South. Then, especially in the southern Appalachians where Sourwood grows 50 and 60 feet tall, is the season to set out afoot, or on horseback, or in your car, to buy Sourwood honey from your country neighbors. Some of them put out little signs along the roadside, but all you have to do is to watch for a row of "bee gums" not far from the farmer's house. For if the southern farmer has hives at all, he has Sourwood honey for sale. Fortunately the blooming period of Sourwood is just after the fading of Mountain Laurel and Rhododendron whose honeys are poisonous. Their honey the beekeeper throws away, but he is very careful to store his Sourwood honey, for it is the finest, in the opinion of many epicures, in the southeastern states and is not surpassed even by the most tangy sage honey of California.

Sourwood honey is medium light in color, of heavy body, and slow to granulate. An average flow of as high as 75 pounds per colony from Sourwood has been recorded. Usually the local demand takes the entire crop at prices above the open market, so that Sourwood is a honey like some of the choicest wines of the vineyards of Europe — that is, it practically does not appear upon the market at all and can be had only by those epicures who will journey far to partake of it. One buys Sourwood honey as one buys any such rare product from its producers — not in a commercial spirit, paying for it and carrying away the wares — but with all the due ceremony observed between a collector and a creative artist. You ride up to the cabin door; a woman appears at the barking of the hounds, with children peeping out from behind her skirts, and mountain courtesy requires that you begin, not by stating your business but by telling where you come from. Then you assure her that she has a "right pretty place"; you praise her portulacas, her turkeys, and so, across the landscape, you arrive at her bee gums. Then you ask if she likes Sourwood honey as much as you do. You tell her that you would go far to obtain a little if only you could find somebody who would give up a few pounds of it. When the honey is produced, as it certainly will be, you accept it before asking the price. This will be shyly stated. You may safely pay it for your haggling was all done, by indirection, in your previous parley. And you are paying no more than a fico for nectar and ambrosia.

The very hard wood scarcely enters into the lumber business but is cut locally by farmers for the handles of tools. Once on a time in the days of home medicine, the leaves were brewed as a tonic, and they still, with their pleasant acid taste, quench the thirst of the hot, perspiring mountain climber.

Desert Ironwood

Olneya Tesota Gray

OTHER NAME: Tesota.

RANGE: From Sonora and Baja California in Mexico north in the valley of the Colorado River through southwestern Arizona and the low deserts of southeastern California (west to Palm Springs).

I F YOU DROP A BLOCK OF DESERT IRONWOOD into water, it sinks like a plummet of lead. For the specific gravity (that is, its weight compared with an equal volume of water) is 1.14. Or, expressed in terms of a balance scale, Ironwood weighs 66 pounds to the cubic foot. This is heavier than any other western wood, heavier indeed than any wood of North America except the Leadwood of southern Florida, which weighs 81 pounds to the cubic foot. Mahogany, which we think of as the heaviest wood in our ordinary experience, weighs only 45 pounds per cubic foot — something to remember next time you are asked to move furniture. And the specific gravity of this famous tropical timber is only 0.7832; it would float in water, at least when dried. The Desert Ironwood, of course, never, where it grows, meets enough water even to sink in!

Weight, to be sure, is no virtue in a wood, of itself; but it is usually associated with great strength and hardness. The strength of Desert Ironwood may never have been tested; this is said to be a brittle wood, though you

432

will not think so if you try to break a limb off a living tree. But in hardness it is unexcelled, earning its name of Ironwood more thoroughly than any of the other trees that, in other parts of the country, claim the name. The ordinary knife blade makes as much impression on it as it would on stone — minute slivers may be sliced off, but as for any attempt really to cut it, it defies the ordinary saw and ax driven by muscle. If you find a piece of steel sharp enough to cut Ironwood, the edge will be so fine that it will be turned by the refractory wood. Only a mechanically powered saw or lathe will cut through this wood in a precise plane, and even then the going is very slow.

Once the surface is planed, however, a beautiful figure appears on the quarter section, the richest walnut brown with darker brown lines; the tangential section looks much like the figure of Mahogany, though far deeper in tone. If only Desert Ironwood attained larger dimensions it would be a cabinet wood of great value. As it is, it is cut only for bookends and other novelties of the tourist trade. Formerly the desert Indians made arrowheads of it, but how they cut it with stone tools is a matter for wonder.

Ironwood grows more abundantly between Desert Center, California, and the Colorado River than anywhere else. You encounter it elsewhere, to be sure, but on the run from Parker or Blythe to Desert Center and Indio it is the dominant species, abundant at every one of the countless bridges and culverts that span the dry washes down which, a few times a year (or once in many years), the flash floods rush. For the most part it is a shrub, but again and again you see it grown to a tree's estate, sometimes 50 feet tall or more, and with a great spread of many-forked branches that may be 80 feet across. You couldn't, on the desert, ask for a finer pool of shade than is cast by the softly gray green leaves. They have no cruel glitter to them, either; thickly set, the foliage bestows a deep shade, and that the year around, for it is evergreen. One specimen about 50 miles from Desert Center has a trunk that two men cannot put their arms around; this should make it about 15 feet in circumference. The age of such a giant can only be guessed; it must run into centuries.

Early in the summer, the Ironwood bursts into a glory which you would never expect from a tree that, at all other times, presents such a sober appearance — gray of bark and gray of leaf. For then the flowers appear, thousands of them on every bough, a beautiful deep indigo to rose purple in shade, much like the corollas of Redbud in form. From the blossoms steals forth on the desert airs a subtle fragrance. Then, when the flowers have faded and fallen on the sands, the new leaves hastily push the old ones off; at this moment Ironwood is as near to being a naked deciduous tree as it ever gets, but it never looks barren, for the tender green of the young leaves clothes it coolly right in the height of the burning summer.

From the time it is young almost every Ironwood struggles with its archenemy the mistletoe, for infection often begins early and in the end may result in the death of the tree. The mistletoe berries are carried by that beautiful desert bird the silky flycatcher or phainopepla, which devours the berries and then, sailing away on those wings that seem to have a translucent patch in them, alights on another bough where it voids the undigested and still living seeds. These lodge in the Ironwood's rough bark, sprout, and send down rootlike suckers that parasitize the host tree. Immense tumorlike growths result; heavier even than normal Ironwood, the abnormal wood of these mistletoe tumors may weigh hundreds of pounds. Sometimes, for no explained reason, the Ironwood exudes great blobs of gummy or gelatinous sap, reddish in color, and said by those who have tasted it to have a pleasant flavor. Bees and hummingbirds come eagerly to sup upon it.

If ever you come upon a procession of rusty red ants marching to and from an Ironwood tree you may notice that those coming away from it are carrying each a tiny leaflet. For these creatures (*Atta desertorum*)* are one of the many kinds of leaf-cutting ants, and the purpose of carrying the Ironwood foliage to the nest is not to devour it, but to allow it to molder and so become a culture medium for certain fungi. On the little spongy masses of the hyphal threads of the fungus the ant workers feed, and when the young "princesses" set out on their marriage flights they carry, in pouches in their mouths, a bit of the fungus with which to start the mushroom garden in their new homes. They do not, however, eat of it at all but carefully divide it, as a gardener divides rootstocks, nurturing each mass with a liquid from their bodies until they have raised a brood of worker-daughters. These, led by their instincts, search out an Ironwood tree and gather its leaves to begin manuring the mushroom garden, and so the strange cycle is complete.

Editor's note: Now *Trachymyrmex desertorum*.

ACACIAS

Sweet Acacia

Acacia farnesiana (Linnaeus) Willdenow

OTHER NAMES: Huisache. Cassie.

RANGE: From northern Chile northward in western South America and parts of Central America to the Big Bend country and the desert between the Rio Grande and Nueces Rivers in Texas; also, apparently as a native, in the Baboquivari Mountains southwest of Tucson, Arizona. Cultivated all over the tropical world and naturalized in many places, as in Florida and extensively in Victoria County, Texas.

"FARNESIANA," ONE OF THE COSTLIEST scents distilled by the French perfumers, and worn by the most knowledgeable *exquises*, is derived from the flowers of this straggling, shrubby little tree which is so common throughout western Texas, as part of the thorn forest. Indeed, the Huisache, as the Texans like to call it, grows thickly around lakes and "tanks" (watering holes) and drainage ditches in the cattle country of the Lone Star State. It grows abundantly on the Mesquite flats, taking over with especial vigor when Mesquite trees have been removed by agencies natural or human. Some will have it that it was first brought to San Patrico County from Mexico by one of the Mexican commissioners sent to represent the government in that colony. He is supposed to have planted it out on his hacienda, and it is a legend that all the Huisaches now growing in Texas have sprung from that source. But this is probably as fictitious as the myth that the bluebonnets (lupine) were brought here by friars and monks from the Holy Land. The Huisache or Sweet Acacia is considered by botanists to be a native of western Texas and also on the lonely Baboquivari Mountains that rise from the desert and Mesquite flats, southwest of Tucson, Arizona.

But long before the first white settlers reached Texas and Arizona from Mexico, the Sweet Acacia was a favorite plant in the gardens of Mediterranean Europe. It seems to have been brought in 1611 from Santo Domingo and first cultivated in the gardens of Cardinal Odoardo Farnese, where the exotic perfume of its little butterballs of bloom was grateful to the exquisitely perceptive senses of that sensual and gifted family, the Farnese. Intermarried with the Borgias and the Medicis, the Farnese family filled the highest offices of the Church in the sixteenth and seventeenth centuries, including the Papal throne. It was a poor Farnese who was not a cardinal or at least a bishop, a duke or at least a ruthless soldier of fortune, the daughter of a cardinal or at least the mistress of one. Alessandro Farnese, son of the bastard son of Pope Paul III, was made a cardinal at the age of fourteen. He it was who founded at Catrarola, near Viterbo, the sumptuous villa and gardens that still bear the family name. Its very walls are 3 miles in circumference, and the Cardinal's son and grandson constantly enriched the flora of this garden with all that was new and rare in plant life. When the garden belonged to Cardinal Odoardo Farnese, he ordered Pietro Castello to draw up a description of its botanical treasures, and in his rare publication of 1625 we find the first mention of this American tree now known as *Acacia farnesiana.*

Perhaps half a century later it was introduced into southern France and rapidly became one of the favorite dooryard trees of Provence. With time it was found that the climate and soil of the Riviera, between Grasse and Cannes, and between the Esterels and the Var River, precisely suited it, so that today that smiling district is a happy home of the Sweet Acacia or *cassie*, as the French call it.

For *cassie* is one of the most important basic materials of a large number of the mixed flower perfumes put out by the great Grasse distilleries. A strain of this tree developed there produces two flower crops a year; the best essence is derived from the flowers of September and October. On account of its cruelly pricking thorns, the *cassie* is no favorite with the peasant women who harvest the blossoms of this tree. They collect them in the morning as soon as the dew has burned off and return two or three times a week for a new cutting. At the Grasse perfumeries the odor is generally extracted with oils, thus preparing a pomade which goes into extracts of violet and aromatic vinegar, into rouges and rice powders; a very concentrated form of extraction with alcohol is known as quintessence of *cassie*.

And what does it smell like, this wonderful perfume? But how can anyone describe an odor to those who have never smelled it, save in terms of some other? The best one can say is that, compared with the fragrance of the Australian Acacias so familiar in the gardens of southern California, Sweet Acacia is far more honeyed and less dry and polleny. It is more intense and, by that same token, more cloying. Certainly it is an odor that once perceived will be identified forever after, so utterly unlike any other in the world it is.

In Texas there is no Grasse, no great perfume trade, yet the beekeepers there value Huisache highly, for it is an important pollen plant, even though it does not, like its relative the *huajillo*, produce the famous Uvalde honey. But bees must have a rich store of pollen to give their youngsters proper protein diet, particularly the future queens. And the pollen is the more precious to the bees because it comes at a time, usually January and February, when not many other plants are in bloom.

Under such names as Popinac and Opopanax, the Sweet Acacia has been grown almost around the world in tropical and subtropical countries. There are few where it has not escaped from cultivation, and in the Hawaiian Islands it has become practically a pest. But it is a pest with many charms, with its feathery foliage consisting in many sensitive leaflets and its butter yellow blooms, which make it, said a French poet, "a load of balm for every wind that stirs."

Desert Cat's-claw

Acacia greggii Gray

OTHER NAMES: Paradise-flower. Texas Mimosa. Devil's-claws.

RANGE: Northern Mexico north to the valley of the Rio Grande and the Big Bend country of Texas, to southern New Mexico and throughout the low deserts of Arizona to southernmost Nevada and the low deserts of California.

D ESERT CAT'S-CLAW IS THE MOST detested and roundly cursed of all trees in the Southwest, for its ferocious armament of spines tears flesh and clothing of all who venture within its grasp. The name of Cat's-claw — *una de gato*, as the Spanish-speaking southwesterners call it — exactly describes its flattened and hooked talons, which, when they sink in, also curl under the skin or the cloth, making extraction worse than penetration. So "Devil's-claws" is one of the mildest epithets applied to this tree, and few creatures save honey bees are voluntarily intimate with it. To many small game animals, however, the dense thickets of Cat's-claw are precious. There the jack rabbit and the Gambel quail can find sanctuary from pitiless hawk and hunter.

Yet it is this hostile little tree that yields that white ambrosia known as Uvalde honey, the most celebrated in Texas. In Uvalde honey is generally mixed with the nectar of another Acacia, a shrub called *huajillo;* their blooming times, though on the whole quite different, just overlap in April, and that is when the bees are most active at this tree, compounding a con-

fection that is unequaled for fragrance and taste. The *huajillo's* flowers —
that you may distinguish them in the field — are nearly white; those of
Cat's-claw are greenish white with the petals creamy margined, and they
wear a fine tuft of some fifty golden stamens in each flower.

The young foliage is gingerly browsed by stock, afraid of the thorns
perhaps, but eagerly taken by antelope. The ribbonlike pods are low in
nutritive value, but the seeds were eaten as pinole by the Pimas and
Papagos, and Gambel quail still fatten on them. The very hard and durable wood, in our times made into trinkets and souvenirs, used to furnish
the Southwest pioneers with all the singletrees and doubletrees of their
home-made wagons. As a fuel wood the Cat's-claw is almost peerless. It
burns with a bluish flame, and long after most wood is reduced to ashes,
Cat's-claw is still a bed of intense coals. In the very depths of the Grand
Canyon, to which Devil's-claw descends, this is considered the best substitute for coal.

Elephant-tree

Bursera microphylla Gray

OTHER NAME: Elephant Bursera.

RANGE: Coasts of the Gulf of California in Mexico, north in the valley of the Colorado to the Gila Desert of Arizona and the Imperial Valley of California.

THIS IS NOT A RARE TREE IN MEXICO. There it is called *toroto* and *copal*. It was first discovered in 1860; but in the United States its occurrence was not suspected until about 1910. And the story of its finding goes back, as all good desert campfire stories should, to a mysterious old desert rat who makes a sudden appearance, telling of a strange tree he has found, while prospecting a gypsum mine — a tree with a gray bark bleached nearly white, and boughs like elephants' trunks, and a wood that bleeds like an animal when you cut it. Then, having delivered himself of this information, and leaving in the hands of his listeners a crude map sketched on a grimy slip of paper, the desert rat vanishes into the shimmering heat waves. You've heard the yarn before — connected with gold mines with a curse placed on them by their dead owners, with mysterious caves, and lost tribes of "white" Indians? Even if you have, you are asked, by an eminently grave and respectable scientific periodical, to believe it for this once. And to believe in the reality of Elephant-trees — even white Elephant-trees.

For it was by the near whiteness of their bark that one Edward H. Davis — the bystander to whom the old desert rat confided the information and the map — recognized them when he set forth to find them and did — along a narrow arroyo tributary to Fish Creek, near Split Mountain. Even today this is a difficult region, in the desertic eastern part of San Diego County, California, to travel. It is best reached by turning south off State Highway 78 at the sun-scorched settlement of Ocotillo, continuing for about 12 miles to the site of a Navy air base and about 5 miles further till you reach an area marked on the Automobile Club of Southern California's map of San Diego County "Elephant Tree Area" — wondrous botanical of them! And here it was that Davis discovered the old desert rat's tree. And its boughs *did* look like the upraised, curling snouts of elephants! And when stabbed with a knife, it *did* exude a blood red sap! And it proved to have not merely one bark but three — a flaky white outer bark, a thin green second layer, and, under that, a thick mass of red cork.

Not content with one old desert rat, this drama is cast for two. For though Mr. Davis was pleased enough with his discovery, the world of science was still only dimly aware that *Busera microphylla* occurred in the United States. Then, in the 1920s, another desert rat — or the same one in disguise — appeared in San Diego and began to tell tales of a grove of trees out in the remote eastern part of the county, that looked like a herd of elephants. This old codger, however, vouchsafed no map; like others of his kind he hugged his secret and disappeared. But in the autumn of 1937, members of the Scripps Institution of Oceanography, of the San Diego Museum of Natural History, and of the state park system began to take rumor seriously and set forth. A party so heavily weighted with intellect could not miss of its quarry, and the Elephant-tree was soon rediscovered and mapped in all of its sporadic occurrences in Fish Creek Canyon, Bow Willow Canyon, and Canebrake Canyon. It is now known to occur in Arizona too, from the Salt River Mountains, in Maricopa County, to the Gila and Tinajas Atlas mountains of Yuma County, up to 2500 feet above sea level. In Arizona it reaches its maximum development — up to 20 feet high — within the borders of the United States.

But mere height, or lack of it, can give no idea of the great, fleshy, dropsical-looking, smooth-barked trunks which start from cracks in the blazing desert rocks without an apparent vestige of soil or moisture. At the height of 3 or 4 feet these boles fork into sharply tapering, brown-barked, curving branches. From these arise abruptly an intricate tangle of very slender, very crooked branchlets, and each of these gives forth, almost at right angles, very rigid, almost thorn-fine bright red twigs. Seen against the naked blue of that arid sky, the whole sprawling, half-absurd, half-lovely tree is hard to believe in even when you see it — as is, indeed, an elephant. The spicy-aromatic foliage is oddly delicate for such a ponderous vegetable — almost ferny, though so small and sparse as to cast but little shade. Equally surprising are the summer clusters of whitish or pink flowers and the red drupes, like chokecherries.

Obviously this tree is quite unlike what comes to our minds when we say the word "tree." And no wonder, for Elephant-tree is the northernmost member of the Torchwood family, and our tree shows this tropical relationship in being very tender to frost. To this family belongs the plant that yields the frankincense mentioned in the Bible and still burned in Roman Catholic churches. Elephant-tree, too, is aromatic and exudes a gum — that red blood mentioned by the anonymous prospector — used in Mexico for a great variety of handy purposes — as a varnish base and a wood preservative, as a remedy in venereal diseases and an adhesive. A fragrant oil extracted from the wood is reported to be burned as incense in Mexican churches.

Bursera odorata T. S. Brandegee* is an extremely fragrant species of Mexico which crosses the frontier into Arizona and is found on the western foothills of the Baboquivari Mountains, where so many rare little tropical trees are found. The foliage has the odor of tangerine peel, while the bark of old trunks is gray brown and peels off in thin papery sheets, like a Birch's. The flowers bloom in July.

---

*Editor's note: Now *Bursera fagaroides* var. *elongata*.

Saguaro

Carnegia gigantea (Engelmann) Britton & Rose*

OTHER NAMES: Pitahaya. Giant Cactus. Suharo. Suguaro. Suwarro. Suwarrow. Sajuaro. Zuwarrow.

RANGE: From western Sonora, Mexico (coast of the Gulf of California to 150 miles inland), north to central Arizona (Gila, Graham, and Yavapai counties and southern Mohave County), usually between 3500 and 4500 feet altitude, sometimes at much lower altitudes near the Colorado River and its tributaries.

THE MOST FASCINATING PART of the American desert is that which lies around the ancient city of Tucson, set in a valley surrounded by rugged mountains, snow-topped in winter, cloud-capped in summer, crowned at all seasons by a forest of Cypress and Juniper, Pine and Fir. The magic of Arizona sunlight and the long shadows cast by the peaks, the strange form of sheer-walled mesas, the nostalgic views of the long *bajadas* or downsloping plains give all of central Arizona a quality unlike that of any other part of the world, so that many persons who have never seen the region can put their fingers unmistakably on a picture of it and say, "That is Arizona." But there is one feature of the land-

---

*Editor's note: Formerly *Carnegia gigantea* Engelmann.

scape more characteristic than any other — the Giant Cactus or Saguaro. Sometimes 30 or 40 feet tall, with enormous branches weighing, themselves, hundreds of pounds, this tree looks like the vegetation of some other planet, and so do the thorny ocotillo bushes, the jumping chollas, the barrel cacti that are its associates.

The Saguaro (pronounced su-wahr-ro) might, one could fancy, be a tree designed by someone who had never seen a tree. With its upraised arms and tall peaked "head," it has a goblin look enhanced by those woodpecker holes in the top that often appear like two eye sockets or slits in a magician's hood. Just as twice the Apaches besieged the walled city of Tucson, so it is beleaguered still by this strange vegetable host armed with fierce spines. Saguaros are seen on most of the approaches to the city; to the east of the town there is a great forest of them set aside as the Saguaro National Monument, embracing 63,284 acres and doubtless several million of these fantastic giants. And as one sees them dotting the stony slopes, as if marching down hill, one is likely to remember the fable of the Sorcerer's Apprentice, who started one automaton to life, struck him with an ax and so made two that divided spontaneously into four, then sixteen, then hundreds, and at last thousands.

One may ask if the Saguaro is rightly called a tree. True that it has at no time in its life any leaves, bark, or solid cylinder of wood. However, palms are trees, yet they have no solid cylinder of wood and no true bark. And the cortex of the Saguaro's green stems and branches is full of chlorophyll and carries on photosynthesis and respiration just as leaves do. One might say that the cortex of a Saguaro is all one vast leaf. Nor does this cactus lack for woody tissue. This is found in the form of long strands of wood, close together at the base of the stem, but spreading apart and tapering above, which might be compared to a bundle of fishing poles. So strong is the wood in these rods that they have been used for centuries in house construction by Indians and Mexicans; as ceiling beams they hold up the thatch of *carrizo* or reed stems; as lath in the walls they furnish a surface for the adobe mud plaster.

Yet there is something about the Saguaro that seems more animal than vegetable, for this strange creation, like a human being, has its skeleton *inside* its soft tissues and, just as with the human animal, when a Saguaro dies the soft parts decay and the skeleton emerges, the woody rods usually so hardened with deposition of mineral crystals as to turn the blade of a knife and appear more like bleached bones than wood.

Nothing, though, so invites the comparison to humanoid forms as the branches or arms of this tree and their strange gesticulations. Leaving the main trunk at 18 to 20 feet above the ground, they are constricted near the point of attachment (so that, ponderous as they are, they rather easily break off), and they soon become, normally, erect instead of pendent like the boughs of other trees. It is this position that, above all others, gives the Saguaros their exclamatory expression, as if they were shouting *hosannah* and testifying to the miracle of their existence upon the desert.

In prolonged droughts, when the turgor of the cells is lowered by falling water pressure, the arms may droop and even curl, and, in the case of heavy old branches, they are likely never to regain their erect position. As a result, the arms may seem to be hugging the ribs of the torso-trunk as if in convulsions of pain or mirth. Or they may touch the ground, like bandy legs, or like a man walking with a cane in each hand. Or they arch gently together, like a tranquil sage thrusting his hands up his sleeves. "Sage of the Desert" is a common allusion to these ancients. Despite their wild fantasies of form, their ponderous awkwardness, they have an inherent dignity. After sitting down among them and laughing at their attitudes till the tears come, one leaves the Saguaros with the feeling that, after all, there is about them something deeply wise, if unconsciously so.

The Saguaro lives in a desert with a peculiar climate, an extension of that of the central highlands of northern Mexico where the cactus family reaches its greatest development. Tucson, for instance, has an average rainfall of about 11 inches a year, but distributed in a special way, and to that odd distribution the Saguaro, which contains as much as 9 tons of water, and is seldom less than 90 percent water, must adapt itself both in its bodily form and life history. In the first three months of the year comes the little rainy season, when the weather is cool and the rains fall gently and intermittently to a total of 2 to 3 inches. This is followed by the little dry season of spring, when the winter annuals and bulbs send briefly up their carpet of wild flowers. By June it is hot and dry in the Saguaro groves, but in July great cumulus clouds gather on the mountains and sweep over the *bajadas* in majestic thunderstorms that wheel and roll and make strange patterns of wet and dry upon the desert's face. In July and August fall about 6 inches of rain, accompanied by strong gusts of wind, flash floods in the arroyos, and slipping down of soil on slopes and banks. Then comes the big dry season, lasting through December, a time of fierce sunlight and drought slowly mitigated by declining temperatures.

To fit itself into this peculiar climate, quite unlike that of the Californian desert with winter rains only and of the New Mexican deserts with summer rains only, the Saguaro has certain equipments common to many cacti but carried out to their greatest expression in this arboreous member of the family. The root system is strangely shallow but far-reaching, so as to catch the maximum of rainfall, which, however, never penetrates deeply. Its roots have been followed by investigators for 40 feet before they become so tenuous as to break when excavated, and doubtless their capillary rootlets extend much farther until, indeed, they reach the only competitor well able to halt them — the periphery of the root system of some other Saguaro.

Then, too, the stem of the Saguaro is, as women would say, accordion pleated. That is, it is fluted in long vertical ridges with deep furrows between them. When low in water supply, these ridges shrink and seem withered; as soon as the rains return, the roots send up to the great storage tank of the trunk enough water to see them through thousands of burning desert hours — and the flutes again expand, the plant that seemed miserable and dying is again bright green, plump, and full of life.

At the close of the little rainy season the flower buds begin to form at the tips of the branches and top of the stem. They grow slowly at first and are ready to bloom when the first hot weather of the year has come, in late April and May. Then one night the great blossoms begin to open. Usually the eclosion commences about eight in the evening; unlike some nocturnal flowers such as the evening primrose of the garden, which can actually be detected in the swift opening of its petals, the old sage of the desert discloses his secret with deliberation; two or three hours are required to complete the performance, and now at last the marvelous blossom stands open to the desert stars. Two or 3 inches across, it is a very heavy blossom, looking with its thick petals as if carved out of wax, and from it there steals forth an odor that, if not a sweet perfume to us, since it is faint and a little like melons, may allure its nocturnal insect visitors.

There is no known relationship between waterlilies and cactus flowers, yet there is something oddly reminiscent, in this queen of the desert night, to the nymph of the tranquil streams, in the serenity of the bloom and the great profusion of the parts. For there are many sepals, many big creamy white petals, and inside them a circle of innumerable heavy stamens wearing a golden rim of anthers. One botanist had the patience to count them and found 3482 in a single blossom. Inside the ovary he counted 1980 ovules. The golden chalice of the stamens contains the exquisite, long columnar style cut into numerous branches at the tip, each branch stigmatic along its inner face. No wonder that the Saguaro has been chosen as Arizona's state flower.

When morning comes, the blossoms are still open. They are often borne so high as to be quite out of reach, and only if a contorted old branch bends downward will the obliging plant put its bouquet in your hands. As the heat of the desert day advances the flowers begin to close and wither, and though there will be others tomorrow they will not be the same blossoms. For each individual bloom is queen of the night for one night only.

Within a month after flowering, and before the onset of the big rainy season of summer, the fruits — the *pitahayas* of the Spanish-speaking people — are ripe. About as big as goose eggs, they split open on the tree, disclosing their pulp, of a watermelon pink, with numberless little black and shiny seeds within them. This is one of the principal wild vegetable foods of the Arizona Indians. The Papagos date their New Year from the fruiting of this great cactus, and the Pimas call July the Saguaro Harvest Moon. To bring down the fruits they use long poles made of the Saguaro's own woody rods, lashed together and fitted with a hook at the top. When the plump fruits fall, the women place them in wide baskets or clay *ollas* which they carry away on their heads. Jam, syrup, and preserves are made from the fruits and kept in sealed clay jars, or some may be dried in the sun like figs, becoming candied in their own sugar, or left to ferment into a strong liquor. Of the fat and oily seeds the Papagos make a sort of butter. The white man prefers his *pitahayas* eaten out of hand; the flesh has much of the crispness of radishes or cucumbers and is cool and sweet. Save for the skin, you devour them seeds and all.

Naturally a fruit so delicious is sought by many desert animals, and usually you find they have first call upon them. Even the coyote is said to eat them, but they are the favorite food of that beautiful game bird, the white-winged dove whose *cook-karra-coo* sweetens the desert morns. What the doves and Indians do not eat, the fierce desert ants soon destroy. Not one seed in a million, it has been surmised, ever escapes to germinate. The great fertility of stamens and ovules is not one germ of life too many.

When a seed does sprout successfully in the high temperatures of the big rainy season, it is usually in the shade of some Mesquite, Palo Verde, or Cat's-claw tree, for the tiny seedling is very sensitive to drying winds and sun. Hence these thorny little leguminous trees are an essential to a Saguaro grove, and they are seldom absent. As a result, too, of this sheltered position, a seedling is seldom detected; by the time it has outgrown its nurse it is already almost as old as an old man.

For the growth of a Saguaro is at first painfully slow. At the end of the second year it is but a quarter of an inch high! A plant 4 inches high is, in general, about eight years old. When it is twenty it will still be only 10 inches high. The growth rate now quickens, but not much. A Saguaro that has seen thirty summers will be only a yard high, and by the time it is 15 feet tall it is some sixty years along in its life. Branching begins now if it has not done so a little earlier, and the first flowers and fruit are borne about this time. For a while growth may be a foot a year, but at 35 or 40 feet, a Saguaro has attained its maximum. It will then be 1 or 2 feet thick in the trunk and will weigh 5 or 6 tons, all precariously balanced on a constricted base (like a fat man with thin ankles and small feet) and a root system that is little effective for purposes of anchorage.

The age of the old Saguaros has been guessed by nonscientific writers as rivaling the Redwoods. But since this type of vegetable does not lay down annual growth rings in solid wood, the age can only be inferred from the growth rate, and how long an old Saguaro may live after growth has practically stopped is unknown. The Arizona botanists believe that 150 years is the average life span of a Saguaro which is not killed violently, with two centuries as exceptional longevity.

During the life of the Saguaro the spines change materially. In youth there is a ferocious armament of them, though old trees may, at base, be spineless where gnawing rodents have torn away the spines and left battle scars. For the first half or three-quarters of a century the cortex bears a crop of heavy reddish brown spines that, with weathering, turn gray and finally black. But as the plant reaches bearing age the new growth puts forth finer needles of a yellowish brown hue much felted with hoary hairs. If we miss the sound of rushing leaves in this leafless tree, the place of that natural music — you will find if you stand in a Saguaro grove when the desert wind is plowing by — is taken by the whistling of the millions of spines, a sound like the far-off seething of surf. So the Saguaro too lifts up its voice with thorny tongues.

All trees have their birds, and the Saguaro is no exception. It is the favorite nesting site of the Gila woodpecker and its relative the golden flicker. Both of them will nest in Willow and Cottonwood when they can find them in a decadent state. But the soft body of the giant cactus is "peckable" at all times. In a very few minutes these birds can thrash out there a globular home for themselves. Oddly, they do this not at the beginning but at the end of the nesting season. The reason seems to be that the very moist interior of the freshly excavated cactus stem is probably not habitable for months — until indeed the soft wet inner cells have formed scar tissue. When this is complete, the following spring, the architects of these apartments proceed to occupy them, providing they do not have to dispute them with some squatter, and here the eggs are laid directly on the hard dry floor of the hole. Sometimes the same nest is used for several years by a pair of birds.

When it is vacated at last it may be appropriated by the tiny elf owl, no bigger than a sparrow, or the Arizona screech owl, the ferruginous pigmy owl, the ash-throated and Arizona crested flycatchers. That sweet, companionable bird, the purple martin, greatly prefers an old woodpecker hole in a nice cool Saguaro to the stuffy, sunbaked bird houses and gourds that humans hang for him.

Later, as these tenements become older and perhaps more disreputable, such unaristocratic society as rats and wild mice may move in, though how they run up the spiny stems is beyond imagining. When at last a Saguaro falls and decays, the scar tissue of these old bird homes will resist the elements as firmly as a wooden shoe, which they vaguely resemble in shape. The Indians then gather these up and use them as storage vessels for preserves and dried fruits of the *pitahaya*.

These holes made by the birds evidently do the tree no harm, but it is not so with some forms of injury. As a shallow stab may give a man blood poisoning by carrying bacteria into the system, so the careless habit of shooting bullets into Saguaros, which idle boys sometimes do, or plunging a pocketknife into their succulent forms, may be fatal to this desert giant. A terrific outbreak of bacterial infection swept through the Saguaro groves some years ago, and the noble vegetables sloughed down in a putrid mass sad to see. Measures of every sort were taken to combat the disease; whether these were effective, or whether the disease ran its course and would have disappeared anyway, the Saguaros around Tucson, at least, are at the present writing apparently in the best of health.

More constant are the inroads of the jack rabbits and other desert rodents, frantic for the water in the soft tissues. Despite the tenderness of their noses, these little mammals are frequently driven to the fanatic courage of thrusting their snouts far enough into the horrid armament to insert their chisel teeth into the cortex. After the first chunk has been ripped out it is then easy to undermine the other thorn clusters. In this way a colossus may soon be gnawed till it topples in the first gust of wind.

Even when intact, the top-heavy, ill-based skyscraper of such a vegetable is subject to overturn by the elements. The summer rains drench and soften the adobe soil to a soft paste; accompanying these thunderstorms are violent gusts of wind. Sooner or later a Saguaro is bound to fall in this way if not laid low by all the other ills and foes that may beset it.

Are the Saguaros holding their own against all these odds? Many close observers are sadly inclined to doubt it. They believe that this species extended its range into Arizona from the great cactus forests of the north Mexican highlands in early post-Pleistocene times, when the climate was perhaps both milder and moister. Since then times have changed for the colder and drier on this desert. In Arizona the Saguaro does very poorly on the north sides of mountains where the frost is deeper and lasts longer in winter. It cannot ascend the mountains much above 4000 feet for similar reasons. However, it does not do well in *bajadas* either, on account of the heat and lack of soil seepage; in muddy or sandy soil it cannot keep itself upright through wind and rain. It is also unsuccessful on very steep slopes. So it strings out on gentle slopes with rocky soil, the long axis of the groves following the contours.

As you drive toward California, after leaving Tucson, you cross "the Gila desert, of dreadful memory" as John W. Audubon called it when his party made its way, starving and dying, in its level wastes. You have left the Saguaro behind and imagine you will never see it again. And then, just as you approach the low desert mountains bordering the valley of the Colorado, the friendly goblin shape of the Saguaro leaps up again. Here the long axis of the groves does not follow but crosses the elevation contours, for the trees are hugging the arroyos, trying to get what moisture they can from the rare freshets that run down these lonely desert ranges.

That will be practically the last of the Saguaros. Beyond Yuma lie the sand dunes, beyond that the soft oppressive airs of the Salton Sink below sea level, and after that come the date gardens of Indio, like a bit of Araby, and then the snows of the San Jacintos and of the strange desert lily at your feet. Beyond those mountains lie the Pacific and great cities — a world so far from the Saguaro forests that you can only wonder there how you imagined such unearthly vegetation.

Coast Madroño

Arbutus menziesii Pursh

OTHER NAMES: Pacific or Menzies Madroño. Pacific Madrone. Madrone-tree. Arbute-tree. Tree Arbutus. Strawberry-tree. Madroña.

RANGE: East coast of Vancouver Island and adjacent islands and immediate mainland coast of British Columbia; in Washington on the west and south shores of Puget Sound; in Oregon all along the coast and western slopes of the Coast Ranges and Siskiyou Mountains, also on the western slopes of the Cascades; south in the California Coast Ranges, both inner and outer, from sea level to 3000 feet, as far south as the mountains of San Diego County; thence only at high altitudes to the San Gabriel Mountains (Mount Wilson); in the Salmon, Trinity, Hayfork, Siskiyou and other northern cross-ranges, and in the foothills (2000 to 3000 feet) of the Sierra Nevada through the old gold-mining country south to the South Fork of the Tuolumne.

AS CHARACTERISTIC OF THE NORTH COAST RANGES of California as the Redwood itself is the Madroño. But it is less an inhabitant of the somber Redwood groves than of a forest belt lying just inland or east of the Redwoods, among the high grassy "balds." Here with the splendid Tan Oak, the California Black Oak with its bold jagged foliage, the bicolored Maul Oak, and the ponderous Oregon Oak, the

Madroño enjoys the brilliant, fog-free sunshine of this region. And even in such distinguished arboreal company it outshines them all.

In midsummer the old foliage begins to drop off the tree, just when the new leaves are pushing out as if in haste to sustain the species' reputation for being evergreen. The old leaves, dejected in position, turn a brilliant scarlet and hang in bunches for a time, then gradually drop off and drift heavily to the ground where they form a deep litter for the wood wanderer to scuff in, like the foliage of eastern deciduous trees in fall. In the meantime the scales of the winter buds are curling back, large as the sepals of some big flower. And the new leaves, very pale green at first, are unfurling like a wrapped standard; then they become plane, and finally concave-convex with recurved margins.

At the same time, the bark of young trunks, of limbs and the upper parts of old trunks is actively exfoliating. A deep terracotta or brownish red, it gleams like the limbs of an Indian through the forest. The skin is tight on the crooked and seemingly muscle-bound limbs and peels off in vertical strips and thin quills, revealing the beautiful green underbark whose destiny it is at last to turn ruddy. It is the brilliance of the bicolored deciduous bark that is the tree's chief charm. But the great compound clusters of creamy white, jug-shaped flowers, which proclaim that this is a tree of the noble heath family, are glorious, high overhead, from March to May. In late summer and autumn they are replaced by the yellow and orange fruits — both colors are seen in the same cluster.

For a hardwood the Madroño is endowed with considerable longevity;

the largest specimens are stated to be 200 to 250 years old. And generous indeed are their dimensions. Professor Jepson in his *Silva of California* (1910) enumerates many of the great specimens of his day, all of them in Sonoma, Mendocino, and Humboldt counties. The Indians, he says, greatly venerated these immense Madroños, and he tells the story of what is perhaps the noblest specimen of its kind:

"From the lower Mattole country in southwestern Humboldt a wagon trail climbs to the Wilder Ridge, heavily wooded with Tan Oak, Douglas Fir and Madroño, and at the end of the ridge drops again to the ford of the Mattole River. On this downward slope a mile above the French and Pixton ranch-house the road passes around a little sharply-defined shoulder, on which, sixty feet from the wagon path, stands the 'Council Madroña.' It is an isolated individual with clean spaces around it and as seen from some little distance up grade the tree suggests an oak, merely on account of its exceptional size. The tree is 75 feet in height and its crown 99 feet wide in the longest direction. . . . The trunk of this tree is round and perfect, and without fire or axe-scars or traces of disease. At its narrowest part (16 inches from the ground), it has a girth of 24 feet 1¼ inches. . . . At ten feet the trunk parts into its main branches, giving rise to a broad but very rounded and symmetrical crown. Under its spreading limbs the coast tribes met the interior tribes in former days for the discussion of intertribal matters and for the conclusion of treaties. Situated on a little knoll on the mountain side it commands a view of the adjacent country and has been saved from destruction or injury by fires through its local isolation in the surrounding forest."

In southern Oregon, Madroños sometimes take on a remarkably symmetrical habit, but in California asymmetry is the rule, and the weirdest eccentricity is not unknown. This seems to be owing to competition with the mighty Tan Oak and the pushing Black Oak. Sometimes the trunk will curve away from its base in a long snaky growth for 30 feet, then, as it gets free of other trees' shade, will shoot up, spindling and narrow spired, for 60 feet. Again, all the limbs will develop on one side of the trunk, producing a most lopsided crown; or the trunk may trail along the ground for many feet, giving off boughs and foliage all the while. Even when granted ample space, a Madroño is apt to have an oddly twisted stem, to develop irregular limbs, and to produce a crown broader than high and often canted over like an umbrella turned to slanting rain. Frequently a curving trunk is much flattened contrary to the direction of the curve, and commonly in old trees great rootlike buttresses are sent out and a big tabular base is developed just above the ground, much as in the case of the California Laurel. When a Madroño is felled close to the ground, hidden and forgotten buds in the stump spring to life and send up crown shoots, producing circles of sister trees much like the "goose nests" of the Redwood.

The name Madroño was given this tree by the first white man who ever saw it — Father Juan Crespí, chronicler of the Portolá expedition which was exploring, in 1769, overland to discover the "lost bay" of Monterey. On November 5 Crespí notes "many madroños, though with smaller fruit than the Spanish." For the word *madroño* means the Strawberry-tree, *Arbutus unedo*, a sister species of the Mediterranean world, and Crespí, who referred every Californian plant to his Spanish frame of reference, perceived at once the resemblance. The Strawberry-tree is commonly grown in California today, and its fruits, which are brilliant red, are indeed larger than those of our Californian Madroño, but the tree is smaller and so are the leaves. The California Indians ate the fruits both raw and cooked. To the white palate they are just barely edible; they have a dry custardy taste that is marred by the sharp if tiny seeds. Overeating of them quickly produces cramps. But band-tailed pigeons devour them, and in the hunting season the Madroño groves ring with the shots of their persecutors.

Texas Madroño, *Arbutus texana* Buckley,* is a closely related shrub or small tree seldom more than 8 feet high, with a short, crooked, slim trunk separating, a foot or more from the ground, into several thick, spreading branches. The leaves are small (1 to 3 inches long, $\frac{2}{3}$ to $1\frac{1}{2}$ inches wide), dark green and smooth above, pale and slightly pubescent on the lower surface with a thick hairy midrib. The flowers appear in March, in compact, hoary-hairy clusters about $2\frac{1}{2}$ inches long. The dark red, scarce fruit is $\frac{1}{3}$ inch thick, with thin glandular flesh and a thick stone containing numerous seeds. This little tree is found on the Edwards Plateau of Texas, in the Guadalupe and Eagle mountains of Culberson and El Paso counties, in southeastern New Mexico, and south in the mountains of Nuevo León to Monterrey, Mexico. The wood is hard and heavy and appears to have been used sometimes in the manufacture of mathematical instruments and small tools.

Editor's note: Now *Arbutus xalapensis* Kunth.

Persimmon

Diospyros virginiana Linnæus

OTHER NAMES: Possumwood. Date Plum.

RANGE: Southern Florida north to the neighborhood of New Haven, Connecticut, the central parts of Ohio, Indiana, Illinois, and Missouri, and west to the eastern part of Kansas, Oklahoma, and Texas.

I F IT BE NOT RIPE," said doughty Captain John Smith, of the persimmon he first tasted near Jamestown, "it will draw a man's mouth awrie with much torment." And your own first bite into a persimmon fruit, unless you have been brought up in the region where it is a familiar article of diet, may, unluckily, be an unforgettable experience. It will be a day before you can get the puckery taste out of your mouth, and in all probability you will be disposed never to make another trial of the fruit whose name, *Diospyros,* means "fruit of Zeus." But that is because most people attempt persimmons before they are truly ripe. At first green, then amber, then glaucous orange, a persimmon is not ripe until the skin is wrinkled and unappetizing in appearance, and the pulp is so mushy that one cannot eat it without washing the hands afterward.

Close relative of the *kaki,* or Japanese persimmon, our native fruit is not usually so large or handsome or firm of flesh. Yet it is esteemed by connoisseurs, who will travel miles to gather the fruit of a particularly fine

tree, and they tell you that the art of eating a persimmon consists (in addition to persuading one's self that a fruit may be a perfect mush and yet delicious) in avoiding the skin altogether, for the intensely tannic taste never leaves that part of the fruit. Certain it is that some trees produce large, some small fruit; some fruits are delicious, some never good at any season; some ripen in August, some in December, and others hold their fruit until spring. Obviously, amidst such variation there are strains well worth propagating and breeding.

During the Civil War, when Confederate soldiers boiled persimmon seeds as a substitute for coffee, Professor F. P. Porcher published in Richmond a book, *Resources of the Southern Fields and Forests*, intended to show the way to meet the blockade of Rebel seaports by utilizing the native products, and in this book he gives as a recipe for persimmon syrup the following:

"The persimmons are mixed with wheat bran, baked in pones, next crushed and put in vessels, water poured on, and all allowed to stand twelve hours. Strain and boil to the consistency of molasses." Porcher adds: "A good vinegar very much like and equal to white wine vinegar is made as follows: Three bushels of ripe persimmons, three gallons of whiskey, and twenty-seven gallons of water. To those who can get the persimmons, the vinegar thus produced will be relatively cheap, even at any price which the elastic conscience can ask for the spirits" — a thrust at war profiteers, that. Perhaps some persons, if they had three gallons of whiskey, would not, even for the sake of obtaining vinegar, mix them with persimmons.

Professor Milton Hopkins* tells us how to make a persimmon pudding: "Three eggs, ½ teaspoon salt, 2 cups sweet milk, 3½ cups flour, 1 qt. seed persimmon fruits, I pint cold water, 1 teaspoon soda, 1 cup granulated sugar.

"Wash and seed the fruit (to make 1 quart, about 3 quarts of whole fresh fruit required) and soak them in cold water for about an hour. Then run them through a colander. Mix the other ingredients in the order given, stirring thoroughly. Pour the batter into a greased pan and bake at 400° for one hour or until the pudding is a dark brown in color. Serve either hot or cold with whipped cream or hard sauce, and garnish with maraschino cherries. The pudding keeps well in the icebox for several days."

*"Wild Plants Used in Cookery," *New York Botanical Garden Journal,* 43:71–76, 1942.

Naturally persimmons were an important article of diet among the Indians. DeSoto was offered loaves made of persimmons by the Indians in the neighborhood of Memphis and discovered dried persimmons (called prunes in the narrative) in the villages deserted before his warlike advance in Arkansas. The English naturalist John Bradbury, while traveling up the Missouri, was received among the Osages and offered a bread called *staninca,* made of the pulp of persimmon pounded with maize; he described the taste as like gingerbread.

Le Page Du Pratz in 1758 wrote, in his *History of Louisiana,* of the persimmon or *placminier* of the Creoles: "When it is quite ripe the natives make bread of it, which they keep from year to year; and the bread has this remarkable property that it will stop the most violent looseness or dysentery; therefore it ought to be used with caution, and only after physic. The natives, in order to make this bread, squeeze the fruit over fine sieves to separate the pulp from the skin and the kernels. Of this pulp, which is like paste or thick pap, they make cakes about a foot and a half long, a foot broad, and a finger's breadth in thickness: these they dry in an oven, upon gridirons, or else in the sun; which last method of drying gives a greater relish to the bread. This is one of their articles of traffick with the French."

But no matter how we humans improve the breed, or cook the fruit, the persimmon will never mean to us what it does in the lives of the wild animals. It is eaten by birds, notably the popular bobwhite, by the half-wild hogs that rule the Ozarks, by flying squirrels and foxes, by raccoons and skunks and white-tailed deer, and above all by the opossum. According to song and story, most 'possum hunts end at the foot of a 'simmon tree, and when Audubon came to paint his great picture of the opossums, he showed them devouring the strange, puckery-looking fruits, high in the branches of this grand old tree.

Anyone can name a Persimmon when it is in fruit; in its winter nakedness or its heavy summer greenery with those dark, gleaming, tropical-looking leaves, it is not so easy to distinguish it; at least it is apt, as to leaves, to be confused with the Black Gum, and both trees have deeply furrowed and cross-checked bark. But Black Gum bark has rather regular narrow ridges cut by remote cross-checks, while the bark of Persimmon is irregularly broken into countless small blocks; it has a distinctly reptilian sort of corky hide. In winter the naked Persimmon is revealed as a not very graceful tree with short crooked branches and fine crooked twigs, and in autumn the leaves, very late in the season, fall without turning the gorgeous colors of the Black Gum. But in the first hot weather of summer the flowers appear, and all that is tropical seeming about this member of a very tropical family is expressed in the blossoms. True, they do not make a brilliant show; they are too small for that and overtopped by the foliage, but, of a waxy white, they breathe forth from their thick, jug-shaped corollas a heavy perfume that is the very spirit of the southern summer.

The Persimmon often forms dense thickets on dry, eroded slopes. Not only has the tree a deep taproot, but it sends out long stolons or subterranean runners which are both wide spreading and deeply penetrating. Trees grown from stolons, however, are apt to be shrubby and are very difficult to eradicate once they have penetrated the soil of an abandoned field. The finest trees, from the point of view of wood production, are, or were, those growing under primeval forest conditions where competition with other trees has forced them to their maximum growth of 100 or even 130 feet in height. Of course the fruit on such a tree is unhandy to pick, and the gatherer of persimmons greatly prefers the dense bushy thickets that spring up on the sides of gullies and in old fields. Although not a fast-growing tree, Persimmon begins sometimes to bear fruit at an early age. It succeeds in the most adverse sites: on the coal lands of Illinois stripped of all the top soil, or in bottomlands where the water may stand for several months. A more adaptable tree would be hard to find, and the extent to which it is cherished in southern farmyards would make one think it common. Actually it seldom occurs in pure stands, and as soon as the lumberman tries to find specimens suitable for cutting, he discovers that, wide though the range of this species, it is not individually so very numerous.

Persimmon belongs to the same genus as Ebony (*Diospyros ebenum*) of the Orient and betrays the relationship in its heartwood, so dark a brown as to be nearly black. This, however, sometimes does not develop until the tree is over a century old; the very thick sapwood is a pale brown. Persimmon belongs in the class of the very strong woods: when green it is not so very hard, but no other wood gains more in hardness when it is well seasoned; it falls in the class of the extremely hard woods. In weight it is in the very heavy class. It shrinks greatly in drying and will crack unless the ends are protected by paint or paraffin. Difficult to glue, it is never used in built-up or ply- or fabricated wood, but when once seasoned properly it retains its shape to perfection. The more it is used, the higher and glossier its polish.

Because the trunk is seldom more than a foot in diameter, this tree can never be an article of great commerce, in spite of its valuable properties and the good price it fetches. Its strength as a beam cannot be utilized, because of the rarity of dimension timber; indeed, Persimmon is commonly sold by the cord. Almost all woods of any value find special employment for which their properties fit them uniquely, and so because of the hardness, smoothness, and nonwarping qualities of Persimmon its chief use is for the making of shuttles for textile looms. Some woods, valuable in many other ways, cannot endure an hour under the terrific wear of the looms without cracking, splitting, or wearing rough; Persimmon, like Apple and Dogwood, can endure one thousand hours of furious activity in the mills. Because it holds its shape so well, it has been employed in the wooden lasts over which children's shoes are built but is too expensive for use in shoes of adults, whose styles in footwear change often. The heartwood has been used extensively for the heads of golf sticks because it does not crack under a sudden or impact load, and takes such a high polish. It is used for billiard cues, beautiful parquet flooring, and, in the days of spinning wheels, the small sort at which the women took their places seated were made of Persimmon wood in the South.

The name of Persimmon is old; the Lenape Indians, with whom William Penn treated, called it *pasimenan*. But older still is the geologic ancestry of this tree. Fifty-five million years ago, when the ancestors of the horse were small and short legged as ponies, Persimmons of numerous species were widespread in North America. On what is now the ranch country of western Oregon grew, for instance, an extinct species (*Diospyros oregana*) whose closest living relatives are now in Java. But many changes in altitude and climate have swept the ancient Persimmons from the West, and today this single species, within the circumscription of our sylva, lives on, as much a reminder of a far-off time as the opossum, our only remaining marsupial.

Common Manzanita

Arctostaphylos manzanita Parry

RANGE: Middle and inner northern Coast Ranges of California from Mount Diablo (Contra Costa County) north to Tehama, Trinity, and Shasta counties, and thence south in the Sierra Nevada foothills to Mariposa County, in the Gray Pine belt.

THERE ARE SOME FORTY KINDS of *Arctostaphylos* or Manzanita in the West (compared with a single species in eastern North America and northern Europe), and most of them are but shrubs; several, though, reach tree size occasionally. The one which most commonly does so is the present species.

Common Manzanita is generally an inhabitant of the valley flats and low hills of much of the Gray Pine belt which, like a big letter O, surrounds the Great Central Valley of California, inhabiting the inner Coast Ranges and the western foothills of the Sierra Nevada. Up to 35 feet tall in exceptional instances, the Common Manzanita may put forth a crown of evergreen foliage that is as broad as the tree is tall. In the case of trees growing close together, however, no such opulent symmetry is possible. The branches are always crooked, flattened this way or that, with twisted grain, so that when these little trees grow densely they lock their brawny red arms and arthritic, haggish fingers into an impenetrable thicket or

low forest of the type that in California is sometimes called an elfin wood. In many places this and other Manzanitas completely dominate the chaparral — that intricate inflammable scrub which covers such immense areas in California.

The flowering of Common Manzanita begins early, in February, during the winter rainy season, which is biologically not winter but spring. Only some of the wild currants, the golden-flowered bush poppy (*Dendromecon*), and a white-flowered *Ceanothus* bloom so early, and the Manzanita surpasses them all, with its prettily blushed, jug-shaped flowers which show by their frosty perfection that they are members of the aristocratic *Ericaceæ* to which belong heather and heath, rhododendron, azalea, mountain laurel, Madroño, and mayflower. The fruits, berrylike drupes, received from the Spanish-speaking pioneers of the Southwest the name of Manzanita, meaning "little apple," but you will be reminded, rather, of blueberries and huckleberries. Bears and chipmunks are fond of them, and so were the California Indians, but to the white man's digestive tract the seeds are most unmerciful.

The Common Manzanita, like others of its tribe, has been commercially exploited of recent years, with no regard to its reproduction, its great importance as a check on erosion, or the property rights of landowners. Because of the fascinating asymmetry of the branches, and the highly colored bark which, skintight, follows every contorted twist in the grain, florists have used these branches, artificially redressed with glued-on foliage shellacked and repainted, and a false "moss," and putting the whole into a bowl with a cheap Chinese figurine, have sold the little horror as a "Ming-tree."

A less banal fancy in Manzanita is the search for "abstractions" — oddities in fragments of Manzanita stems, branches, and roots which bear resemblance to anything (or nothing) else on earth. These bits of "mountain driftwood" as they are called are collectors' items among hobbyists. In order to prevent the collectors from stealing surreptitiously into national forest lands and breaking down the Manzanitas with violent hands (while setting the forest alight with cigarette stubs in a hundred places every Sunday), the Forest Service opened in the summer of 1951 a "Manzanita Area," up in the old Mother Lode country. Here where the Manzanitas are superabundant and a ranger is at hand to enforce certain restrictions, collectors may "pick" their mountain driftwood, providing they are amateurs and not florists' scouts. But a sharp saw or ax will be necessary to cut this immensely tough, hard wood.

Desert Smoketree

Psorothamnus spinosus (Gray) Barneby*

OTHER NAMES: Smokethorn Dalea. Indigobush.

RANGE: Low deserts of Sinaloa, Sonora, and Baja California, in Mexico, north in the basin of the Colorado River in western Arizona and eastern California (west to Palm Springs).

SAVE FOR A FEW BRIEF WEEKS IN SUMMER, when the little Smoketree puts forth the merest token of evanescent foliage — it stands perfectly leafless. But not unclothed or barren, for its twigs, up to their third year, are wrapped in a dense felting of translucent gray hairs. Sometimes the Smoketrees look almost like eastern deciduous trees coated in hoarfrost — but with no glitter to them, only a soft, smoky or silvery halo. Under the desert moon they are positively ghostly.

The Smoketree, which is seen at its best around Palm Springs and below sea level in the Salton Sink, is never much more than 20 feet high, and seldom that; nor does it usually stand up straight — how could it, with its inherent crookedness of growth? — and its thorny boughs are all zigzag. One would expect such a tree to be utterly shapeless, yet it cannot help falling into picturesque attitudes; in its wildly unsymmetrical form it

Editor's note: Formerly *Dalea spinosa* Gray.

somehow achieves a sort of Japanese artistry. Add to this the dramatic setting of canyon walls and boulder-strewn washes, of dreamy mesas or snow-capped peaks.

When the low deserts are flaming with full summer heat, and all the tourists have departed, the little Smoketree bears its profusion of deep violet purple flowers, like so many tiny sweet peas in form. From them breathes out a tender fragrance to "waste its sweetness on the desert air," but with few then to praise it.

Desert Catalpa

Chilopsis linearis (Cavanilles) Sweet

OTHER NAME: Desert, Flowering, or Bow Willow.

RANGE: Low deserts of Mexico, north to the valley of Rio Grande throughout its length in Texas, and well into southern Arizona, generally below 5000 feet altitude, and north in the Colorado River valley to extreme southern Nevada, extreme southwestern Utah, and the Colorado desert of California (but not the Mohave desert), inland to Palm Springs and along the Mexican boundary within 40 miles of the sea in San Diego County.

AS YOU GO FLYING OVER THE SOUTHWESTERN DESERTS, anywhere in the vast arid domain from the Big Bend of Texas to the Salton Sea of California, you may see, at the culverts and along the washes, this little tree, which never grows over 30 feet tall. It is often called Desert Willow from its long narrow leaves; yet, close relative of the true Catalpa and the trumpetvine, it is at the opposite end of the evolutionary scale from the primitive Willows. Perhaps there is something willowy in the way it overleans the banks of washes, but there is nothing kin to the weak-limbed Willows about the sinewy branches of this desert tree. So stiff is its wood that it is, or was, a favorite with the Indians for the making of bows. And Bow Willow Canyon in eastern San

Diego County, California, is named for this tree, for here the Indians used to come to cut their bow wood.

Most visitors go to the deserts in winter, when this tree stands naked save for a few long, empty pods, swinging disconsolately and weathered silver, on the twigs. Then in early spring the leaves appear. The flowers, though, do not open until most of the tourists have gone to their far-off homes, when the sound of the grinding of gears is low, and the wrangler of dudes has fallen asleep at his post. Then the lovely blossoms, much like those of the true Catalpa, pink or whitish with purple veins and yellow spots in the throat, open in stately masses, each flower a silent trumpet. So all summer, off and on, the flowers bloom, with few to praise them.

If anyone has read this book in something like sequence, he may have wondered, unless botanically trained, at the order of succession of the more than two hundred species which comprise the sylva of western North America. That sequence is the one usually followed by botanists who assume (or hope) that it represents the order of evolution from olden types of trees to the most modern. If that is so, one may ask in what way this spindling and unimportant little tree is "higher" than the mighty conifers, which endure for centuries and tower above all other trees in majesty, as they do in utility to man. But biological order is not a question of splendor or worth; what sets the noble conifers in an early rank is the primitive naked flowers, which have no petals or sepals, and not even ovaries, for their ovules are borne naked on the scales of the female conelets.

Obviously, the highly developed, tubular corolla of the Desert Catalpa is far more complex and perhaps more efficient, and it is believed, from fossil evidence, to represent millions of years of advance over the coniferous flower.

More — if we think of such titanic trees as the Sequoias in terms of modern conditions in western North America, it seems that, for all their stature and their years, they are adapted to no more than a narrow range of conditions. Such were perhaps found more widely in other geologic times, when Sequoias were widespread and the sylva of the West consisted in a somewhat different assemblage of species. Today, though, it is in but two restricted localities that the Sequoias have survived. Quite the contrary with the Desert Catalpa; this modest little tree occupies a vast tract of the West as it is in our times. Call it a world of harsh contrasts, filled with wind and drought, heat and cold. But here this drought-resistant little tree holds its own remarkably well. It is even able to utilize the gusts of the desert that sear the land and make it uninhabitable for many trees with great reputations; for on the winds go sailing, from the Desert Catalpa's opened pods, the tiny seeds that are flat and light as bits of confetti and borne on silken wings. Thus they cross vast arid spaces, to populate the sands of other waterless washes, the cobbles of other arroyos. Swiftly the new seedlings spring up, enduring as readily as a Papago the long blazing summer days that know no shade until, from the lunar and jagged ranges, the sundown shadows rush forth across the long *bajadas* to the edge of the world. When the summer stars come forth, and hot Antares blazes in the Scorpion, then and then only there steals forth from the lips of the Desert Catalpa's blossoms the odor of sweet violets.

GLOSSARY

Aborted. Incompletely developed, defective in form.

Acidulous. Having acid properties and taste.

Akene (also *achene*). A dry, often seedlike fruit not opening or splitting by any natural sutures. Examples: the fruits of Mountain Mahogany, the "seeds" or "straws" of strawberries.

Alternate. Growing singly at the nodes (q.v.) of the stem or axis or rachis; not opposite (q.v.) nor in whorls (q.v.).

Anther. The part of a stamen which contains the pollen. Anthers consist of one or more pollen sacks opening variously by pores or slits. If there is no stalk or filament, then the anther of itself constitutes the entire stamen (q.v.) and is exactly synonymous with it.

Apetalous. Without petals.

Apex. The tip; the upper or outer end, farthest removed from the stalk, axis, or stem.

Appressed. Closely and flatly pressed against.

Aril. An appendage or outer covering of a seed, an outgrowth of the hilum (q.v.), sometimes appearing pulpy. Example: the Yew fruit.

Awl shaped. Sharp pointed and narrow.

Axil. The inner (upper) angle of a leaf with the stem, or of a scale with the axis.

Axillary. In the position of an axil.

Axis. The central shoot of a compound leaf, cone, inflorescence, root, etc.

Balsamic. Having the qualities of balsam; soft, mucilaginous, often aromatic.

Bark. The outermost, often more or less corky or leathery cell layers on stems, branches, twigs, and roots, formed by the cambium cells. The bark of trees usually has at least two layers, the outer and the inner, more or less distinct in structure, texture, color, etc.

Base. The lower end of an organ, that is, the part nearest the stalk, stem, or axis on which an organ is borne.

Bast. The soft tissue of the fibers of the inner bark, which are often employed in making thread and rope.

Beard. Long, bristlelike hairs, especially upon petals or styles.

Bearded. Having a beard (q.v.).

Berry. As defined by botanists (only), a fleshy fruit proceeding from the ripening of a single pistil but with more than one seed, the seeds not enclosed in a "stone." Example: tomatoes. Practically all fruits called "berry" by berry growers, as strawberry, blackberry, raspberry, blueberry, cranberry, are excluded by botanists from their definition of the word. The berries of the Juniper are really cones whose scales have become fused and pulpy but are in effect, if not in origin, berries.

Biconvex. Convex on both surfaces.

Bisexual. Having the parts or organs of both sexes simultaneously, as a flower which contains both pollen and ovules.

Blade. The expanded leaf, apart from its stalk.

Board foot. A unit of lumber measurement 1 foot long, 1 foot wide, and 1 inch thick, or an equivalent volume.

Bole. A tree trunk, especially that of a large tree.

Bract. A more or less modified leaf, generally subtending a flower, fruit, stalk, or flowering or fruit cluster, head, or spike.

Branchlet. The ultimate division of a branch.

Bud. An embryonic shoot bearing embryonic leaves or flowers or both.

Bushy. Having the growth form of a bush; that is, with numerous branches or shoots from the base but little or no central trunk.

Calyx (pl. *calyces*). The outer envelope of a flower, generally green and more or less leaflike but, in the absence of petals, sometimes petal-like. Usually the term used when the sepals are united.

Cambium. In trees, the thin layer of tissue just under the inner bark and just outside the wood, which by cell division increases the tree in diameter, giving off bark cells on the outside and wood cells on the inside.

Capsule. A compound pod (q.v.); a dry, few- or many-seeded fruit splitting at maturity by longitudinal sutures. Examples: fruits of Poplar, Willow, Horse Chestnut.

Carpel. One of the units of a compound pistil (q.v.) or ovary — the basic ovule-bearing unit of the female reproductive organ. Examples: the segments of an apple core; the fruits of Catalina Ironwood.

Cartilaginous. Parchmentlike, hard and tough.

Catkin. A more or less compact spike of mostly unisexual flowers. A term used generally of the peculiar inflorescences of certain trees, such as the Willows, Poplars, Walnuts, Hickories, Oaks and, more loosely, of the conifers, having few or very reduced floral envelopes and those often consisting of bracts and scales rather than sepals and petals, while the flowers or florets are often reduced to the organs of one sex or the other.

Checked. Said of bark, when it is marked by horizontal cracks or grooves.

Claw. The narrowed or stalklike base of the petals or sepals of certain flowers. Example: Plum.

Compound. Said of any organ composed of two or more similar parts. A compound leaf is one composed of two or more leaflets, as in the case of Walnuts and Locusts (see *simple,* for contrast). A leaf is once compound when the leaflets are arranged on a single, unbranched axis or rachis. It is twice compound when the axis or rachis is branched. A compound leaf may be known from a twig bearing simple leaves by the fact that there is a bud in the axil of a leaf but not of a leaflet. A compound fruit is composed of many more or less united fruitlets. Example: Mulberry. A compound ovary is one composed of the union of two or more pistils and possesses two or more cells.

Cone. A dense and more or less conical mass of flowers or fruits, or (more strictly) of seed-bearing scales, on a central axis. Loosely used for the fruits of Alders, etc., but more specifically for the female inflorescence of the Pine family. The cones of Pines and their relatives consist in the more or less woody, leathery, papery, or fleshy seed-bearing scales of the female catkins after fertilization, these arranged on a central axis forming a homogeneous fruit which generally detaches as a unit.

Conelet. A small, or immature, or ungrown cone. Commonly said of the female catkin of the Pine family.

Confluent. Running together, or uniting, as the tissues of two organs.

Conifer. A member of the Pine family.

Coniferous. Of or pertaining to the conifers.

Corolla. The inner series (petals, q.v.) of floral envelopes; used especially where the petals are fused at base into a common tube. Examples: Madroño, Desert Catalpa.

Cortex. Surface, as of bark, or the barklike rind of stems.

Deciduous. Naturally falling; said especially of the foliage of trees that become naked during the unfavorable seasons.

Declined. Bent downward.

Decurrent. Running down, as of the blades of leaves on their stalks.

Deflexed. Abruptly turned down.

Disc, disk. A more or less fleshy development of the receptacle (q.v.) of a flower around the pistil.

Dorsal. On the upper ("back") or outer face of an organ or part.

Drupe. A fleshy, one-seeded fruit which contains a single stone which in turn contains the seed; a stone fruit. Examples: Plum, Cherry, Almond, Peach, Dogwood.

Drupelet. A little drupe; more particularly one of a number of similar fruitlets in a compound fruit. Example: Mulberry.

Duct. A pit, chamber, or gland, usually filled with sap, resin, or other secretion.

Ecologist. One who studies ecology.

Ecology. The life habits and interrelations of plants and animals with each other and with environmental influences. Botanical ecology has been picturesquely characterized as "the sociology of plants."

Endophytic. Within the tissues of a plant. Said particularly of certain fungi living symbolically in the root and other tissues of trees.

Epidermis. The thin layer of cells forming the outer coating of plants.

Evergreen. Remaining green through the seasons; never naked of foliage. All evergreens eventually shed their leaves but not as do deciduous trees (all at once or before new growth appears).

Exfoliating. Peeling away in papery plates or strips, as the bark of Sycamore, Birch, Eucalyptus, etc.

Exserted. Projecting beyond, as stamens which stand out beyond the corolla.

Female. Said of the flowers having ovules and (except in the conifers) ovaries, but not male organs (stamens, pollen). Said of inflorescences or of trees having only female flowers. See also *male, fertile, perfect, unisexual, bisexual.*

Fertile. Capable of producing fruit. Sometimes used to denote flowers wholly female, or a pollen-bearing anther, as contrasted with a sterile one or staminodium. Also seed-bearing fruits.

Fertilization. Impregnation within the ovule of the egg cells by union with the sperm cells.

Filament. The stalk of an anther.

Flesh. The pulpy part of a fruit.

Flora. The plant population (or more strictly the flowering plants) of an area. Also a book dealing with their enumeration and identities.

Floral. Of or pertaining to flowers or inflorescences.

Floret. A little flower, especially when it is a part of a compact and specialized type of inflorescence (q.v.) such as a catkin (q.v.).

Flower. There are two definitions of a flower. The older and more popular conceives the flower as consisting in the organs of one or both the sexes enveloped in sepals and, commonly, also in petals. This, however, could not include the Pines, Oaks, and fully one-third of our trees which yet have stamens and pistils, pollen, and ovules and bear fruits. The more scientific and inclusive definition depicts the flower as consisting primarily in reproductive organs (stamens and pistils, or pollen-bearing and ovule-bearing bracts and scales, as in the Pine family). This definition does not, however, entirely exclude some of the fern allies, which are considered flowerless. There is, therefore, no perfect definition of this highly evolutionary and variable group of organs, the flower, but the second definition is much the better.

Fluted. Channeled or grooved.

Follicle. A free podlike fruit opening only on the front suture.

Free. Not joined to other organs; said, for instance, of stamens free from the petals or an ovary free from the calyx.

Frond. Used sometimes for a compound leaf (as of a fern, palm, etc.) or for a spray of foliage.

Fruit. The seed-bearing organ; the ripened ovary or pistil and sometimes adjacent and cohering parts.

Fruitlet. A little fruit when it is a part of a compound fruit.

Fulvous. Dull brownish or reddish yellow; tawny.

Furrowed. Marked with longitudinal grooves.

Genus. A group of species (q.v.) which resemble each other more than they differ, or an isolated species showing marked differentiation from any other. The first of the two Latin names of a plant.

Gland. A secreting pore or part or prominence often exuding resinous, sticky, oily, or sweet substances; said also of hairs terminating in a knoblike tip, especially when exuding clammy substances, and of the teeth of leaves when glandlike in appearance (thickened and colored), and of any colored prominences of glandlike appearance — as those on the leafstalks of Plums and Cherries.

Glandular. Of or pertaining to a gland or of glandlike appearance.

Glaucous. With a bloom or cast of a bluish white appearance.

Globose. Approaching the form of a sphere.

Habit. The growth form of a plant.

Habitat. The situation, with regard to soil, light, temperature, and associated species, in which a plant grows.

Head. A compact cluster; a very short dense spike.

Heartwood. The hard, inner cylinder of a woody stem, consisting of dead and heavy and more or less dense wood elements, usually darker, from the deposition of tannin, gums, resins, and pigments, than the sapwood.

Hilum. The scar or mark on a seed indicative of its point of attachment to the placenta of the parent plant.

Horizontal. At right angles to the (normally) up-and-down axis of growth.

Husk. The outermost covering of a fruit, usually of a heavy character — woody as in the case of the Walnut husk, leathery in the Locust pod, heavy in the hazelnut, and papery in the Hop Hornbeam's fruits.

Inferior. In a lower position. Said especially of ovaries which are adherent to, or surmounted by, the calyx, as in the case of Apples and Hawthorns.

Inflexed. Bent inward.

Inflorescence. The flower cluster; the mode of bearing the flowers.

Integument. Covering or coat; outer tissues.

Involucre. A whorl (q.v.) of small leaves or bracts subtending a flower or an inflorescence or fruit cluster. Example: Dogwood.

Irregular. Said of a flower when the parts or members of any one of the sets or series (particularly the petals) are unlike the others or eccentrically placed, or when the flower is bilaterally symmetrical, as in sweet pea, Locust, and certain other flowers of the pea family.

Keel. A ridge like the keel of a boat, especially on a fruit or seed. Also the keel-shaped pair of united petals on the lower side of a flower of the pea family.

Lateral. On or at the side; not terminal.

Leader. A growing shoot, especially when extending beyond the rest of the crown of a tree.

Leaf. The lateral outgrowth of a stem or shoot, appearing from a bud, and usually flattened (but needlelike in Pines, Larches, etc.), veinous, and, at maturity, green from the presence of chlorophyll; the principal photosynthetic organ of a tree. A leaf may consist in two parts, the stalk (when present) and the blade or leaf proper. Dimensions of leaves are usually given to include only the blade.

Leaflet. A single division of a compound leaf. The ultimate unit of division of a twice-compound leaf.

Legume. A pod opening by longitudinal sutures. Examples: the pod of a pea, bean, Mesquite, Locust.

Lenticel. A pore in the bark.

Limb. The flat or expanded part of an organ; in particular the flaring and lobed part of a corolla or calyx as distinct from its throat or tube. "Limb" in the sense of a branch of a tree is not usually employed in formal botanical descriptions.

Lobe. A segment of an organ usually separated from similar parts by a regular space or sinus, as in the lobed leaves of some Oaks, or the lobed corolla of Desert Catalpa.

Male. Said of flowers which bear pollen and, except in the Pine family, stamens. Said of a tree that bears only male flowers and never fruit.

Mammillate. Having the form of breast and nipple.

Medullary ray. A vertical band or plate radiating between pith and bark.

Membranous. Thin and wide, membranelike or filmy.

Midrib. The central or main and heaviest rib or nerve or vein, of a leaf or leaflet.

Needle. The peculiar, very long and narrow leaf, commonly triangular or piano-convex in cross section, of Pines and (more loosely) of some of the relatives of Pines.

Nerve. A principal vein or slender rib of a leaf, especially when it is one of several arising from the base of the blade.

Node. The level, on a shoot, at which a branch, bud, leaf, flower, or other organ appears.

Nut. A dry, usually large, nonsplitting fruit with thick, hard outer walls, produced from a two- or more-celled ovary, but usually one-seeded.

Nutlet. A small nutlike part, usually one of several, within a fruit.

Opposite. Said of leaves when they appear in pairs at the same node (q.v.) of the stem but on opposite sides of it; not alternate (q.v.) nor whorled (q.v.).

Ovary. The part of the pistil enclosing and bearing the ovules.

Ovule. The minute body, borne within the ovary and containing the female cells (eggs) which after fertilization become the seeds.

Palmate. Veined, lobed, or divided as the fingers of the hand or like the leaf of a fan palm. Examples: Sycamore, Horse Chestnut.

Perfect. Said of flowers when they are bisexual (q.v.).

Persistent. Remaining attached, not falling off.

Petal. A member of the inner series of floral envelopes, standing between the sepals and the stamens, and usually thin and colored (not green). See also *corolla.*

Pinna (pl. *pinnæ*). The primary division of a compound leaf.

Pinnate. Said of a compound leaf with leaflets arranged along a common axis.

Pinnule. The secondary division of a pinna on a leaf which is twice or more compound.

Pistil. The ovule-bearing and seed-bearing organ of a flower, consisting in the ovary (q.v.), the stigma (q.v.), and, when present, the style (q.v.); the whole female organ.

Pith. The soft, spongy, loosely cellular tissue found within the woody cylinder of a stem, most characteristic of twigs and seedlings.

Placenta. Attachment point of ovules in an ovary.

Pod. A simple (not compound) usually thick-walled, dry fruit, splitting or otherwise opening at maturity.

Pollen. The spores or grains containing the male element (sperm) and originating in an anther (q.v.).

Pollination. The transfer of pollen from the anther to the stigma.

Polygamous. Bearing both perfect (q.v.) and unisexual flowers.

Pome. Fruit with papery or cartilaginous carpels (q.v.) at the center and fleshy outer tissue, of which the apple is a type; also pear, quince, and the fruits of Hawthorn, Mountain Ash, etc.

Polypetalous. Having separate, not united, petals.

Precocious. Coming to flower or fruit early in the year, or early in the life of a plant.

Pubescence. Soft short hairs.

Pubescent. Covered with short soft hair.

Punctate. Having translucent dots or pits.

Rachis. Axis shoot of a compound leaf or inflorescence; the central stalk or midrib.

Radial. Developed around a central axis.

Receptacle. The elongated or enlarged end of a shoot or flower axis on which some or all of the flower parts are borne.

Regular. Said of a flower when the parts of members in each series (as sepals, petals, stamens, pistils) are like each other and symmetrically disposed on three or more radii.

Resin. Secretions, usually formed in special passages or chambers, either hard or liquid, usually aromatic, insoluble in water, soluble in alcohol, ether, or carbon disulfide, and burning with a sooty flame.

Resinous. Containing, bearing, or impregnated with resin.

Ribbed. Having ribs.

Ribs. Principal nerves, usually parallel or all arising from the base of a leaf, sometimes, also, the ridges between furrows on fruits, seeds, etc.

Rind. The firm close layer of cells covering many fruits and some trunks which do not have true bark, as Palms.

Root. The usually underground part of a plant distinguished from a stem by its origin at the opposite end of the embryo, and by its generally downward growth.

Rosin. The hard, brittle resin (q.v.) remaining after the oil of turpentine has been driven off by distillation.

Sack (also *sac*). A pouch or receptacle or cavity in an organ, as the pollen sacks of an anther.

Samara. A dry, winged fruit not naturally splitting even at maturity. Examples: fruits of Maples, Elms, Ashes.

Sapwood. The woody cylinder between the bark and the heartwood, usually paler than the heartwood, less heavy and dense, and more permeable.

Scale. A term used variously for different organs and appendages; often employed in connection with much-reduced stem leaves and other thin, papery bodies, but in the cones of conifers denoting more or less woody, bractlike organs bearing the seeds.

Scurfy. Flaky.

Seed. The ovule (q.v.) after fertilization, containing the embryonic plant, within one or more coats, and often accompanied by a store (the endosperm or "meat") of fats, proteins, carbohydrates.

Sepal. One of the segments or lobes of the calyx (q.v.); usually said when the parts are not united at base.

Sheath. Any tubular structure surrounding an organ or part; the sheaths of Pines are short, papery tubes enclosing the base of the bundle of needles.

Shoot. Any growing axis of a stem, or a new plant or branch growing from an old one.

Short-shoot. A shortened and condensed and usually thickened branch or twig usually bearing flowers, or a tuft of foliage, or spines.

Simple. Said of leaves that are not compound, that have a single un-branched midrib engaged continuously with the blade.

Sinus. The space or bay between two lobes of an organ.

Species. The unit of classification, composed, as a rule, of individuals which resemble each other more than they differ, are usually inter-fertile, are frequently sterile to other species, and breed true, repro-ducing their own kind.

Sperm. A male reproductive cell.

Spike. A simple elongated cluster.

Spore. A simple reproductive body, usually consisting in a detached cell.

Spreading. Standing outward or horizontally, not hanging deflexed or flattened to the stem.

Springwood. Growth made in the spring, as contrasted with the denser, darker summerwood.

Spur. A thickened short-shoot (q.v.), often bearing leaves, flowers, or thorns.

Stalk. The stem of any organ as of a leaf, flower, inflorescence, anther, etc.

Stamen. The pollen-bearing or male organ. A single stamen, with or with-out floral envelopes, may, in the case of certain unisexual flowers, constitute a male flower. In bisexual flowers, the stamens usually stand outside the female organs but within or upon the floral enve-lopes.

Staminodium (pl. *staminodia*). A sterile or aborted stamen, without an-thers or pollen, usually more or less modified in form (club shaped, flattened, etc.) or even petal-like.

Standard. The upper petal of a flower of the pea family.

Stem. The main axis of growth above ground, bearing the buds, leaves, and flowers, as contrasted with the root-bearing axis.

Stigma. The part of the pistil that receives the pollen. Generally it is some-what sticky and of a definite form, but it may occupy only an in-definite (see *stigmatic*) area on the style.

Stigmatic. Of or pertaining to the stigma; often said of that portion of a style functioning as, but not clearly separated as, a stigma (q.v.).

Stipulate. Accompanied by stipules.

Stipule. Generally, a little appendagelike part of a leaf, growing one on each side of the base of the leafstalk and sometimes fused with it, sometimes deciduous.

Stoma (pl. *stomata*). A minute opening between two guard cells in the epidermis, especially on undersides of leaves, through which gaseous interchange between inner cells and atmosphere is effected.

Stomatal. Of or pertaining to stomata (see *stoma*).

Style. The stalklike or columnar part of the pistil surmounting the ovary and upholding the stigma (q.v.). Frequently the style is branched, thus representing a union of styles. Sometimes the styles are separate to the base, representing a union of carpels (q.v.). Sometimes no stigma is present, and the styles merely exhibit a stigmatic surface on one or more sides.

Subtend. To stand under, in a bractlike position.

Summerwood. Growth of darker, more compact wood made after the springwood.

Superior. Placed above; said of an ovary that is free from, and not surmounted by, the calyx. Example: Plum flowers.

Suture. A natural groove or line along which splitting takes place, especially in fruits, seeds, etc.

Sylva (also *silva*). The forest trees of a region, collectively considered. A book dealing with the trees of an area.

Taproot. A vertical, strong, central root that continues growth, in line with the axis of the stem, straight down in the ground.

Terminal. At the end of a branch, shoot, style, etc.

Throat. The opening or orifice in a flower with united petals or united sepals at the point where the tube (q.v.) expands into the limb (q.v.).

Tortuous. Twisted, sinuous.

Transverse. Crosswise, across.

Tridentate. Three-toothed, especially at the apex of a part or organ.

Truncate. Appearing as if cut off along a straight or essentially straight margin. Example: the bases of the leaves of some Cottonwoods.

Tube. The unexpanded, more or less cylindrical and basal portion of a calyx (q.v.) or corolla (q.v.). See also *throat* and *limb*.

Tumid. Swollen.

Turgid. Distended by pressure from within.

Twig. A branchlet; the ultimate division of a woody shoot.

Umbo. The central boss on a cone scale.

Unarmed. Without thorns, prickles, or spines.

Underbark. The inner, often brightly colored bark beneath the corky or scaly outer bark.

Unisexual. Composed of one sex only; said of a flower having pollen *or* ovules, but not both.

Valve. The separable part of a pod or capsule; the walls of such fruits, between the sutures (q.v.).

Variety. A fraction of the unit of classification (species, q.v.); a group of individuals within a species set aside from others by their exclusive resemblances in minor ways.

Vein. A branch of the sap-conducting tissue of a leaf, petal, scale, bract, seed coat, etc. See also *veinlet, midrib, nerve.*

Veinlet. A secondary vein.

Veiny. With the veins heavily or darkly or intricately marked.

Venation. The system (variously patterned) of midribs, nerves, and veins in a leaf, petal, etc.

Venous. Of or pertaining to the veins or system of veins.

Ventral. On the under ("belly") or inner face of an organ or part. (See *dorsal.*)

Vesicle. A chamber, blister, hollow, pit, or duct, usually filled with sap, resin, or other secretion.

Whorl. Three or more leaves or other organs arising in a circle from one node (q.v.) of a shoot.

Wing. A flat, thin expansion of an organ, as the papery wings of Elm and Maple fruits, or the winged seeds of Pines. The word is also used to denote the lateral petals of a flower of the pea family.

Winter bud. A dormant, much-condensed shoot formed during the previous season.

INDEX OF

SCIENTIFIC NAMES

INDEX OF
COMMON NAMES

Donald Culross Peattie (1898–1964) was one of the most influential American nature writers of the twentieth century. Peattie was born in Chicago and grew up in the Smoky Mountains of North Carolina, a region that sparked his interest in the immense wonders of nature. He studied at the University of Chicago and Harvard University. After working for the U.S. Department of Agriculture, he decided to pursue a career as a writer. In 1925 he became a nature columnist for the *Washington Star* and went on to pen more than twenty fiction and nonfiction books over the next five decades. Widely acclaimed and popular in his day, Peattie's work has inspired a modern age of nature writing.